# The Tolerant Cook

## The Allergy and Food Intolerance Cookbook

*Tish Richardson PhD*

Lothian
BOOKS

**To Maggie B**
**I love and miss you so much**

Thomas C. Lothian Pty Ltd
132 Albert Road, South Melbourne, 3205
www.lothian.com.au

Copyright © Tish Richardson 2004

First published 2004

National Library of Australia
Cataloguing-in-Publication data:

Richardson, Tish.
The tolerant cook : the allergy and food intolerance cookbook.

ISBN 0 7344 0666 5.

1. Food allergy - Diet therapy - Recipes.  I. Title.

   641.5631

Cover design by Lee Burgemeestre
Typeset by Lee Burgemeestre in Baskerville and Lucida Grande
Printed in China by SNP Leefung

**Disclaimer**
The author has made every effort to ensure that the information and advice in this book is complete and accurate. However, the information, ideas, suggestions and dietary advice contained in this book are not intended as a substitute for consulting your healthcare practitioner and obtaining medical supervision regarding any action that may affect your well-being. Individual readers must assume responsibility for their own actions, safety and health. Neither the author nor the publisher shall be liable or responsible for any loss, injury or damage allegedly arising from any information or suggestion in this book.

## Acknowledgements

First and foremost, to my gorgeous husband and best friend Jonathan, who has supported, encouraged, eaten, programmed, eaten, critiqued and eaten!

To my dear friend Mary Malone, who prompted, cajoled and hassled me to get on and actually write this book, and who was always ready with a score out of ten for any dish—and an appetite to match.

To Robin James, thank you for looking at the project as a whole, being a much-needed touchstone, and for introducing Julie as the next step in the publication process.

To Julie Stanton, for her mentoring on the ways of the publishing world, for her belief in the principles underpinning the book, and for personally taking on the task of finding a publisher.

To Averill Chase, Sharon Mullins, Clare Coney and Lothian Books for making publication a reality.

To my many friends, especially Sam and Charlie, Bobbie, Angie, the Bashinsky family, Jo and family, Noreen, Terry and Col, Maureen and Pete, Alrie and B, who have patiently munched their way through my forays into the various cuisines.

And lastly to my son, for his outstanding contribution—particularly in the final phase of writing the manuscript.

This is a cookbook full of innovative, contemporary, mouth-watering recipes that tackle today's most common food allergies and intolerances head on! But it is not just written for the health conscious or for those dealing with food sensitivities, it is a collection of dishes infused with flavours that will tempt any cook. It contains recipes that cross many cuisines—from traditional European to Mediterranean, Indian and Thai to Australian bush tucker—and have a unique style of their own.

Have a change from the cookbooks where every recipe is drowned by today's 'fashionable' flavours and get away from the overpowering taste of garlic or soy in seemingly every dish. Skip the lashings of saturated fats—the dollops of cream and butter—and the inevitable dairy base used by many of today's celebrity cooks and cookbooks. Enjoy cooking with a wide range of foods, herbs and spices to develop a spectrum of flavours; flavours that are deliciously crisp and clean on the palate and dishes that leave you replete and satisfied, not bloated or holding your breath!

Today, with the enormous growth in health awareness, what we eat and just how it is grown or produced are increasingly being recognised as fundamental to our health and well-being. What we eat affects us mentally, emotionally and physically. The dependence of so much of our diet on both the obvious 'bad guy' junk or fast foods and on a handful of foods that are regarded as 'staples', such as wheat, dairy, eggs and soy, is leading to more and more people being diagnosed with food intolerances or dietary problems that require radical changes to their diet. In addition to the now accepted links between diet and obesity, and saturated fats and heart disease, current medical research is concerned with links between such diverse conditions as autism and cancer with foods—including wheat and dairy.

But are such links and the resultant need to radically review our diet surprising? Our bodies are like finely tuned engines: to function properly they need to be fuelled with foods that suit them. Eating a food your body can't tolerate is like expecting a car to run smoothly with water added to the petrol. While the benefits of tailoring your diet to your body's needs are easily recognised when looking at the diets of athletes who are working to optimise their performance or, in the extreme, with children who have life-threatening allergies to foods such as peanuts, for the majority of people the effects of food on their body can be subtle and hidden. For example, how many people with hay fever realise that what they eat can increase their sensitivity to the culprit airborne pollens or dust mites? A breastfeeding mum may not realise that her baby's continuous colic, disrupted sleep or eczema may be caused by a food she is eating and passing on to her food-sensitive baby. Even a continual lack of energy or just feeling 'a bit off' may simply be due to eating something that doesn't suit you. Just because a food is generally regarded as 'healthy' doesn't mean everybody can tolerate it.

## The 'one cookbook and one meal' approach

How do you avoid 'problem' foods in your diet? How do you make sense of product labels with complex ingredient names? How do you cater in a simple way if different family members have different dietary requirements—when some can eat everything but others cannot? How do you cater for friends who can't eat certain foods, when you want to invite them round but haven't the vaguest idea what to cook? Do you have to cook a different meal for everyone?

Worse, how many times have you picked up a recipe and tried to modify it to suit your family or friends' dietary needs, only to end up with a tasteless flop? Or browsed through an 'allergy' cookbook trying to avoid dairy products or wheat, to find they are replaced by soy—and you don't like or can't tolerate soy either?

There is no need to feel like a social outcast or be deprived, eating a dreary diet full of dull and flavourless food, because you can't eat the handful of foods that seems to be the base of every product in the supermarket. The principle behind this book is to simplify the task of managing a range of common dietary requirements: each recipe caters for an extensive range of food allergies and intolerances, as well as other dietary needs, such as low salt and low saturated fat, without compromising core nutritional requirements or flavour. By following the recipes in this book you can cook a dish suitable for both a family member with a food intolerance and another on a low-fat diet, creating meals that will meet their needs while tickling the rest of the family's tastebuds. *The Tolerant Cook* thus allows you to address a wide range of dietary needs easily with one set of recipes, making catering for family and friends a breeze— and avoiding the uneconomic and time-consuming need to cook separate meals.

## The 'No-Go' foods

All the 240-plus recipes in this book are free of what I have called the 'No-Go' foods: wheat, gluten, dairy, eggs, peanuts, soy, onion and garlic. There is no need to scan icons or text to check; select any recipe and you will safely avoid all these foods, as well as ingredients derived from them.

Many of the recipes also are free of corn, fish and tree nuts (like walnut, almond, pistachio or cashew, see Avoiding Nuts, page 169), and are vegetarian. The Key to Recipes—How to Select Recipes that Suit You on page viii provides a full explanation of how to select and tailor recipes to suit specific dietary requirements. Additionally, every recipe includes an analysis of core nutrients per serve, to make watching your dietary intakes easy; this is also explained in more detail in Key to Recipes—How to Select Recipes that Suit You.

There is a brief overview on how to balance your diet in Healthy Eating Guidelines, page 198. But remember, when you must avoid one or more of the 'No-Go' foods, working with your healthcare practitioner is a key building block to ensuring you eat a healthy, properly balanced diet.

Why avoid all the 'No-Go' foods if you don't need to? It's simple—you don't have to! All the entrées, mains and desserts are designed to provide a complete, stand-alone dish and include full serving suggestions, so they are perfect to eat just as they are. While for best results I recommend you do not modify an individual recipe, for example by replacing egg substitute with eggs, by starting with basic recipes that suit a wide range of diets, you can simply adapt the menu to meet each individual's requirements by adding any 'No-Go' foods to a meal on an 'as-wanted-and-can-eat' basis. This allows you to optimise flexibility and variety in any family or social situation. For example, if soy is not a problem, then serve one of the delicious tarts and dessert cakes with a commercially made soy-based ice-cream—but if it is, then just follow a recipe for one of the sorbets, ice-creams or gelati free of all the 'No-Go' foods.

To keep the dishes economical, most recipes are based on products readily available from supermarkets, greengrocers, fishmongers and butchers; for more esoteric products, advice on sourcing and manufacturers' contact details are provided in the extensive Glossary. Where relevant, details of suggested or specific brands of commercially made ingredients are included—together with what to watch out for when selecting these products.

Catering, once you understand your family's individual dietary requirements, is simply a matter of having well-stocked cupboards, fridge and freezer and planning meals in advance. Have basic stocks of the foods you can *all* eat, plus a range of supplementary foods for family members with less restricted diets—so that they can snack on or cook with these if they wish. However, importantly, where you have a family member with an allergy or a high-level sensitivity to a particular food, such as eggs, gluten or peanuts, it is best to *totally avoid* bringing those foods into the home. Whenever you are managing a food sensitivity and you do choose to bring a 'No-Go' food through the door, at an absolute minimum set in place (and make sure everyone follows) strict procedures for food storage and preparation (see Managing the Kitchen, page 201) to minimise any risk of cross-contamination of safe foods.

I do hope you enjoy the wide range of dishes and wonderful flavours in this book—free from today's all-pervasive 'staples' and their myriad derivatives. If you have queries or comments about any of the recipes or ingredients, please feel free to e-mail me at TishRichardson@intoleranz.com.au or visit my website at www.intoleranz.com.au.

Happy cooking!

## Key to Recipes—How to Select Recipes that Suit You

### Checking ingredients

An extensive section on ingredients is contained in the Glossary, page 173, and all ingredients with an entry are flagged '*' in the recipes.

Where an ingredient requires careful selection, it is flagged '(ingredient check)'. This is important for two reasons:

1 There is often a difference in the ingredients used in different brands of commercially made products; one brand may be suitable for use because it is free of all the 'No-Go' foods while another may not.

2 No commercially made brand free of all the 'No-Go' foods may be readily available, in which case I have included a recipe for making that ingredient from scratch, and have given a cross-reference to the recipe to simplify preparing the dish.

In each case, the Glossary entry includes details of what to watch out for when selecting the ingredient, and in many cases a suitable brand is nominated together with contact details for its manufacturer, to help you track down stockists of the ingredient in your area, or for double-checking with the manufacturer about its suitability.

Remember, manufacturers can and do change ingredients at any time, so **always** check a product label before buying to ensure it is *definitely* free of your 'No-Go' foods. Use the lists of the various forms in which each of the 'No-Go' foods may appear on a product label, in the section Avoiding 'No-Go' Foods and Their Derivatives on page 159, to help you understand a product's contents from its label.

In some instances the 'ingredient check' is also flagged with a ⓒ as '(ingredient check; ⓒ)' to indicate care is also required in selecting a corn-free brand for people with a corn sensitivity, see below.

### The 'No-Go' foods

All the recipes in this book are designed to be free of the following foods, including commercially made ingredients containing or derived from any of them:

- wheat and gluten;
- dairy;
- eggs;
- peanuts—many recipes include tree nuts; where peanuts and all tree nuts must be avoided, select recipes that are annotated with Ⓝ or Ⓝ at the end of the recipe title, indicating they are nut-free (see below);
- soy—some recipes include the Nuttelex brand of margarine, a dairy-free margarine which as of early 2004 contains lecithin derived from sunflower seeds not soy beans; refer to Glossary, page 181, for full details;
- garlic and onions—green shallots (see Glossary, page 179) are used, along with a very limited use of chives, but no onions (white, brown, red, Spanish), garlic or leeks;

ⓒⒻⓃⓥ

In addition, many of the recipes are vegetarian ⓥ and are also free of one or more of:

- corn ⓒ
- fish Ⓕ
- tree nuts Ⓝ

In each case the recipe title is flagged to indicate which of these food sensitivities the recipe suits. For example, a recipe flagged with Ⓒ Ⓕ Ⓥ is corn- and fish-free, and vegetarian.

The *absence* of one or more of these flags indicates that the recipe *cannot* be easily modified to avoid that food (in this example, the Ⓝ is missing since nuts are a core ingredient and so cannot easily be avoided). Where the vegetarian Ⓥ flag is absent, the recipe includes a core ingredient that is of animal origin.

In some recipes, one or more of these flags is outlined with a black circle to indicate careful selection of an ingredient is required to avoid that food. For example, where a recipe is annotated with Ⓝ, one or more of the ingredients may require careful selection to ensure they are nut-free. Information about how to select or replace that ingredient is included in the introduction to the recipe.

Corn can be a difficult ingredient to avoid since it is used in so many commercially produced products, as are corn derivatives, such as corn starch, a common thickener, or corn syrup, a sweetener. Please take time to read the section on Avoiding Corn, page 161, for a full explanation. Where a recipe is flagged Ⓒ, information about the avoidance of corn is included in two ways:

1  If the information is specific to the avoidance of corn *only*, information on brand selection is included in the introduction to the recipe.
2  If the ingredient requires careful selection because it may contain one or more of the 'No-Go' foods in addition to corn, the relevant ingredient is flagged with '(ingredient check; Ⓒ)'. Information about why care is required in selecting that ingredient is included in the relevant ingredient entry in the Glossary.

## Cooking hints and methods, and cooking tools

The section on Cooking Hints and Methods, page 201, is designed to explain and simplify certain cooking techniques and to help you to get the best results from the recipes. It covers topics from setting up a 'No-Go' food safe kitchen to a basic quickie 'how to' guide. For example, where a recipe includes terms such as 'pin-boned' or 'dry roasted' it is flagged '**' to indicate the technique is described in the Cooking Hints section.

You should also take the time to read the entry Checking the Oven Temperature on page 202 for hints to get the best out of your baking—including fully preheating the oven before you start baking, and pre-checking the stabilised oven temperature carefully to make sure you are baking at the temperature stated in the recipe, as even relatively small variations in temperature can lead to disappointing results when baking cakes and desserts. All dishes, except casseroles (because of their size), are cooked on the middle or top shelves of the oven.

For accuracy of measurement, given the sensitivity of many of the recipes (and in particular the flours) to small variations in the amount of an ingredient added, the amount of a non-liquid ingredient is generally stated as a weight rather than a volume. Exception is made where the weight of a dry or solid ingredient is not as critical since they will only be used, for example, for coating or dusting. In some cases, weight measures are also included for liquids such as syrups and honey since these can be measured by pouring them slowly into the pan or mixing bowl, rather than measuring out a tablespoonful at a time. A good set of electronic scales which also allow you to reset to zero, or tare ingredients as you add them is, therefore, invaluable (see Cooking Tools—Kitchen Scales, page 205).

The appendices also include a description of some really useful, time-saving cooking tools (page 204) to assist in recipe preparation.

### Please note

In all recipes, the volume of a tablespoon is 15 mL (not the Australian 20 mL) since most tablespoon measures commonly available through department and specialist kitchen shops are in fact 15 mL! The tablespoon volume (or weight) is given in each recipe to ensure accuracy of measurement. Again, it is critical to be accurate about volume when adding liquids to a recipe, particularly when making desserts, cakes and biscuits.

Unless otherwise specified in the recipe:

- all herbs, vegetables, salad leaves and fruit are washed, and thoroughly drained before use;
- potatoes are used with their skins on;
- fresh ginger, galangal and turmeric are peeled before being grated, chopped or sliced;
- green shallots* are 0.75–1 cm in diameter, so increase the number of shallots used in a recipe proportionately if only thinner shallots are available;
- all nuts and seeds are to be purchased raw and dry roasted** before use because of the industry practice of adding of wheat flour and other ingredients to many commercially roasted nuts;
- allow fish, meat, poultry and marinated dishes that have been stored chilled to warm at room temperature for a short period immediately before cooking to ensure the inside of the food is not cold when it is cooked rapidly, e.g. by char-grilling, or equivalent;
- microwave oven cooking times are given for a 850 watt microwave; increase or decrease cooking times depending on the relative power of your microwave oven.
- for all recipes using cooked beans, the weights and nutritional information stated are for the *rinsed, drained* weight of beans cooked from dried; if using canned beans note the '(ingredient check–Canned beans)' and see corresponding Glossary entry (page175).

### Core nutritional data

The core nutritional data included in each recipe are *per serve* unless otherwise stated. Where a recipe yields a range of serves, such as 4–6, the nutritional data are provided for the larger number of serves, which in this example would be 6.

The following data are included:

- energy supplied per serve in both kilojoules (kJ) and calories (cal);
- protein in grams (g);
- fat, as both total fat and saturated fat, in grams (g);
- carbohydrate, as both carbohydrate and total sugars, in grams (g);
- dietary fibre in grams (g);
- sodium in milligrams (mg).

---

### Symbols & abbreviations used in this book

- ● Indicates recipe is free of a particular food
- ◉ Careful selection of ingredient needed to avoid food that causes sensitivity
- \* Ingredient has entry in the Glossary
- \*\* Cooking method has entry in Cooking Hints and Methods
- † Kitchen tool has entry in Cooking Tools
- tsp Teaspoon
- tbs Tablespoon

---

## Soups

### ⓒ Artichoke and Red Capsicum Soup

ⓕ
ⓝ *This simple soup combines the delicate and very different flavours of globe and Jerusalem artichokes. The soup may be prepared in*
ⓥ *advance and the fresh parsley added after it is reheated.*

**Serves 4**

200 g Jerusalem artichokes (about 4), peeled and sliced

3 green shallots*, trimmed and sliced

½ red capsicum, seeded and diced

200 g red-skinned potatoes (such as Desiree), skin on, cleaned and diced

1 tsp finely chopped lemon thyme leaves

6 curry leaves*, bruised

freshly ground black pepper

1 L water

1 x 400 g can artichoke hearts in brine, rinsed, drained and shredded (ingredient check)

½ cup fresh flat-leaf (Italian) parsley, finely shredded

**Per serve**

Energy 375 kJ (90 cal)

Protein 5.1 g

Total fat 0.5 g

Saturated fat <0.1 g

Carbohydrate 14.9 g

Total sugars 4.4 g

Dietary fibre 5.9 g

Sodium 112 mg

**1** Put all the ingredients except the artichoke hearts and parsley in a pan, partially cover with a lid. Bring to the boil over a medium heat, reduce heat and simmer for 20 minutes or until the Jerusalem artichokes are tender when tested with a sharp knife.

**2** Remove from the heat. Add the artichoke hearts and mash lightly with a potato masher to partially break up the vegetables. Return to the heat and bring back to simmering point. Stir through two-thirds of the parsley and simmer for 1 minute.

**3** Serve immediately, garnished with the rest of the parsley.

### ⓒ Bean and Vegetable Soup—with or without Meatballs

ⓕ
ⓝ *Strange name, but this recipe offers three ways of using a delicious, home-made vegetable stock base! It makes a wholesome, flavour-*
ⓥ *filled soup for a starter or light lunch, served with suitable bread, and a more substantial meal by serving over bean-thread or rice*
*vermicelli or fresh rice noodles—or you can 'beef' it up with some tasty meatballs. If a using commercial stock check suitability of ingredients carefully (ingredient check—Stock; ⓒ). ⓥ omit meatballs.*

**Serves 6 as starter or 4 as a main**

Soup

2 L Vegetable Stock (page 12)

200 g cooked chickpeas** or red kidney beans** (if using canned, ingredient check)

200 g cooked cannellini beans** (if using canned, ingredient check)

370 mL tomato passata* (ingredient check)

freshly ground black pepper

1 tbs (15 mL) lemon juice

250 g bean-thread* or rice vermicelli* (optional)

Meatballs (optional)

350 g lean beef mince, well chilled (to keep meatballs intact while cooking)

¼–½ tsp sambal oelek* (ingredient check)

½ tsp ground cumin

1 tbs finely chopped herb used in Vegetable Stock

freshly ground black pepper

about ½ cup rice crumbs (Orgran brand)*

**Per serve with meatballs**

Energy 1082 kJ (258 cal)

Protein 20.4 g

Total fat 4.1 g

Saturated fat 1.4 g

Carbohydrate 33.0 g

Total sugars 7.2 g

Dietary fibre 7.9 g

Sodium 91 mg

Garnish
2 tbs each chopped flat-leaf (Italian) parsley, coriander and mint leaves

1 *Bean and Vegetable Soup* Strain Vegetable Stock and return to the pan. Discard the spice parcel. Roughly slice the carrots, celery and cabbage from the stock and return to the pan. Add all remaining soup ingredients except lemon juice and vermicelli and return to boiling point. Reduce heat, and simmer for 1–2 minutes to heat through thoroughly. Stir through the lemon juice and serve immediately garnished with the chopped herbs.

2 *Plus vermicelli* While the soup is heating, prepare the vermicelli as per the packet instructions where specified, or place the dried vermicelli in a pan, cover with boiling water and leave to stand for 5 minutes or until rehydrated and soft. Drain thoroughly and divide between serving bowls. Stir the lemon juice through the soup and ladle the hot soup over the vermicelli. Serve immediately garnished with the herbs.

3 *Plus meatballs* Prepare meatballs in advance and refrigerate until ready to cook. To make the meatballs, place all the ingredients except the rice crumbs in a bowl and combine well. Spread the rice crumbs on a small plate. Taking a rounded teaspoon at a time, roll the mix into balls—it will make about 36—and then roll in rice crumbs. Repeat until all the mix is used up.

   Prepare the soup as described in Step 1 and bring to the boil. Reduce heat so the soup is gently simmering and add meatballs. Simmer for 8–10 minutes or until the meatballs are cooked. Meanwhile, prepare vermicelli as described in Step 2, drain and divide between serving bowls. Stir the lemon juice through the soup and ladle the soup and meatballs over the vermicelli. Serve immediately garnished with chopped herbs.

##  Carrot, Sweet Pumpkin and Fennel Soup

*The colours of this wonderful soup are enough to make you want to eat it—but just wait until you taste it! You only need a small amount of liquid at the start as the vegetables release extra as they cook. The soup can be prepared 24–48 hours in advance and refrigerated; it is equally delicious served hot or cold. ⓥ use vegetable stock.*

**Serves 4–6**

600 g carrots, peeled and finely sliced
600 g Aussie sweet pumpkin (or Butternut or Jap), peeled, seeded and diced
300 g fennel, leaves and central stem removed, sliced
1 red capsicum, seeded and roughly chopped
500 mL (2 cups) chicken* or vegetable stock* (ingredient check—Stock; Ⓒ)
⅓ cup finely chopped fresh flat-leaf (Italian) or curly parsley leaves
freshly ground black pepper
dash of chilli oil* (optional; ingredient check)

Garnish
fresh flat-leaf (Italian) parsley, finely chopped

| Per serve |
| --- |
| Energy 450 kJ (108 cal) |
| Protein 4.8 g |
| Total fat 0.8 g |
| Saturated fat 0.1 g |
| Carbohydrate 19.0 g |
| Total sugars 14.3 g |
| Dietary fibre 5.5 g |
| Sodium 80 mg |

1 Place vegetables and stock in a large pan over a medium-high heat. Cover and heat until simmering. Reduce the heat and simmer gently for 20 minutes or until the vegetables are tender.

2 Remove from the heat. Roughly mash the vegetables with a potato masher (do not totally mash or purée). Add the parsley, black pepper and chilli oil, if using. Return to the heat to warm through.

3 Serve garnished with the parsley. If serving chilled, refrigerate after cooking and serve garnished as above.

## Celery Leaf and Roast Chestnut Soup with Lemon-Infused Olive Oil Garnish

*Celery leaves are used to make the stock base for this soup. I like to serve the soup really thick and creamy, so you'll find a small portion is quite filling. To make a thinner soup, add additional celery stock to taste. Serve with a suitable warm herb bread. The soup may be made 24 hours in advance and reheated immediately before serving.*

*Note: Chestnuts are not classified as a true nut; if cooking for someone with a nut sensitivity, check that they can safely eat chestnuts.*

**Serves 4-6**

450 g fresh chestnuts
leaves and top of stalks of 1 celery head (about 300 g)
1.5 L water
2 green shallots*, trimmed and roughly chopped
250 g red-skinned potatoes (such as Desiree), skin on, cleaned and diced
1 tsp fresh thyme or lemon thyme leaves
freshly ground black pepper

Garnish
small swirl of lemon-infused olive oil*
lemon zest

**Per serve**
Energy 708 kJ (169 cal)
Protein 2.4 g
Total fat 1.0 g
Saturated fat 0.2 g
Carbohydrate 34.7 g
Total sugars 8.7 g
Dietary fibre 4.3 g
Sodium 18 mg

1   Preheat oven to 200°C (180°C fan forced). Line a baking tray with baking paper.

2   With a sharp paring knife, cut a cross in flat side of each chestnut, deep enough to pierce the brown peel and reveal the flesh underneath. Place the chestnuts in a single layer in the tray and roast in the oven for 20–30 minutes, or until the slit widens to about 0.5 cm and the chestnut starts to brown slightly. Shake the tray every 10 minutes during roasting.

3   Wrap chestnuts in a towel immediately and set aside for 5 minutes. As soon as the chestnuts are cool enough to handle, peel, removing the shells and furry inner coat (pellicle).

4   While the chestnuts are roasting, place the celery leaves and water in a large pan, cover and bring to the boil. Reduce the heat and simmer for 30 minutes. Drain the stock, discard the celery leaves, and return the stock to the pan.

5   Add chestnuts and all remaining ingredients, place over a medium-high heat and bring to the boil. Reduce the heat and simmer gently, partially covered, for 45 minutes. Set aside to cool.

6   Transfer to a food processor and blend to a smooth consistency.

7   Immediately before serving, reheat the soup over a low-medium heat, stirring regularly to ensure the soup does not catch. Serve in pre-warmed bowls garnished with a small swirl of lemon-infused olive oil, and a pinch of lemon zest.

## Chilled Avocado and Curried Prawn Soup

*Simplicity plus—the two parts of this soup can be prepared 24 hours in advance and simply 'assembled' in the bowls just before serving. It is best served in wide, flat bowls rather than the traditional soup bowl, to show off the prawns. A small amount of this soup goes a long way on a hot summer's day.*

**Serves 6**

Soup
2 ripe avocados (about 225 g each), halved, stoned and peeled
1 green shallot*, trimmed and roughly chopped
5 tbs (75 mL) lime juice
750 mL (3 cups) chicken stock*, chilled (ingredient check—Stock; ⬤)

**Per serve**
Energy 571 kJ (136 cal)
Protein 8.7 g
Total fat 10.1 g
Saturated fat 2.2 g

generous pinch of cayenne pepper or hot paprika

freshly ground black pepper

1 tsp finely chopped fresh lemon thyme leaves

Prawns

200 g cooked peeled prawn meat

generous pinch of curry powder* (ingredient check)

tiny pinch of sea salt

Garnish

fresh lemon thyme leaves, finely chopped

**Carbohydrate 2.4 g**
**Total sugars 1.6 g**
**Dietary fibre 1.6 g**
**Sodium 135 mg**

1 Put all the soup ingredients in a food processor and blend until smooth. Transfer to a large jug, cover, refrigerate and chill well.

2 Mix the prawns with the curry powder and season with a tiny pinch of salt to taste. Cover and chill until ready to serve.

3 To serve, arrange the prawns as a small mound in the centre of 6 serving dishes. Stir the soup well and pour around the prawns. Garnish with the lemon thyme and serve immediately.

## Ⓒ Hot and Sour Prawn Soup
Ⓝ

*A great way to serve prawns as a starter, or for a light lunch, with a leafy salad and a crisp white wine. The soup stock may be made in advance, then just before serving cook the prawns and herbs in the stock.*

**Serves 4**

500 g large green prawns

2 tsp extra-light olive oil*

2 stalks lemon grass* (white part only), shredded lengthways and cut into 3 cm lengths

4 tsp finely chopped fresh ginger

1.5 L water

1 bunch fresh coriander, including roots*

freshly ground black pepper

6 kaffir lime leaves*, finely shredded

grated zest of ½ lime

juice of 2 limes

3 green shallots*, trimmed, shredded and cut into 3 cm lengths

½–1 large red chilli, seeded and very finely sliced into 1 cm lengths

½–1 large green chilli, seeded and very finely sliced into 1 cm lengths

Garnish

fresh coriander leaves, roughly chopped

**Per serve**
**Energy 363 kJ (87 cal)**
**Protein 13.4 g**
**Total fat 2.7 g**
**Saturated fat 0.3 g**
**Carbohydrate 1.7 g**
**Total sugars 1.4 g**
**Dietary fibre 1.6 g**
**Sodium 219 mg**

1 Shell and devein the prawns, leaving the tail intact. Place in a bowl, cover and refrigerate.

2 Place the oil in a large frying pan or wok over a high heat. Add the prawn heads, lemon grass and ginger and sauté for 3 minutes, stirring frequently.

3 Add the water and bring to the boil, skimming any scum off the surface. Cover and simmer over a low heat for 10 minutes. Strain the stock into a large, clean pan and discard solids.

4 Trim coriander roots (retaining the leaves for garnish), wash and chop finely. Place in a pestle and mortar with the pepper, work together to form a rough paste and add to the stock.

5   Reheat the stock until simmering gently and add prawns and all remaining ingredients. Simmer gently for 3–4 minutes or until the prawns turn pink.

6   Season to taste. Serve immediately garnished with the coriander leaves.

## Jerusalem Artichoke and Fennel Soup with Warm Cashew and Bacon Garnish

*The natural sweetness of the smooth fennel and artichoke base is complemented by the slightly salty, crunchy bacon and cashew garnish. The soup may be made in advance and reheated just before serving. It presents best served in flat soup bowls with the cashew and bacon piled in the centre. ⓢ use sunflower seeds in place of cashews. ⓥ omit bacon.*

**Serves 6-8**

1.5 L water

1 tsp lemon juice

350 g fine-skinned Desiree or Coliban potatoes (about 4), cleaned

500 g Jerusalem artichokes, cleaned

3 green shallots*, trimmed and roughly sliced

200 g fennel, roughly sliced

2 stalks celery (about 100 g) peeled, trimmed and roughly sliced

bouquet garni of 5 juniper berries, 1 bay leaf, 2 sprigs fresh basil tops, tied in muslin

1 tsp fresh dill tips, finely chopped

freshly ground black pepper (lots!)

Garnish

50 g raw cashews pieces, dry roasted**

75 g short-cut, rindless bacon (ingredient check; Ⓖ), trimmed of fat and finely diced

2 tbs finely shredded fresh flat-leaf (Italian) parsley

**Per serve**

Energy 518 kJ (124 cal)

Protein 5.8 g

Total fat 4.1 g

Saturated fat 0.8 g

Carbohydrate 14.9 g

Total sugars 3.6 g

Dietary fibre 3.7 g

Sodium 163 mg

1   Put the water and lemon juice in a large pan. Dice the potatoes and artichokes and place immediately in the lemon-water. Add the shallots, fennel, celery and bouquet garni. Partially cover with a lid, place over a high heat and bring to the boil. Reduce the heat and simmer gently for 40 minutes. Set aside to cool slightly.

2   Discard the bouquet garni and blend the soup to a smooth purée in a food processor (or with a Bamix blender) and place in a clean pan. Stir through the chopped dill. Season to taste with plenty of pepper.

3   Put the diced bacon in a small, non-stick pan and cook over a low-medium heat, tossing regularly, until browned and crunchy. Transfer to a paper towel to drain.

4   Reheat the soup over a low heat, stirring regularly.

5   Just before the soup is ready, put the cashew pieces and bacon in a small pan and warm gently. Remove from the heat and stir through the parsley.

6   To serve, ladle the soup into warmed soup dishes and place a spoonful of the cashew and bacon garnish in the middle of each.

## Minted Baby Pea and Crispy Pancetta Soup

*Using frozen minted baby peas and crisp and spicy pancetta, this soup has a wonderful blend of subtle flavours. The soup may be prepared 24–48 hours in advance and reheated just before serving.*

**Serves 4**

100 g hot (spicy) pancetta*, trimmed of excess fat and rind (ingredient check; ⊚)
extra–light olive oil spray* (ingredient check)
3 green shallots*, trimmed and finely sliced
500 g frozen baby mint green peas (Bird's Eye brand)*
1 L chicken* or vegetable stock* (ingredient check—Stock; ⊚)
4 sprigs fresh mint
freshly ground black pepper

Garnish
shredded fresh mint leaves
paprika

**Per serve**
Energy 675 kJ (161 cal)
Protein 12.8 g
Total fat 4.6 g
Saturated fat 1.7 g
Carbohydrate 12.5 g
Total sugars 6.3 g
Dietary fibre 7.0 g
Sodium 379 mg

1 Heat a non-stick frying pan to very hot. Add the pancetta and fry until crisp. Place on kitchen towels to drain then chop finely. Transfer to a medium-sized pan.

2 Very lightly spray a non-stick frying pan with oil, place over a high heat, add the shallots and sauté 1 minute. Add the peas and cook for 2 minutes, tossing regularly. Add to the pan with the pancetta.

3 Add the chicken stock and mint and bring to the boil over a medium heat. Reduce the heat and simmer for 3–4 minutes or until the peas are tender. Set aside to cool slightly.

4 Remove the mint and transfer the soup to a food processor. Blend until smooth. Sieve into a clean pan, pressing the solids through with the back of a metal spoon. Discard the remaining solids.

5 Season to taste with freshly ground black pepper.

6 Reheat just before serving. Serve immediately garnished with the shredded mint and a pinch of paprika.

## Parsnip, Apple and Celery Soup

*This recipe offers an unusual combination of fruit and vegetables to make a delicately flavoured soup.*
Ⓝ *use olive oil and omit walnut garnish.* Ⓥ *use vegetable stock.*

**Serves 6**

2 tsp macadamia* or extra–light olive oil*
6 green shallots*, trimmed and coarsely chopped
3 Granny Smith apples or equivalent, peeled, cored and chopped
2 stalks celery, finely chopped (retain leaves for bouquet garni)
6 medium parsnips, peeled and finely shredded
¼ bunch chives, chopped
1 L chicken* or vegetable stock* (ingredient check—Stock; ⊚)
500 mL (2 cups) water
bouquet garni of celery leaves, 3 sprigs fresh thyme, 5 sprigs fresh parsley, tied in muslin
freshly ground black pepper

Garnish
10 walnuts, coarsely chopped
chopped chives

**Per serve**
Energy 487 kJ (116 cal)
Protein 3.4 g
Total fat 2.3 g
Saturated fat 0.3 g
Carbohydrate 20.5 g
Total sugars 14.7 g
Dietary fibre 5.4 g
Sodium 55 mg

1  Place the oil in a large heavy-based pan over a medium-high heat, add shallots and sauté for 3–4 minutes, stirring regularly, or until the shallots are starting to soften.

2  Add the apple, celery and parsnips and sauté for 3–4 minutes.

3  Add half the chives, the stock, water, bouquet garni and black pepper. Partially cover with a lid and simmer gently for 20–25 minutes or until the fruit and vegetables are soft.

4  Blend in food processor (or with a Bamix blender) until smooth. Season to taste.

5  Reheat the soup gently just before serving, stirring frequently.

6  Divide the chopped walnuts equally between 6 bowls, ladle the hot soup over the top. Serve immediately garnished with remaining chopped chives.

## Seafood Bisque

*A bisque with a difference—not the usual cream base but a light coconut- and herb-based stock to bring out the wonderful seafood flavours. It may be served as is with suitable warm crusty bread, or over a bed of rice for a more substantial meal. The stock may be made in advance and the soup cooked just before serving. If using mussels in shells, scrub well and de-beard before cooking.*

**Serves 4**
300 g green large king prawns

Stock
250 mL (1 cup) white wine (ingredient check—Wine)
750 mL (3 cups) water
3 green shallots*, trimmed and roughly chopped
5 kaffir lime leaves*, bruised
1 stalk lemon grass* (white part only), roughly chopped and bruised
½–1 tsp tamarind paste* (ingredient check)
zest and juice of 1 lemon
1 stalk celery, with leaves
2 coriander roots*, roughly chopped
freshly ground black pepper

Soup
2 tsp arrowroot plus 1 tbs water, mixed to a smooth paste
750 g mixed seafood (white fish fillet, tuna cubed, mussel and prawn meat, calamari, scallops)
1 bird's eye red chilli, seeded and finely chopped
freshly ground black pepper
100 mL light coconut milk* (ingredient check; ⊚)
⅓ cup finely shredded fresh coriander leaves

Garnish
sprigs of fresh coriander

**Per serve**
Energy 1036 kJ (247 cal)
Protein 40.0 g
Total fat 3.0 g
Saturated fat 1.5 g
Carbohydrate 4.2 g
Total sugars 2.3 g
Dietary fibre 1.2 g
Sodium 246 mg

1  Shell and devein the prawns, leaving the tails intact. Put prawns in a glass or ceramic bowl, cover and refrigerate. Place the prawn heads and shells and all the stock ingredients in a pan over a medium heat. Cover and bring to the boil. Reduce the heat and simmer for 20 minutes. Strain the stock into a large pan and discard the solids.

2  Return the stock to the heat, stir through the arrowroot paste and add the mixed seafood, chilli and black pepper. Simmer gently for 5 minutes or until the seafood is cooked (discard any unopened mussels if using mussels in their shells).

3  Stir through the coconut milk and coriander leaves and cook for 1 minute. Serve immediately garnished with the sprigs of coriander.

## Smoked Salmon, Chive and Green Shallot Soup

*The soup may be prepared in advance to the completion of the vegetable broth stage. Simply reheat the broth and add the smoked salmon 2–3 minutes before serving.*

**Serves 6**

6 large green shallots*, trimmed and finely shredded

1 baby fennel bulb (about 100 g trimmed), tips removed, very finely shredded

1 stalk celery, very finely sliced

400 g chat or small Coliban potatoes, skin on, cleaned and finely diced

grated zest of ¼ lemon

375 mL (1½ cups) dry white wine (ingredient check—Wine)

1 L fish stock* (ingredient check—Stock; ◎)

250 mL (1 cup) water

freshly ground black pepper

200 g smoked salmon* pieces, finely shredded (ingredient check)

Garnish

½ bunch chives, finely chopped

Bouquet garni (wrap in a small square of muslin)

1 star anise

3 celery leaves

1 bay leaf

½ tsp fresh lemon thyme leaves

3 sprigs fresh parsley

1 tsp shredded lemon grass* (white part only)

**Per serve**

Energy 787 kJ (188 cal)

Protein 11.2 g

Total fat 2.1 g

Saturated fat 0.4 g

Carbohydrate 13.2 g

Total sugars 3.4 g

Dietary fibre 3.1 g

Sodium 641 mg

1 Place all the ingredients except the smoked salmon in a large pan over a medium-high heat, cover and bring to the boil. Reduce the heat and simmer for 15 minutes or until the vegetables are tender.

2 Remove the bouquet garni, add the smoked salmon and simmer for a further 2–3 minutes, stirring occasionally. Serve immediately garnished with the chopped chives.

## Stocks

At the outset it may look as though making your own stock is time consuming—but in most cases it is just a matter of throwing everything together in a large pan and leaving it to simmer away for a couple of hours while the lovely flavours develop. Plus stocks freeze well (for up to 6 months), so they are an excellent and economical way to make use of left-over bones or carcasses, or get the last scrap of goodness out of a roast leg of lamb or a chicken. Home-made stock adds a whole new dimension to soups, stews and sauces. Refrigerating the stock overnight results in the fat settling and solidifying on top, making skimming it off in one go easy.

## Beef Stock

*Of all the stocks, beef stock really benefits from oven-roasting the bones and vegetables before making the stock. If you are in a hurry, you can omit that step, but the stock will lack the deep and robust flavour. Ask your butcher to crack and cut the bones for you.*

**Makes 2 litres**

1 kg beef knuckle, cracked

1 kg beef soup bones with meat (such as shin or shank)

2 large carrots, scrubbed and quartered

1 parsnip, scrubbed and quartered

2 stalks celery, stalks quartered and leaves trimmed

250 mL (1 cup) water

500 mL (2 cups) boiling water

4 green shallots*, trimmed and halved

5 sprigs fresh parsley

2 bay leaves

2 sprigs fresh thyme or 1 tsp dried thyme

¼ tsp black peppercorns

2.5 L water

Per 100 mL

Energy 88 kJ (21 cal)

Protein 1.6 g

Total fat 0.4 g

Saturated fat 0.2 g

Carbohydrate 2.7 g

Total sugars 1.3 g

Dietary fibre 1.0 g

Sodium 17 mg

1  Preheat the oven to 240°C (220°C fan forced).

2  Wash the bones, place in a large roasting tray and roast for 30 minutes. Turn the bones and add the carrots, parsnip, celery pieces (not leaves) and 250 mL water. Loosely cover with aluminium foil and roast for a further 30 minutes, turning once (the bones should be well browned).

3  Transfer the bones, vegetables and juices to a large pan or stockpot. Deglaze the tray with 2 cups boiling water and add the resulting gravy to the pan. Add all the remaining ingredients including the celery leaves to the pan, cover and slowly bring to the boil. Reduce the heat and simmer for 2–3 hours or until a good flavour has developed.

4  Remove the bones and strain the stock. Set aside to cool slightly before cooling fully, uncovered, in the refrigerator. Skim the fat from the surface before using.

5  Use the stock fresh as required; refrigerate for up to 3 days or freeze for up to 6 months.

## Ⓖ Chicken Stock

Ⓕ
Ⓝ
*This stock may be made from a left-over chicken carcasses or from fresh chicken bones. If you are short of time, for a real quick 'n' easy chicken stock see page 12.*

**Makes 2 litres**

2 chicken carcasses or 1 kg chicken bones (neck, back, feet, etc.)

4 green shallots*, trimmed and halved

2 carrots, washed and quartered

2 stalks celery with leaves, cut into 5-6 cm pieces

¼ tsp black peppercorns

¼ tsp coriander seeds

2 cm knob fresh ginger, peeled

2 sprigs fresh oregano or ½ tsp dried oregano

2 bay leaves

2.5 L water

Per 100 mL

Energy 52 kJ (12 cal)

Protein 0.8 g

Total fat 0.3 g

Saturated fat 0.1 g

Carbohydrate 1.5 g

Total sugars 0.9 g

Dietary fibre 0.7 g

Sodium 13 mg

**1** Put all the ingredients in a large pan or stockpot. Bring to the boil slowly, cover and simmer slowly for 2–3 hours.

**2** Strain the stock, discard the solids and set aside to cool slightly before cooling fully, uncovered, in the refrigerator. Skim the fat from the surface before using.

**3** Use the stock fresh as required; refrigerate for up to 3 days or freeze for up to 6 months.

## Ⓖ Dashi and Quick Dashi Soup

Ⓝ
*Dashi* is soup stock used extensively in Japanese cooking and is usually made with bonito flakes* and kombu*. Ready-made dashi (sold as hon dashi or dashi-no-moto) is available as granules, powder and concentrate in Japanese supermarkets but usually contains MSG. This very delicately flavoured stock is easily transformed into a nutritious soup—see suggestions below.*

**Makes 1 litre—serves 4**

Stock

2 g dried kombu*

4 g dried sliced shiitake mushrooms*

2 green shallots*, trimmed and finely sliced

1.25 L cold water

3 g bonito flakes*

Soup

250 g raw prawn meat or 12 oyster or button mushrooms, cleaned

zest of ½ lemon

4 tbs kizami nori*

½ sheet roasted nori*, roughly chopped

Garnish

reserved green tops of shallots, finely sliced

¼ cup fresh coriander leaves

2 tbs sushi-style pickled ginger*, finely chopped (optional; ingredient check—Ginger; Ⓖ)

Per serve

Energy 297 kJ (71 cal)

Protein 14.1 g

Total fat 0.5 g

Saturated fat 0.1 g

Carbohydrate 2.2 g

Total sugars 1.9 g

Dietary fibre 2.0 g

Sodium 272 mg

**1** Place the kombu, shiitake mushrooms, shallots and water in a pan over a low heat and bring to the boil slowly (takes 12–15 minutes); do not boil the kombu. Remove the kombu and leave to stand for 20 minutes. Strain and discard the shiitake and shallots (these can be retained for use in the soup if desired).

**2** Return to the boil and add the bonito. Remove from the heat and let the bonito sink. Strain and discard the bonito.

3  To make the soup, reheat the stock, add the prawns (or mushrooms) and lemon zest and simmer for 1–2 minutes or until the prawns (or mushrooms) are just cooked through. Divide the nori between 4 soup bowls and ladle the hot soup over the top. Serve immediately garnished with the shallots tops, coriander leaves and ginger, if using.

## Fish Stock

*The left-overs from a large whole baked fish, such as a kingfish, Australian salmon or snapper, make an excellent stock, particularly if the fish has been baked stuffed with lemon and fresh herbs—make sure to retain the stuffing as well as the head, bones and any skin to make your stock. Alternatively, start from scratch with fresh fish trimmings from your fishmonger. Fish stock only needs to simmer for 15–20 minutes to bring out the best flavour; longer and it becomes bitter.*

**Makes 1 litre**

head, bones and skin from 1 medium-large whole baked fish or 750 g fish trimmings
2 green shallots*, trimmed and halved
1 carrot, cleaned and quartered
1 stalk celery, with leaves, halved
zest and juice of 1 lime
1 bay leaf
½ tsp fennel seeds
¼ tsp black peppercorns
pinch of ground mace
250 mL (1 cup) white wine (ingredient check— Wine)
1 L water

**Per 100 mL**
Energy 120 kJ (29 cal)
Protein 0.7 g
Total fat 0.3 g
Saturated fat 0.1 g
Carbohydrate 1.5 g
Total sugars 0.8 g
Dietary fibre 0.4 g
Sodium 23 mg

1  Put all the ingredients in a large pan or stockpot. Bring to the boil slowly, cover and simmer slowly for 15–20 minutes.

2  Strain the stock, discard the solids and set aside to cool slightly before covering and refrigerating, or cooling fully before freezing.

3  Use the stock fresh as required; refrigerate for up to 3 days or freeze for up to 6 months.

## Prawn Stock

*When you buy raw prawns be sure to reserve the heads and shells to make this simple stock. It always adds a great depth of flavour to any sauce for char-grilled seafood or a seafood risotto. The stock can be frozen in ice-cube trays and transferred, once frozen, to freezer bags—a cube or two can then be added to a sauce for extra flavour. Simply vary the amount of white wine you use according to the weight of raw prawns being used.*

**Makes 500 mL**

heads and shells from 750 g — 1 kg green prawns
500 mL (2 cups) white wine (ingredient check—Wine)
250 mL (1 cup) water
2 sprigs fresh lemon thyme
6 black peppercorns, lightly crushed

**Per 100 mL**
Energy 341 kJ (81 cal)
Protein 3.4 g
Total fat 0.1 g
Saturated fat <0.1 g
Carbohydrate 0.3 g
Total sugars 0.3 g
Dietary fibre <0.1 g
Sodium 77 mg

1  Put all the ingredients in a large pan or wok. Cover and simmer over a low heat for 10 minutes, stirring occasionally.

2  Strain the stock, discard the solids and set aside to cool slightly before cooling fully in the refrigerator.

3  Use the stock fresh as required; refrigerate for up to 3 days or freeze for up to 6 months.

## Quick Chicken Stock

*This is a quick way to make use of a left-over chicken carcass. While it may not provide the depth of flavour of a chicken stock made the traditional way (page 10), it does provide an easy base for soups or chicken-based dishes. Use the same method to make a quick fish stock—simply replace the chicken carcass with a barbecued or baked fish head, skin and carcass, shrimp paste\* and lemon.*

**Sodium 14 mg**

**Makes 1 litre**

1 cooked chicken carcass

10 black peppercorns, lightly crushed

6 coriander seeds, lightly crushed

2 green shallots\*, trimmed and sliced

2 stalks celery, finely sliced

2 sprigs sage or other fresh herbs

3 x 375 mL (3 x 1½ cups) water

**Per 100 mL**

**Energy 46 kJ (11 cal)**

**Protein 0.7 g**

**Total fat 0.3 g**

**Saturated fat 0.1 g**

**Carbohydrate 1.2 g**

**Total sugars 0.6 g**

**Dietary fibre 0.5 g**

1  Place the chicken carcass and the remaining ingredients with the first 375 mL water in a covered, microwave-proof dish.

2  Microwave on high for 5 minutes. Strain stock into a bowl or jug and return chicken, vegetables and herbs to dish.

3  Add the second 375 mL water to dish, cover and microwave on high for 5 minutes; strain stock into bowl and return solids to dish.

4  Repeat with the third 375 mL water. Strain the stock, discard the solids and set stock aside to cool slightly before cooling fully, uncovered, in the refrigerator. Skim the fat from the surface before using.

5  Use the stock fresh as required: refrigerate for up to 3 days or freeze for up to 6 months.

## Vegetable Stock

*An easy stock to 'throw' together. Tie the juniper berries, star anise and peppercorns in a muslin square to make separating the stock and vegetables easy. The vegetables take on the wonderful flavours of the spices, so can be reheated and served as is or used as part of a soup such as Bean and Vegetable Soup—with or without Meatballs (page 1).*

**Makes 2 litres**

2.5 L water

3 large green shallots\*, trimmed and roughly chopped

3 stalks celery with leaves, trimmed and quartered

2 large carrots, peeled and quartered

300 g white cabbage, roughly chopped

10 juniper berries

1 star anise

1 tbs black peppercorns

1 tbs (15 mL) balsamic vinegar\* (ingredient check—Vinegar; ◯)

2 bay leaves, bruised

mixture of 3–4 types of fresh herbs:

rosemary, dill, coriander roots\*, sage, tarragon, lemon thyme, oregano

**Per 100 mL**

**Energy 33 kJ (8 cal)**

**Protein 0.4 g**

**Total fat <0.1 g**

**Saturated fat <0.1 g**

**Carbohydrate 1.2 g**

**Total sugars 1.1 g**

**Dietary fibre 0.7 g**

**Sodium 13 mg**

1  Place all the ingredients in a large pan and bring to the boil slowly. Cover and simmer gently for 1–1½ hours, or until the stock has developed a good flavour.

2  Strain the stock, discard the spice parcel, retaining the vegetables for a side dish. Set aside to cool slightly before cooling fully in the refrigerator.

3  Use the stock fresh as required; refrigerate for up to 3 days or freeze for up to 6 months.

Starters

## Avocado Stuffed with Citrus-Dressed Chicken Salad

*Avocados are wonderful fruits at the best of times, but stuffed with a tasty chicken salad they make a great light lunch served on a large platter with a green leafy salad or alone as a starter for a luncheon or dinner. If you have no roasted cold chicken handy, see the recipe for Blood Orange and Poached Chicken Salad on page 59 for a simple method of poaching chicken fillets.*
*use virgin olive oil in place of the nut oil.*

**Serves 4**

Filling
150 g cooked chicken breast, chilled and finely diced
50 g pepitas, dry roasted**
⅓ cup finely chopped watercress
2 tbs finely chopped fresh coriander
1 small Lebanese cucumber (about 12 cm), ends trimmed, seeded and finely diced
freshly ground black pepper

Dressing
zest and juice of ½ chilled orange
1 tbs (15 mL) balsamic vinegar* (ingredient check—Vinegar; )
1 tbs (15 mL) walnut* or macadamia oil*
½ tsp freshly grated ginger
½ red chilli, seeded and very finely chopped
pinch of palm sugar* or soft brown sugar
freshly ground black pepper

Avocado
2 large ripe avocados, chilled
2 tbs (30 mL) lemon juice, chilled

Garnish
fresh coriander leaves

**Per serve**
Energy 1274 kJ (304 cal)
Protein 13.2 g
Total fat 25.4 g
Saturated fat 5.1 g
Carbohydrate 5.6 g
Total sugars 4.0 g
Dietary fibre 3.7 g
Sodium 39 mg

1  Put all the filling ingredients in a mixing bowl.

2  Mix all the dressing ingredients together.

3  Cut the avocados in half and discard the stones. Carefully slice an oval of skin off the uncut side of each avocado to form a flat base to stand the avocado on. Carefully scoop out the flesh into the mixing bowl with the filling, leaving a 1 cm thick lining in the shell. Coat the lining with lemon juice to prevent discolouration.

4  Quickly dice the scooped avocado flesh in the mixing bowl and add the dressing. Gently toss to mix and dress the filling. Pile into the prepared avocado shells. Serve immediately garnished with the coriander leaves.

## ⓒ Buckwheat Pasta, Smoked Salmon and Cucumber Salad

ⓝ *A simple salad starter based on the lovely nutty flavour of buckwheat\*. You can use either buckwheat spiral pasta\* for this dish or Japanese buckwheat (soba) noodles\*. The key is to ensure that you do not overcook the pasta.*

**Serves 4**

300 g buckwheat pasta\* (ingredient check—Pasta)

1 Lebanese cucumber (about 125 g), ends trimmed

2 green shallots\*, trimmed and finely sliced

175 g smoked salmon\*, roughly chopped (ingredient check)

2 tbs finely chopped coriander root\*

freshly ground black pepper

Dressing

2 tbs (30 mL) lemon juice

½ tsp lemon zest

2 tbs (30 mL) apple cider vinegar\*

4 tsp apple juice concentrate\*

2 tbs pure sesame oil\*

Garnish

40 g wild or baby rocket leaves

4 tsp sesame seeds, dry roasted\*\*

**Per serve**

**Energy 1666 kJ (398 cal)**

**Protein 20.5 g**

**Total fat 10.2 g**

**Saturated fat 1.3 g**

**Carbohydrate 61.0 g**

**Total sugars 8.7 g**

**Dietary fibre 4.7 g**

**Sodium 760 mg**

1  Cook the buckwheat pasta following the packet instructions—do not overcook. Drain immediately, rinse with cold water. Drain thoroughly. Transfer to a mixing bowl, cover and chill.

2  Blend the dressing ingredients together well.

3  Using a vegetable peeler, stripe peel the cucumber lengthways so about half the skin remains intact. Slice the cucumber in half lengthways. Remove the seeds with a teaspoon, and slice into 0.5 cm pieces crossways.

4  Add the cucumber, shallots, smoked salmon, coriander and dressing to the pasta, and toss gently to combine and dress. Season to taste.

5  Arrange a bed of rocket leaves on 4 serving plates. Spoon the pasta mix on top. Garnish with the sesame seeds and serve immediately.

## ⓒ Bush Tomato Tartlets

Ⓕ *Bush tomatoes have a very distinct flavour—one that is quite unlike traditional tomatoes. These tartlets make a simple, tasty*
ⓝ *appetiser to serve with champagne or chilled white wine. This bush tomato sauce mix also makes a great stir-through sauce for*
Ⓥ *pasta. I make the bases in advance and assemble and heat just before serving.*

**Makes 20**

½ quantity Shortcrust Pastry (page 155)

extra-light olive oil spray\* (ingredient check)

Topping

3 Roma tomatoes, very finely chopped

1 tsp ground bush tomato\*

3 sun-dried tomatoes\*, finely chopped (ingredient check; ⓒ)

2 tsp tomato paste (ingredient check)

3 tbs (45 mL) water

**Per tart**

**Energy 209 kJ (50 cal)**

**Protein 0.9 g**

**Total fat 2.9 g**

**Saturated fat 0.5 g**

**Carbohydrate 5.2 g**

**Total sugars 0.6 g**

**Dietary fibre 1.0 g**

**Sodium 26 mg**

¼ tsp ground lemon myrtle*

¼ tsp ground mountain pepper* or freshly ground black pepper

10 black olives, pitted and halved (ingredient check; ⬤)

Garnish

finely chopped fresh parsley

1   Preheat the oven to 200°C (180°C fan forced). Line a baking tray with baking paper.

2   Roll the pastry out between 2 sheets of baking paper to a 2–3 mm thickness. Using a 5 cm diameter pastry cutter, cut out 20 tartlet bases, remove excess pastry from around the bases (to retain their shape). Transfer the bases to the tray. Repeat with the left-over pastry to make additional bases. Bake in the oven for 10–12 minutes or until just starting to lightly brown. Set aside to cool.

3   If cooking the tartlets immediately, reduce the oven temperature to 180°C (160°C fan forced).

4   Place all the topping ingredients except the lemon myrtle, mountain pepper and olives in a small pan and simmer gently until a thick sauce is formed, stirring occasionally. Remove from the heat and stir through the lemon myrtle and mountain pepper.

5   Spoon a teaspoonful of the bush tomato mix onto the centre of each base, top with an olive and warm in the oven for 4–5 minutes. Transfer to a serving plate and serve immediately, garnished with chopped parsley.

## Chickpea Patties with Mint Chutney on Green Apple and Tomato Salsa

*These vegetarian patties with the crunchiness of fresh corn and kohlrabi are delicious dressed with the fresh, minty chutney. The chutney is best made 24–48 hours in advance so the flavours have time to develop fully.*

**Serves 4—makes 16 patties**

1 quantity Mint Chutney (page 88)

Apple and Tomato Salsa

1 green apple

1 tsp lemon juice

3 Roma tomatoes, diced

⅓ cup roughly chopped fresh coriander leaves

1 tsp extra-virgin olive oil*

2 tsp balsamic vinegar* (ingredient check—Vinegar)

freshly ground black pepper

Chickpea Patties

480 g cooked chickpeas** (if using canned, ingredient check)

4 tsp freshly grated ginger

¼–1 tsp sambal oelek* or chilli paste* (ingredient check)

1 tsp tamarind paste* (ingredient check)

1 tsp ground cumin

freshly ground black pepper

2 coriander roots*, finely chopped

10 fresh basil leaves, shredded

100 g fresh corn kernels (if using canned, rinse and drain well)

100 g finely diced kohlrabi* or daikon*

1½ cups rice crumbs (Orgran brand)*

extra–light olive oil spray* (ingredient check)

Per serve

Energy 1709 kJ (408 cal)

Protein 15.5 g

Total fat 9.0 g

Saturated fat 2.3 g

Carbohydrate 63.9 g

Total sugars 9.4 g

Dietary fibre 11.9 g

Sodium 42 mg

1  Prepare the Mint Chutney as described on page 88 and refrigerate.

2  Core and dice the apple, place in a mixing bowl and quickly coat with the lemon juice. Mix through all the remaining salsa ingredients. Cover and set aside.

3  Put all the patty ingredients except the corn kernels, kohlrabi (daikon), rice crumbs and oil in a food processor and process until coarsely chopped. Add the corn kernels and kohlrabi; pulse for 2–3 seconds. Transfer to a bowl and stir through 1 cup of rice crumbs.

4  Put the remaining rice crumbs on a plate. Roll about 2 tablespoonfuls of the patty mix in the crumbs and flatten to form a patty. Place on a clean plate. Repeat with the remaining patty mix.

5  Spray a large, non-stick frying pan lightly with oil and place over a high heat. When hot, add half the patties and cook for 2–3 minutes on each side, or until browned and cooked through. Transfer to a plate and repeat with remaining patties.

6  To serve, divide the salsa between 4 plates, top each with 4 patties. Stir the mint chutney and spoon over the top of the patties. Serve immediately.

## Chilled Calamari Salad

*My favourite way of eating calamari—served alone as a starter or as part of a platter with oysters and Mediterranean Octopus Salad (page 19). The calamari is wonderfully tender—but be careful not to overcook it. Make the salad 24 hours in advance and refrigerate to allow the flavours to develop fully.*

**Serves 4**

500 g cleaned calamari tubes
3-4 cos lettuce leaves, washed, drained and shredded

Dressing
¾–1 tsp sambal oelek* or chilli paste* (ingredient check; ◉)
1 tbs (15 mL) brown rice vinegar* (ingredient check—Vinegar)
1 tbs (15 mL) fish sauce* (ingredient check; ◉)
½ tsp pure sesame oil*
1 tbs (15 mL) extra–virgin olive oil*
3 tbs (45 mL) lime juice
¼ tsp soft brown sugar
¼ tsp tamarind paste* (ingredient check)
½ Lebanese cucumber, seeded and finely diced
2 tbs finely chopped coriander root*

Garnish
roughly chopped fresh coriander leaves
freshly ground black pepper

**Per serve**
**Energy 604 kJ (144 cal)**
**Protein 21.7 g**
**Total fat 5.5 g**
**Saturated fat 1.0 g**
**Carbohydrate 1.4 g**
**Total sugars 1.2 g**
**Dietary fibre 0.5 g**
**Sodium 770 mg**

1  Put all the dressing ingredients except the cucumber and coriander in a glass or ceramic mixing bowl and whisk to combine. Stir through the cucumber and coriander and set aside.

2  Bring a pan of water to a fast boil. Add one calamari tube and cook for 20 seconds; do not overcook or the calamari will be tough. Quickly remove the calamari and slice finely crossways while hot. Toss through the dressing immediately.

3  Repeat with the remaining calamari tubes. Cover and refrigerate for a minimum of 2 hours, preferably overnight.

4  To serve, arrange a bed of shredded lettuce on each plate and spoon the calamari and dressing on top. Serve immediately garnished with the coriander leaves and black pepper.

## Cider, Chicken, Apple and Walnut Terrine

*This makes a wonderful light starter or, by serving a slightly larger wedge, an excellent main. Pickled Cucumber Salsa (page 88) is a great salad accompaniment. To make slicing into wedges simple, use a plate or bowl with a flat base of the same diameter as the terrine tin so that the terrine can be evenly weighted while setting. Don't overfill the terrine with the cider–gelatine mix; the chicken mix should not float off the bottom of the tin to avoid the liquid overflowing the tin when weighted. ⊙ sparkling apple juice may contain vitamin C (see Avoiding Corn, page 161).*

**Serves 8 as a starter, 6 as a main**

500 g skinless chicken breast fillets, trimmed and cut into bite-sized pieces

600 mL dry cider (ingredient check) or non–alcoholic sparkling apple juice

zest of 1 lemon

2 tsp pure sesame oil*

1 tbs (15 mL) lemon juice

1 crisp red apple

75 g raw walnuts, dry roasted** and broken into sixths

15 g red capsicum, very finely diced

1 tsp finely chopped fresh marjoram leaves

freshly ground black pepper

1 crisp green apple

25 g powdered gelatine

1 x 20 cm round non–stick baking tin (1.5 litre capacity)

**Dressing**

stock from the chicken (above)

½ medium-sized red chilli, seeded and very finely diced

juice of ½ lemon

½ tsp pure sesame oil*

½ tsp finely chopped fresh marjoram leaves

50 mL water

**Garnish**

wild or baby rocket leaves

| Per serve |
| --- |
| Energy 945 kJ (226 cal) |
| Protein 17.6 g |
| Total fat 11.4 g |
| Saturated fat 1.7 g |
| Carbohydrate 8.5 g |
| Total sugars 8.2 g |
| Dietary fibre 1.4 g |
| Sodium 59 mg |

1 Poach the chicken in 100 mL of the cider in a pan for 4 minutes over a medium heat or until just cooked through. Transfer the chicken into a mixing bowl using a slotted spoon; retain the stock for the dressing. Stir the sesame oil and lemon zest through while the chicken is still warm. Cover and set aside to cool.

2 Core, cube and coat the red apple with lemon juice. Add to the cooled chicken and mix through the walnuts, capsicum, marjoram and seasoning.

3 Core the green apple and cut into wedges (8 wedges if serving the terrine as a starter or 6 if serving as a main). Coat immediately with lemon juice. Arrange in a ring on the bottom of the tin, so that each wedge of terrine, when cut, will have an apple crescent in the top.

4 Gently spoon the chicken mix on top of the apple crescents mix without disturbing their placement. Smooth surface lightly.

5 Heat 150 mL of the cider in a small pan until just boiling. Reduce the heat and whisk in the gelatine until fully dissolved; do not boil. Remove from the heat and whisk in the remaining cider. Pour over the chicken mix until almost covered; the chicken should not lift off the bottom of the tin. Set aside any left-over jelly mix.

6 Cover with plastic wrap, place a flat-bottomed plate on top and weigh down with a packet of rice or equivalent. Refrigerate overnight. (If there is any jelly mix left over, refrigerate the terrine for 1 hour or until it has started

to set, warm the left-over jelly in a microwave or in a basin of hot water to re-liquify and pour over the chicken mix until it is just covered. Recover with plastic wrap, replace the weight and refrigerate overnight.)

7  To make the dressing mix all the ingredients together well in a small jug, cover and refrigerate.

8  10–20 minutes before serving, dip the terrine tin in hot water very quickly and invert on a large serving dish. Return to the refrigerator to allow any liquid to reset.

9  Arrange a bed of rocket leaves on serving plates. Slice the terrine into wedges between the green apple and place on the rocket. Drizzle 1–2 tablespoons of dressing over each and serve immediately.

## Ⓒ Fig and Pancetta Parcels with Pickled Ginger Stuffing

Ⓕ *A wonderful light snack or starter, the flavours of the fig parcels contrast with the Green Olive Dressing on the salad bed. As an*
Ⓝ *alternative in out-of-fig season, try using firm ripe pears (such as Beurre Bosc or Nashi), cored from their base and stuffed with the ginger or char-grilled capsicum. Pears need 8–10 minutes to warm through at the same oven setting.*

**Serves 4**

Dressing
4 tsp extra-virgin olive oil*
4 tsp apple cider vinegar*
4 tsp lemon juice
½ tsp apple juice concentrate*
25 g green olives, pitted and finely chopped (ingredient check)
½ tsp finely chopped fresh oregano or thyme leaves

Figs
4 fresh figs
2 tsp finely shredded sushi-style pickled ginger* (ingredient check—Ginger; Ⓒ)
12 slices very finely sliced pancetta* (hot or mild; ingredient check; Ⓒ)
4-5 cos lettuce leaves, shredded

Garnish
2 tbs (30 mL) sesame seeds, dry roasted**

**Per serve**
**Energy 572 kJ (137 cal)**
**Protein 6.9 g**
**Total fat 9.5 g**
**Saturated fat 2.2 g**
**Carbohydrate 6.7 g**
**Total sugars 6.1 g**
**Dietary fibre 3.1 g**
**Sodium 466 mg**

1  Preheat oven to 220°C (200°C fan forced). Line a baking tray with baking paper.

2  Put all the dressing ingredients in a screw-top jar and shake to mix thoroughly.

3  Cut a cross in the top of each fig and fill with the ginger. Close up the fig. On a flat surface, arrange 3 slices of the pancetta so they overlap as shown.

4  Place a fig in the centre and wrap the pancetta up around the fig to form a parcel. Secure with toothpicks and transfer to the baking tray. Repeat with the remaining figs.

5  Bake the figs in the oven for 5 minutes or until the pancetta is just to starting to brown and crisp round the edges.

6  Arrange lettuce as a bed on 4 serving plates. Divide the dressing over the top. Place a fig parcel on the salad bed, carefully remove and discard the toothpicks. Garnish with the sesame seeds and serve immediately.

## Fruit Kebabs with Savoury Strawberry Dressing

*Fruit with a savoury sauce makes an excellent starter for summer lunches and dinners. This dish lends itself to the fruits in season, so choose a selection for the kebabs but ensure you include strawberries to get the contrasting flavour of the whole strawberry with those in the dressing. The kebabs can also be served as a dessert—try a spoonful of chilled Hot Chocolate Sauce (page 140) to top them off.*

**Serves 4**

8 bamboo skewers
12 strawberries, chilled and hulled

Additional well-chilled fruit such as:
2 nectarines, stoned and cut into eighths
8 lychees, peeled and seeded
2 kiwi fruit, peeled and cut into large dice
8 cubes of rockmelon

Dressing
150 g strawberries, hulled
2 tbs (30 mL) extra-virgin olive oil*
3 scant tbs balsamic vinegar* (ingredient check—Vinegar; ⬤)
1 tsp apple juice concentrate*
1 tsp lemon juice
5 fresh mint leaves, finely chopped

Garnish
sprigs of fresh mint

Per serve
Energy 647 kJ (154 cal)
Protein 3.5 g
Total fat 7.1 g
Saturated fat 0.8 g
Carbohydrate 18.3 g
Total sugars 18.3 g
Dietary fibre 5.9 g
Sodium 14 mg

1   Put all the dressing ingredients in a food processor and blend to a purée. Cover and chill.

2   Thread the fruits onto the bamboo skewers. Place on serving plates and drizzle the dressing over the top. Serve immediately garnished with the mint sprigs.

## Mediterranean-Style Octopus Salad

*The combination of lemon, herbs and good olive oil makes this salad an excellent starter or light lunch on a warm, sunny day. Serve on a bed of shredded cos lettuce with suitable crusty bread to soak up the dressing or as part of a platter with Chilled Calamari Salad (page 16) and oysters.*

**Serves 4**

1 kg cleaned baby octopus

Dressing
3 tbs (45 mL) red wine vinegar* (ingredient check—Vinegar; ⬤)
3 tbs (45 mL) extra-virgin olive oil*
1 tbs (15 mL) lemon-infused olive oil*
⅓ cup finely shredded fresh flat-leaf (Italian) parsley leaves
½ tsp finely chopped fresh lemon thyme leaves
1 tbs capers* (ingredient check; ⬤)
freshly ground black pepper

Per serve
Energy 1384 kJ (330 cal)
Protein 37.7 g
Total fat 16.1 g
Saturated fat 2.2 g
Carbohydrate 5.8 g
Total sugars 0.3 g
Dietary fibre 0.4 g
Sodium 601 mg

1   Check the octopus have been cleaned and all beaks removed; remove and discard any remaining beaks.

2   Put the vinegar and oils in a bowl and whisk well. Add the remaining dressing ingredients and stir to combine.

3   Bring a large pan of water to a fast boil. Add the octopus and cook for 45–60 seconds (do not overcook or the

octopus will become chewy). Drain well and toss through the dressing while still hot. Cover and refrigerate for a minimum of 3 hours, preferably overnight.

4 Serve on a bed of shredded cos lettuce with extra freshly ground black pepper to taste.

## Ocean Trout Kibbeh Nayee on Lime and Mango Salad

*The clean flavours of the lime-dressed mango salad make a perfect base for these delicately flavoured trout patties.*

**Serves 4**

Trout Kibbeh Nayee
200 g skinless ocean trout, pin-boned** and well chilled
1 large green shallot (about 10 g), trimmed and finely sliced
¼ tsp ground allspice
1 small red chilli, seeded and finely sliced
1 tbs (15 mL) extra-virgin olive oil*
zest of 1 lime
juice of ½ lime
¼ cup very finely chopped fresh coriander leaves and roots*
freshly ground black pepper
10 g rice crumbs (Orgran brand)*

Dressing
4 tbs (60 mL) lime juice
2 tsp fish sauce* (ingredient check; ◎)
1 tbs soft brown sugar

Salad
2 Lebanese cucumbers (about 225-250 g total), ends trimmed and very finely sliced
1 medium ripe mango (about 400 g), peeled and diced
½ cup coriander leaves (about 10 g), shredded
½ cup mint leaves (about 10 g), shredded
60 g bean sprouts

Garnish
2 tsp shredded sushi-style pickled ginger* (ingredient check—Ginger; ◎)
2 tsp salmon caviar* (optional; ingredient check)
4 sprigs fresh mint

**Per serve**
Energy 730 kJ (174 cal)
Protein 13.0 g
Total fat 5.8 g
Saturated fat 0.9 g
Carbohydrate 17.0 g
Total sugars 14.5 g
Dietary fibre 3.5 g
Sodium 312 mg

1 Finely mince the trout and mix with all the remaining kibbeh nayee ingredients, except the rice crumbs, in a glass or ceramic bowl. (If not using a mincer, dice the fish and place in a food processor with all the kibbeh nayee ingredients except the rice crumbs. Process lightly; the fish should be finely chopped not blended to a smooth paste.) Cover and chill well.

2 Put all the dressing ingredients in a mixing bowl and stir until the sugar has dissolved. Add all the salad ingredients and toss to mix through the dressing. Cover and chill for 30 minutes.

3 Just before serving, mix the rice crumbs through the chilled fish mix. Divide the mix into 4 and form into neat patties in an egg ring (or in your hands).

4 Re-toss the salad and divide between 4 serving plates, drizzling any remaining dressing over the top. Place a trout patty on top. Garnish each patty with a quarter of the shredded ginger, the caviar and a sprig of mint. Serve immediately.

## Portugese-Style Chicken Wingettes

*You can use drumsticks, drumettes, or a combination of drumettes and wingettes—just vary the cooking time according to the thickness of the meat. They are delicious served hot as a pre-dinner nibble, or chilled for snacks, lunch-boxes and the like. They are also suitable to barbecue—brush occasionally with left-over marinade while cooking.*

**Serves 6**

1 kg chicken wingettes

Marinade

3 tbs (45 mL) lemon juice

2 tbs (30 mL) apple juice concentrate*

1 tbs (15 mL) finely chopped fresh ginger

½ tsp smoked sweet paprika* or mild paprika

1 tsp dried oregano

1 tsp pure sesame oil*

½–1 tsp sambal oelek* or chilli paste* (ingredient check; ◯)

**Per serve**

Energy 651 kJ (155 cal)

Protein 23.8 g

Total fat 6.3 g

Saturated fat 1.9 g

Carbohydrate 4.2 g

Total sugars 3.8 g

Dietary fibre 0.1 g

Sodium 86 mg

1   Put all the marinade ingredients together in a large mixing bowl and mix well. Add the chicken and toss to coat well. Cover and refrigerate for a minimum of 2 hours or overnight.

2   Preheat the oven to 220–240°C (200–220°C fan forced). Line a baking tray with aluminium foil. Transfer the chicken to the baking tray. Bake for 12–15 minutes or until cooked through and browning, turning and basting once during cooking.

3   Transfer to a serving platter and set aside to cool for a few minutes before serving as finger food.

## Smoked Salmon, Prawn and Herb Risotto with Grape Tomato and Caper Garnish

*This is best prepared with a good home-made prawn or fish stock (see page 11), served on a watercress and rocket bed. The risotto also makes excellent fish cakes that can be served with a tasty dipping sauce (see Thai-style Fish Cakes, page 24) on a salad bed. To make fish cakes, add an extra 250 mL water to the risotto while cooking, cover and refrigerate when cool. Roll tablespoonfuls of the mix into a ball in rice crumbs\*, flatten out to a patty and fry in a very lightly oiled non-stick pan or char-grill until golden.*

**Serves 4**

Risotto

500 mL Prawn Stock (page 11) plus 1 L water, or 1.5 L fish stock* (ingredient check; ◯)

1 tbs (15 mL) virgin olive oil*

2 green shallots*, trimmed and finely sliced

440 g arborio rice*

250 mL (1 cup) dry white wine (ingredient check—Wine)

3 tbs (45 mL) lemon juice

zest of ½ lemon

150 g raw prawn meat, deveined

2 stalks celery (about 100 g), peeled and finely diced

6 button mushrooms, cleaned and finely sliced

100 g smoked salmon pieces, shredded (ingredient check)

⅓ cup finely shredded fresh flat-leaf (Italian) parsley leaves

2 tbs chopped fresh dill tips

freshly ground black pepper

Salad

½ bunch watercress (about 125 g), trimmed and roughly chopped

75 g wild or baby rocket leaves

**Per serve**

Energy 2750 kJ (656 cal)

Protein 27.6 g

Total fat 5.7 g

Saturated fat 0.8 g

Carbohydrate 90.5 g

Total sugars 3.5 g

Dietary fibre 4.1 g

Sodium 733 mg

Garnish
10 grape tomatoes, diced
15 capers*, drained and halved (ingredient check; ⊙)
2 tsp chopped fresh dill tips
1 tsp lemon juice
freshly ground black pepper

1   Prepare the garnish by mixing the ingredients together in a small bowl. Cover and set aside.

2   To make risotto, place the stock in a pan over a medium heat and bring to boiling point. Reduce the heat until the stock is just simmering.

3   Place the olive oil in a large, heavy-bottomed pan over medium heat. Add the shallots and sauté for 1 minute. Add the rice and stir with a wooden spoon for 1 minute or until the rice appears to be partly translucent or glassy. Add the wine and lemon juice and cook, stirring continuously, until almost all the liquid is absorbed (about 5 minutes).

4   Add a ladleful of the stock (about 125 mL) and stir continuously over a medium heat until the liquid is completely absorbed. Continue to add the stock a ladleful at a time, stirring continuously, waiting until the stock is almost completely absorbed before adding more. When only 1–2 ladles of stock remain, add the lemon zest, prawn meat, celery and mushrooms together with the remaining stock and continue to stir until the stock is just absorbed. Cooking to this stage will take 25–30 minutes, at which point the rice grains should be tender but still firm when bitten.

5   Stir though the smoked salmon, fresh herbs and seasoning, cover and leave to stand for 5 minutes.

6   Arrange a watercress and rocket bed on 4 serving plates. Spoon the risotto on top. Serve immediately garnished with the tomato and caper mix.

## Ⓝ Spicy Ginger Scallops on a Two Rice Bed

*Using a wild rice and long-grain rice blend really sets off these delicate scallops with their watercress garnish. I usually cook the rice in advance, rinse well with cold water, cover and reheat in the microwave just before serving.*

**Serves 4**

2-3 cups cooked wild rice blend* or basmati rice*
½ bunch watercress (about 125 g), trimmed
½ tsp virgin olive oil*
2 green shallots*, trimmed and finely sliced
⅛-¼ tsp sambal oelek* or chilli paste*, to taste (ingredient check)
5 tbs (75 mL) Ginger Refresher (Buderim brand)*
2 tbs (30 mL) lime juice
3 tbs (45 mL) water
12-16 scallops, roe on (increase to 20 if very small)
1 tbs finely chopped fresh dill
freshly ground black pepper

Garnish
freshly ground black pepper
fresh dill tips, finely chopped

**Per serve**
**Energy 1383 kJ (330 cal)**
**Protein 17.9 g**
**Total fat 1.4 g**
**Saturated fat 0.3 g**
**Carbohydrate 108.6 g**
**Total sugars 3.2 g**
**Dietary fibre 2.5 g**
**Sodium 179 mg**

1   Pre-cook rice following instructions on the packet, rinse well with cold water and drain. Transfer to a microwave-proof dish and cover. Reheat in a microwave just before cooking the scallops.

2   Arrange the watercress in the centre of 4 serving plates.

3  Heat the oil in a non-stick frying pan over a medium heat. Add the shallots and sambal oelek and sauté, stirring regularly, for 1 minute.

4  Add the Ginger Refresher, lime juice and water, and heat until simmering gently.

5  Add the scallops and dill, and poach for 1–2 minutes on each side (do not overcook, the scallops should just be opaque).

6  Divide the steaming rice between 4 serving plates and arrange 3–4 scallops on top of each. Spoon the sauce over the top. Serve immediately, garnished with freshly ground black pepper and the fresh dill tips.


## Thai Beef Salad

*This salad is a favourite. I usually use topside or silverside if I cook the meat in a kettle-style barbecue over charcoal, but if oven roasting I prefer to use a fillet. Ideally select or trim the meat to a piece 6–8 cm square for its length (see figure below) for quick, even cooking and good presentation when carved and served. 'Hedgehogged' mango cheeks garnished with pickled ginger\* (ingredient check;* ◉*) make a wonderful accompaniment to convert this dish into a light lunch. ◉ use Asian Marinade recipe (page 110). ◎ omit the brazil nuts.*

**Serves 6**

500–600 g beef fillet (or topside if barbecuing), trimmed of fat
1 tsp extra-light olive oil\*

Marinade (not corn-free)
2 tbs (30 mL) pure sesame oil\*
2 tbs dry vermouth (ingredient check—Wine)
2 tbs fish sauce\* (ingredient check)
4 tsp oyster sauce\* (ingredient check)

6–8 cm  12–15 cm
6–8 cm

Garnish
500 g baby spinach leaves
½ char-grilled red capsicum\*, finely sliced (ingredient check; ◉)
10–12 fresh Vietnamese mint leaves\*, finely shredded (regular mint can substituted)
6–8 brazil nuts, dry-roasted\*\*
freshly ground black pepper

| Per serve | |
|---|---|
| Energy 829 kJ (198 cal) | |
| Protein 19.9 g | |
| Total fat 10.8 g | |
| Saturated fat 2.8 g | |
| Carbohydrate 2.8 g | |
| Total sugars 2.6 g | |
| Dietary fibre 0.8 g | |
| Sodium 860 mg | |

1  If cooking in a kettle barbecue over charcoal, or equivalent: sear outside of meat on wire rack directly over hot coals, then place the meat on a foil tray and cook with the lid on for 15–20 minutes or until the meat is rare (the meat should be springy when tested with the back of a pair of tongs or the internal temperature is 60°C on a meat thermometer); cover with an aluminium foil tent and leave to rest for 10 minutes.

   If cooking in an oven: preheat to 240°C (220°C fan forced). Lightly oil the meat. Heat a non-stick frying pan to hot and sear meat for 1 minute on each side. Transfer to a baking tray and roast for 6–7 minutes or until the meat is rare (see above). Cover and rest as above.

   Note: Do not overcook the beef—it should be on the rare side of rare to medium-rare.

2  While the meat is resting, combine all the marinade ingredients in a glass or ceramic bowl. Carve the beef in slices 3–5 mm thick across the grain and place in the marinade, coating each slice thoroughly. Cover and refrigerate for a minimum of 1 hour, preferably overnight.

3  Arrange a spinach leaf bed on 4 serving plates. Place the beef slices on the bed. Drizzle over the marinade. Garnish with the sliced capsicum, shredded mint, nuts and black pepper. Serve immediately.

## Thai-Style Fish Patties with Dipping Sauce

*A simple version of the classic Thai fish cakes, Tod Man Pla. This recipe is eggless, using potato and the refrigerator to bind the patties together, to give a lighter consistency. The high salt content of the dish is due to the fish sauce; for a less salty result replace half the fish sauce with water.*

**Makes 18—serves 6**

Dipping Sauce

1 tbs (15 mL) white vinegar (ingredient check—Vinegar; ◯)

3 tbs (45 mL) fish sauce* (ingredient check; ◯)

1 tbs soft brown sugar

½ medium red chilli, seeded and very finely chopped

2 coriander roots* (about 10 g), very finely chopped

Fish Cakes

300 g red-skinned potatoes such as Desiree (about 2 medium-sized), skin on, cleaned

400 g white or red fish fillets

1 tbs (15 mL) fish sauce* (ingredient check; ◯)

½ tsp lemon grass* (white part only), finely chopped

¼ tsp tamarind paste* (ingredient check)

½ red chilli, seeded and roughly chopped

2 tbs (30 mL) virgin olive oil*

zest of 1 lime

1 green shallot*, trimmed and finely chopped

1 coriander root* (about 5 g), roughly chopped

50 g green beans, trimmed and very finely chopped

¼ cup finely chopped fresh coriander leaves

1 cup brown rice flour*, for dusting patties

extra-light olive oil spray* (ingredient check)

Garnish

50 g salad leaves

sprigs of fresh coriander

**Per serve**

Energy 981 kJ (234 cal)

Protein 15.8 g

Total fat 5.4 g

Saturated fat 0.7 g

Carbohydrate 30.2 g

Total sugars 3.4 g

Dietary fibre 3.0 g

Sodium 1110 mg

1  Put all sauce ingredients in a bowl and stir until the sugar dissolves.

2  Place potatoes in a pan, cover with hot water and cook over a medium heat for 10 minutes or until just undercooked when tested with a sharp knife (do not overcook or the potatoes will not grate easily). Drain, place in a bowl and refrigerate for a minimum of 2 hours.

3  Grate the potatoes into a mixing bowl (the skins provide holders for the potato for grating—discard them once all the potato flesh has been grated).

4  Chop the fish fillets coarsely, place in a food processor and blend until smooth (about 20 seconds). Add the fish sauce, lemon grass, tamarind paste, chilli, oil, lime zest, shallot and coriander root. Blend until well combined.

5  Scrape the fish mixture into a bowl. Mix through the beans, coriander leaves and grated potato.

6  Place the rice flour on a plate. Roll a dessertspoon of the fish mixture into a ball in the rice flour. Flatten out into a patty and transfer to a large plate. Repeat until all the mixture has been used. Cover and refrigerate for a minimum of 1 hour—this is important to bind the patties together for cooking.

7  Divide the dipping sauce between 4 small dishes.

**8** Spray a large, non-stick frying pan lightly with oil and place over a medium heat. Place sufficient patties in the pan to fill the base of the pan without touching, and cook for 2–3 minutes on each side or until golden brown. Set aside and keep warm while cooking the remaining patties.

**9** Serve immediately on a bed of salad leaves with the Dipping Sauce and coriander garnish.

## Toasted Sesame-Seed Coated Avocado and Almond Balls

*These can be served as pre-dinner nibble with toothpicks, as a starter or a light lunch with a salad—they are surprisingly filling! If serving as a starter or lunch, make larger balls using a dessertspoonful of the mix, and serve with a rosette of smoked salmon topped with baby capers\* (ingredient check ◯), lemon juice and black pepper.*

### Makes 18—serves 6

| | |
|---|---|
| ½ cup white sesame seeds plus ½ cup black sesame seeds (or 1 cup white sesame seeds) | **Per ball** |
| 1 ripe avocado (about 225 g) | Energy 422 kJ (101 cal) |
| 2 tsp lemon juice | Protein 3.3 g |
| 1 tsp sumac\* | Total fat 9.3 g |
| ¼ tsp sambal oelek\* or chilli paste\* (ingredient check; ◯) | Saturated fat 1.2 g |
| freshly ground black pepper | Carbohydrate 1.1 g |
| 2 tbs rice crumbs (Orgran brand)\* | Total sugars 0.4 g |
| 100 g almond meal | Dietary fibre 1.6 g |
| 75 g celery (about 1½ stalks), very finely chopped | Sodium 7 mg |
| 1 tbs finely chopped fresh parsley | |

Garnish
mixed salad leaves
18 small pieces sushi-style pickled ginger\* or red pickled ginger straws\*
   (ingredient check—Ginger; ◯)

**1** Place the white sesame seeds in a non-stick frying pan over a low-medium heat. Roast for 5 minutes, tossing constantly, or until golden brown. Set aside to cool.

**2** Put the avocado flesh in a bowl with the lemon juice and mash with a fork to combine.

**3** Add all the remaining ingredients, except the sesame seeds, and mix thoroughly. Cover and refrigerate for 30 minutes.

**4** Mix the white and black sesame seeds together. Spoon 2 tablespoonfuls onto a small plate. Spoon 1 teaspoonful of the avocado mix onto the seeds and roll into a ball in the seeds. Transfer the ball to a serving dish. Repeat the process until all the avocado mix is used, replenishing the sesame seeds for coating as required. Cover and chill well.

**5** Just before serving, arrange the salad leaves around the Avocado Balls and garnish each ball with a piece of pickled ginger. Serve immediately with toothpicks.

## Dips 'n' Pâtés

Dips and pâtés make a quick and tasty snack served with savoury biscuits, julienned vegetables or with any suitable dipper or crusty bread of choice … or try making your own, low-fat, low-salt corn chips by slicing White Corn Tortilla (Diego brand) into 8, gently shaking in a plastic bag with 1 teaspoon each ground cumin and mild or hot paprika and toasting in an oven preheated to 200°C (180°C fan forced) for 4–5 minutes or until crisp and light gold.

### Ⓒ Avocado and Tomato Dip

Ⓕ *Similar to guacamole, this recipe skips the usual onion and dairy ingredients and includes chickpeas to make a light, nutritious dip.*
Ⓝ *Roughly mash the chickpeas and dice the tomatoes very finely to make a salsa for tacos and tortilla wraps, or Chilled Minted Lamb*
Ⓥ *Salad (page 46).*

**Makes 1½ cups—serves 4-6**

| | |
|---|---|
| 2 medium-sized ripe avocados (about 150-175 g each), stoned and peeled | **Per serve** |
| 2 vine-ripened, hydroponic or Roma tomatoes (about 150 g), diced | **Energy 581 kJ (139 cal)** |
| 200 g cooked chickpeas** (if using canned, ingredient check) | **Protein 3.9 g** |
| 4 tbs (60 mL) lemon juice | **Total fat 10.4 g** |
| 1 green shallot*, trimmed and very finely sliced | **Saturated fat 2.2 g** |
| 1 red chilli, seeded and very finely chopped or ¼-½ tsp sambal oelek* (ingredient check) | **Carbohydrate 6.8 g** |
| ½ tsp mild paprika | **Total sugars 1.6 g** |
| ¼ tsp ground cumin | **Dietary fibre 3.3 g** |
| ⅓ cup finely chopped fresh coriander leaves and roots* | **Sodium 8 mg** |
| freshly ground black pepper (lots!) | |

Garnish
mild paprika
fresh coriander leaves

1  Put all the ingredients in a food processor and blend until an even consistency. Transfer to a serving dish, cover and chill.

2  Serve garnished with paprika and coriander, and with dipper of choice.

### Ⓒ Beetroot Pâté

Ⓕ *This naturally sweet pâté is excellent served with raw julienned vegetables or rice crackers, as a spread on toast or warm bread*
Ⓝ *rolls—or as a starter with a naturally smoked fish (such as Yarra Valley Smoked Baby Salmon) on a watercress bed. Ⓥ use agar*
Ⓥ *powder* to set the pâté.*

**Makes 2½ cups or 4 individual pâtés**

| | |
|---|---|
| 4 fresh beetroot (about 500 g), trimmed | **Per pâté** |
| 1 tbs powdered gelatine or ¾ tsp agar powder* | **Energy 297 kJ (71 cal)** |
| 150 mL hot water | **Protein 4.8 g** |
| extra-light olive oil spray* (ingredient check) | **Total fat 0.2 g** |
| 3 green shallots*, trimmed and roughly chopped | **Saturated fat <0.1 g** |
| ¼ tsp paprika (mild or smoked sweet*) | **Carbohydrate 11.6 g** |
| ¼ tsp ground cardamom | **Total sugars 11.4 g** |
| 1 tsp freshly grated ginger | **Dietary fibre 4.3 g** |
| freshly ground black pepper | **Sodium 80 mg** |
| 2 tbs (30 mL) balsamic vinegar* (ingredient check—Vinegar; Ⓒ) | |
| zest of 1 lemon | |
| 1 tbs finely chopped fresh parsley | |

1  Place the beetroot in a pan of water, over a medium-high heat, cover and bring to the boil. Reduce the heat and simmer for 30 minutes or until tender when tested with a sharp knife. Drain and set aside to cool.

2  Very lightly oil a small bowl (2$^1\!/_2$–3 cup capacity or 2 smaller bowls for 2 dips) or 4 x 1-cup capacity moulds if serving as a starter.

3  Sprinkle the gelatine (agar) over the hot water and set aside.

4  Very lightly spray a small non-stick pan with oil and place over a medium heat. Add the shallots and sauté for 2 minutes, stirring occasionally. Add the spices and lightly roast for 1 minute or until fragrant, stirring frequently.

5  Add the pepper, vinegar and zest and bring to the boil. Reduce the heat, add the gelatine mix and stir constantly until the gelatine has fully dissolved; do not boil. Set aside to cool slightly.

6  Peel the cooled beetroot, roughly slice and place in a food processor with the shallot mix and parsley. Blend until smooth. Transfer the mixture to the bowl or divide between the moulds, cover and refrigerate for a minimum of 2 hours or until set.

7  Immediately before serving, turn the pâté out by dipping the base of the moulds in hot water for a few seconds and inverting onto serving plate(s). (The pâté may served in the bowl(s) if serving as a dip.)

## Bruschetta Mix

*This wonderful tomato-basil-capsicum mix can be served as a dip with corn chips, as a great summery snack or starter with suitable lightly toasted, crusty bread, or just tossed through salad leaves. As optional extra, try tossing 100 g of roughly chopped smoked salmon pieces (ingredient check) through the mix.*

**Serves 4**

| | |
|---|---|
| 750 g Roma tomatoes, diced | **Per serve** |
| 25 g capers*, roughly chopped (ingredient check; ) | **Energy 190 kJ (45 cal)** |
| 1 green shallot*, trimmed and very finely sliced | **Protein 2.9 g** |
| zest and juice of 1 large lemon | **Total fat 0.4 g** |
| 100 g char-grilled capsicum*, finely sliced (ingredient check; ) | **Saturated fat <0.1 g** |
| 3 tbs (45 mL) char-grilled capsicum oil* (ingredient check; ) or virgin olive oil* | **Carbohydrate 6.6 g** |
| 1 tbs (15 mL) balsamic vinegar* (ingredient check—Vinegar; ) | **Total sugars 6.4 g** |
| 20 large, fresh basil leaves, finely shredded | **Dietary fibre 3.2 g** |
| ½ tsp caraway seeds | **Sodium 56 mg** |
| freshly ground black pepper | |

Garnish
fresh basil leaves, roughly shredded

1  Mix all the ingredients together in a bowl. Cover and chill for 3 hours, preferably overnight.

2  Serve with accompaniment of choice as a dip or on lightly toasted bread, garnished with the shredded basil.

## Red Lentil Dip

*A tasty, high-fibre dip that is equally good served hot, at room temperature or chilled! Serve with dippers of choice, or use as a spread in wraps.*

**Makes 1½ cups—serves 6-8**

| | |
|---|---|
| 150 g dried red lentils, picked over | **Per serve** |
| extra-light olive oil spray* (ingredient check) | **Energy 238 kJ (57 cal)** |
| 3 green shallots*, trimmed and sliced | **Protein 5.0 g** |
| 2 tsp grated fresh ginger | **Total fat 0.5 g** |

½ red chilli, seeded and finely chopped

½ tsp ground turmeric

1 tsp sumac*

1 tsp ground cumin

freshly ground black pepper

500 mL (2 cups) water

2 tbs (30 mL) tomato paste (ingredient check)

½ cup roughly chopped fresh coriander

Garnish

sprig of fresh coriander

Saturated fat 0.1 g

Carbohydrate 8.4 g

Total sugars 1.3 g

Dietary fibre 3.3 g

Sodium 4 mg

1   Rinse the red lentils thoroughly under cold water and drain well.

2   Lightly spray a non-stick frying pan with oil, place over a medium-high heat, add the shallots and sauté for 2 minutes, stirring occasionally. Add the spices and roast gently for 1 minute or until fragrant, stirring constantly to prevent them from catching or burning.

3   Add the drained lentils, water and tomato paste and bring to the boil. Reduce the heat and simmer gently for 15–20 minutes or until the lentils are just soft. (Note: If the mixture is simmered too fast it will thicken before the lentils have softened adequately; add an additional 3–4 tbs (45–60 mL) of water to complete the cooking.) Stir the coriander through and set aside to cool slightly.

4   Transfer the lentil mix to a food processor and blend to an even consistency. Transfer to a serving bowl and cover. Serve warm, at room temperature or chilled, garnished with the coriander.

## Smoked Mackerel and Butter Bean Pâté

*This light, creamy pâté uses butter beans as its base, so it offers the nutritious combination of the 'good oils' and dietary fibre. Serve either in ramekins or turn out immediately before serving. The pâté may also be made with other white beans, such as cannellini.*

**Makes 2½ cups—serves 8-10**

10 g powdered gelatine

150 mL boiling water

extra–light olive oil* to grease the moulds

240 g cooked butter (lima) beans** (if using canned, ingredient check)

1 x 200 g can kippers in brine (John West brand), rinsed and well drained

2 tsp lemon–infused olive oil* or 2 tsp extra–virgin olive oil* plus zest of ½ lemon

1 tsp finely chopped fresh dill tips

freshly ground black pepper

Per serve

Energy 320 kJ (76 cal)

Protein 6.1 g

Total fat 4.0 g

Saturated fat 0.1 g

Carbohydrate 4.2 g

Total sugars 0.3 g

Dietary fibre 1.7 g

Sodium 96 mg

Garnish

sprigs of fresh dill

1   Dissolve gelatine in the boiling water and set aside to cool for a few minutes.

2   Very lightly oil 3 x 1-cup capacity ramekins or moulds. If serving turned out, place the dill garnish in the bottom of each.

3   Put all ingredients in a food processor and blend to a smooth paste. Transfer to the moulds (or ramekins) and smooth tops. Cover and refrigerate for a minimum of 1 hour.

4   To serve turned out, place the moulds in hot water for a few seconds and turn out onto a serving plate. If serving in the ramekins, garnish the top of each with a dill sprig.

# Sun-Dried Tomato Dip with Crudités

*This tasty dip is excellent served with crudités, rice crackers or corn chips.*

**Makes ¾ cup—serves 4-6**

Dip

8 sun-dried tomatoes* (dehydrated, e.g. not in oil)

4 tbs (60 mL) tomato passata* or 1 tbs tomato paste plus 3 tbs water (ingredient checks)

2 tsp tomato paste (ingredient check)

4 tbs (60 mL) balsamic vinegar* (ingredient check—Vinegar; ◯)

4 tbs water

1 tsp finely chopped fresh oregano leaves, or ¼ tsp dried oregano

1 large red chilli, seeded (optional)

3 tbs (45 mL) extra-virgin olive oil*

freshly ground black pepper

Selection of chilled, julienned vegetables:

carrots, celery, snow peas, cucumber, green beans

**Per serve**

Energy 337 kJ (80 cal)

Protein 0.6 g

Total fat 7.4 g

Saturated fat 0.9 g

Carbohydrate 2.6 g

Total sugars 1.5 g

Dietary fibre 1.3 g

Sodium 9 mg

1 Soak the tomatoes in water until plump and soft (5–10 minutes). Drain. (If using sun-dried tomatoes in oil, drain well and omit soaking, but check ingredients carefully.)

2 Put tomatoes, tomato passata and paste, vinegar and oregano in a food processor. Blend until smooth. For a spicier dressing, add a seeded red chilli with the tomatoes or sambal oelek* (ingredient check) to taste. With the processor running, stream in the olive oil and process until the oil is thoroughly mixed through the tomato base.

3 Season to taste with freshly ground black pepper. Transfer to a small bowl and serve with the chilled, julienned vegetables.

## Fish and Seafood

### Baked Blue-Eye Cod with Lemon Grass Paste

*Simply baked in paper, the flavours of the Lemon Grass Paste permeate the fish. Serve with steaming rice (try one of the Fragrant Rice recipes, page 93). This recipe is suitable for other fish cutlets or steaks, such as jewfish, salmon and swordfish. The paste is also delicious in a salmon-tail roast—slit the salmon from the underside along the backbone, stuff with the paste and bake wrapped in foil at 200°C (180°C fan forced) for 12–15 minutes, or until flesh flakes when tested.*

**Serves 4**

Lemon Grass Paste

3 green shallots*, trimmed and sliced

2 cm piece of fresh ginger (about 15 g), peeled and roughly sliced

12 kaffir lime leaves*, stalks trimmed

12 curry leaves*

40 g fresh coriander (about ½ bunch), trimmed and roughly chopped

1 tsp ground coriander

1 stalk lemon grass* (white part only), finely chopped

¼ tsp sambal oelek* or chilli paste* (ingredient check; ◉)

¼ tsp ground turmeric

2 tbs (30 mL) virgin olive oil*


Blue-eye Cod

4 x 125–150 g blue-eye cod cutlets

4 tbs (60 mL) white wine (ingredient check—Wine)

zest and juice of 1 lime

75 g button mushrooms, cleaned and finely sliced

200 g baby spinach leaves


Garnish

freshly ground black pepper

lemon wedges

**Per serve**

Energy 771 kJ (184 cal)

Protein 23.9 g

Total fat 7.4 g

Saturated fat 0.9 g

Carbohydrate 2.1 g

Total sugars 1.6 g

Dietary fibre 1.6 g

Sodium 220 mg

1   Preheat the oven to 220°C (200°C fan forced). Cut 4 squares of baking paper large enough to enclose the fish.

2   Put all the lemon grass paste ingredients in a food processor and blend to a smooth paste.

3   Pat the fish dry with a paper towel. Place the mushrooms in the centre of the 4 paper squares. Place a cutlet on top of each. Spread each with a generous dessertspoon of the lemon grass paste (freeze any left-over paste for later use). Divide the lime zest, juice and white wine over the top of each cutlet.

4   Wrap the baking paper to form a parcel round the fish to seal in all the juices. Place the parcels on a baking tray and bake in the oven for 10–12 minutes or until tender (the parcels should puff up when the fish is cooked.)

5   Arrange a bed of steaming rice in the centre of 4 serving plates. Surround with the spinach leaves. Arrange the fish and juices on top of the rice. Serve immediately garnished with freshly ground black pepper and a lemon wedge.

## ⓒ Char-Grilled Salmon on Kumara Purée with Maple Syrup and
## ⓝ Macadamia Nut Garnish

*The delicate flavours of the orange-pink kumara bed and salmon are perfect topped with a hint of maple syrup and dry-roasted macadamia nuts. Serve with a leafy herb or mesclun salad and a light citrus vinaigrette. Prepare the Kumara Purée in advance and reheat in the microwave just before serving* ⓝ *use virgin olive oil and replace the macadamia nut garnish with 2 tablespoonfuls dry-roasted\*\* sesame seeds*

**Serves 4**

1 quantity Kumara Purée (page 94)
4 x 125–150 g skinless salmon fillets, pin-boned\*\*

Marinade
3 tbs (45 mL) lemon juice
1 tbs (15 mL) macadamia\* or virgin olive oil\*
freshly ground black pepper

Garnish
100 g raw, unsalted macadamia nuts, halved
4 tsp pure maple syrup
2–3 tsp finely chopped fresh parsley
freshly ground black pepper

Per serve
Energy 2154 kJ (514 cal)
Protein 27.7 g
Total fat 26.8 g
Saturated fat 3.4 g
Carbohydrate 40.9 g
Total sugars 19.3 g
Dietary fibre 6.0 g
Sodium 82 mg

1   Prepare the Kumara Purée as described on page 94.

2   Mix the marinade ingredients together in a bowl. Coat the salmon with the marinade, cover and set aside for a minimum of 30 minutes.

3   Place the macadamia halves in a small pan over a low heat and gently roast, shaking regularly for 5–10 minutes or until golden brown. Set aside to cool.

4   Reheat the kumara purée. Cover and keep warm.

5   Heat a char-grill or non-stick frying pan to very hot. Sear the salmon for 1 minute on each side, basting with the marinade, or until cooked to taste.

6   To serve, divide the kumara purée between 4 serving plates and top with a salmon fillet. Drizzle 1 teaspoon of maple syrup over the top of each. Serve immediately garnished with the macadamia nuts, parsley and black pepper.

## ⓒ Crispy Potato and White Fish Pie

ⓝ *This tasty fish pie is a family favourite and can be made as a single pie or in individual ramekins—my son likes to polish off any left-overs for breakfast! Serve with blanched spinach tossed with Pickled Ginger Sesame Sauce (page 79) or with steamed green vegetables.*

**Serves 4–6**

Potato Topping
1 kg Sebago potatoes, skin on, cleaned and diced
2 tbs margarine (Nuttelex brand)\* or extra-light olive oil\*
3 tbs (45 mL) light coconut milk\* (ingredient check; ⓒ)
1 tsp fish sauce\* (ingredient check; ⓒ)
freshly ground black pepper
extra-light olive oil spray\* (ingredient check)
extra 1 large potato, skin on and cleaned

Per serve
Energy 1161 kJ (277 cal)
Protein 19.3 g
Total fat 7.7 g
Saturated fat 2.2 g
Carbohydrate 31.5 g
Total sugars 5.0 g
Dietary fibre 4.1 g
Sodium 479 mg

Filling

1 tsp extra-light olive oil*

3 green shallots*, trimmed and sliced

1 small red capsicum, seeded and diced

500 g firm, boneless fish fillets (such as hake or ling), cut into 1 cm dice

5 kaffir lime leaves*, bruised

zest of 1 lemon

2 coriander roots* (about 10 g), chopped

50 g baby spinach or rocket leaves, roughly chopped

Sauce

1 tbs arrowroot

250 mL (1 cup) rice milk* (ingredient check)

4 tbs (60 mL) light coconut milk* (ingredient check; Ⓒ)

4 tsp lemon juice

1 tbs fish sauce* (ingredient check; Ⓒ)

1 tsp sumac*

freshly ground black pepper

1  Preheat the oven to 200°C (180°C fan forced).

2  Place the diced potatoes in a pan of cold water over a high heat. Bring to the boil, reduce the heat and simmer, covered, until the potatoes are just cooked when tested with a sharp knife. Drain immediately, retaining ½ cup of the water. Add the margarine, coconut milk, fish sauce and black pepper and mash until smooth and creamy, adding back the retained water as required to achieve the desired consistency. Set aside.

3  Place the oil in a medium-sized pan over a medium heat, add the shallots and capsicum and sauté for 1 minute. Remove from the heat and add all the remaining filling ingredients. Set aside.

4  Mix the arrowroot with 2 tablespoons rice milk to a smooth paste. Place remaining rice milk and other sauce ingredients in a pan over a medium heat and heat until starting to simmer gently. Mix through the arrowroot paste and stir continually until the arrowroot is cooked and the sauce thickened.

5  Add the fish filling to the sauce and cook for 1–2 minutes. Divide between 6 ovenproof ramekins or place in a single 2.5–3 litre capacity ovenproof dish. Spread the mashed potato over the top. Slice the remaining potato very finely and very lightly spray with oil. Arrange over the top of the mashed potatoes.

6  Bake in the oven for 30–35 minutes or until the potatoes are golden brown and the filling is bubbling. Serve immediately accompanied by vegetables of choice.

## Ⓒ Green King Prawn Curry

Ⓝ *This easy curry uses the Green Curry Paste (page 82) as its base—the paste is flavour packed, but very mild to allow you to adjust the heat of the dish to taste with sambal oelek* or chilli paste* (ingredient check; Ⓒ). If using a commercially made paste, check ingredients carefully and adjust the amount of paste added to desired level of spiciness. Serve over a bed of steaming rice.*

**Serves 4 as a main or 6 as a starter**

| | |
|---|---|
| 1 kg green king prawns, peeled and deveined, tails intact (retain heads and shells) | **Per serve** |
| 500 mL (2 cups) water | **Energy 774 kJ (185 cal)** |
| 125 mL (½ cup) white wine (ingredient check—Wine) or extra water | **Protein 26.8 g** |
| 3 tbs (45 mL) Green Curry Paste (page 82) | **Total fat 4.2 g** |
| 1 baby fennel (about 100 g), trimmed and finely sliced | **Saturated fat 2.2 g** |
| 3 green shallots*, trimmed and diagonally sliced | **Carbohydrate 3.8 g** |
| 4 kaffir lime leaves* | **Total sugars 3.0 g** |

1 tbs (15 mL) lime juice

1 tbs finely sliced coriander root*

150 mL light coconut milk* (ingredient check; ⊙)

½–1 tsp sambal oelek* or chilli paste* (optional; ingredient check; ⊙)

100 g okra or sugar snap peas, trimmed

Garnish

fresh coriander leaves

Dietary fibre 1.6 g

Sodium 473 mg

1  Place the prawn shells, water and wine in a pan over a medium heat. Simmer for 5–6 minutes, stirring occasionally. Strain stock into a wok or large, non-stick frying pan and discard shells.

2  Add all the remaining ingredients except the peeled prawns, sambal oelek and okra (or peas). Simmer together 3–4 minutes, stirring occasionally. Adjust heat of the sauce to taste with sambal oelek.

3  Add prawns and cook for 2–3 minutes or until they turn pink. Stir through the okra or peas, simmer for 1 minute. Serve immediately over a bed of rice garnished with coriander leaves.

## ⊙ King Prawn and Dill Risotto

Ⓝ *Serve this risotto, bursting with the flavour of prawns and herbs, with a large, green leafy salad. The prawn stock may be made in advance and reheated to a gentle simmer just as you make the risotto. Any left-over risotto can be made into fish cakes to serve with a tasty dipping sauce (page 24)—I often make extra risotto just to have left-overs!*

**Serves 4**

1 kg green king prawns

Prawn Marinade

½ tsp balsamic vinegar* (ingredient check—Vinegar; ⊙)

2 tbs (30 mL) lemon juice

200 mL white wine (ingredient check—Wine)

¼ tsp paprika

freshly ground black pepper

Stock

2 cups (500 mL) white wine (ingredient check—Wine)

1.5 L water (plus extra to make stock up to 2 litres)

4 kaffir lime leaves*, bruised

3 tbs (45 mL) lemon juice

Risotto

4 tsp (20 mL) virgin olive oil*

3 green shallots*, trimmed and finely sliced

550 g (2½ cups) arborio rice*

2 stalks celery (about 100 g), peeled and finely diced

rind of ¼ preserved lemon* (flesh removed), rinsed, dried and finely chopped (ingredient check)

½ cup finely shredded fresh flat-leaf (Italian) parsley leaves

2 tbs chopped fresh dill tips

6 button mushrooms, cleaned and finely sliced

¼ small red capsicum, seeded and very finely chopped

freshly ground black pepper

Garnish

sprigs of fresh dill

**Per serve**

**Energy 3236 kJ (772 cal)**

**Protein 35.7 g**

**Total fat 5.9 g**

**Saturated fat 0.8 g**

**Carbohydrate 112.0 g**

**Total sugars 3.4 g**

**Dietary fibre 2.8 g**

**Sodium 505 mg**

1 Peel and devein the prawns, leaving the tail intact (retain heads and shells for stock).

2 Put all the marinade ingredients in a large bowl and mix to combine. Add the prawns and toss well to coat, cover and refrigerate until ready to cook.

3 Put the prawn heads and shells in a large pan with the wine, 1.5 L water and the lime leaves. Bring to the boil, reduce the heat and simmer for 20 minutes. Strain off the stock into a measuring jug and make up to 2 L with extra water. Transfer to a large pan, add the lemon juice, return to the heat and adjust heat so that the stock remains at a gentle simmer. Discard the prawn heads and shells.

4 Place the olive oil in a large pan over a medium heat. Add the shallots and sauté for 1 minute. Add the rice and stir with a wooden spoon for 1 minute or until the rice appears translucent or glassy. Add 2 ladles of stock (about 1 cup) and cook, stirring continuously, for 5 minutes or until almost all the stock is absorbed.

5 Add a ladle of stock and continue to stir continuously over a medium heat until the liquid is completely absorbed. Continue to add the stock a ladle at a time, stirring continuously, until all the stock has been absorbed—about 25–30 minutes, at which point the rice should be tender but still firm to bite. Stir though the celery, preserved lemon rind, fresh herbs, mushrooms, red capsicum and seasoning, cover and leave to stand for 5 minutes.

6 Place the prawns and marinade in a wok or non-stick frying pan and poach over a medium heat for 3–4 minutes or until the prawns turn pink and are cooked.

7 Spoon the risotto onto warmed serving plates, arrange the prawns over the top. Drizzle over a spoonful of the jus. Garnish each with a sprig of dill and serve immediately.

## ⊙ Lightly Spiced Fennel Mussels

Ⓝ *A light and spicy alternative to the usual tomato-based sauce. This uses a home-made green curry paste to give the mussels a not-too-hot Thai-style flavour base. Prepare the sauce in advance for ease and reheat just before serving. Serve over a bed of fresh rice spaghetti\*, bean-thread vermicelli\* or jasmine rice\* in pasta bowls.*

**Serves 4**

1 kg black mussels

Sauce
1 tsp extra-light olive oil\*
1 baby fennel (about 100 g), trimmed and finely chopped
3 large green shallots\*, trimmed and coarsely chopped
½ large red chilli, seeded and finely sliced
2 tsp Green Curry Paste (page 82)
500 mL (2 cups) fish stock\* (ingredient check—Stock; ⊙)
juice of 1 lime
1 tbs apple cider vinegar\*
2 tsp fish sauce\* (ingredient check; ⊙)
2 tsp soft brown sugar
freshly ground black pepper
200 mL light coconut milk\* (ingredient check; ⊙)
1 tbs chopped fresh Vietnamese mint leaves\*
½ cup chopped fresh coriander

Garnish
sliced mild red chilli rings
fresh coriander leaves

**Per serve**
**Energy 794 kJ (190 cal)**
**Protein 14.7 g**
**Total fat 6.5 g**
**Saturated fat 3.4 g**
**Carbohydrate 12.6 g**
**Total sugars 6.5 g**
**Dietary fibre 2.3 g**
**Sodium 1006 mg**

1 Scrub the mussel shells thoroughly under cold running water and de-beard. Cover with damp kitchen towel and refrigerate in the warmest part of the refrigerator until ready to cook.

2 Put the oil in a large pan over a medium heat. When hot, add the fennel, shallots and chilli and cook for 2–3 minutes, stirring regularly. Add the curry paste and sauté for 1 minute. Add all the remaining ingredients except the mussels, coconut milk and fresh herbs, and simmer slowly over a low heat for 10–15 minutes. Stir through the coconut milk and herbs.

3 Add the mussels to the simmering sauce and cook for 2–3 minutes or until the mussels have opened (discard any that do not open).

4 Serve immediately in pasta bowls on a bed of jasmine rice or fresh rice noodles, garnished with the chilli rings and coriander leaves.

## Marinated Ocean Trout Fillets on Warm Bean Salad with Minted Coconut Dressing

*The ingredient list may look lengthy but the dish is very simple to prepare. The bean salad on top of the lightly roasted potatoes provides a perfect bed for the char-grilled ocean trout.*

**Serves 4**

4 x 110–125 g skinless ocean trout fillets (middle not tail fillets), pin-boned**

Minted Coconut Dressing

⅓ cup finely chopped fresh mint

4 tbs (60 mL) light coconut milk* (ingredient check; )

1 tbs desiccated coconut

⅛ tsp sambal oelek* or chilli paste* (ingredient check; )

1 tbs (15 mL) lime juice

1 tsp fish sauce* (ingredient check; )

½ tsp grated palm sugar* or soft brown sugar

freshly ground black pepper

Marinade

2 tsp extra-virgin olive oil*

1 tbs (15 mL) lime juice

2 tsp sumac*

Potatoes

12–16 Pink Fir potatoes (about 800 g), skin on and cleaned, or other chat potatoes

1 tsp extra-light olive oil*

Salad

150 g green beans (select baby to medium-sized, tender beans), trimmed

150 g sugar snap peas, trimmed

150 g snow peas, trimmed

1 bunch asparagus, trimmed (thin shoots are best)

25 g Lebanese cucumber, very finely sliced

Garnish

paprika (if serving on plain white plates)

salmon caviar* (ingredient check) or a sprig of fresh mint

Per serve
Energy 1398 kJ (334 cal)
Protein 30.4 g
Total fat 8.9 g
Saturated fat 2.2 g
Carbohydrate 31.9 g
Total sugars 5.2 g
Dietary fibre 7.8 g
Sodium 202 mg

1   Put the minted coconut dressing ingredients in a glass jar and shake well to combine. Leave to stand at room temperature for 1 hour to allow the coconut to swell and thicken the dressing.

2   Preheat the oven to 220°C (200°C fan forced).

3   Mix the marinade ingredients together in a bowl and coat the fish fillets. Cover and refrigerate for a minimum of 30 minutes.

4   Line a baking tray with baking paper and add the oil. Roll the potatoes in the oil to coat and roast in the oven for 35–40 minutes or until potatoes are golden brown. Shake the tray twice during cooking to ensure the potatoes roast evenly.

5   15 minutes before the potatoes are ready, bring a large pan of water to the boil and preheat a char-grill or grill pan to very hot.

6   Add all the salad vegetables except the cucumber to the boiling water and blanch for 45–60 seconds or until the vegetables turn bright green. Do not overcook. Drain immediately into a colander and very quickly refresh under cold running water. Drain well and place in a mixing bowl with the cucumber. Add the minted coconut dressing and toss it through the vegetables.

7   Just before the potatoes are ready, place the trout on the grill and sear for 1 minute on either side or until cooked to taste.

8   Build your dish to serve. Arrange 3–4 potatoes in the centre of each plate and lightly flatten with a potato masher. Spoon the salad over and top with a fish fillet. Garnish the outside of the plate with a sprinkle of paprika and the fish with a small spoonful of caviar or a mint sprig. Serve immediately.

## Melt-in-the-Mouth Calamari and Parsley Ragú

*Not the usual ragú since the dish is made with calamari rather than the traditional ground beef—but the wonderfully tender calamari in the light tomato-parsley-white wine sauce offers a depth of flavour that is totally unexpected from the simplicity of the ingredients. Serve over rice or pasta of choice, or as a warm salad tossed through mixed leafy greens.*

**Serves 4**

2 tbs (30 mL) extra-light olive oil*
4 green shallots*, trimmed and sliced
750 g calamari tubes, cleaned and cut into 0.75–1 cm wide rings
1 bunch fresh parsley, very finely chopped (reserve 1 tablespoon as garnish)
freshly ground black pepper (lots!)
125 mL (½ cup) white wine wine (ingredient check—Wine) or water
3 tbs (45 mL) tomato paste (ingredient check)
zest of ½ lemon

**Garnish**
reserved finely chopped fresh parsley

Per serve
Energy 1010 kJ (241 cal)
Protein 33.0 g
Total fat 8.6 g
Saturated fat 1.5 g
Carbohydrate 2.7 g
Total sugars 2.4 g
Dietary fibre 2.7 g
Sodium 565 mg

1   Heat the oil in a medium-sized pan over a medium heat. Add the shallots and cook for 2 minutes. Add the calamari, parsley and black pepper, cover and cook over a very low heat for 30 minutes.

2   Add the wine, tomato paste and lemon zest and simmer gently, uncovered, for 10 minutes.

3   Serve immediately over a bed of rice or pasta garnished with the reserved parsley. If serving as a warm salad, allow to cool slightly before tossing through the salad leaves.

## Orange Ginger Salmon Fillets on Dressed White Beans

*Another simple but flavour-packed way to serve salmon. This marinade is also excellent with ocean or rainbow trout, or a firm white fish fillet such as ling. Serve white beans on a bed of steamed bok choy or raw baby spinach leaves topped by the poached salmon.*

**Serves 4**

4 x 110-125 g skinless salmon fillets, pin-boned**

4 baby bok choy, washed and leaves separated

Marinade

zest of ½ large orange

6 tbs (90 mL) fresh orange juice

5 tbs (75 mL) Ginger Refresher (Buderim brand)*

10 fresh mint leaves, finely shredded

2 green shallots*, trimmed and finely chopped

freshly ground black pepper

Dressed White Beans

480 g cooked cannellini beans** (if using canned, ingredient check)

10 fresh mint leaves, finely shredded

¼ cup finely chopped fresh flat-leaf (Italian) parsley leaves

3 tbs (45 mL) lemon juice

1 tsp yellow mustard seeds, lightly crushed

2 tsp apple cider vinegar*

1 tbs (15 mL) extra-virgin olive oil*

freshly ground black pepper

Garnish

sprigs of fresh mint

**Per serve**

Energy 1083 kJ (259 cal)

Protein 30.7 g

Total fat 5.3 g

Saturated fat 0.7 g

Carbohydrate 23.4 g

Total sugars 7.0 g

Dietary fibre 10.7 g

Sodium 82 mg

1   Pat the salmon dry with kitchen towels. Mix the marinade ingredients together in a bowl. Add the salmon and coat well. Cover and refrigerate for a minimum of 30 minutes.

2   Place a large pan of water on to boil.

3   Mix the white beans with the dressing ingredients in a microwave-proof bowl. Cover and microwave the beans for 2 minutes on high, stir and heat for another 1–2 minutes or until warmed through. Keep warm.

4   Transfer the salmon and marinade to a large, non-stick frying pan and poach for 1–2 minutes on each side (depending on the thickness of the fillet). Remove and keep warm.

5   Blanch the bok choy in the boiling water for 1–2 minutes or until just wilted. Drain well.

6   Arrange bok choy in the centre of 4 serving plates, spoon over the white beans and top with salmon fillets and marinade. Serve immediately garnished with the mint sprigs.

## Ⓒ Prawn and Pumpkin Curry

Ⓝ *This recipe uses a home-made Laksa Paste (page 83) as the base—a paste that has all the depth and breadth of flavour without the usual 'heat', so that you can 'chilli up' the dish to taste. Serve on a bed of rice with steamed Asian greens or green leafy salad.*

**Serves 4**

1 kg peeled butternut pumpkin, cut into 2 cm dice
150 g green beans, trimmed and cut to 2-3 cm lengths
extra-light olive oil spray* (ingredient check)
3 tbs (45 mL) Laksa Paste (page 83)
¼ tsp sambal oelek* (optional; ingredient check)
juice of 1 lime (zest the lime before squeezing and reserve for garnish)
400 mL light coconut milk* (ingredient check; Ⓒ)
500 g prawn meat or 750 g green prawns, shelled and deveined, tails intact
  (reserve shells to make Prawn Stock, page 11)
20 fresh mint leaves, shredded

Garnish
shredded mint leaves
reserved lime zest

**Per serve**
Energy 1402 kJ (335 cal)
Protein 33.0 g
Total fat 11.0 g
Saturated fat 5.7 g
Carbohydrate 23.9 g
Total sugars 17.3 g
Dietary fibre 1.3 g
Sodium 478 mg

1 Bring a pan of water to the boil. Add the pumpkin, return to the boil and simmer for 5 minutes or until the pumpkin is starting to soften. Turn off the heat and add the green beans. Leave to stand for 1 minute. Drain thoroughly.

2 Very lightly spray a non-stick frying pan or wok with oil and place over a medium heat. Add the Laksa Paste and sambal oelek (optional) and sauté for 1 minute, stirring continuously. Add the pumpkin and beans and sauté for 2 minutes, stirring regularly.

3 Add the lime juice, coconut milk and prawns and simmer for 2–3 minutes or until the prawns turn pink. Stir through the shredded mint leaves.

4 Serve immediately over a bed of rice, garnished with the extra shredded mint leaves and lime zest.

## Ⓒ Salmon and Tuna Ceviche

Ⓝ *This simple way of 'cooking' fish in lime juice results in a lovely, light summery dish. I use a wide variety of fish to prepare this dish, including ocean trout, ling, barramundi and snapper, to name a few. Serve the marinated fish as is with suitable bread, or on top of chilled Warm Bean Salad with Minted Coconut Dressing (page 35) used as the base for Marinated Ocean Trout Fillets. Refrigerate the dressing for 1 hour after combining (this allows the coconut to swell and thicken the dressing) before tossing through the chilled salad.*

**Serves 4 as a light main or 6 as a starter**

250 g skinless salmon fillet, pin-boned**
250 g tuna steaks

Marinade 1
zest of 1 lime
125 mL (½ cup) lime juice

Marinade 2
½–1 tsp sambal oelek* (ingredient check)
125 mL (½ cup) light coconut milk* (ingredient check; Ⓒ)
4 tbs (60 mL) lime juice

**Per serve**
Energy 733 kJ (175 cal)
Protein 27.1 g
Total fat 5.9 g
Saturated fat 3.1 g
Carbohydrate 1.8 g
Total sugars 1.3 g
Dietary fibre 0.5 g
Sodium 201 mg

1 tsp fish sauce* (ingredient check; ⓖ)

¼ cup finely shredded fresh basil leaves

¼ cup finely shredded fresh coriander leaves

freshly ground black pepper

Garnish

150 g mixed leaf salad or mesclun salad mix

1   Using a sharp knife carefully slice the fish thinly. Place in a non-metallic bowl with the lime zest and coat thoroughly with the pure lime juice. Cover and refrigerate for 2 hours or until the fish becomes opaque, looking 'cooked'. Drain well.

2   Mix the second marinade ingredients together and pour over the fish, turning the fish to coat well. Cover and chill for a minimum of 1 hour (up to 4 hours).

3   To serve, divide the fish and marinade between 4 serving plates and garnish with the salad leaves.

## ⓖ Seared Crusted Salmon With Coriander Salsa

ⓝ *The refreshing Coriander Salsa sets off the moist salmon sealed in the lightly spiced, crushed linseed, sunflower seed and almond (LSA) crust. Try serving on bed of 'Dilled' Celeriac and Carrots (page 92) or Fragrant Rice (page 93) with spicy leafy greens— such as wild rocket or watercress. The salsa may be made in advance, covered and refrigerated for up to 1 week; it is also delicious served alone on Shortcrust Pastry tartlets (page 155). ⓝ use flax meal, quick-cook (instant) polenta\* or rice crumbs\* in place of the LSA mix\*.*

**Serves 4**

4 x 125 g salmon cutlets (or tuna, marlin or swordfish steaks), pin-boned\*\*

extra-light olive oil spray* (ingredient check)

Salsa

25 g fresh coriander roots* and leaves (about ⅓ bunch), roughly chopped

1 green shallot*, trimmed and roughly chopped

30 g desiccated coconut

1 tbs roughly chopped sushi-style pickled ginger (ingredient check—Ginger; ⓖ)

1 tsp grated palm sugar* or soft brown sugar

juice of 1 lime

chilli oil* to taste (⅛–½ tsp) or sambal oelek* (ingredient check)

1 tsp fish sauce* (ingredient check; ⓖ)

2 tsp extra-virgin olive oil*

freshly ground black pepper

Crust

¾ cup LSA mix*

2 tsp sumac*

grated zest of 1 lemon

freshly ground black pepper

Garnish

sprigs of coriander

lemon wedges

| Per serve | |
|---|---|
| **Energy 1556 kJ (371 cal)** | |
| **Protein 26.1 g** | |
| **Total fat 26.5 g** | |
| **Saturated fat 2.9 g** | |
| **Carbohydrate 6.7 g** | |
| **Total sugars 1.9 g** | |
| **Dietary fibre 5.6 g** | |
| **Sodium 191 mg** | |

1   Put all the salsa ingredients in a food processor and process to an evenly chopped consistency (not to a paste). Cover and refrigerate until required.

2   Mix the crust ingredients together on a flat plate. Press the salmon cutlets into the mix to coat both sides well.

3   Lightly spray a large, non-stick frying pan with oil and place over a high heat. When hot transfer the salmon to the pan and sear for 2 minutes on each side or until the crust has started to brown.

4   Serve immediately topped with a heaped teaspoon of the salsa, garnished with coriander and lemon wedges.

## Warehou Fillets with Smoked Salmon Sauce

*This simple light marinade makes a sauce that does justice to the delicately flavoured warehou fillets, or other boneless white fish fillets, such as ling or perch. The dish may be prepared up 24 hours in advance, then cook in a large flat-bottomed frying pan or in the microwave. Serve with steaming Lemon Long-Grain Rice (page 95) or with minted, boiled chat potatoes and steamed greens.*

**Serves 4**

50 g smoked salmon* pieces, roughly chopped (ingredient check)
200 mL light coconut milk* (ingredient check; ◯)
zest and juice of ½ lemon
6 kaffir lime leaves*, bruised
½ tsp mild paprika
freshly ground black pepper
4 warehou fillets (125–150 g each)
6–8 button mushrooms, cleaned (optional)
1 cup bean sprouts (optional)

Garnish
finely chopped fresh parsley
lemon wedges

**Per serve**
Energy 694 kJ (166 cal)
Protein 28.9 g
Total fat 4.3 g
Saturated fat 2.8 g
Carbohydrate 2.4 g
Total sugars 1.3 g
Dietary fibre 0.8 g
Sodium 401 mg

1   Combine the smoked salmon, coconut milk, lemon zest and juice, kaffir lime leaves, paprika and black pepper together in a bowl large enough to hold the fish fillets. Coat the fish fillets in the marinade, cover and refrigerate for at least 1 hour, or overnight.

2   To cook, place the marinade in a large flat-bottomed frying pan over a medium heat and bring to a simmer, stirring occasionally. Add the fish fillets and poach for 2 minutes on each side or until the fish flakes when tested in the thickest part of the fillet. (Hint: warehou fillets break up easily when cooked so turn and serve carefully to ensure the fish remains intact.)

3   If including the mushrooms and bean sprouts, add these into the sauce 2 minutes before the end of cooking so that they are warmed through but retain their texture.

4   Serve immediately on a bed of rice or with minted baby potatoes, garnished with the parsley and lemon wedges.

## Whole Baked Harissa-Seasoned Barramundi

*The fish flesh is deliciously moist, gently flavoured by the home-made harissa paste stuffing. Great served with fresh green beans and potatoes—Roast Pink Fir Potatoes (page 99) are excellent—or a bed of Fragrant Rice (page 93). The fish may be cooked in pairs in aluminium foil as described, or in individual parcels in baking paper.*

**Serves 4**

2 lemons, washed and finely sliced
4 small barramundi, cleaned and scaled
4 sprigs fresh rosemary (3–4 cm each)
8 tsp Green Harissa Paste (page 83)

**Per serve**
Energy 1186 kJ (283 cal)
Protein 46.2 g
Total fat 6.1 g

2 large green shallots*, trimmed and roughly chopped

125 mL (½ cup) Ginger Refresher (Buderim brand)* mixed with 2 tbs (30 mL) water

1 tbs capers*, drained (ingredient check)

1 red capsicum, seeded and finely sliced

Saturated fat 1.3 g

Carbohydrate 9.2 g

Total sugars 8.1 g

Dietary fibre 2.7 g

Sodium 220 mg

Garnish

lemon wedges

mizuna or other salad leaves

1   Preheat the oven to 220°C (200°C fan forced). Line 2 baking trays with aluminium foil, allowing sufficient excess to enclose the fish when folded over. Arrange 2 beds of sliced lemon in each tray.

2   Wash and dry the barramundi. Make 3–4 diagonal cuts through the skin and flesh of 'meaty' section of both sides of each fish. Place a sprig of rosemary in the cleaned cavity and divide 2 teaspoons of the harissa paste between the cuts of each fish. Place each fish on a lemon bed and top with more slices of lemon.

3   Divide the shallots, ginger juice, capers and capsicum between the baking trays. Fold the foil over to seal the fish. Bake in the oven for 20–25 minutes or until the fish flesh flakes when tested with a sharp knife.

4   Serve immediately garnished with lemon wedges and mizuna.

## ⊙ Wild Lime Chilli Prawns

Ⓝ *This exquisite blend of flavours makes the effort of tracking down the wild limes well worth while. It is best served in large white pasta bowls. Serve over a bed of fresh rice spaghetti or other suitable pasta, or a bed of wild rice. If wheat or gluten are not a problem, the prawn sauce is wonderful served over black squid ink pasta. I prefer to use a coconut cream (such as Kara brand) for this dish but a thickened light coconut milk (such as Taste of Thai brand) works well too for a low saturated fat version. The stock and sauce can be prepared in advance.*

**Serves 4**

750 g medium–sized green prawns

250 mL (1 cup) dry white wine (ingredient check—Wine)

250 mL (1 cup) water

Per serve

Energy 978 kJ (233 cal)

Protein 20.7 g

Total fat 3.7 g

Saturated fat 2.7 g

Carbohydrate 18.6 g

Total sugars 16.0 g

Dietary fibre 2.1 g

Sodium 619 mg

Sauce

extra–light olive oil spray* (ingredient check)

3 large green shallots*, trimmed and diagonally sliced (2–3 cm long)

½ cup fennel (about 75 g), finely chopped

½ red capsicum (about 75 g), finely sliced lengthways

150 mL Wild Lime Chilli Sauce (page 80)

200 mL coconut cream* or light coconut milk* (ingredient check; ◯)

2 tsp fish sauce* (ingredient check; ◯)

zest of ½ lime

juice of 1 lime

freshly ground black pepper

1 tbs arrowroot plus 1 tbs water, mixed to a smooth paste

½ cup finely chopped fresh coriander roots* and leaves

Garnish

sprigs of fresh coriander

1   Peel and devein the prawns, leaving the tails intact; place in a bowl, cover and refrigerate until just before cooking (retain the heads and shells for the stock).

**2** Place the prawn heads and shells in a pan, add the wine and water and simmer gently for 10 minutes. Strain the stock into a wok or large frying pan and discard the heads. (The stock may be refrigerated until just before cooking the prawns.)

**3** Very lightly spay a non-stick frying pan with oil and place over a high heat. Add the shallots, fennel and capsicum and sauté for 1 minute, tossing regularly.

**4** Reduce the heat and add the Wild Lime Sauce, coconut cream, fish sauce, lime zest and juice and black pepper. Simmer gently for 2 minutes, stirring occasionally. Add the arrowroot paste and simmer for 1–2 minutes to thicken the sauce. Remove from the heat.

**5** While the sauce is simmering, bring the prawn stock to simmering point. Add the prawns and simmer gently until the prawns turn pink (about 2–3 minutes). Add the lime-coconut sauce and return to simmering point. Stir through the chopped coriander.

**6** Serve immediately over a pasta or rice bed garnished with the sprigs of coriander.

## Meat

Often all you need to turn a simple piece of meat into a great dish is a good sauce, so in addition to the mouth-watering dishes included here, browse through the serving suggestions for Sauces (page 75) for more tasty ideas.

## Aromatic Pork, Chickpea and Spinach Curry

*Forget ready-made curry powder: this delicious curry builds its flavours by the addition of a few simple spices. Delicious served hot over basmati rice\* or rice noodles\*, at room temperature or lightly chilled as part of a buffet, or tossed through salad leaves. Vary the amount of sambal oelek added to alter the 'heat' of the curry; as a rule of thumb, 1 teaspoon makes a warmish curry and ½ teaspoon a mild one.*

**Serves 4**

extra-light olive oil spray\* (ingredient check)

350 g lean pork fillet, finely sliced

4 green shallots\*, trimmed and sliced

1 tbs (15 mL) brown mustard seeds

1 tsp ground turmeric

1 tsp ground fennel

½–1 tsp sambal oelek\* or chilli paste\* (ingredient check; ⓒ)

400 mL light coconut milk\* (ingredient check; ⓒ)

250 mL (1 cup) water

240 g cooked chickpeas\*\* (if using canned, ingredient check)

15 curry leaves\*

2 hydroponic or vine-ripened tomatoes, cut into wedges

150 g spinach (leaves and stalks), trimmed, washed and shredded

20 fresh mint leaves, shredded

Garnish
fresh mint leaves, finely shredded

**Per serve**

Energy 1128 kJ (269 cal)

Protein 26.6 g

Total fat 10.6 g

Saturated fat 6.2 g

Carbohydrate 15.6 g

Total sugars 4.4 g

Dietary fibre 4.9 g

Sodium 154 mg

1  Lightly spray a large, non-stick frying pan with oil and place over a high heat. Add the pork and cook for 2 minutes to sear and seal the meat. Transfer to a bowl with any pan juices.

2  Lightly re-oil the pan, return to a medium heat and add the shallots. Cook for 3 minutes, or until starting to brown lightly and soften, stirring occasionally. Add the mustard seeds and stir for 1 minute or until the seeds start to pop (watch your eyes).

3  Add the turmeric, fennel and sambal oelek and roast, stirring constantly, for 1 minute or until fragrant.

4  Add the coconut milk, water, chickpeas and curry leaves and simmer gently for 10 minutes.

5  Add the pork with any meat juice and tomatoes and cook for 1 minute to heat through. Stir through the spinach and mint, simmer for 30 seconds or until wilted.

6  Serve immediately over steaming basmati rice or noodles garnished with the shredded mint leaves—or set aside to cool and serve at room temperature or lightly chilled, tossed through salad leaves.

## Ⓒ Balsamic Syrup-Dressed Sirloin on a Caramelised Mango and Roast
Ⓕ Vegetable Bed

Ⓝ *A wonderful blend of flavours and textures. Serve with wilted Asian greens, steamed green beans or green leafy salad. This combination works equally well with other meat—for pork, lamb and white fish replace the orange juice in the balsamic syrup with lemon juice, for salmon, ocean trout or chicken serve as is.*

**Serves 4**

Balsamic Syrup

4 tbs (60 mL) balsamic vinegar* (ingredient check—Vinegar; Ⓒ)

6 tbs (90 mL) water

2 tbs (30 mL) orange juice

50 g caster sugar

freshly ground black pepper

Batons and Beef

1 quantity Carrot, Parsnip and Kumara Batons (page 91)

2 small mangoes or 4 slices fresh pineapple

4 tsp soft brown sugar

4 x 125 g sirloin steaks, trimmed of excess fat

extra-light olive oil spray* (ingredient check)

Garnish

fresh flat-leaf (Italian) parsley leaves, roughly chopped

**Per serve**

Energy 2168 kJ (517 cal)

Protein 32.7 g

Total fat 10.5 g

Saturated fat 3.6 g

Carbohydrate 70.8 g

Total sugars 46.4 g

Dietary fibre 9.3 g

Sodium 124 mg

1   Preheat the oven to 240°C (220°C fan forced). Line 2 baking trays with baking paper.

2   Place all the syrup ingredients in a small pan over a high heat. Bring to the boil, stirring continuously. Reduce the heat and simmer gently for 10–12 minutes or until starting to turn slightly syrupy. Set aside.

3   Prepare the carrot, parsnip and kumara batons as described on page 91, place on the baking trays and roast in the oven for 25–30 minutes or until starting to brown lightly, tossing once during cooking.

4   While the vegetables are roasting, preheat a char-grill, or grill pan and grill, to very hot. Remove the mango cheeks by slicing down both sides of the mango stone. Score the mango flesh at 1 cm intervals and repeat in the opposite direction to form a diamond pattern, invert the skin to 'hedgehog' the mango cheeks. Transfer to a grill tray and sprinkle a teaspoon of sugar over each.

5   Very lightly oil both sides of the steak. Ten minutes before the roast vegetables are ready, place the steaks on the grill and cook for 2–3 minutes each side or until cooked to taste. Cover and set aside to rest for 5 minutes. Grill the mangoes for 5 minutes or until warmed through and the sugar caramelised (or roast in the oven for 5–10 minutes). Re-warm the balsamic syrup over a low heat.

6   To serve arrange a nest of the roast vegetables on serving plates, place a mango cheek in the centre of each and top with a steak. Drizzle the warm balsamic syrup over the top. Serve immediately garnished with the parsley, accompanied by green vegetables or salad of choice.

## Ⓒ Butterfly Pork on Apple and Wild Rice Risotto with Stuffed Baby Peppers

Ⓕ *The Wild Rice Risotto makes a wonderful bed for the char-grilled, marinated butterfly pork. It is equally good served with lamb—*
Ⓝ *simply swap the teaspoon of marjoram with 2 teaspoons finely shredded mint. Serve with a green leafy salad.*
Ⓥ Ⓒ *for a vegetarian dish, substitute 2 cups cooked du Puy green lentils* for the pork; add to the risotto with the apple mix. Serve garnished with the roasted baby pepper.*

**Serves 6**

Pork

750 g butterfly–cut pork loin steaks, trimmed of excess fat

2 tbs (30 mL) apple cider vinegar*

½ tsp ground cumin

3-4 drops chilli oil* (ingredient check)

1 tbs (15 mL) virgin olive oil*


Wild Rice Risotto

1 tbs (15 mL) virgin olive oil*

3 green shallots*, trimmed and sliced

150 g celery (about 3 stalks), trimmed and sliced

1 red apple (about 150 g), washed, cored, diced and coated in lemon juice

1 tsp wholegrain mustard (ingredient check—Mustard)

750 mL (3 cups) dry cider (ingredient check) or 3 tbs (45 mL) apple juice concentrate*

   plus 700 mL water

150 mL water

200 g wild rice*, rinsed and drained well

1 tsp finely chopped fresh marjoram or thyme

freshly ground black pepper


Baby Capsicum

6 baby red capsicums

100 g cherry or grape tomatoes

1 tsp finely chopped fresh oregano or ½ tsp dried oregano

15 baby spinach leaves, shredded

½ tsp virgin olive oil*

1 tsp balsamic vinegar* (ingredient check—Vinegar; ◯)

freshly ground black pepper

**Per serve**

**Energy 1861 kJ (444 cal)**

**Protein 34.2 g**

**Total fat 10.9 g**

**Saturated fat 2.5 g**

**Carbohydrate 43.9 g**

**Total sugars 18.0 g**

**Dietary fibre 6.3 g**

**Sodium 135 mg**

1   Preheat the oven to 180°C (160°C fan forced). Line a baking tray with baking paper.

2   Mix the vinegar, cumin and oil together in a bowl, toss the pork in the marinade, cover and refrigerate.

3   Place the oil in a small pan over a high heat, add the shallots, celery, apple and mustard and sauté, stirring occasionally, for 3 minutes. Set aside.

4   Place the cider (or diluted apple juice concentrate) and water in a large pan over a high heat and bring to the boil. Stir in the rice and chopped herb, reduce the heat, partially cover and simmer for 30 minutes, stirring occasionally. Add the celery and apple mix and cook gently for a further 20–25 minutes or until all the liquid is absorbed and the rice grains have opened and curled. Remove from the heat, season with pepper, then cover and keep warm.

5   While the rice is cooking, slice the top off the capsicums and carefully remove the seeds. Mix all the remaining ingredients together in a small bowl and spoon into the capsicums. Place in the oven and roast for 30 minutes or until the capsicums have softened and the skin has started to brown. Turn off the oven off. Cover the tray with foil, and return to the oven to keep warm until ready to serve.

6   10 minutes before the rice is cooked, heat a char-grill or grill pan to very hot. Cook the pork for 1–2 minutes on each side or until just cooked. Remove from the grill, cover and set aside to rest for 5 minutes. Slice the pork diagonally across the grain of the meat.

7   Stir the risotto and spoon into the centre of 6 warmed serving plates. Top with the sliced pork. Serve immediately garnished with the baby capsicum accompanied by a green leafy salad.

## Chilled Minted Lamb Salad with Roasted Sticky Rice

*A refreshing cold meat salad ideal for a light lunch. It is also great served with Avocado Dip (page 26). The meat is dressed after it is cooked.*

**Serves 4**

Dressing

½–1 tsp chilli oil* (ingredient check)

zest of ½ lime

1 tbs (15 mL) lime juice

20 fresh mint leaves, finely shredded

1 green shallot*, very finely chopped

2 tbs roughly chopped fresh coriander leaves

1 tsp freshly grated ginger

freshly ground black pepper

Rice and Lamb

100 g white glutinous rice*

water

600 g lamb backstrap (eye of loin)

extra–light olive oil spray* (ingredient check)

100 g baby rocket leaves or mesclun salad mix

Garnish

2 tbs sesame seeds, dry roasted**

**Per serve**

Energy 1148 kJ (274 cal)

Protein 33.3 g

Total fat 6.2 g

Saturated fat 2.5 g

Carbohydrate 21.1 g

Total sugars 0.8 g

Dietary fibre 0.9 g

Sodium 106 mg

1  Mix all the dressing ingredients together in a small jug.

2  To roast the rice, heat a heavy-based pan or skillet to very hot. Add the rice and roast until golden brown, stirring regularly and adding a tablespoon of water at intervals. Set aside to cool. Grind in a pestle and mortar or coffee grinder to a very coarse, grainy texture.

3  Preheat a char-grill or grill pan to very hot. Lightly spray the lamb with oil and sear for 1–2 minutes each side or until cooked to rare to medium-rare. Cover and set aside for 5 minutes. Slice the meat diagonally across the grain and place in a bowl. Pour the dressing over the lamb and coat thoroughly. Cover and refrigerate for 1 hour or until well chilled.

4  Immediately before serving, toss the ground rice through the lamb. Serve on a bed of baby rocket leaves, garnished with the sesame seeds.

## Goat Vindaloo

*Vindaloo normally has the reputation of being very hot, but this recipe has all the wonderful spice flavours without the heat. For a hotter curry, add sambal oelek* (ingredient check) to taste 10 minutes before the end of cooking. Serve with poppadums* (ingredient check), sambals such as banana tossed in coconut, and tomato, parsley and cucumber in lemon juice with Mint Chutney (page 88) over basmati rice*. The curry is just as delicious made with lean gravy or stewing beef or mutton pieces.*

**Serves 4**

1 tbs (15 mL) ground coriander

1 tbs (15 mL) ground turmeric

2 tsp ground ginger

1 tsp ground cumin

175 mL white vinegar (ingredient check—Vinegar; )

5 green shallots*, trimmed and finely sliced

**Per serve**

Energy 1251 kJ (299 cal)

Protein 52.0 g

Total fat 6.1 g

Saturated fat 1.8 g

Carbohydrate 3.2 g

1 kg goat pieces, bone in (4-5 cm pieces), trimmed of excess fat

3 large bay leaves

Total sugars 1.7 g

Dietary fibre 0.7 g

Sodium 210 mg

1 Put the spices and vinegar in a large ovenproof, non-reactive casserole dish and mix to a smooth paste. Stir through the shallots. Add the meat and coat thoroughly with the spice paste. Cover and refrigerate for 24 hours.

2 Preheat the oven to 210°C (190°C fan forced). Add the bay leaves to the curry and stir to re-coat the meat. Place a sheet of aluminium foil over the top of the casserole dish and cover with the lid to ensure a good fit. Cook in the oven for 1½–1¾ hours or until the meat is tender and most of the liquid has evaporated.

3 Stir well and serve immediately over steaming basmati rice with accompaniments of choice.

## Kangaroo Fillets on Wilted Chinese Greens with Mountain Pepper Plum Sauce

*This is a simple and delicious dish that combines the very lean and tender loin fillet of kangaroo with a lovely plum sauce based on the distinctive native mountain pepper. Since kangaroo is so lean, it cooks very rapidly and it should be served rare to medium-rare, so be careful not to overcook. The sauce can be made in advance and reheated just before serving—it makes a great condiment for cold meat or as a dipping sauce. Frenched kangaroo racks are equally good served with this sauce—to cook, lightly oil the racks, drizzle with balsamic vinegar (ingredient check; ◉) and roast at 240°C (220°C fan forced) for 15–20 minutes. Serve with Orange Zested Roast Parsnips (page 97). ◉ canned plums may contain vitamin C (see Avoiding Corn, page 161).*

**Serves 4**

Sauce

825 g canned plums in natural juice

2 tbs (30 mL) plum or balsamic vinegar* (ingredient check—Vinegar; ◉)

10 drops chilli oil* (ingredient check) or to taste

1 tbs Dijon mustard (ingredient check—Mustard)

2 x 5 cm strips lemon zest

1 bay leaf

3 kaffir lime leaves*, bruised

1 star anise

freshly ground black pepper

¼ tsp mountain pepper* or additional black pepper

Gai Lum and Kangaroo

1-2 bunches gai lum* (Chinese broccoli) or other Asian greens

4 x 125 g kangaroo loin fillets*, lightly flattened

2 tsp lemon-infused olive* or extra-light olive oil*

Garnish

long strands of lemon zest

Per serve

Energy 1213 kJ (289 cal)

Protein 29.7 g

Total fat 4.7 g

Saturated fat 0.8 g

Carbohydrate 31.0 g

Total sugars 28.9 g

Dietary fibre 4.3 g

Sodium 170 mg

1 To make the sauce, drain the plum juice into a medium-sized pan. Stone the plums and chop the flesh very finely. Add to the plum juice. Add all remaining ingredients except the mountain pepper and place over medium heat. Bring to the boil, reduce the heat and simmer steadily for 25–30 minutes or until sauce has reduced to a thin syrupy consistency, stirring occasionally.

2 Wash and trim the gai lum and place in cold water until ready to cook. Bring a large pan of water to the boil.

3 Heat a char-grill or grill pan to very hot. Reheat the sauce until simmering gently. Stir through the mountain pepper.

**4** Very lightly oil the kangaroo fillets and sear for 1 minute on each side, then transfer to the simmering sauce. Turn the meat to coat both sides, remove the pan from the heat and cover to keep warm.

**5** Add the gai lum to the boiling water and blanch for 1–2 minutes or until wilted and the stalks are just starting to soften; do not overcook. Drain well and arrange as a bed in the centre of serving plates. Place a kangaroo fillet on top and spoon over the sauce. Serve immediately garnished with the lemon zest accompanied by the roast parsnips.

## Kashmir Curry

*A sweeter-style, mild lamb and fruit curry to serve with rice, poppadums\* (ingredient check), and sambals, such as banana slices tossed in lemon juice and desiccated coconut, Mint Chutney (page 88) and diced cucumber, tomatoes and shredded flat-leaf (Italian) parsley tossed in lemon juice. As with any curry, the flavour develops if the curry is refrigerated overnight and reheated.*

**Serves 4**

| | |
|---|---|
| extra-light olive oil spray\* (ingredient check) | **Per serve** |
| 2 green shallots\*, trimmed and sliced | **Energy 1565 kJ (374 cal)** |
| 1 medium-sized red capsicum, seeded and diced | **Protein 25.1 g** |
| 1 tsp freshly grated ginger | **Total fat 11.5 g** |
| 2 tsp curry powder\* (ingredient check) | **Saturated fat 3.2 g** |
| ½ tsp sumac\* | **Carbohydrate 43.9 g** |
| ¼ tsp cumin seeds | **Total sugars 38.6 g** |
| 400 g lean lamb mince | **Dietary fibre 6.0 g** |
| zest and juice of ½ lemon | **Sodium 98 mg** |
| 250 mL (1 cup) tomato passata\* (ingredient check) | |
| 125 mL (½ cup) water | |
| 25 g desiccated coconut | |
| 100 g natural sultanas | |
| 2 firm bananas | |

**1** Lightly spray a large, non-stick frying pan or wok with oil and place over a medium heat. Add the shallots and capsicum and sauté for 1–2 minutes. Add the spices and roast for 1 minute or until fragrant, stirring regularly.

**2** Add the lamb mince and cook until lightly browned and well mixed with the spices. Add all the remaining ingredients except the bananas and heat until simmering slowly. Peel and slice the bananas, add to the pan, reduce the heat and simmer very slowly for 15 minutes.

**3** Serve over steaming rice with accompaniments of choice.

## Lamb and Quandong Pies

*The quandongs provide a wonderful fruity sauce to complement the rich flavour of the lamb. The pie is simply topped by browned potatoes—I usually prepare an individual pie for each person but the dish may be prepared as a single pie in a larger ovenproof dish if preferred. The filling may be prepared in advance and reheated before topping with the potato. Slice the potatoes immediately before layering on the pies so that they do not discolour. The cooked quandongs can be substituted with 150 g quandong jam (such as Beerenberg brand), in which case omit the soft brown sugar. Serve with steamed green vegetables or a leafy salad.*

**Serves 4**

| | |
|---|---|
| Pie filling | **Per serve** |
| extra-light olive oil spray\* (ingredient check) | **Energy 1500 kJ (358 cal)** |
| ½ green capsicum, seeded and thinly sliced into 2 cm lengths | **Protein 33.4 g** |
| ½ tsp ground cumin | **Total fat 5.5 g** |
| 500 g lamb backstrap (eye of loin), sliced thinly across the fillet | **Saturated fat 2.0 g** |
| ⅛–⅓ tsp sambal oelek\* (optional; ingredient check) | **Carbohydrate 42.9 g** |

½ cup cooked quandongs, roughly chopped (see Quandong Compote, page 127)

2 tsp wholegrain mustard (ingredient check—Mustard)

2 sun-dried tomatoes*, finely chopped (ingredient check; ⊙)

zest and juice of ½ lime

100 g tender green beans, trimmed and cut to 2 cm lengths

1 tsp soft brown sugar

125 mL (½ cup) vegetable* or chicken stock* (ingredient check—Stock; ⊙) or water

1 tsp very finely chopped fresh rosemary leaves

freshly ground black pepper

2 tbs arrowroot plus 5 tbs (75 mL) water, mixed to a smooth paste

Topping

600 g fine-skinned Desiree potatoes (about 4 medium-sized), cleaned and lightly pricked

extra-light olive oil spray*

Garnish

sprigs of fresh rosemary

Total sugars 18.4 g

Dietary fibre 8.4 g

Sodium 107 mg

1   Preheat the oven to 220°C (200°C fan forced).

2   Very lightly spray a non-stick frying pan with oil and place over a high heat. Add the capsicum and sauté for 1 minute. Add the cumin and cook for 1 minute, stirring regularly to prevent the spice from catching. Add the lamb and sambal oelek and cook for 2–3 minutes to seal the meat, tossing regularly. Add all the remaining filling ingredients (see Note) except the arrowroot, and simmer for 4–5 minutes or until the lamb is almost cooked, stirring occasionally—do not overcook the lamb.

Note: If the beans are not tender, blanch in boiling water for 1 minute and refresh under cold running water before adding to the lamb mix with the other ingredients.

3   Stir the arrowroot paste through the lamb mix. Simmer gently for 1–2 minutes, while stirring, or until the sauce has thickened. Place the mixture in individual ovenproof ramekins or pie dishes and set aside.

4   Wrap each potato in a sheet of kitchen towel and place in the microwave; cook on high for 3 minutes, turn and cook for a further 3 minutes or until the potatoes are just soft when tested with a sharp knife. Remove the potatoes, unwrap and set aside for 5 minutes to cool. (Alternatively, the potatoes may be pre-cooked in boiling water.) Slice the potatoes thinly crossways and place in layers on top of the lamb. Very lightly brush the top layer of potatoes with oil. Bake in the oven for 15–20 minutes or until the potatoes start to turn golden and the filling bubbles.

5   Serve immediately garnished with the rosemary, accompanied by a green leafy salad or a mixture of steamed green vegetables.

## Lamb Shanks Baked in Red Wine, Preserved Lemon and Smoked Paprika Sauce

*A casserole just bursting with wonderful flavours. To really develop the flavours and minimise fat levels in the sauce, cook the casserole a day in advance, refrigerate overnight, skim off the fat and reheat. If serving immediately, skim the surface of the gravy to remove any excess oil—I find a gravy separator† really handy. Serve with fluffy jacket potatoes or brown rice and steamed fresh vegetables.*

1 tsp sweet smoked paprika*

rind of ¼ preserved lemon* (flesh removed), rinsed and finely chopped (ingredient check)

1 sprig fresh rosemary

2 sprigs fresh thyme

1 medium-sized red capsicum, seeded and diced

Per serve

Energy 1760 kJ (420 cal)

Protein 41.6 g

Total fat 17.3 g

3 green shallots*, trimmed and sliced

100 g celery, diced

2 medium-sized carrots, cleaned and sliced

140 g tomato paste (ingredient check)

freshly ground black pepper

250 mL (1 cup) red wine (ingredient check—Wine)

250 mL (1 cup) water

4 lamb shanks, trimmed of excess fat

2 tbs arrowroot plus 3 tbs (45 mL) water mixed to a smooth paste

Saturated fat 7.8 g

Carbohydrate 13.9 g

Total sugars 9.0 g

Dietary fibre 4.0 g

Sodium 231 mg

Serves 4

1   Preheat the oven to 200°C (180°C fan forced).

2   Place all ingredients except the lamb shanks and arrowroot paste in a large ovenproof casserole dish and mix well. Add the shanks, ensuring they are covered with the sauce. Place a piece of aluminium foil over the top of the dish and cover with the lid (to ensure a good seal).

3   If serving without cooling and reheating, cook in the oven for 1½–1¾ hours or until lamb is tender and starting to fall off the bones, stirring twice during cooking. Five minutes before the casserole is ready, skim off any surface fat (see recipe introduction). Stir through the arrowroot paste, replace the lid and return to the oven for 5 minutes to cook the paste and thicken the gravy.

4   For the very low-fat version, cook the casserole for 1¼–1½ hours or until the lamb is tender. Set aside to cool before refrigerating. Skim off any solidified surface fat and reheat in an oven preheated to 200°C (180°C fan forced) or in a microwave, thickening the sauce as above.

5   Serve immediately with fluffy jacket potatoes or over brown rice, with steamed vegetables.

## Ⓒ Lamb with Minted Green Pea Mash and Mushroom Salsa

Ⓕ
Ⓝ
*This is such a simple way to serve lamb, either cutlets or chops of your choice or my favourite cut, backstrap (eye of loin). The Green Pea Mash and Mushroom Salsa are both quick and easy to prepare, while the fresh mint and lemon flavours provide a perfect foil for the lamb. Prepare the Mash ahead of time (particularly if using dried peas) and reheat in the microwave just before serving; the salsa is best made fresh. Serve with steamed fresh vegetables or Lemon Oil Infused Green Beans (page 95). Ⓝ use olive oil in place of walnut oil.*

**Serves 4**

1 tsp balsamic vinegar* (ingredient check—Vinegar; Ⓒ)

1 tbs (15 mL) lemon-infused olive oil* or 2 tsp virgin olive oil* plus 1 tbs lemon juice

4 lean leg lamb chops or 4 x 125 g portions lamb backstrap (eye of loin)

Minted Green Pea Mash

2 x 440 g cans green peas, rinsed and drained (ingredient check; Ⓒ) or 1½ cups
   cooked dried peas** (green split peas or blue broilers; retain some of the cooking
   water to moisten when mashing if required)

zest and juice of ½ lemon

20 fresh mint leaves, finely chopped

freshly ground black pepper (lots!)

Mushroom Salsa

6 firm mushrooms (about 175 g), cleaned and diced

1 green shallot*, finely sliced

1 tsp water

2 tsp walnut* or virgin olive oil*

2 tsp balsamic vinegar* (ingredient check—Vinegar; Ⓒ)

Per serve

Energy 1816 kJ (433 cal)

Protein 43.3 g

Total fat 16.5 g

Saturated fat 5.4 g

Carbohydrate 22.7 g

Total sugars 5.4 g

Dietary fibre 9.3 g

Sodium 406 mg

4 fresh mint leaves, finely chopped

freshly ground black pepper

Garnish

sprigs of fresh mint

1   Mix the balsamic vinegar and lemon-infused olive oil (or lemon juice and oil) together in a glass or ceramic bowl. Coat the meat with the marinade, cover and refrigerate for a minimum of 1 hour before cooking.

2   Preheat a char-grill, grill pan or barbecue to very hot. While the grill is heating, place the mushrooms, shallot and water in a small microwave-proof bowl. Cover and microwave on high for 1 minute or until the mushrooms are hot and just starting to soften. Mix the oil, vinegar, mint and black pepper through the mushrooms, cover and set aside. The salsa is best served at room temperature or just warm.

3   While the salsa is warming, mash the peas to an even consistency in a microwave-proof bowl with a fork. Mix through the lemon zest and juice, mint and black pepper. Cover and heat in the microwave on high for 2–3 minutes. Remove and stir the mash and return to the microwave for a further 2 minutes or until the mash is hot. Cover and keep warm.

4   Place the lamb on the grill and sear for 2 minutes on each side or to taste. Cover and rest for 5 minutes.

5   To serve, pile the pea mash into the middle of 4 serving plates and arrange the meat on top (if using backstrap, slice the meat diagonally across the grain before serving). Spoon the salsa over the top, and serve immediately garnished with the mint sprigs accompanied by vegetables of choice.

## Ⓒ Lancashire-Style Beef Hot Pot with Lemon and Mace-Dressed Spinach

Ⓕ
Ⓝ
*Lancashire Hot Pot is usually based on a cheap cut of lamb, but I prefer to use a lean cut of beef for a flavour-packed, low-fat version which takes less time in the oven. Home-made beef (page 9) or vegetable stock (page 12) makes a wonderful gravy base— but any good, suitable stock can be used. Accompanied by dressed, lightly blanched spinach and a suitable, traditional pickled red cabbage, this makes a delicious meal for a wintery night. Ⓖ use sea salt instead of fish sauce.*

**Serves 4**

650–700 g economy rump steak or topside, trimmed of fat and diced

3 rashers short-cut, rindless bacon, roughly chopped (ingredient check; Ⓖ)

5 green shallots*, trimmed and roughly chopped

3 tbs (45 mL) tomato paste (ingredient check)

75 g button mushrooms, cleaned

240 g cooked chickpeas** (if using canned, ingredient check)

1 tsp dried oregano

½ tsp fish sauce* (ingredient check; Ⓖ) or tiny pinch of sea salt

freshly ground black pepper

2 tbs arrowroot

375 mL (1½ cups) beef*, chicken* or vegetable stock* (ingredient check—Stock; Ⓖ)

150 g fresh or frozen peas (ingredient check)

3 carrots (about 250 g), peeled and sliced

650 g fine-skinned Desiree potatoes (about 4–5), cleaned and thinly sliced

extra-light olive oil spray* (ingredient check)

Spinach

1 bunch spinach

½ tsp lemon zest

¼ tsp mace

**Per serve**

Energy 2348 kJ (560 cal)

Protein 56.0 g

Total fat 12.1 g

Saturated fat 4.2 g

Carbohydrate 50.3 g

Total sugars 11.5 g

Dietary fibre 14.1 g

Sodium 1024 mg

1 Preheat the oven to 220°C (200°C fan forced).

2 Place the beef, bacon, shallots, tomato paste, mushrooms, chickpeas, oregano and seasoning in a casserole (about 3-litre capacity). Mix the arrowroot with 4 tablespoons of stock and add to the casserole. Add the remaining stock and stir to mix ingredients evenly.

3 Scatter the peas over the meat mix. Top with the carrot followed by the potato slices, ensuring the potatoes are laid evenly across the top of the casserole. Cover and cook in the oven for 1 hour.

4 Remove the casserole and very lightly spray the top layer of potatoes with oil. Return to the oven and cook uncovered for 20–30 minutes or until the top layer of potatoes is golden brown and crispy.

5 While the potatoes are browning, place a large pot of water on to boil. Wash, trim and finely shred the spinach stalks. Roughly shred the spinach leaves. Five minutes before the casserole is ready, blanch spinach in the boiling water for 3–4 minutes or until the stalks are just softened. Drain immediately, return to the pan and toss through the lemon zest and mace. Cover to keep warm.

6 Serve the casserole immediately accompanied by the spinach and pickled red cabbage.

## Osso Bucco and Red Wine Braise

*A rich and hearty dish which is excellent served with jacket potatoes or Carrot, Parsnip and Kumara Batons (page 91)—anything, in fact, that will soak up the wonderful sauce. The potatoes thicken the sauce as they soften and start to break up.*
*use sea salt instead of fish sauce.*

**Serves 6**

1 green capsicum, seeded and diced

5 green shallots*, trimmed and sliced

4 fine–skinned, floury potatoes (about 600 g) such as Nicola, Russet, Spunta or Sebago, cleaned and cut to 1 cm dice

2 large carrots, peeled, sliced to 3 cm lengths and quartered

1 x 425 g can chopped tomatoes (no added thickener, no added salt)

200 g tomato paste (ingredient check)

375 mL (1½ cups) red wine (ingredient check—Wine)

2 bay leaves

1 tbs (15 mL) dried oregano leaves

zest of 1 lemon

freshly ground black pepper

½ tsp fish sauce* (ingredient check; ⊙) or a pinch of sea salt

1–1.25 kg osso bucco (shin of beef), trimmed of excess fat

**Per serve**

Energy 1390 kJ (332 cal)

Protein 33.4 g

Total fat 7.4 g

Saturated fat 3.5 g

Carbohydrate 23.7 g

Total sugars 9.3 g

Dietary fibre 5.5 g

Sodium 144 mg

1 Preheat the oven to 200°C (180°C fan forced). Place all the ingredients except the beef in a large ovenproof casserole and mix well.

2 Heat a non-stick frying pan over a medium heat, add the beef and brown lightly on both sides to seal. Transfer to the casserole, ensuring the meat is covered with liquid.

3 Place a sheet of aluminium foil over the top of the casserole dish and cover with the casserole lid. Cook in the oven for 1¾–2 hours, or until the meat is tender and the potatoes are soft, stirring twice during cooking to ensure the meat is covered with the sauce.

4 Skim off any surface fat and serve immediately with 'sauce mopper' of choice and steamed green vegetables.

## Pork a–top a Pancake

*A great way to serve the humble chop! The 'pancake' can be served whole and cut into wedges immediately before serving, or as individual patties.*

**Serves 4**

1 quantity Potato and Apple Pancake (page 98)

4 lean pork loin chops

extra–light olive oil spray* (ingredient check)

50 g baby spinach or rocket leaves

Sauce

1 large firm red apple (such as Jonagold or Braeburn), cored and diced

juice of ½ lime

seeds from 3 cardamom pods or 3 whole cloves

250 mL (1 cup) water

Garnish

sprigs of fresh mint

**Per serve**

**Energy 1330 kJ (317 cal)**

**Protein 30.8 g**

**Total fat 5.6 g**

**Saturated fat 2.0 g**

**Carbohydrate 34.9 g**

**Total sugars 10.7 g**

**Dietary fibre 5.6 g**

**Sodium 114 mg**

**1** Put all the sauce ingredients in a small pan and simmer over a low heat for 10 minutes, stirring occasionally, or until the fruit has softened and the sauce has reduced to about half the original volume. Set aside.

**2** Prepare pancake as described on page 98 for Potato and Apple Pancake. Transfer the cooked pancake(s) to a baking tray lined with baking paper and place in a slow oven or warming drawer to keep warm while cooking the pork.

**3** While the pancake is cooking, preheat a barbecue, char-grill or grill; if using a char-grill or grill pan, very lightly spray the chops with oil before cooking. Cook the chops for 2–3 minutes each side or until cooked to taste (do not overcook or the pork will be dry). Cover and rest for 2–3 minutes.

**4** Reheat the sauce gently. Arrange a bed of baby spinach or rocket leaves on 4 serving plates, top with a pancake wedge or patty, divide the sauce over the pancake and top with the pork. Serve immediately garnished with mint.

## Pork in Ginger on Roast Kumara Wedges

*This is simple—and can only be described as absolutely delicious!*

**Serves 4**

Marinade

200 mL Ginger Refresher (Buderim brand)*

3 tbs (45 mL) water

2 tsp pure sesame oil*

zest of 1 lime

freshly ground black pepper

Pork and Kumara

2 pork fillets (about 600 g)

3-4 kumara or orange sweet potatoes (about 750 g), peeled and sliced into wedges

1-2 tsp extra–light olive oil*

**Per serve**

**Energy 1458 kJ (348 cal)**

**Protein 37.2 g**

**Total fat 7.3 g**

**Saturated fat 1.7 g**

**Carbohydrate 33.9 g**

**Total sugars 17.4 g**

**Dietary fibre 3.8 g**

**Sodium 138 mg**

Garnish

50 g baby rocket leaves

2 green shallots*, trimmed and slivered

6 fresh mint leaves, finely shredded

1   Mix the marinade ingredients together in a bowl. Place the pork fillet in the marinade, cover and refrigerate for a minimum of 1 hour, turning once if the meat is not totally covered.

2   Preheat the oven to 220°C (200°C fan forced). Line a baking tray with baking paper and add oil. Roll the kumara wedges in the oil to coat. Roast for 30–40 minutes or until the wedges are browning and starting to crisp slightly. Shake the tray twice during cooking to ensure even browning.

3   While the kumara is cooking, preheat a char-grill, grill pan or barbecue to very hot. Ten minutes before the kumara is ready, cook the pork fillet for 2–3 minutes each side (depending on the thickness of the fillet), or until cooked to taste (do not overcook). Cover and set aside to rest for 5 minutes.

4   While the pork is resting, place the remaining marinade in a small pan and reduce over a high heat until two-thirds the original volume, then lower the heat to keep warm.

5   To serve, arrange the rocket leaves on 4 serving plates and top with the kumara wedges. Slice the pork fillet diagonally against the grain of the meat and arrange on top of the kumara. Drizzle the reduced sauce over the top. Serve immediately garnished with the shallots and mint.

## ⓒ Pork Fillet and Prosciutto Parcels on Cinnamon–Poached Quince and
## ⓕ Spinach Bed

ⓝ *The quinces take time to poach—but the rest of the dish is quick to prepare and cook. A great dish for a formal dinner party, where the sweetness of the quinces is perfectly complemented by the saltiness of the prosciutto and the citrus of the spinach and sumac. Prepare the quinces 1–2 days in advance and store refrigerated in a covered glass or ceramic bowl; reheat just before serving.*

**Serves 4**

Poached Quinces

250 mL (1 cup) sweet wine (ingredient check—Wine)

125 mL (½ cup) water

50 g caster sugar

1 cinnamon quill

3 x 5 cm strips lemon rind

2 quinces (about 450 g), washed to remove all fur

Pork Parcels

4 x 125-150 g portions of pork fillet

extra-light olive oil spray* (ingredient check)

4 tsp pure quince paste*

2 tsp sumac*

freshly ground black pepper

12 fresh basil leaves, finely shredded

4 slices prosciutto* (ingredient check; ⓒ)

Potatoes

750 g Desiree chat potatoes (12-16) or other fine-skinned, small potatoes, cleaned

1 tsp extra-light olive oil*

Spinach

¾-1 bunch spinach, stalks trimmed and roughly shredded

2 tbs (30 mL) lemon juice

**Per serve**

**Energy 1968 kJ (470 cal)**

**Protein 37.3 g**

**Total fat 5.3 g**

**Saturated fat 1.3 g**

**Carbohydrate 56.5 g**

**Total sugars 32.5 g**

**Dietary fibre 13.4 g**

**Sodium 671 mg**

1   To prepare the quinces, place all the poached quince ingredients except the quince in a medium-sized pan. Cut the quinces into quarters, peel and core. Wrap the skin and cores in a muslin square, tie it up and put it in the pan. Cut the quince quarters into 3–4 pieces lengthways and add to the pan. Bring to simmering point over a medium heat. Place a layer of aluminium foil over the top of the pan and cover with a lid. Reduce the heat and simmer the quinces gently for 1 hour or until soft and pink. Remove the muslin parcel, squeezing it well to return any quince juices to the pan before discarding.

2   To prepare the pork parcels, place 2 of the fillets in a plastic bag and flatten out to half the original thickness with a meat mallet. Repeat with the remaining fillets. Very lightly oil one side of the fillets and lay out on a plate oil-side down. Spread a teaspoon of quince paste on each fillet and sprinkle ½ teaspoon sumac over the top of each. Top with black pepper, the shredded basil and a slice of prosciutto. Cover and set aside.

3   To roast potatoes, preheat the oven to 220°C (200°C fan forced) and follow recipe for Roast Chat, Pink Fir and Kipfler Potatoes on page 99.

4   15 minutes before the potatoes are ready, put a large pan of water on to boil.

5   10 minutes out, place the quinces over a medium-low heat to warm through, stirring occasionally. Place a large, non-stick frying pan or skillet over a high heat and add the pork parcels, prosciutto-side down. Reduce heat to medium-high and cook for 2 minutes or until the prosciutto is well coloured and crispy (lift up the corner of the pork to check). Carefully turn the parcels using a spatula and tongs and cook for 2–3 minutes or until the pork is just cooked through.

6   While the pork is cooking, blanch the spinach for 2 minutes in the boiling water. Drain immediately, return to the pan and toss through the lemon juice. Cover to keep warm.

7   To assemble the dish, arrange 3–4 roast potatoes in the centre of each plate and semi-flatten with a potato masher. Top each potato bed with a serve of spinach. Spoon 2–3 tablespoonfuls of quince into the middle and top with a pork parcel. Serve immediately.

## Porterhouse Steak on Char-Grilled Tri-Colour Capsicum and Preserved Lemon Salad

*The flavours of the capsicum salad are outstanding and provide a perfect bed for a lightly char-grilled porterhouse steak. The salad may be made in advance up to the addition of the parsley: simply cover, refrigerate and add the parsley just before reheating. Serve with a green salad and Carrot, Parsnip and Kumara Batons (page 91), roast Desiree chat potatoes (see Roast Chat, Pink Fir and Kipfler Potatoes, page 99) or Lemon Long-Grain Rice (page 95) or Fragrant Rice (page 93).*

**Serves 4**

Salad

3 large capsicums, 1 each of green, red and yellow, char-grilled**

2 tbs capers*, drained (ingredient check; ◎)

2 tsp extra-virgin olive oil*

rind of ½ preserved lemon* (flesh removed), rinsed and finely chopped (ingredient check)

⅓ cup finely shredded fresh flat-leaf (Italian) parsley

Steaks

4 x 125 g porterhouse steaks, trimmed of fat

lemon-infused olive oil* or extra-light olive oil spray* (ingredient check)

Garnish

snow pea sprouts

freshly ground black pepper

**Per serve**

Energy 892 kJ (213 cal)

Protein 28.7 g

Total fat 8.4 g

Saturated fat 2.9 g

Carbohydrate 4.9 g

Total sugars 4.9 g

Dietary fibre 1.9 g

Sodium 100 mg

1   Peel the char-grilled capsicums; remove stalks, membranes and seeds. Slice into thin strips and place in a glass or ceramic bowl with the capers, olive oil and preserved lemon. (If making the salad in advance, cover and refrigerate. Warm to room temperature before completing.)

2   Preheat a char-grill or grill pan to very hot. Lightly oil the steak. Sear the meat for 1–2 minutes on each side or to taste. Rest, covered, for 5 minutes.

3   While the meat is resting, mix the parsley through the salad. Microwave on high for 1–2 minutes to warm through.

4   Slice the meat diagonally across the grain. Divide the salad between 4 serving plates and top with the sliced meat. Serve immediately, garnished with snow pea sprouts and black pepper.

## Red Capsicum Beef Stir-Fry on Red Lentil Risotto

*A quick beef stir-fry served on a red lentil risotto bed. You'll find this 'risotto' also makes an excellent accompaniment for chicken, pork and char-grilled vegetables. The lentil risotto may be made in advance and reheated as the beef is being cooked, but don't add the rocket until just before you serve.*

**Serves 4**

Red Lentil Risotto
400 g red lentils, picked over, rinsed and drained
1 L water
2 tbs (30 mL) tomato paste (ingredient check)
10 sun-dried tomatoes*, finely sliced (ingredient check; ⊙)
½ tsp ground cardamom
freshly ground black pepper
100 g wild or baby rocket leaves

Beef
extra-light olive oil spray* (ingredient check)
1 red capsicum, seeded and sliced into 3 cm lengths
1 large green shallot*, trimmed and diagonally sliced
½ tsp cumin seeds
1 tsp wholegrain mustard (ingredient check—Mustard) or Green and Pink Peppercorn
   Mustard (page 82)
freshly ground black pepper
600 g lean stir-fry beef

Garnish
extra wild or baby rocket leaves

**Per serve**
**Energy 2045 kJ (488 cal)**
**Protein 58.8 g**
**Total fat 9.8 g**
**Saturated fat 3.2 g**
**Carbohydrate 45.5 g**
**Total sugars 6.2 g**
**Dietary fibre 17.0 g**
**Sodium 110 mg**

1   Place all the risotto ingredients except the rocket in a medium-sized pan over a high heat and bring to the boil. Cover and reduce the heat until simmering steadily. Cook the lentils for 12–13 minutes or until al dente; do not overcook or the lentils will become mushy. Remove from the heat, add the rocket and cover.

2   Very lightly spray a non-stick frying pan or wok with oil and place over a high heat. Add the capsicum, shallot, cumin seeds, mustard and black pepper and sauté for 1–2 minutes, stirring regularly. Add the beef and cook for 1–2 minutes (the beef should be rare to medium-rare; do not overcook).

3   Spoon the lentil risotto into the centre of serving plates, top with the pepper-beef. Serve immediately garnished with the rocket.

# Red Pork Curry

*A light Thai-style pork curry that is equally good with chicken or prawns. Serve on a bed of steaming jasmine rice\* and be careful not to overcook the pork or it will become chewy.*

**Serves 4**

| | |
|---|---|
| 400 mL light coconut milk\* (ingredient check; ◎) | **Per serve** |
| 2 tbs (30 mL) Red Thai Curry Paste (page 84) | Energy 1161 kJ (277 cal) |
| 6 kaffir lime leaves\*, torn | Protein 35.3 g |
| 600 g lean pork stir-fry (make sure it is finely sliced so it cooks quickly) | Total fat 11.6 g |
| 2 tbs (30 mL) fish sauce\* (ingredient check; ◎) | Saturated fat 6.7 g |
| 150 g green beans, trimmed and sliced diagonally to 2-3 cm lengths | Carbohydrate 8.0 g |
| 50 g Lebanese eggplant, trimmed and finely sliced | Total sugars 6.3 g |
| 1 tbs grated palm sugar\* or soft brown sugar | Dietary fibre 1.7 g |
| 12 large fresh basil leaves, shredded | Sodium 913 mg |

Garnish
shredded fresh basil leaves

1  Heat half the coconut milk in a large pan to simmering point. Add the curry paste and lime leaves and simmer rapidly for 2 minutes, stirring occasionally.

2  Add the pork, fish sauce, beans, eggplant and sugar. Simmer fast for 2 minutes or until the pork is just cooked, stirring occasionally.

3  Add the remaining coconut milk and basil leaves. Heat until just boiling.

4  Serve immediately on a bed of steaming rice, garnished with the basil leaves.


# Spiced Crusted Topside of Beef with Orange and Port Sauce

*A lean topside roast or fillet is rolled in a dry spice marinade and compressed in plastic wrap, then seared and served warm with a light citrussy-port sauce, salad leaves tossed in a vinaigrette or citrus dressing (see Dressings and Marinades, page 106) and minted baby potatoes. The meat is also delicious served chilled, very finely sliced with salad leaves as starter or main. I usually buy a larger joint, then divide it into 2 lengthways and make 2 spiced rolls of the right dimensions—the correct thickness is important if you are to cook the meat to the right level of 'doneness' without burning the spice coat.*

**Serves 4-6**

| | |
|---|---|
| 650-700 g beef topside or fillet (dimensions about 8 x 8 x 16 cm long), trimmed of fat | **Per serve** |
| 2 tsp lemon-infused olive\* or extra-light olive oil\* | Energy 733 kJ (175 cal) |
| | Protein 24.4 g |
| Spice Mix | Total fat 6.3 g |
| 1 heaped teaspoon each of caraway seeds, cumin seeds, fennel seeds, coriander seeds, | Saturated fat 2.3 g |
|    Sichuan peppercorns\*, black peppercorns, sumac\* | Carbohydrate 4.0 g |
| | Total sugars 1.9 g |
| Sauce | Dietary fibre 0.9 g |
| 500 mL (2 cups) beef stock\* (ingredient check—Stock; ◎) | Sodium 78 mg |
| 1 tsp orange zest | |
| 2 tablespoons (30 mL) port (ingredient check—Wine; ◎) | |
| 1 bay leaf | |
| freshly ground black pepper | |
| 1 tsp arrowroot plus 1 tablespoon (15 mL) water mixed to a smooth paste | |

**1**  Put all the spices together in a coffee grinder or pestle and mortar and grind to an even, slightly grainy mix. Transfer to a large plate. Roll the beef in the spice mix to coat completely.

**2**  Place a 40 cm length of plastic wrap on a bench top lengthways away from you, with the bottom end hanging over the edge of the bench. Lean against the wrap overhang to hold it in place. Place the beef across the top end of the wrap and start to roll the beef up in the film towards you, at the same time pulling the wrap very tight by stretching the wrap backwards away from you as you roll. When completely rolled up, twist the ends of the wrap tightly and lay them back across the meat.

**3**  Repeat the process with a second piece of wrap. The beef should be a very tightly bound, cylindrical shape. Refrigerate for a minimum of 2 hours or preferably overnight.

**4**  To prepare the sauce, place all the ingredients except the arrowroot paste in a small pan and simmer gently for 15 minutes, stirring occasionally. Add the arrowroot and cook for 1–2 minutes or until the sauce has thickened. Set aside and reheat just before serving.

**5**  Unwrap the beef. Place the lemon-infused olive oil in a large, non-stick frying pan over a high heat. When hot, reduce the heat to medium-high, add the beef and cook for 2 minutes, turn and cook for another 2 minutes. Repeat the turning-cooking process 2–3 times until all the outside of the beef has been seared. Transfer to a plate, cover and leave to rest for 5 minutes.

**6**  To serve, slice the beef in 1–1.5 cm thick slices. Arrange 2–3 slices on each plate and top with the sauce. Serve immediately accompanied by minted boiled chat potatoes and a dressed mixed leaf salad.

## Poultry

### Ⓒ **Baked Spiced Chicken**

Ⓕ *A simple twist to roast chicken—the chicken meat is flavoured with one of three home-made Thai pastes. Minted and Spiced*
Ⓝ *English Spinach (page 96) or Asian greens dressed with Pickled Ginger Sesame Sauce (page 79, not corn-free) make a great accompaniment. The chicken is best roasted with the skin on but it can be removed to minimise fat.* Ⓕ *use Green Harissa Paste or Vietnamese Mint Pesto.* Ⓝ *avoid Vietnamese Mint Pesto.*

**Serves 4**

| | |
|---|---|
| 4 chicken marylands, trimmed of excess fat | **Per serve** |
| 4 rounded tsp Green Curry Paste (page 82) Ⓒ Ⓝ | **Energy 932 kJ (222 cal)** |
| or Green Harissa Paste (page 83) Ⓒ Ⓕ Ⓝ | **Protein 29.7 g** |
| or Red Thai Curry Paste (page 84) Ⓒ Ⓝ | **Total fat 11.4 g** |
| or Vietnamese Mint Pesto (page 85) Ⓒ Ⓕ | **Saturated fat 3.4 g** |
| | **Carbohydrate 0.3 g** |
| Garnish | **Total sugars 0.2 g** |
| sprigs of coriander | **Dietary fibre 0.1 g** |
| wedges of lime | **Sodium 160 mg** |

**1**  Preheat the oven to 220°C (200°C fan forced). Line a baking tray with baking paper.

**2**  Cut 5–6 slits diagonally across the top of each chicken piece. Place a teaspoon of the paste of choice on top of each, spread into each slit and over the top of the skin. Place chicken in the baking tray. Cover and refrigerate for a minimum of 1 hour to marinate.

**3**  Roast for 30–35 minutes or until the chicken is just cooked (juices run clear when thickest part of meat is tested with a sharp knife), basting with the juices 2–3 times during cooking. Leave to rest for 5 minutes before serving with selected vegetables, garnished with the coriander and lime wedges.

## Ⓒ Blood Orange and Poached Chicken Salad

Ⓕ *A flavour-filled salad to serve for a lunch or light dinner. I love blood oranges, but out of season substitute any sweet, juicy oranges, such as Navels. Try using half and half oranges and ruby grapefruit for a salad with an extra dimension.*

**Serves 4**

3 skinless chicken breast fillets, trimmed
3 green shallots*, trimmed and roughly sliced
1 bay leaf, bruised
6 black peppercorns
2 tbs (30 mL) lemon juice
cold water to cover

Salad
50 g pepitas, dry roasted**
50 g pistachio kernels, dry roasted**
2 blood oranges, peeled, seeded and segments cut into thirds
2 kiwi fruit, peeled and diced
175 g mixed salad leaves including baby spinach leaves, baby rocket leaves, chervil, cress
1 Lebanese cucumber, ends trimmed and sliced

Dressing
zest and juice of ½ orange
2 tbs (30 mL) red wine vinegar* (ingredient check—Vinegar; Ⓒ)
½ tsp balsamic vinegar* (ingredient check—Vinegar; Ⓒ)
1 tbs (15 mL) extra-virgin olive oil*
1 tsp pure sesame oil*
1 sprig fresh tarragon, leaves picked, finely chopped
pinch of grated palm sugar* or soft brown sugar
freshly ground black pepper

**Per serve**
Energy 2047 kJ (489 cal)
Protein 41.7 g
Total fat 25.0 g
Saturated fat 4.7 g
Carbohydrate 23.4 g
Total sugars 20.2 g
Dietary fibre 8.5 g
Sodium 124 mg

1 Place the chicken fillets in a medium-sized pan with the shallots, bay leaf, peppercorns, lemon juice and enough cold water to just cover the chicken. Bring to the boil over a high heat, reduce the heat and poach for 10 minutes or until the chicken is just cooked (the juices run clear when the thickest part of the breast is pierced with a sharp knife). Remove from the heat, cover and set aside to cool.

2 Combine all the dressing ingredients in a screw-top jar and shake well. Set aside for 30 minutes to allow the flavours to develop.

3 Place all the salad ingredients in a large mixing bowl. Remove the chicken from the poaching liquid and shred or dice.

4 Immediately before serving, add the chicken to the salad. Shake the dressing well and pour over the salad. Toss and serve.

## Ⓕ Cashew and Chicken Ginger Stir-Fry

*Such a simple dish for the wealth of flavours. It is equally good served on a bed of steaming rice or buckwheat noodles* (ingredient check—Pasta).*

**Serves 4**

1 tsp extra-light olive oil*
2 green shallots*, trimmed and diagonally sliced
½ red capsicum (about 75 g), seeded and finely sliced

**Per serve**
Energy 1328 kJ (317 cal)
Protein 30.8 g

seeds from 3 cardamom pods or ⅛ tsp cardamom seeds

freshly ground black pepper

500 g skinless chcken breast fillets, trimmed and sliced into bite–sized pieces

125 mL (½ cup) Ginger Refresher (Buderim brand)*

125 mL (½ cup) water

2 tsp lime juice

2 tsp finely chopped fresh coriander root*

2 tsp arrowroot plus 2 tbs (30 mL) water, mixed to a smooth paste

10 fresh mint leaves, finely shredded

75 g raw cashews, dry roasted**

Garnish

fresh coriander leaves, roughly chopped

Total fat 17.4 g

Saturated fat 3.9 g

Carbohydrate 10.0 g

Total sugars 6.5 g

Dietary fibre 1.7 g

Sodium 99 mg

1 Heat the oil in a large, non-stick frying or wok over a medium-high heat. Add the shallots, capsicum, cardamom seeds and black pepper and sauté for 1 minute. Add the chicken and cook for 2–3 minutes to seal, stirring frequently.

2 Add the Ginger Refresher, water, lime juice and coriander root and simmer for 3 minutes or until the chicken is just cooked.

3 Stir through the arrowroot paste, mint leaves and cashews and simmer for 1–2 minutes or until the sauce has thickened.

4 Serve immediately on a bed of rice or buckwheat noodles, garnished with the coriander leaves.

## Chicken, Chickpea and Potato Ragout

*Serve this hearty dish with a green leafy salad and suitable warm bread—it makes an excellent lunch or light supper.*

**Serves 4**

extra–light olive oil spray* (ingredient check)

500-600 g chicken breast chunks or skinless breast fillets, trimmed and cut into 3 cm dice

2 tsp lemon juice

500 g fine-skinned Desiree potatoes, cleaned and cut into 1 cm dice

3 green shallots*, trimmed and sliced

¼ tsp caraway seeds

½ tsp fennel seeds

1 x 810 g can chopped tomatoes (no added thickener, no added salt)

240 g cooked chickpeas** (if using canned, ingredient check)

2 tbs capers* (ingredient check; ◯)

2 artichoke hearts in brine, roughly chopped (ingredient check)

1 tsp balsamic vinegar* (ingredient check—Vinegar; ◯)

125 mL (½ cup) water

⅓ cup chopped fresh parsley

freshly ground black pepper

**Per serve**

Energy 1601 kJ (382 cal)

Protein 37.0 g

Total fat 8.9 g

Saturated fat 2.4 g

Carbohydrate 36.5 g

Total sugars 9.0 g

Dietary fibre 9.1 g

Sodium 149 mg

Garnish

fresh parsley, roughly chopped

1 Lightly spray a large, non-stick frying pan or wok with oil and place over a medium heat. Add the chicken and cook for 2–3 minutes or until sealed and lightly browned. Stir through the lemon juice, transfer to a bowl and set aside.

2   Respray the pan lightly with oil and return to the heat. Add the potatoes and shallots and cook, stirring frequently, for 10 minutes. Add the caraway and fennel seeds and cook for 1 minute.

3   Add the tomatoes and chickpeas and cook for 5 minutes. Return the chicken to the pan with the capers, artichokes and vinegar and simmer uncovered for 5 minutes, stirring occasionally. Add up to 125 mL of water if required to thin sauce slightly. Stir through the parsley and season with black pepper.

4   Serve immediately accompanied by salad and bread.

## Chicken Maryland Casserole

*This dish can be prepared up to 48 hours in advance: marinated, cooked, chilled and reheated just before serving. This allows the lovely variety of flavours in the dish to develop and any fat to be skimmed off the top with ease; if preparing the dish in advance, I leave the skin on the chicken but trim any excess fat. The sauce requires no thickening as the potatoes included in the dish do it all for you. Serve with fluffy jacket potatoes to soak up the wonderful sauce—or on a bed of brown rice—and a mixed leaf salad. The dish is also delicious made with lamb shanks. (Cooking time will vary according to the microwave power, see Key to Recipes, page viii.) ◯ omit the corn kernels.*

**Serves 4**

| Ingredients | Per serve |
|---|---|
| 4 chicken marylands, skinned and trimmed of excess fat (see above) | Energy 2180 kJ (520 cal) |
| 2 carrots, peeled and julienned | Protein 44.6 g |
| ½ red capsicum, seeded and diced | Total fat 12.5 g |
| 4 medium-sized floury potatoes (about 600 g) such as Sebago or Nicola, skin on, cleaned and cut into 1 cm dice | Saturated fat 3.5 g |
| 150 g fresh corn kernels (if using canned, rinse and drain well) | Carbohydrate 52.1 g |
| 240 g cooked cannellini beans** (if using canned, ingredient check) | Total sugars 16.8 g |
| 8 green shallots*, trimmed and coarsely chopped | Dietary fibre 16.2 g |
| 1 small eggplant, trimmed and diced | Sodium 203 mg |
| 1 x 810 g can chopped tomatoes (no added thickener, no added salt) | |
| 2 tbs tomato paste (ingredient check) | |
| 125 mL (½ cup) red wine (ingredient check—Wine) or water | |
| 2 bay leaves | |
| ½ red chilli, seeded and finely chopped (optional) | |
| 2 tsp Italian herbs (ingredient check) or dried oregano | |
| freshly ground black pepper | |

1   Place all the ingredients in a large microwave-proof casserole, mix thoroughly and cover. The dish may be cooked immediately or refrigerated and marinated for 2–3 hours or overnight before cooking. (If the dish is cooked straight from the refrigerator allow an extra 15 minutes cooking time.)

2   Microwave on high for 20 minutes. Remove and stir, ensuring the chicken pieces are covered by the sauce. Return to the microwave and cook on high for 15 minutes, remove and stir again. Microwave on medium-high for a final 30–40 minutes or until the chicken is cooked and the potatoes tender. Set aside to cool and refrigerate overnight. (If serving immediately, skim off any surface fat and microwave on medium-high for a further 10–15 minutes if the chicken has not started to come away from the bone and the potatoes started to break up and thicken the sauce).

3   Before reheating, skim any excess fat from the surface and microwave on high for 35–40 minutes or until piping hot. Serve immediately with jacket potatoes or brown rice and salad or steamed greens.

Note: The casserole may be cooked in an oven preheated to 200°C (180°C fan forced) for 1½–2 hours or until the chicken is cooked and the potatoes are tender. Stir the casserole at least once during cooking and ensure the chicken is covered with the sauce.

## Ⓒ Chicken Tangine
Ⓕ
Ⓝ *'Tangine' or 'tagine' is a Moroccan stew named after the cooking utensil in which it is cooked. The stews may be based on meat, poultry, fish or vegetables and are highly spiced but not hot, with sweet overtones imparted by the fruit in the dish. Try cooking other meat or fish in this wonderful sauce. I serve the chicken on a bed of rice accompanied by steamed green beans and Mint Chutney (page 88). Ⓝ omit the almonds.*

**Serves 6**

2 tbs arrowroot

1 tsp each ground cinnamon and turmeric

2 tsp each ground cumin, coriander and ginger

½ tsp ground cardamom or 5 cardamom pods, lightly bruised

12 chicken pieces, skinned and trimmed of fat, or skinless chicken breast or thigh fillets

extra-light olive oil spray* (ingredient check)

1 tsp extra-light olive oil*

3 green shallots*, trimmed and sliced

1 cinnamon quill

½ tsp sambal oelek* or chilli paste* (ingredient check; Ⓒ) or chilli powder

250 mL (1 cup) water

425 g Roma tomatoes, peeled and finely chopped

2 bay leaves

125 g pitted dates, halved, or prunes, apricots or currants (ingredient check—Dried fruit)

240 g cooked chickpeas** (if using canned, ingredient check)

75 g blanched almonds, dry roasted**

25 g fresh coriander or flat-leaf (Italian) parsley, finely chopped

freshly ground black pepper

Garnish
roughly chopped coriander leaves

| Per serve | |
| --- | --- |
| Energy 1988 kJ (474 cal) | |
| Protein 42.5 g | |
| Total fat 21.8 g | |
| Saturated fat 4.9 g | |
| Carbohydrate 27.6 g | |
| Total sugars 17.8 g | |
| Dietary fibre 6.7 g | |
| Sodium 197 mg | |

1  Mix the arrowroot and spices together in a medium-sized bowl (if using cardamom pods, add them with the cinnamon quill in Step 3). Roll the chicken pieces in the mixture to coat.

2  Lightly spray a large, non-stick frying pan with oil and place over a medium heat. Sear the chicken in batches for 1 minute on each side or until lightly browned. Set aside.

3  Place the teaspoon of oil in a large, heavy-bottomed pan. Add the shallots and sauté for 2–3 minutes. Add any remaining spiced flour mixture, cinnamon quill and sambal oelek and cook for 12 minutes or until fragrant, stirring constantly.

4  Add the chicken, water, tomatoes and bay leaves and simmer, partially covered, for 30–35 minutes, stirring occasionally.

5  Add the dates and chickpeas and simmer uncovered for 5 minutes. Stir through the almonds, coriander and black pepper. Simmer for 1 minute.

6  Serve immediately on a bed of rice garnished with the coriander leaves.

## Ⓝ Chicken Thigh and Gai Lum Casserole

*A simple but very different casserole that can be prepared 24 hours in advance, allowing the chicken to take up all the flavours of the marinade. Serve on a bed of basmati rice\*, bean-thread\* or rice vermicelli\*.*

**Serves 4**

10 g dried sliced shiitake mushrooms\*

Marinade

3 green shallots\*, trimmed and very finely chopped

1 tbs (15 mL) oyster sauce\* (ingredient check)

1 tbs (15 mL) fish sauce\* (ingredient check)

3 tbs (45 mL) lime juice

2 tbs very finely chopped lemon grass\* (white part only)

1 large, mild red chilli, seeded and finely chopped (or hotter, use 1–2 bird's eye chillies)

2 tsp soft brown sugar

Chicken and Gai Lum

8 skinless chicken thighs (about 700–750 g), trimmed of excess fat

1 bunch gai lum\* (Chinese broccoli; about 350 g), trimmed, washed and roughly chopped

250 mL (1 cup) chicken stock\* (ingredient check—Stock)

2 tbs arrowroot plus 2 tbs water, mixed to a smooth paste

**Per serve**

Energy 1286 kJ (307 cal)

Protein 36.6 g

Total fat 13.6 g

Saturated fat 4.0 g

Carbohydrate 9.4 g

Total sugars 5.2 g

Dietary fibre 2.9 g

Sodium 727 mg

1 Place the mushrooms in a small bowl and cover with boiling water. Leave to soak for 5 minutes. Drain well.

2 Place all the marinade ingredients in a 3 litre casserole and mix well. Add the chicken and mushrooms and toss to coat the chicken thoroughly. Cover and refrigerate for a minimum of 1 hour or preferably overnight.

3 Preheat the oven to 200°C (180°C fan forced). Add the gai lum and stock to the casserole and toss to coat the vegetables in the marinade. Cover and cook in the oven for 35–40 minutes or until the chicken is cooked and tender, stirring the dish after 20 minutes, ensuring the vegetables are covered by sauce.

4 Stir through the arrowroot paste 5 minutes before the end of cooking.

5 Serve immediately over a bed of rice, or bean-thread or rice vermicelli.

## Ⓒ Chilli-Basil Chicken Curry

Ⓕ *This resembles a green Thai curry—its depth of flavour is delicious. Serve on a bed of steaming jasmine\* or basmati rice\* with a green or Asian salad (page 101).*

**Serves 4**

extra-light olive oil spray\* (ingredient check)

4 skinless chicken breast fillets, trimmed and cut into strips

3 tbs (45 mL) Chilli-Basil Paste (page 81)

4 kaffir lime leaves\*, finely shredded

200 mL light coconut milk\* (ingredient check; Ⓒ)

125 mL (½ cup) water

**Per serve**

Energy 1418 kJ (338 cal)

Protein 43.8 g

Total fat 17.2 g

Saturated fat 6.3 g

Carbohydrate 2.1 g

Total sugars 1.4 g

Dietary fibre 0.6 g

Sodium 129 mg

1 Lightly spray a large, non-stick frying pan or wok with oil and place over a medium-high heat. Add the chicken and cook, turning frequently, for 3–4 minutes.

2 Add the remaining ingredients. Simmer gently for 7–10 minutes, stirring occasionally.

3 Serve on a bed of steaming rice with the salad of choice.

## Chook à L'Orange

*This low-fat, wonderfully citrussy dish is very simple to prepare, unlike the lengthy and often fatty duck version. The chicken is poached in the sauce and so is tender and moist. Serve on top of 'smashed' Roast Chat Potatoes (page 99), or with minted boiled chats accompanied by a green salad or lightly steamed green vegetables. use lemon thyme garnish.*

**Serves 4**

extra-light olive oil spray* (ingredient check)

4 green shallots*, trimmed and diagonally sliced

6 sun-dried tomatoes*, sliced (ingredient check; )

1 small char-grilled capsicum*, sliced (ingredient check; )

¼ tsp cumin seeds

¼ tsp caraway seeds

zest of 1 orange

375 mL (1½ cups) fresh orange juice

zest and juice of ½ lime

2 sprigs fresh lemon thyme, leaves picked, or ½ tsp Italian herbs (ingredient check)

4 skinless chicken breast fillets, trimmed of any fat and tenderloins removed

freshly ground black pepper

1 tsp arrowroot plus 1 tbs water, mixed to a smooth paste

Garnish

¼ cup flaked almonds, dry-roasted** or sprigs of fresh lemon thyme

**Per serve**

Energy 1369 kJ (327 cal)

Protein 44.5 g

Total fat 11.9 g

Saturated fat 3.5 g

Carbohydrate 11.3 g

Total sugars 9.4 g

Dietary fibre 2.0 g

Sodium 132 mg

1 Lightly oil a large, non-stick frying pan and place over a medium-high heat. Add the shallots, tomatoes, capsicum and spices and cook for 1–2 minutes or until fragrant, stirring regularly.

2 Add the zests, juices and herbs. Simmer gently for 2–3 minutes.

3 Add the chicken and poach in the sauce for 4–5 minutes on each side or until just cooked (juices run clear when the thickest part of the fillet is pierced with a knife). Stir through the arrowroot paste and cook for 1 minute or until the sauce thickens.

4 Serve immediately with potatoes and vegetables of choice, garnished with the almonds or lemon thyme.

## Green Chicken Curry

*A lovely light, mildly spicy Thai-style curry made using the Green Curry Paste on page 82; for a hotter curry add sambal oelek* (ingredient check) or chilli to the sauce. If using a commercially made paste, modify the amount of paste used according to its 'heat'. The chicken can be substituted with 600 g lean finely sliced pork. Serve over steaming jasmine rice*.*

**Serves 4**

375 mL (1½ cups) light coconut milk* (ingredient check; )

125 mL (½ cup water

3 tbs (45 mL) Green Curry Paste (page 82)

600 g skinless chicken breast fillets, trimmed and cut into bite-sized pieces

3 green shallots*, trimmed and coarsely chopped diagonally

6 kaffir lime leaves*, crushed

100 g flat or round green beans, trimmed and sliced finely diagonally

4 tsp fish sauce* (ingredient check; )

2 tbs (30 mL) lime juice

2 tsp soft brown sugar

¼ cup finely chopped fresh coriander root*

1 large handful bean sprouts (optional)

¼–½ tsp sambal oelek* or chilli paste* (optional; ingredient check; )

**Per serve**

Energy 1277 kJ (305 cal)

Protein 34.8 g

Total fat 15.0 g

Saturated fat 7.6 g

Carbohydrate 7.4 g

Total sugars 5.6 g

Dietary fibre 2.1 g

Sodium 669 mg

Garnish
fresh coriander leaves

1  Place the coconut milk and water in a wok (or large pan) over a high heat, bring to the boil, reduce heat and simmer gently for 2 minutes.

2  Stir through the Green Curry Paste and simmer gently for 5 minutes.

3  Add chicken, shallots, lime leaves and beans, and simmer gently uncovered for 10 minutes or until the chicken is cooked, stirring occasionally.

4  Add the remaining ingredients and simmer for 1–2 minutes.

5  Serve immediately on a bed of jasmine rice garnished with the coriander leaves.

## Maple Syrup Turkey Strips on a Double Bed of Balsamic Roasted Vegetables

*This triple-layered dish is surprisingly easy to prepare and uses the maple syrup dressing on the turkey to complement the naturally sweet flavours of the roasted vegetables. The secret is to slice the different vegetables to equivalent sizes so that they cook at the same rate and toss them in oil as soon as they are peeled to prevent discolouration.*

**Serves 4**

Vegetables

Tray 1

600 g Desiree and/or Coliban chat potatoes, skin on, cleaned and halved

300 g kumara or orange sweet potato, peeled and cut into wedges

300 g swede, peeled, cut into wedges and/or 300 g parsnip, peeled, cut into thick slices

150 g Jerusalem artichoke (in season), peeled and cut into wedges

1 tbs (15 mL) extra-light olive oil*

4 tsp balsamic vinegar* (ingredient check—Vinegar; ◯)

½ tsp ground cumin

½ tsp paprika

tiny sprinkle of sea salt

Tray 2

300 g fennel, trimmed and coarsely sliced or celery if fennel is out of season

4 large Roma tomatoes, quartered lengthways

2 medium-sized red capsicum, seeded and cut into 3 cm wide wedges

1 tbs (15 mL) extra-light olive oil*

4 tsp balsamic vinegar* (ingredient check—Vinegar; ◯)

½ tsp ground cumin

½ tsp paprika

Turkey

extra-light olive oil spray* (ingredient check)

3 green shallots*, trimmed and roughly sliced

600 g lean turkey strips

zest of ½ lemon

freshly ground black pepper

1 tsp chopped fresh marjoram or ½ tsp dried marjoram

3 tbs (45 mL) pure maple syrup

1 tbs sesame seeds, dry roasted**

**Per serve**

Energy 2466 kJ (589 cal)

Protein 54.8 g

Total fat 14.2 g

Saturated fat 2.3 g

Carbohydrate 56.6 g

Total sugars 26.3 g

Dietary fibre 12.3 g

Sodium 304 mg

Garnish
50 g mixed salad leaves

1  Preheat the oven to 240°C (220°C fan forced). Line 2 baking trays with baking paper.

2  Place the vegetables for Tray 1 in a baking tray. Sprinkle remaining Tray 1 ingredients over the top and toss to coat the vegetables thoroughly. Spread vegetables out to form a single layer. Place on the top shelf of the oven.

3  Repeat coating and tossing process with ingredients for Tray 2. Cover the tray with a sheet of aluminium foil. Place on the middle shelf of the oven.

4  Bake for 30 minutes, shaking and rotating Tray 1 at least once during roasting. Remove foil cover from Tray 2 and continue to roast Trays 1 and 2 for 15 minutes or until Tray 1 vegetables golden and Tray 2 vegetables soft and starting to brown lightly on edges.

5  7–10 minutes before the vegetables are ready, lightly spray a non-stick frying pan with oil and place over a medium heat. Add the shallots and cook for 1 minute. Add the turkey strips and cook for 5 minutes or until just starting to brown, stirring regularly. Stir the lemon zest, black pepper, marjoram and maple syrup through the turkey and remove from the heat. Cover.

6  Divide the vegetables from Tray 1 between 4 serving plates. Top with the vegetables from Tray 2 and any roasting juices. Top with the turkey strips. Sprinkle the sesame seeds over the top. Serve immediately with the salad garnish arranged to one side of the plate.

## Ⓒ Mock Soy Stir-Fried Chicken with Cashews

Ⓕ *Apple juice concentrate combined with apple cider vinegar makes a great soy-style, stir-fry base without the saltiness. Serve on a bed of salad leaves or steamed Asian greens.*

**Serves 4**

extra-light olive oil spray* (ingredient check)

2 green shallots*, trimmed and sliced diagonally

½ tsp caraway seeds

500 g chicken breast chunks or skinless breast/thigh fillets cut into bite-sized pieces

100 g green beans, trimmed and cut to 2 cm lengths

1 tbs (15 mL) apple juice concentrate*

1 tbs (15 mL) apple cider vinegar*

freshly ground black pepper

50–100 mL water, as required

⅓ cup raw cashews, dry roasted**

**Per serve**

Energy 1014 kJ (242 cal)

Protein 29.3 g

Total fat 12.5 g

Saturated fat 3.1 g

Carbohydrate 6.1 g

Total sugars 4.2 g

Dietary fibre 1.6 g

Sodium 77 mg

Garnish
fresh coriander leaves, roughly chopped

1  Lightly spray a large, non-stick frying pan or wok with oil and place over a high heat. Add the shallots and caraway seeds and cook for 1 minute, tossing regularly.

2  Add the chicken and cook, stirring occasionally, for 3–4 minutes or until almost cooked. Add beans, apple juice concentrate, vinegar and black pepper and cook for 2 minutes. Add water as required to make a sauce (the amount depends on the amount of juice released by the chicken).

3  Stir through cashews. Serve immediately on the salad or Asian greens bed, garnished with the coriander.

## Pesto and Sun-Dried Tomato Stuffed Chicken Pockets with Pesto Sauce

*Another delicious way to use the Vietnamese Mint Pesto (page 85) to flavour a dish. Serve on a bed of 'smashed' Roast Chat Potatoes (page 99) with lightly steamed spinach and Oven-Roasted Roma Tomatoes (page 97).*

**Serves 4**

4 skinless chicken breast fillets, trimmed of fat and sinew, tenderloins removed

**Stuffing**

2 tsp Vietnamese Mint Pesto (page 85)

4 large sun-dried tomatoes*, roughly chopped (ingredient check; ⓒ)

**Sauce**

125 mL (½ cup) light coconut milk* (ingredient check; ⓒ)

4 tbs (60 mL) water

1 tbs (15 mL) Vietnamese Mint Pesto (page 85)

2 tbs (30 mL) apple juice concentrate*

| Per serve | |
| --- | --- |
| Energy 1347 kJ (322 cal) | |
| Protein 44.0 g | |
| Total fat 15.3 g | |
| Saturated fat 5.3 g | |
| Carbohydrate 8.3 g | |
| Total sugars 6.7 g | |
| Dietary fibre 1.2 g | |
| Sodium 129 mg | |

**1** Using a sharp knife, carefully slice horizontally through the side of the thickest section of each chicken fillet to create a pocket about 5–6 cm square (depends on the size of the fillet).

**2** Spread ½ teaspoon of pesto on the inside of one half the chicken breast pocket and top with ¼ of the sun-dried tomatoes. Repeat with the remaining chicken breasts. Secure the pocket opening with 2 toothpicks. Very lightly oil the chicken breasts with the oil from the sun-dried tomatoes.

**3** Preheat a char-grill or grill pan to very hot (the chicken may also be cooked in a heavy-bottomed non-stick pan).

**4** Place all the sauce ingredients in a small pan over a low-medium heat and simmer for 1–2 minutes; do not boil.

**5** Cook the chicken breasts on the grill for 3–4 minutes on each side or until just cooked through (the juices run clear when the thickest part of the breast is tested with a sharp knife).

**6** Serve the chicken immediately on a bed of smashed roast chat potatoes, topped with the pesto sauce and accompanied by lightly steamed spinach.

## Potato and Chicken Laksa

*This dish uses Laksa Paste (page 83) to make this tasty, mild curry; you can make it hotter by adding sambal oelek* (ingredient check). If using a commercially made paste, reduce the amount of paste unless you want a very hot curry. Serve over jasmine* or basmati rice* or bean-thread vermicelli* with steamed Asian greens or a green leafy salad.*

**Serves 4**

500 g Coliban or chat potatoes, skin on, cleaned and diced (2 cm dice)

50 g green beans, trimmed and sliced to 2 cm lengths

extra-light olive oil spray* (ingredient check)

3 tbs (45 mL) Laksa Paste (page 83)

¼ tsp sambal oelek* (optional; ingredient check)

500–600 g skinless chicken breast fillets, trimmed and diced into bite-sized pieces

1 tbs (15 mL) lime juice (zest the lime before squeezing and reserve for garnish)

200 mL light coconut milk* (ingredient check; ⓒ)

100 mL chicken stock* (ingredient check—Stock; ⓒ) or water

100 g bean sprouts

20 fresh mint leaves, shredded

| Per serve | |
| --- | --- |
| Energy 1350 kJ (322 cal) | |
| Protein 31.6 g | |
| Total fat 12.6 g | |
| Saturated fat 5.1 g | |
| Carbohydrate 19.9 g | |
| Total sugars 2.7 g | |
| Dietary fibre 4.0 g | |
| Sodium 110 mg | |

Garnish
shredded fresh mint
reserved lime zest

1  Bring a pan of water to a fast boil. Add the potatoes and simmer for 5 minutes or until the potatoes are starting to soften. Turn off the heat and add the green beans. Leave to stand for 1 minute. Drain thoroughly.

2  Very lightly spray a non-stick frying pan or wok and place over a medium heat. Add the Laksa Paste (and sambal oelek if using) and chicken and cook for 1–2 minutes, stirring regularly. Stir through the potato and beans and cook for 2 minutes.

3  Add the lime juice, coconut milk and stock and simmer for 3–4 minutes. Stir through the bean sprouts and shredded mint.

4  Serve immediately over a bed of rice or bean-thread vermicelli, garnished with the shredded mint leaves and lime zest.

## Ras el Hanout Chicken

*Originating from Morocco, ras el hanout\* is a wonderfully aromatic blend of up to 50 spices for which there is no fixed recipe— traditionally it is very much the secret blend of the shop owner, so the flavour of the curry will vary slightly depending on the spices in the mix you use. Serve over a bed of rice such as Lemon Long-Grain Rice (page 95) with lightly wilted spinach, Asian greens or a leafy salad.*

**Serves 4**

extra–light olive oil spray\* (ingredient check)
4 green shallots\*, trimmed and diagonally sliced
4 tsp ras el hanout\* (ingredient check)
700 g skinless chicken breast fillets, trimmed and diced into generous bite–sized pieces
1 green capsicum, seeded and sliced into 5 cm lengths
1 red capsicum, seeded and sliced into 5 cm lengths
400 mL light coconut milk\* (ingredient check; ⊚)
1 tbs chopped coriander root\*
2 tbs (30 mL) lime juice
3 kaffir lime leaves\*, bruised
100 g tender sugar snap peas, trimmed
20 fresh mint leaves, shredded

| Per serve | |
|---|---|
| Energy 1456 kJ (347 cal) | |
| Protein 41.2 g | |
| Total fat 15.9 g | |
| Saturated fat 8.2 g | |
| Carbohydrate 10.0 g | |
| Total sugars 6.9 g | |
| Dietary fibre 2.2 g | |
| Sodium 127 mg | |

Garnish
shredded fresh mint leaves

1  Lightly spray a large, non-stick frying pan with oil and place over a high heat. Add the shallots and sauté for 2 minutes. Reduce the heat, add the ras el hanout and roast for 15–20 seconds or until fragrant, stirring constantly to prevent the spices catching or burning.

2  Toss the chicken in the shallot–spice mix. Cook, stirring regularly, for 3–4 minutes or until chicken is well coated with the spice mix and lightly browned. Add the capsicum and cook for 1 minute.

3  Add the coconut milk, coriander, lime juice and lime leaves, bring to simmering point and cook for 1 minute. Stir through the sugar snap peas and mint, turn off the heat, leaving the flavours to infuse while the rice is served.

4  Serve immediately over the rice, garnished with the shredded mint leaves.

## Warm Moroccan Turkey Salad

*This delicious salad can be served as is for a lighter meal, or add roasted Jerusalem artichoke or chat potatoes for a more substantial main.*

**Serves 4**

Salad
200 g baby spinach leaves
½ cup fresh finely chopped flat-leaf (Italian) parsley
1 punnet mustard sprouts
⅓ cup fresh finely chopped coriander roots* and leaves
12 grape or cherry tomatoes, halved
75 g broad beans, cooked and peeled (optional)

Dressing
4 tsp extra-virgin olive oil*
2 tbs (30 mL) fresh orange juice
4 tsp apple cider vinegar*
freshly ground black pepper

Turkey
1 tsp extra-light olive oil*
⅛–¼ tsp sambal oelek* or chilli paste* (ingredient check; ◉) or to taste
1 tsp paprika
¼ tsp ground cinnamon
½ tsp ground cumin
¼ tsp ground ginger
1 tsp ground coriander
freshly ground black pepper
600 g lean turkey chunks or strips
3 tbs (45 mL) fresh orange juice
1 green shallot*, trimmed and diagonally sliced

Garnish
3 tbs sesame seeds, dry roasted**

**Per serve**
Energy 1356 kJ (324 cal)
Protein 47.6 g
Total fat 12.0 g
Saturated fat 2.1 g
Carbohydrate 4.8 g
Total sugars 3.5 g
Dietary fibre 2.8 g
Sodium 353 mg

1  Place all the salad ingredients in a mixing bowl. Mix all the dressing ingredients to combine and toss through the salad. Divide the salad between 4 serving plates.

2  Heat the oil in a non-stick frying pan over a medium heat. Add the spices and cook, stirring continually, for 1–2 minutes or until fragrant. Add the turkey, coat with the spices and cook over a high heat for 3 minutes. Add the orange juice and shallot. Cook for 1–2 minutes or until the turkey is just cooked through. Leave to stand for 2–3 minutes to cool slightly.

3  Spoon the turkey over the salad, garnish with the sesame seeds and serve immediately.

## Pasta

These dishes can be prepared with one of the myriad gluten-, wheat-, soy-, egg- and corn-free pastas now widely available—a range of these is described in the Glossary (page 185). Of course, if wheat and gluten are not a problem, one the many wheat-based pastas may also be used for these recipes.

### Bacon And d'Anjou Pear Pasta Salad

*The red skin of the d'Anjou pear is a contrast to the other ingredients, but any firmish pear in season can be used. The salad dressing is best made in advance and chilled to allow the flavours to develop. Serve as a light meal with Warm Roast Vegetable Salad (page 104) or a green leafy salad, as part of a buffet, or a salad accompaniment to char-grilled meat or fish.*

**Serves 6**

| | |
|---|---|
| 1 quantity Coconut and Chilli Dressing (page 107) | **Per serve** |
| 500 g dry pasta shapes of choice* | **Energy 1549 kJ (370 cal)** |
| extra-light olive oil spray* (ingredient check) | **Protein 13.0 g** |
| 150 g short-cut, rindless bacon (ingredient check; ⊚), trimmed of fat, cut into 1 cm dice | **Total fat 4.6 g** |
| 2 d'Anjou pears (about 300 g), washed, or other firm, ripe pear | **Saturated fat 1.8 g** |
| 1 tsp lime juice | **Carbohydrate 73.3 g** |
| 50 g celery (about 1 stalk), finely diced | **Total sugars 6.8 g** |
| ⅓ cup finely shredded fresh flat-leaf (Italian) parsley | **Dietary fibre 4.6 g** |
| | **Sodium 646 mg** |

Garnish
1 tbs sesame seeds, dry roasted **

1 Prepare dressing as described on page 107.

2 Cook pasta to al dente following the packet instructions; do not overcook. Rinse thoroughly with cold water and drain well. Spray the pasta very lightly with oil and gently mix to coat evenly (this prevents the pasta from sticking together and replaces the need for oil in the dressing).

3 Dry fry the diced bacon in a small non-stick pan until crispy, tossing regularly. Set aside on a kitchen towel to drain and cool.

4 Core and dice the pears into 0.5–0.75 cm dice and toss in the lime juice to prevent them from discolouring.

5 Toss the cooled bacon, pears, celery, parsley and dressing through the pasta and transfer to a serving bowl.

6 Garnish with the sesame seeds immediately before serving.

### Mixed Mushroom Pasta

*The great range of mushrooms available in the fruit and vegetable sections of many supermarkets these days makes this dish as easy to source as it is to prepare!*

**Serves 4**

| | |
|---|---|
| 400 g dry pasta of choice* (fresh noodles can be used) | **Per serve** |
| 1 tsp virgin olive oil* | **Energy 1539 kJ (367 cal)** |
| 1 large green shallot*, trimmed and finely sliced | **Protein 11.4 g** |
| 1 green chilli, seeded and finely chopped | **Total fat 2.4 g** |
| 300 g mixed mushrooms—select 3 or 4 of: | **Saturated fat 0.2 g** |
| shiitake, enoki, Swiss brown, button and oyster, cleaned | **Carbohydrate 80.6 g** |
| 4 sun-dried tomatoes*, finely chopped (ingredient check; ⊚) | **Total sugars 1.9 g** |
| zest of ½ lemon | **Dietary fibre 6.2 g** |
| ½ cup shredded fresh flat-leaf (Italian) parsley | **Sodium 20 mg** |

Garnish
roughly shredded flat–leaf (Italian) parsley leaves

1   Cook pasta of choice according to the instructions on the packet; do not overcook.

2   5 minutes before the pasta is cooked, heat the oil in a non-stick frying pan or wok over a medium heat. Add the shallot and chilli and cook for 1 minute. Add the mushrooms, sun-dried tomatoes and lemon zest and cook for 3–4 minutes. Stir through the parsley and heat for 30 seconds to warm through.

3   Drain the pasta and combine with the mushroom mix. Serve immediately garnished with the parsley leaves.

## Pasta Putanesca

*A wonderfully tasty sauce. Serve it with a large green salad and a full-bodied red wine. If you can eat sheep's milk cheese, a good pecorino parmesan really tops it off. The sauce makes a great base for a seafood marinara—simply prepare the sauce as described and cook 500–600 g mixed fish and seafood (for example, prawns, scallops, diced tuna, salmon, perch) in the sauce immediately before serving. It is also a delicious sauce to serve over char-grilled or pan-fried white fish fillets, such as barramundi.*

**Serves 4**

extra–light olive oil spray* (ingredient check)
2 green shallots*, trimmed and sliced
1 medium–sized red capsicum, seeded and diced
1 bird's eye chilli, seeded and finely chopped
30 fresh basil leaves, shredded
20 g anchovy fillets*, finely chopped (ingredient check)
175 g black olives, pitted and chopped (ingredient check; 🌀)
2 tbs (30 mL) capers* (ingredient check; 🌀)
1 x 810 g can chopped tomatoes (no added thickener, no added salt)
4 tsp tomato paste (ingredient check)
freshly ground black pepper
400 g dry pasta of choice*

**Per serve:**
**Energy 1951 kJ (466 cal)**
**Protein 13.2 g**
**Total fat 6.2 g**
**Saturated fat 0.7 g**
**Carbohydrate 93.8 g**
**Total sugars 11.5 g**
**Dietary fibre 15.8 g**
**Sodium 495 mg**

Garnish
fresh basil leaves, shredded

1   Very lightly spray a non-stick frying pan with oil and place over a medium-high heat. Add the shallots, capsicum, chilli and basil leaves. Cook for 1 minute, stirring regularly.

2   Add all the remaining ingredients except pasta. Simmer slowly, uncovered, over a low heat for 20 minutes, stirring occasionally. The sauce will reduce and thicken during this time.

3   While the sauce is cooking, cook the pasta as per the packet instructions. Drain and divide between 4 serving plates.

4   Spoon sauce over the pasta and serve immediately, garnished with shredded basil.

## Smoked Salmon Spirals

*A quick and simple pasta dish which also makes a great starter. It is best cooked just before serving. Serve with a crisp green leafy salad, or steamed baby bok choy or other Asian greens. Alternatively, add 2 cups bean sprouts at the same time as the mushrooms or use very lightly steamed fresh asparagus as a garnish.*

**Serves 4**

| | |
|---|---|
| extra–light olive oil spray* (ingredient check) | **Per serve** |
| 3 green shallots*, trimmed and finely chopped | **Energy 1903 kJ (454 cal)** |
| ⅛ tsp sambal oelek* (ingredient check) | **Protein 21.1 g** |
| 2 stalks celery, finely sliced | **Total fat 6.7 g** |
| 1 char–grilled capsicum*, finely sliced (ingredient check; ◯) | **Saturated fat 3.5 g** |
| juice of 1 lemon | **Carbohydrate 78.7 g** |
| zest of ¼ lime | **Total sugars 8.4 g** |
| 250 mL (1 cup) light coconut milk* (ingredient check; ◯) | **Dietary fibre 7.4 g** |
| 1 tbs capers*, drained (ingredient check; ◯) | **Sodium 483 mg** |
| freshly ground black pepper | |
| 400 g buckwheat* or rice spiral pasta*, or equivalent (ingredient check—Pasta) | |
| 100 g smoked salmon* pieces (ingredient check), roughly shredded | |
| 10 button mushrooms, cleaned and sliced | |
| ½ cup fresh coriander leaves | |

Garnish
sprigs of fresh coriander
sprinkle of paprika
freshly ground black pepper

1 Lightly spray a non-stick pan with oil and place over a medium heat. Add the shallots, sambal oelek, celery and capsicum and cook for 2 minutes, stirring regularly. Add the lemon juice, lime zest, coconut milk, capers and black pepper. Simmer gently for 2 minutes.

2 Cook the pasta according to the instructions on the packet; do not overcook. Just before the pasta is cooked, add the smoked salmon, mushrooms and coriander to the sauce and simmer for 1 minute to warm through.

3 Drain the pasta and return to the pan. Pour the smoked salmon sauce over the top and gently mix through. Serve immediately garnished with the coriander, paprika and freshly ground black pepper.

## Spaghetti Bolognese

*The use of beef and lamb mince in this classic adds a wonderful taste dimension to the sauce. Simply serve over suitable pasta, use to stuff jacket potatoes, taco shells or for making individual pies. The sauce may be served as soon as it is cooked, but it is best when refrigerated overnight to allow the flavours to develop fully. By adding 400 g of cooked red kidney beans and ¼–1 teaspoon sambal oelek* or chilli paste* (ingredient check; ◯), the sauce is easily converted into Chilli Con Carne—or try the serving suggestion below for stuffed red capsicum.*

**Serves 6**

| | |
|---|---|
| 1 tsp extra–light olive oil* | **Per serve** |
| 6 shallots*, trimmed and chopped | **Energy 1518 kJ (362 cal)** |
| 1 large red or green capsicum, seeded and chopped | **Protein 40.7 g** |
| 2 tsp ground cumin | **Total fat 11.2 g** |
| 2 tsp ground coriander | **Saturated fat 4.5 g** |
| 2 tsp paprika | **Carbohydrate 19.1 g** |
| freshly ground black pepper | **Total sugars 14.5 g** |

500 g lean beef mince

500 g lean lamb mince

1 tbs (15 mL) fish sauce* (ingredient check; ◯)

1 tsp tamarind paste* (ingredient check)

200 mL red wine (ingredient check—Wine)

1 x 810 g can chopped tomatoes (no added thickener, no added salt)

400 g tomato paste (ingredient check)

2 bay leaves

1 tsp Italian herbs (ingredient check) or dried oregano

12 button mushrooms, cleaned and sliced (optional)

Dietary fibre 5.5 g

Sodium 397 mg

1   Place the oil in a large pan over a high heat, add the shallots and capsicum and sauté for 2 minutes, stirring occasionally. Add the spices and cook, stirring regularly, for 2 minutes or until the spices are fragrant.

2   Add the mince and cook for 5–6 minutes, stirring regularly to ensure the mince browns evenly and is lump free.

3   Add the remaining ingredients and simmer over a low-medium heat for 35–40 minutes.

4   Serve immediately over pasta of choice or cover, set aside to cool and refrigerate and reheat just before serving.

*Serving suggestion* For a simple and tasty variation try this recipe for stuffed red capsicum. The sauce is best if it is thicker than for serving over pasta, so if time allows refrigerate overnight or stir through 1 tablespoon psyllium* while hot and allow to stand for 15 minutes to thicken. Preheat the oven to 220°C (200°C fan forced) and line a large baking tray with baking paper. Halve 6 large red capsicums lengthways through the stalk. Remove the seeds and membranes, place on the baking tray and bake for 12–15 minutes. Fill the capsicum halves with the bolognese mixture. Mix ½ cup finely chopped flat-leaf (Italian) parsley with 10 fresh mint leaves, zest of 1 lemon, 1 tablespoon sesame seeds and freshly ground black pepper and press onto the top of the filled capsicum. If allowed, add ⅓ cup grated hard sheep's milk cheese. Bake for 25–30 minutes or until the capsicums are tender. Serve immediately on a bed of rice pasta* (such as Buonotempo brand) lightly dressed with lemon-infused olive oil*.

## ◯ Spaghetti Marinara

Ⓝ *An age-old favourite, this gently spicy, tomatoey recipe is a great base for the mixed seafood! The tomato sauce may be made in advance and refrigerated until you're ready to cook the seafood—I usually refrigerate the sauce for up to 24 hours to really let the flavours develop. The dish can be easily dressed up by cooking the prawns and mussels separately and arranging these on top of the marinara sauce just as you are serving.*

**Serves 6**

12 green king prawns, or equivalent

12 black mussels

1 cup (250 mL) white wine (ingredient check—Wine)

1 red capsicum, seeded and sliced

3 large green shallots*, trimmed and sliced

½ cup chopped fennel (optional if out of season)

2 tsp extra-light olive oil*

1 x 810 g can chopped tomatoes (no added thickener, no added salt)

6 sun-dried tomatoes*, finely sliced (ingredient check; ◯)

4 tsp tomato paste (ingredient check)

zest of ½ lemon

juice of 1 lemon

1 tbs fish sauce* (ingredient check; ◯)

3 kaffir lime leaves*, bruised

2 coriander roots*, finely chopped

Per serve

Energy 2427 kJ (579 cal)

Protein 45.0 g

Total fat 4.1 g

Saturated fat 0.5 g

Carbohydrate 88.7 g

Total sugars 8.9 g

Dietary fibre 6.3 g

Sodium 522 mg

6 fresh basil leaves, finely shredded
¼ tsp sambal oelek* (ingredient check)
freshly ground black pepper (lots!)
1 kg mixed seafood, such as:
white fish and tuna cubes, mussel and prawn meat, calamari rings and scallops
600 g pasta of choice*

Garnish
fresh coriander leaves
lemon wedges

1   Peel and devein the prawns leaving the tails in tact. Place in a bowl, cover and refrigerate until just before serving. Scrub the mussel shells thoroughly under cold running water and de-beard. Cover and refrigerate.

2   Place the prawn heads, shells and wine in a pan over a medium heat, cover and simmer gently for 10 minutes. Strain, discard the prawn heads and shells, and set the stock aside.

3   Place the capsicum, shallots and fennel in a large pan with the olive oil over a medium-high heat and sauté for 3 minutes, stirring occasionally. Add the tomatoes (chopped and sun-dried), tomato paste, lemon juice and zest, fish sauce, herbs and spices. Cover, reduce the heat and simmer gently for 10–15 minutes, stirring occasionally. Set aside to cool, cover, and refrigerate until just before serving.

4   Cook the pasta of choice as per the packet instructions. Drain well, return to the pan, cover and keep warm.

5   Meanwhile, bring the sauce to a simmer and add the mixed seafood. Simmer gently for 4–5 minutes or until the seafood is just cooked, stirring occasionally.

6   *To serve quickly* Add the prawn stock, prawns and mussels to the marinara sauce and simmer gently until the prawns have turned pink and the mussel shells have opened (discard any mussels that do not open). Divide the pasta between pasta bowls or plates and spoon over the marinara mix. Serve immediately garnished with the coriander leaves and lemon wedges.

7   *To dress it up* In a separate pan reheat the prawn stock and add the prawns and mussels. Cover and simmer for 5 minutes or until the prawns have turned pink and the mussel shells have opened (discard any mussels that do not open). Strain the prawn and mussel stock into the simmering marinara sauce; cover the drained prawns and mussels to keep warm. Divide the pasta between pasta bowls or plates and spoon over the marinara sauce. Arrange 2 prawns and 2 mussels in the marinara sauce on each plate. Serve immediately, garnished with the coriander leaves and lemon wedges.

## Sauces

Short of time, short on flavour or want a simple way to dress up a chop, a fillet, fish or steamed vegetables? A tasty sauce is the answer. I've included a number of sauces with serving suggestions in this section—but also check out the sauces in the Mains chapter for some other delicious saucy ideas.

## BBQ Sauce

*This is wonderful with American-style pork ribs or other barbecued red meats. I usually serve it in a bowl and let everyone just help themselves … which they do! The sauce is best prepared 24 hours in advance and refrigerated to develop the flavours—it also freezes really well so make in it bulk and freeze meal-sized portions in freezer bags.*

**Serves 4—6**

1 tsp extra-light olive oil*
3 large green shallots*, trimmed sliced
1 large green capsicum, seeded and diced
1 tsp dry mustard powder* (ingredient check)
1 tsp ground cumin
1 x 810 g can chopped tomatoes (no added thickener, no added salt)
2 tsp tomato paste (ingredient check)
2 zucchini (about 125 g), trimmed and sliced
4 tbs (60 mL) white wine vinegar* (ingredient check—Vinegar; )
1 tbs (15 mL) balsamic vinegar* (ingredient check—Vinegar; )
¼ tsp sambal oelek* or chilli paste* (ingredient check; )
2 tbs (30 mL) fish sauce* (ingredient check; )
1 tsp tamarind paste* (ingredient check)
½ tsp dried oregano
½-1 tsp soft brown sugar
freshly ground black pepper (lots!)

**Per serve**
Energy 276 kJ (66 cal)
Protein 3.1 g
Total fat 1.2 g
Saturated fat 0.1 g
Carbohydrate 9.6 g
Total sugars 7.4 g
Dietary fibre 2.0 g
Sodium 550 mg

1 Place the oil, shallots and capsicum in a medium-sized pan over a high heat. Cook for 3 minutes, stirring regularly.

2 Add the mustard powder and cumin. Cook for 1 minute, stirring constantly.

3 Add the remaining ingredients and simmer gently for 30 minutes, stirring occasionally.

4 Set aside to cool, cover and refrigerate overnight or freeze.

5 Serve hot with barbecued meat of choice.

## Chilled Pickled Zucchini and Capsicum Salsa

*While this is not a sauce per se, it can served either as a sauce over meat or as a side dish. It is excellent served over barbecued lamb chops or steak. The addition of the yellow capsicum adds extra colour and flavour to the salsa. For those who can tolerate soy, try replacing the vinegar with a wheat-free tamari sauce.*

**Serves 4**

2 tbs (30 mL) virgin olive oil*
1 red capsicum, seeded and finely sliced
1 green capsicum, seeded and finely sliced
1 yellow capsicum, seeded and finely sliced (optional)
1 small red chilli, seeded and finely chopped

**Per serve**
Energy 410 kJ (98 cal)
Protein 2.9 g
Total fat 6.5 g
Saturated fat 0.7 g

1 tbs (15 mL) balsamic vinegar* (ingredient check—Vinegar; ◯)

1 medium zucchini, trimmed and shredded

1 medium carrot, trimmed and shredded

Carbohydrate 6.4 g

Total sugars 6.3 g

Dietary fibre 2.1 g

Sodium 12 mg

1   Place the oil in a pan over a medium heat. When hot, add the capsicum and chilli. Reduce the heat, and cook for 10 minutes partially covered, stirring occasionally.

2   Add the vinegar and cook uncovered for 5 minutes, stirring occasionally.

3   Stir in the zucchini and carrot, cook for a further 2 minutes uncovered.

4   Transfer to a bowl, cover and chill for a minimum of 1 hour before serving.

## Cumberland Sauce

*A variation of a classic sauce traditionally served with mutton or game. It is good served hot or cold with lamb or as a dipping sauce for hot chips! For a sweeter sauce, use port (ingredient check—Wine; ◯) in place of the red wine.*

**Serves 4**

zest and juice of 1 orange

zest and juice of 1 lemon

4 tbs (60 mL) water

6 tbs (90 mL) redcurrant jelly (ingredient check)

4 tbs (60 mL) soft red wine, such as merlot (ingredient check—Wine)

¼ tsp dry mustard powder* (ingredient check)

¼ tsp ground ginger

1 tbs (15 mL) balsamic vinegar* (ingredient check—Vinegar; ◯)

freshly ground black pepper

5 fresh mint leaves, finely shredded

2 tsp arrowroot plus 2 tbs water, mixed to a smooth paste

**Per serve**

Energy 538 kJ (128 cal)

Protein 0.9 g

Total fat 0.2 g

Saturated fat <0.1 g

Carbohydrate 26.3 g

Total sugars 23.6 g

Dietary fibre 1.3 g

Sodium 5 mg

1   Place the orange and lemon zest and water in a small pan over a low heat and simmer gently for 5 minutes. Add all the remaining ingredients except the fruit juice, mint and arrowroot paste, and stir continuously until the jelly is completely melted.

2   Stir through the fruit juice, mint and arrowroot paste. Cook, stirring continuously, for 2–3 minutes or until the sauce thickens. Serve hot or cold.

## Creamy Mustard Sauce

*This is a creamy, dairy-free sauce to serve with any red meat—it is excellent with lamb. It may be prepared in advance and reheated just before serving.*

**Serves 4**

½ tsp extra-light olive oil*

2 green shallots*, trimmed and coarsely chopped

4 tsp wholegrain mustard (ingredient check—Mustard)

1 tsp paprika (mild or hot to taste)

freshly ground black pepper

1 tsp lemon juice

150 mL light coconut milk* (ingredient check; ◯)

150 mL water

**Per serve**

Energy 185 kJ (44 cal)

Protein 1.0 g

Total fat 3.4 g

Saturated fat 2.1 g

Carbohydrate 2.4 g

Total sugars 1.3 g

Dietary fibre 0.4 g

Sodium 10 mg

1  Heat the oil in a small pan over a medium heat. Add the shallots and cook until softened (2–3 minutes). Add the mustard, paprika and black pepper and cook for 1 minute, stirring regularly.

2  Add the remaining ingredients and simmer over a low heat for 5 minutes.

3  Serve drizzled over the meat and garnish with fresh herbs.

## Cumquat and Vermouth Fish Sauce

*A very quick sauce that is just excellent for dressing up lightly cooked white fish fillets, marlin steaks or other light-flavoured fish of choice, served on a bed of baby spinach leaves and bean sprouts. Try rolling very lightly oiled white fish fillets in a mixture of rice flour and desiccated coconut before searing in a non-stick pan for a delicate, crunchy coat.*

**Serves 4**

| | |
|---|---|
| 100 g cumquats, finely sliced and seeded | **Per serve** |
| ½ tsp finely chopped fresh ginger | Energy 303 kJ (72 cal) |
| 125 mL (½ cup) water | Protein 1.0 g |
| 100 mL dry vermouth (ingredient check—Wine) | Total fat 0.2 g |
| juice of ½ lemon | Saturated fat <0.1 g |
| 1 tsp palm sugar* or caster sugar | Carbohydrate 9.7 g |
| 2 kiwi fruit, peeled and diced | Total sugars 9.2 g |
| ¼ tsp paprika | Dietary fibre 2.9 g |
| freshly ground black pepper | Sodium 8 mg |
| 1 tsp psyllium* or 1 tsp arrowroot plus 2 tsp water, mixed to a smooth paste | |
| 1 tbs finely chopped fresh parsley | |

1  Place the cumquats, ginger, water, vermouth and lemon juice in a small pan over a low-medium heat and simmer gently for 10 minutes.

2  Add all the remaining ingredients except the parsley and simmer for 2–3 minutes to soften the kiwi fruit and thicken the sauce. Stir through the parsley and serve immediately spooned over fish.

## Macadamia and Cashew Satay Sauce

*Usually sauces to accompany satay are based on peanuts—the macadamia and cashews give a new dimension to this versatile sauce. It is excellent served drizzled over or as a dipping sauce for meat, chicken or vegetable satays or kebabs or as the sauce base for pizza. Try the recipe on page 112 for a simple Satay Marinade.*

*Note: The first 5 ingredients can be substituted with 2 tablespoons Red Thai Curry Paste (page 84).*

**Serves 4**

| | |
|---|---|
| 3 green shallots*, trimmed and roughly chopped | **Per serve** |
| 1 tsp sambal oelek* (ingredient check) or 2 small red chillies, seeded and roughly chopped | Energy 1349 kJ (322 cal) |
| 1 stalk lemon grass* (white part only), roughly chopped | Protein 6.1 g |
| zest of 1 lime | Total fat 30.0 g |
| 2 tsp grated fresh ginger | Saturated fat 7.8 g |
| ¼ tsp ground turmeric | Carbohydrate 10.1 g |
| 1 tsp extra-light olive oil* | Total sugars 7.0 g |
| 250 mL (1 cup) light coconut milk* (ingredient check; ◯) | Dietary fibre 2.0 g |
| 5 tbs (75 mL) pure macadamia spread* (Naytura brand) | Sodium 560 mg |
| 50 g cashew pieces, dry roasted** | |
| 2 tbs (30 mL) lime juice | |
| 1 tsp tamarind paste* (ingredient check) | |
| 4 tsp fish sauce* (ingredient check; ◯) | |

1 tbs grated palm sugar* or soft brown sugar

½ cup finely chopped fresh coriander stalks and roots*

Garnish

fresh coriander leaves, roughly chopped

1  Put the shallots, sambal oelek, lemon grass, lime zest, ginger and turmeric in a food processor and blend to a paste.

2  Heat the oil in a non-stick frying pan over a medium heat. Add the paste and cook, stirring, for 2–3 minutes or until fragrant. Add all the remaining ingredients except the coriander. Bring to the boil then reduce the heat and simmer for 6–7 minutes, stirring regularly. Stir through the coriander. Remove from the heat and set aside for 1 hour to allow the flavours to develop.

3  Reheat gently before serving. Serve spooned over char-grilled or barbecued satay or in individual bowls as a dipping sauce, garnished with a little extra chopped coriander leaves.

## Parsley and White Bean Sauce

*A variation of the classic sauce to serve with corned silverside, white fish or steamed vegetables. I like to use both flat-leaf (Italian) and curly parsley, adding them just before serving to get the best flavour.*

**Serves 4**

| | |
|---|---|
| 240 g cooked white cannellini beans** (if using canned, ingredient check) | **Per serve** |
| 300 mL vegetable stock* (ingredient check—Stock; 🌀) or water | Energy 314 kJ (75 cal) |
| 5 tbs (75 mL) light coconut milk* (ingredient check; 🌀) | Protein 5.9 g |
| freshly ground black pepper | Total fat 1.4 g |
| tiny pinch of sea salt | Saturated fat 1.0 g |
| 1 cup very finely chopped fresh parsley (packed) | Carbohydrate 10.0 g |
| ½ cup very finely chopped fresh flat-leaf (Italian) parsley leaves | Total sugars 1.7 g |
| | Dietary fibre 5.8 g |
| | Sodium 26 mg |

1  Blend all the ingredients except the parsley in a food processor until smooth. Either transfer to a medium-sized pan or press through a metal sieve with the back of a metal spoon for a smoother sauce.

2  Bring to simmering point over a medium heat, stirring regularly. Adjust thickness of the sauce with additional water if required. Immediately before serving, stir through the parsley and cook for 1 minute. Season to taste and serve over silverside, fish or steamed vegetables.

## Pesto Pasta Sauce

*Using the Vietnamese Mint Pesto, this pasta sauce is so easy. Serve tossed through pasta of choice, or with very lightly cooked button mushrooms—or top the pasta with lightly poached chicken and serve garnished with freshly ground black pepper, suitable crispy bacon or prosciutto pieces and shredded, seasoned or char-grilled capsicum\* (ingredient checks on all; 🌀).*

**Serves 4**

| | |
|---|---|
| 5 tbs (75 mL) light coconut milk* (ingredient check; 🌀) | **Per serve** |
| 3 tbs (45 mL) water | Energy 268 kJ (64 cal) |
| 4 tbs (60 mL) Vietnamese Mint Pesto (page 85) | Protein 1.4 g |
| 1 tbs (15 mL) apple juice concentrate* | Total fat 5.7 g |
| freshly ground black pepper | Saturated fat 1.6 g |
| | Carbohydrate 4.7 g |
| | Total sugars 3.8 g |
| | Dietary fibre 1.1 g |
| | Sodium 7 mg |

1   Put all the ingredients in a small pan over a low-medium heat and bring to simmering point, stirring occasionally. Do not boil.

2   Toss though pasta and serve immediately.

## Ⓝ Pickled Ginger Sesame Sauce

*Dress up any lightly steamed or blanched Asian green vegetable with this simple sauce—or serve it over lightly poached or char-grilled fish.*

**Serves 4**

1 tsp oyster sauce* (ingredient check)

1 tbs finely chopped sushi-style pickled ginger* (ingredient check—Ginger)

1 tsp pure sesame oil*

1 tbs (15 mL) white wine (ingredient check—Wine)

**Per serve**

**Energy 72 kJ (17 cal)**

**Protein <0.1 g**

**Total fat 1.1 g**

**Saturated fat 0.2 g**

**Carbohydrate 1.1 g**

**Total sugars 0.9 g**

**Dietary fibre 0.1 g**

**Sodium 49 mg**

1   Place all the ingredients in a small pan over a low heat and simmer for 2 minutes, stirring occasionally.

2   Drizzle sauce over vegetables or fish of choice.

## Ⓒ Port Wine and Sun-Dried Tomato Sauce

Ⓕ *This sauce is excellent served over char-grilled or barbecued meat—or if you are using lamb backstrap or fillet, lightly poach the*
Ⓝ *meat in the sauce. I usually make the sauce 24 hours in advance and refrigerate it to allow the flavours to develop. Excellent served*
Ⓥ *accompanied by Roast Chat Potatoes (page 99) or on a bed of Kumara Purée (page 94) with a spicy salad such as Watercress, Rocket and Marigold Salad (page 105). For a simple variation, add 6–8 sliced button mushrooms at the same time as the lamb.*

**Serves 6**

extra-light olive oil spray* (ingredient check)

3 large green shallots*, trimmed and sliced into 1 cm lengths

½ tsp ground cumin

6 sun-dried tomatoes*, finely chopped (ingredient check; Ⓒ)

250 mL (1 cup) port (ingredient check—Wine; Ⓒ)

1 tsp tomato paste (ingredient check)

2 kaffir lime leaves*, bruised

1 tsp finely chopped fresh lemon thyme or rosemary leaves

500 mL (2 cups) water

1 tbs finely chopped fresh coriander root*

freshly ground black pepper

**Per serve**

**Energy 298 kJ (71 cal)**

**Protein 0.6 g**

**Total fat 0.5 g**

**Saturated fat 0.1 g**

**Carbohydrate 7.2 g**

**Total sugars 6.2 g**

**Dietary fibre 1.0 g**

**Sodium 12 mg**

1   Very lightly spray a large, non-stick frying pan with oil. Add the shallots and sauté over a medium-high heat for 2 minutes. Add the cumin and sauté for 1 minute or until the cumin is fragrant, stirring constantly.

2   Add the sun-dried tomatoes, port, tomato paste, lime leaves and lemon thyme and simmer gently to reduce the sauce to ¼ of its original volume. Add 250 mL of the water and repeat the reduction process. Add the remaining water, coriander and black pepper and simmer for 2 minutes.

3   If poaching lamb in the sauce, place the meat portions in the hot sauce and poach for 2–3 minutes each side (do not overcook—the meat should still be rare to medium-rare.)

## Quick Pasta Sauce

*This simple sauce turns the pasta of your choice into a ready meal—just serve with a big bowl of salad. It is easy to modify by adding any of a variety of toppings or sauce ingredients (making sure you select suitable brands—see Glossary, page 173): top with crispy pancetta or bacon pieces, a good shaved pecorino cheese (if sheep's milk is OK), or when cooking the sauce add one or more as suitable: 240g cooked white beans or 10–12 button mushrooms, 2 tablespoons capers\*, 2–3 chopped anchovy fillets\*, 3 sliced artichoke hearts\*.*

**Serves 4**

extra-light olive oil spray* (ingredient check)
3 green shallots*, trimmed and sliced
1 medium-sized green capsicum, seeded and finely sliced
10-12 black olives, pitted and halved (ingredient check; ○)
½ cup shredded fresh basil leaves
1 bottle (700 mL) tomato passata* (ingredient check)
juice of ½ lemon
freshly ground black pepper

Garnish
fresh basil leaves, roughly shredded

**Per serve**
Energy 338 kJ (81 cal)
Protein 3.8 g
Total fat 1.6 g
Saturated fat 0.2 g
Carbohydrate 12.0 g
Total sugars 10.7 g
Dietary fibre 7.0 g
Sodium 85 mg

1 Lightly spray a non-stick frying pan with oil and place over a medium-high heat. Add the shallots and capsicum and cook for 2–3 minutes, stirring frequently. Add all the remaining ingredients and simmer for 5 minutes, stirring occasionally.

2 Serve tossed through pasta of choice garnished with the shredded basil leaves.

## Wild Lime Chilli Sauce

*This sauce is excellent as a marinade for char-grilling meat or fish, or for making a sauce with coconut milk for poaching prawns or white fish that guarantees the plates will be licked clean! Wild limes can take some tracking down but they have an exquisite flavour—refer to the Glossary for suppliers' contact details. ♥ use agar powder.*

**Makes 1—1¼ cups**

1 sterilised screw-top glass jar**
50 g wild limes*, very finely chopped
2 bird's eye chillies, seeded and very finely chopped
1 tsp freshly grated ginger
100 g caster sugar
6 tbs (90 mL) white vinegar (ingredient check—Vinegar; ○)
1 tbs (15 mL) lemon juice
125 mL (½ cup) water
½ tsp agar powder* or 2 tsp powdered gelatine plus 1 tbs boiling water

**Per 100 g**
Energy 448 kJ (107 cal)
Protein 0.2 g
Total fat <0.1 g
Saturated fat <0.1 g
Carbohydrate 26.2 g
Total sugars 26.2 g
Dietary fibre 0.4 g
Sodium 2 mg

1 Place all the ingredients except the agar in a small pan over a medium-high heat. Bring to the boil, reduce the heat and simmer for 10 minutes, stirring regularly. Remove from the heat.

2 Sprinkle the agar over the sauce and stir to dissolve. (If using gelatine, dissolve in the boiling water and stir through the sauce.) Transfer the sauce to the sterilised jar. Label and store refrigerated for up to 6 weeks unopened and up to 4 weeks after opening.

## Pastes and Mustards

Make a few pastes and store them in tablespoon portions in the freezer and you will have a wealth of flavours to knock up a quick curry or masala dish any time. As with many spiced dishes, you will find that freezing enhances the flavour of these pastes. The mini-sized food blenders found in many supermarkets are ideal for processing the relatively small quantities of pastes.

## Chilli–Basil Paste

*This paste can be used in a similar way to a pesto or a green masala paste—it is very versatile. Two recipe suggestions are Chilli-Basil Chicken Curry (page 63) and Baked Spiced Chicken (page 58).*

**Makes 1¼—1½ cups**

1 bunch fresh basil, leaves picked
1 bunch fresh coriander, trimmed and roughly chopped
2 red chillies, seeded and roughly chopped
50 g pine nuts
juice of 1 lemon
1 red banana capsicum, seeded and roughly chopped
2 fresh tomatoes, roughly chopped
2 green shallots*, trimmed and roughly chopped
½ tsp ground cumin
2 tsp balsamic vinegar* (ingredient check—Vinegar; ○)
freshly ground black pepper (lots!)
3 tbs (45 mL) extra–light olive oil*
1 sterilised glass jar** (if not freezing)

**Per tablespoon**
**Energy 195 kJ (47 cal)**
**Protein 0.8 g**
**Total fat 4.4 g**
**Saturated fat 0.4 g**
**Carbohydrate 0.9 g**
**Total sugars 0.8 g**
**Dietary fibre 0.8 g**
**Sodium 3 mg**

1  Put all ingredients in a food processor and blend to a fine paste.

2  Transfer to a sterilised glass jar, cover with a thin layer of oil, seal, label with the 2-week 'use-by' date and refrigerate, or freeze in 1 tablespoon portions in an ice cube tray, transfer to a freezer bag, label and store frozen for up to 6 months.

## Curry Powder—Ready-Ground Spices

*This makes a good curry powder blend from ready-ground spices. Store in a tightly sealed glass jar. To use, roast or cook the curry powder in a small amount of oil to bring out the fragrance and flavours of the spices.*

**Makes 1 cup**

3 tbs ground cinnamon
3 tbs ground coriander
2 tbs ground turmeric
3 tbs ground cumin
1 tbs ground fenugreek
4 tsp dry mustard powder* (ingredient check)
4 tsp ground cardamom
2 tbs ground chilli
2 tbs freshly ground black pepper
1 tbs ground ginger

**Per teaspoon**
**Energy 26 kJ (6 cal)**
**Protein 0.2 g**
**Total fat 0.2 g**
**Saturated fat <0.1 g**
**Carbohydrate 0.9 g**
**Total sugars 0.2 g**
**Dietary fibre 0.1 g**
**Sodium 1 mg**

1  Put all ingredients in a glass jar and mix thoroughly.

2  Seal tightly and use as required.

## Green and Pink Peppercorn Mustard

*A twist on the regular seeded mustard, using a predominance of peppercorns in place of the more usual mustard seeds. Excellent served with cold meats such as beef and lamb or as a flavouring for beef stir-fries.*

**Makes ½ cup**

1 tbs green peppercorns, rinsed and dried (ingredient check)

1 tbs pink peppercorns, rinsed and dried (ingredient check)

2 tbs yellow mustard seeds

¼ tsp ground allspice

¼ tsp mace

4 tbs (60 mL) white wine vinegar* (ingredient check—Vinegar; ⓒ)

1 tbs honey

1 small sterilised jar**

**Per teaspoon**

**Energy 32 kJ (8 cal)**

**Protein 0.2 g**

**Total fat 0.3 g**

**Saturated fat <0.1 g**

**Carbohydrate 0.8 g**

**Total sugars 0.7 g**

**Dietary fibre 0.1 g**

**Sodium 2 mg**

**1** Put the spices in a food processor and grind coarsely. Add the remaining ingredients and blend to a coarse, grainy mix. (The mixture will be quite runny when first made, but thickens over the 7 days as it matures.)

**2** Transfer to the sterilised jar, seal and label. Set aside for 7 days at room temperature to mature. The mustard will keep unopened for up to 6 weeks in a sterilised screw-top jar. Refrigerate after opening and it will keep for a further 6 weeks.

## Green Curry Paste

*Unlike most commercially prepared green curry pastes this recipe is very mild, so it can be used in a number of different recipes to provide a wonderful flavour base. For a hotter curry simply spice the sauce with sambal oelek* or chilli paste* (ingredient check; ⓒ) to taste. The paste can be used to make Green Chicken Curry (page 64), Baked Spiced Chicken (page 58) or Green King Prawn Curry (page 32), amongst other dishes.*

**Makes 1 cup**

2 tsp cumin seeds

1 tbs (15 mL) coriander seeds

1 tsp shrimp paste* (ingredient check; ⓒ)

½ tsp freshly ground black pepper

½ tsp ground turmeric

6 large green chillies, seeded and roughly chopped (8 for a hotter paste)

5 green shallots*, trimmed and chopped

5 cm piece of fresh galangal*, peeled and finely sliced

6 kaffir lime leaves*, shredded

3 stalks lemon grass* (white part only), finely sliced

zest and juice of 2 limes

½ cup shredded fresh coriander roots* and leaves

2 tbs (30 mL) extra-light olive oil*

1 sterilised glass jar** (if not freezing)

**Per tablespoon**

**Energy 81 kJ (19 cal)**

**Protein 0.4 g**

**Total fat 1.6 g**

**Saturated fat 0.2 g**

**Carbohydrate 0.8 g**

**Total sugars 0.5 g**

**Dietary fibre 0.4 g**

**Sodium 24 mg**

**1** Dry roast the cumin and coriander seeds in a small heavy-bottomed pan over a low heat for 2–3 minutes or until fragrant, shaking the pan regularly. Grind the seeds in a coffee grinder or pestle and mortar and put in a food processor.

**2** Wrap the shrimp paste in an envelope of aluminium foil and roast for 2–3 minutes in the spice pan or under a hot grill, turning the envelope at least twice during cooking to prevent the paste from burning.

**3** Add the shrimp paste and all the remaining ingredients to the food processor. Blend thoroughly to a paste, scraping down the sides of the blender as required.

4   Transfer to a sterilised jar, seal and refrigerate for up to 2 weeks (mark your 'use-by' date on the jar) or freeze in tablespoon-sized portions in an ice cube tray; transfer to a freezer bag, label and store for up to 6 months frozen.

## Green Harissa Paste

*This paste is excellent with fish, such as Whole Baked Harissa-seasoned Barramundi (page 40), or chicken—try Baked Spice Chicken (page 58).*

**Makes ½—¾ cup**

| | |
|---|---|
| 70 g fresh coriander (about ¾–1 bunch), trimmed and roughly chopped | **Per tablespoon** |
| 4 tsp caraway seeds | **Energy 212 kJ (51 cal)** |
| 4 tsp ground coriander | **Protein 0.4 g** |
| 4 tsp ground cumin | **Total fat 4.7 g** |
| 2 large red chillies, seeded and finely chopped, or ¾ tsp sambal oelek* (ingredient check) | **Saturated fat 0.6 g** |
| ½ tsp ground turmeric | **Carbohydrate 1.8 g** |
| freshly ground black pepper | **Total sugars 0.6 g** |
| 3 tbs (45 mL) extra–light olive oil* | **Dietary fibre 0.5 g** |
| 1 sterilised glass jar** (if not freezing) | **Sodium 3 mg** |

1   Put all the ingredients except the oil in a food processor and blend until finely chopped. With the motor running, gradually add the oil and process to a paste.

2   Transfer to a sterilised glass jar, seal and refrigerate marking the 2-week expiry date on the jar, or freeze in tablespoon-sized portions in an ice-cube tray, transfer to a freezer bag, label and store up to 6 months frozen.

## Laksa Paste

*This paste is excellent for making quick and easy curries, such as Prawn and Pumpkin Curry (page 38) and Potato and Chicken Laksa (page 67). It is a mild, flavour-packed paste designed to allow you to build the level of 'heat' you want in a dish. Ⓝ replace macadamia nuts with 2 tbs ground rice or rice crumbs*.*

**Makes 1 cup**

| | |
|---|---|
| 6 large red chillies (about 75 g), seeded and roughly chopped | **Per tablespoon** |
| 4 large green shallots* (about 120 g), trimmed and roughly chopped | **Energy 153 kJ (36 cal)** |
| 4 cm piece fresh ginger (about 30 g), peeled and roughly chopped | **Protein 0.4 g** |
| 2 cm piece fresh turmeric (about 15 g), peeled, roughly chopped, or 2 tsp ground turmeric | **Total fat 3.5 g** |
| 3 stalks lemon grass* (about 100 g; white part only), sliced | **Saturated fat 0.4 g** |
| 25 g raw, unsalted macadamia nuts | **Carbohydrate 0.9 g** |
| 1 tsp shrimp paste* (ingredient check; Ⓢ) | **Total sugars 0.6 g** |
| zest of 2 limes | **Dietary fibre 0.3 g** |
| 4 tbs (60 mL) lime juice | **Sodium 23 mg** |
| 2 tsp ground coriander | |
| 1 tsp grated palm sugar* or soft brown sugar | |
| 3 tbs (45 mL) extra–light olive oil* | |
| extra–light olive oil spray* (ingredient check) | |
| 1 sterilised glass jar** (if not freezing) | |

1   Place all the ingredients except extra-light olive oil spray in a food processor and blend to an evenly textured paste.

2   Lightly spray a non-stick frying pan or wok with oil. Place over a medium heat and add the paste. Cook gently, stirring continuously, for 5–6 minutes or until a golden brown and fragrant.

3   Transfer the paste to the glass jar, seal and label with use-by date, or freeze in tablespoon-sized portions in an ice-cube tray, transfer to a freezer bag, label and store up to 6 months frozen.

## Red Thai Curry Paste

*A very versatile paste—great for making Thai curries such as Red Pork Curry (page 57), Baked Spiced Chicken (page 58), Macadamia and Cashew Paste for Satay (page 77). It is an excellent paste to make in bulk and freeze.*

**Makes ½ cup**

| | |
|---|---|
| 5 green shallots* (about 125 g), trimmed and chopped | **Per tablespoon** |
| 5 medium-sized red chillies (about 30 g), seeded and roughly chopped | **Energy 187 kJ (45 cal)** |
| 4 thin slices fresh galangal (about 5 g) | **Protein 0.4 g** |
| 2 tbs finely chopped lemon grass* (white part only) | **Total fat 4.5 g** |
| 20 g fresh coriander roots* | **Saturated fat 0.5 g** |
| ½ tsp ground cumin | **Carbohydrate 0.8 g** |
| ¾ tsp shrimp paste* (ingredient check; ◉) | **Total sugars 0.7 g** |
| 3 tbs (45 mL) extra-light olive oil* | **Dietary fibre 0.5 g** |
| 1 small sterilised glass jar** (if not freezing) | **Sodium 35 mg** |

1 Put all the ingredients except the oil in a food processor. Blend to a smooth paste.

2 Heat a non-stick frying pan on a medium-high heat and add the oil.

3 Reduce the heat and add the paste. Slow fry for 5 minutes or until the paste is fragrant, stirring regularly.

4 Transfer to the sterilised glass jar, seal and label with the 3-week use-by date and refrigerate, or freeze in tablespoon-sized portions in an ice cube tray, transfer to freezer bags, label and store frozen for up to 6 months.

## Sweet Chilli Sauce

*A sweet chilli sauce without the usual garlic dose of commercially made sauces. Store in sterilised glass bottles or jars in the refrigerator for up to 1 month after opening. Reduce sugar to 100 g for a less sweet sauce. ⓋUse agar instead of gelatine.*

**Makes 2 cups**

| | |
|---|---|
| 10 large red chillies, seeded and roughly chopped | **Per tablespoon** |
| 1 small red capsicum, seeded and roughly chopped | **Energy 110 kJ (26 cal)** |
| 2 green shallots*, trimmed and roughly chopped | **Protein 0.3 g** |
| 250 mL (1 cup) white vinegar (ingredient check—Vinegar; ◉) | **Total fat <0.1 g** |
| 400 mL water | **Saturated fat <0.1 g** |
| 200 g soft brown sugar | **Carbohydrate 6.1 g** |
| freshly ground black pepper | **Total sugars 6.1 g** |
| 2 tsp powdered gelatine sprinkled over 3 tbs (45 mL) water or ½ tsp agar powder* | **Dietary fibre 0.1 g** |
| 1 x 500 mL sterilised glass bottle or jar** | **Sodium 3 mg** |

1 Place all the ingredients except the gelatine (include agar if using) in a pan over a low-medium heat. Simmer gently for 30 minutes.

2 Transfer to a food processor and blend until the chillies, capsicum and shallots are finely and uniformly chopped. Return to the pan and reheat to simmering point, reduce the heat add the gelatine mix and stir until dissolved and the sauce has thickened slightly; do not boil. (Omit the reheating if using agar.)

3 Transfer to labelled, sterilised glass container(s) and seal.

## Vietnamese Mint Pesto

*The blend of Vietnamese mint and Thai basil makes this a very versatile pesto for use with pasta (Pesto Pasta Sauce, page 78) or for such goodies as Baked Spiced Chicken (page 58), Pesto and Sun-dried Tomato Stuffed Chicken Pockets with Pesto Pasta Sauce (page 67), for noodle stir-fries or simply as a salsa on char-grilled fish fillets or steamed vegetables.*

**Makes 1 cup**

| | |
|---|---|
| 75 g raw cashew nuts, pine or macadamia nuts | **Per tablespoon** |
| 1 bunch Thai basil or regular basil (about 35 g), leaves picked | **Energy 213 kJ (51 cal)** |
| ½ bunch Vietnamese mint* (about 10 g), leaves picked | **Protein 1.2 g** |
| 1 small bunch coriander (about 50 g), trimmed | **Total fat 4.6 g** |
| 1 large red chilli, seeded and roughly chopped | **Saturated fat 0.6 g** |
| 1 tsp freshly grated ginger | **Carbohydrate 1.4 g** |
| 1 green shallot*, trimmed and roughly chopped | **Total sugars 0.8 g** |
| 1 tsp brown sugar | **Dietary fibre 1.1 g** |
| 2 tbs (30 mL) lime juice | **Sodium 3 mg** |
| freshly ground black pepper | |
| 3 tbs (45 mL) extra-light olive* or macadamia oil* | |
| 1 x 250 mL sterilised glass jar** (if not freezing) | |

1   Place the nuts in a small, heavy-bottomed pan over a low heat and dry roast for 4–5 minutes or until golden brown, shaking regularly. Allow to cool.

2   Put all the ingredients in a food processor and blend to an evenly textured paste.

3   Transfer the pesto to the sterilised glass jar. Cover pesto with a layer of oil, seal, label and refrigerate for up to 2 weeks, or freeze in tablespoon-sized portions in an ice cube tray. Transfer to a freezer bag, and store frozen for up to 6 months.

## Wholegrain Mustard

*This simple recipe for a tasty home-made mustard is like most good condiments: the mustard needs to be allowed to mature for the flavours to develop. It will keep unopened for up to 6 weeks in a sterilised glass jar. After opening, refrigerate and it will keep for a further 6 weeks.*

**Makes ½ cup**

| | |
|---|---|
| 2 tbs (25 g) brown mustard seeds | **Per teaspoon** |
| 2 tbs (25 g) yellow mustard seeds | **Energy 41 kJ (10 cal)** |
| ½ tsp caraway seeds | **Protein 0.5 g** |
| ½ tsp green peppercorns, rinsed and dried (ingredient check) | **Total fat 0.6 g** |
| ¼ tsp mixed spice | **Saturated fat <0.1 g** |
| ½ tsp dried tarragon | **Carbohydrate 0.4 g** |
| 4 tbs (60 mL) white wine vinegar* (ingredient check—Vinegar; ) | **Total sugars 0.2 g** |
| 1 tsp grated palm sugar* or soft brown sugar | **Dietary fibre 0.2 g** |
| 1 small sterilised glass jar** | **Sodium 2 mg** |

1   Put the spices and tarragon in a food processor and grind coarsely. Add the remaining ingredients and blend to a coarse, grainy mix.

2   Transfer to the sterilised jar, seal and label. Set aside for 7 days at room temperature to mature. Refrigerate after opening.

## Salsas, Relishes and Pickles

Like a good sauce, a good salsa or relish can add a new dimension to a meal, turning it from simple to very tasty.

### Apple Relish

*Served warm, a great way to top off a pork chop or roast—or chilled, as an accompaniment for pork or ham salad. For a more textured sauce leave the apples unpeeled.*

**Serves 4**

| | |
|---|---|
| 5 green apples (about 750 g), cored and thinly sliced (peeled or unpeeled) | **Per serve** |
| 25 g currants (ingredient check—Dried fruit; ) | **Energy 479 kJ (114 cal)** |
| 100 g celery (about 2 stalks), medium or finely diced | **Protein 1.2 g** |
| 2 tbs (30 mL) apple juice concentrate* | **Total fat 0.4 g** |
| 3 tbs (45 mL) apple cider vinegar* | **Saturated fat <0.1 g** |
| zest of ½ lemon | **Carbohydrate 32.9 g** |
| 2 tbs (30 mL) lemon juice | **Total sugars 30.4 g** |
| 5 tbs (75 mL) water | **Dietary fibre 4.6 g** |
| 1 tsp curry powder* (ingredient check) | **Sodium 28 mg** |
| 3 sprigs fresh oregano or ¼ tsp dried oregano | |
| freshly ground black pepper | |

1  Put all the ingredients in a pan over a medium heat. Simmer for 10 minutes or until the apples are soft.

2  Spoon warm over cooked meat or transfer to a small bowl set aside to cool, cover and chill.

### Beetroot Relish

*A flavoured-packed relish that is great served chilled or at room temperature with char-grilled or barbecued cuts of lamb or beef. The relish will keep for up to 1 week refrigerated.*

**Makes 1 cup—serves 8-10**

| | |
|---|---|
| 200 g raw beetroot, peeled and grated | **Per serve** |
| 1 tsp yellow mustard seeds | **Energy 112 kJ (27 cal)** |
| 2 tbs (30 mL) balsamic vinegar* (ingredient check—Vinegar; ) | **Protein 0.6 g** |
| 2 tbs (30 mL) white wine vinegar* (ingredient check—Vinegar; ) | **Total fat 0.2 g** |
| 1 green apple (about 250 g), washed, cored and diced | **Saturated fat <0.1 g** |
| 25 g currants (ingredient check—Dried fruit; ) | **Carbohydrate 5.2 g** |
| 3 tbs (45 mL) water | **Total sugars 5.0 g** |
| freshly ground black pepper | **Dietary fibre 1.1 g** |
| | **Sodium 14 mg** |

1  Put all the ingredients in a small pan over a medium heat. Simmer, covered, for 10 minutes.

2  Transfer to a small serving bowl, cover and leave to cool. Store refrigerated.

## Capsicum and Coriander Relish

*This relish is so easy to make, but its wonderful colour and flavours belie the ease of preparation. An excellent topping for grilled fish, seafood and lamb or chicken—and kebabs.*

**Serves 4**

| | |
|---|---|
| 1 green chilli, seeded and roughly chopped | **Per serve** |
| 1 medium-sized red capsicum (about 150 g), seeded and roughly chopped | Energy 114 kJ (27 cal) |
| 1 green shallot*, trimmed and roughly chopped | Protein 1.8 g |
| 3 Roma tomatoes, skinned, seeded and chopped | Total fat 0.2 g |
| 20 g fresh coriander roots* and leaves, roughly chopped | Saturated fat <0.1 g |
| ¼ tsp lime zest | Carbohydrate 3.8 g |
| 4 tbs (60 mL) lime juice | Total sugars 3.7 g |
| freshly ground black pepper | Dietary fibre 1.8 g |
| | Sodium 6 mg |

1  Put all the ingredients in a food processor and blend to an even, very finely chopped consistency (do not purée).

2  Transfer to a serving dish. Cover and chill. Stir well before serving as a serve-yourself relish or drizzled over cooked meat or fish of choice.

## Cranberry Relish

*Forget the usual bland cranberry jelly accompaniment for turkey, as this relish does justice to any turkey! It can be made in advance and stored refrigerated in a sterilised jar** for up to 6 weeks. omit the walnuts.*

**Makes 1½ cups**

| | |
|---|---|
| 250 mL (1 cup) water | **Per tablespoon** |
| 50 g honey | Energy 214 kJ (51 cal) |
| 125 g Craisins* (dried cranberries) | Protein 0.5 g |
| zest and juice of 1 orange | Total fat 1.0 g |
| 1 small green apple, peeled, cored and diced | Saturated fat 0.1 g |
| 50 g sun-dried apricots (ingredient check—Dried fruit; ) | Carbohydrate 10.2 g |
| 65 g natural sultanas | Total sugars 9.8 g |
| 1 cinnamon quill | Dietary fibre 1.0 g |
| ¼ tsp nutmeg | Sodium 3 mg |
| 4 tsp apple cider vinegar* | |
| 35 g walnuts, dry roasted** and chopped | |

1  Place the honey and water in a medium-sized pan over a medium heat and bring to the boil, stirring until the honey has dissolved. Reduce the heat until the syrup is simmering gently.

2  Stir through all the remaining ingredients. Partially cover with a lid and simmer for 15 minutes, or until the relish reduces and thickens, stirring occasionally. Fully cover and simmer gently for a further 10 minutes or until the fruit is soft and the relish thickened.

3  If the relish is to be stored for more than 4–5 days, transfer to a sterilised jar**, seal and set aside to cool. If to be used within 5 days, transfer to a glass or ceramic serving bowl, cover and set aside to cool before refrigerating.

## Mint Chutney

*This is a great alternative to the yoghurt-based sauce often served up with spicy dishes. Serve as an accompaniment to dishes such as Chicken Tangine (page 62) and Chickpea Patties (page 15), or as a dressing for salads. The chutney can be stored in the refrigerator for up to 3 days.*

**Makes 1½ cups—serves 6**

⅔ cup very finely chopped fresh mint leaves

125 mL (½ cup) light coconut milk* (ingredient check; ◯)

2 tbs desiccated coconut

¼ tsp sambal oelek* or chilli paste* (ingredient check; ◯)

2 tbs (30 mL) lime juice

1 tsp grated palm sugar* or soft brown sugar

**Per serve**

Energy 29 kJ (7 cal)

Protein 0.1 g

Total fat 0.6 g

Saturated fat 0.3 g

Carbohydrate 0.3 g

Total sugars 0.2 g

Dietary fibre 0.1 g

Sodium 1 mg

1  Put all the ingredients in a glass jar and shake well to combine. Refrigerate for a minimum of 1 hour to allow the chutney to thicken.

2  Shake well before serving.

## Pickled Cucumber Salsa

*This very refreshing dish can be served as a salsa or as a stand-alone salad with fish, poultry or meat. It may be prepared 2–3 days in advance, but needs to marinate overnight as a minimum to bring out the lovely flavours. Select fine-skinned cucumbers; they are best cut on a mandoline† or food slicer.*

**Serves 4**

500 g cucumber, very finely sliced (Lebanese are best)

1 tsp sea salt

1 large green shallot*, trimmed and very finely sliced

Dressing

1 tsp yellow mustard seeds

3 tbs (45 mL) white wine vinegar* (ingredient check—Vinegar; ◯)

200 mL water

2 tsp caster sugar

¼ tsp paprika

freshly ground black pepper

**Per serve**

Energy 139 kJ (33 cal)

Protein 1.0 g

Total fat 0.5 g

Saturated fat <0.1 g

Carbohydrate 5.5 g

Total sugars 5.3 g

Dietary fibre 1.7 g

Sodium 195 mg

1  Mix the salt through the cucumber and shallot in a bowl. Cover and leave to stand at room temperature for 40 minutes.

2  Lightly crush the mustard seeds in a mortar and pestle (or small plastic bag with a rolling pin). Transfer to a medium-sized ceramic or glass bowl and add the remaining dressing ingredients. Mix well.

3  Squeeze the sliced cucumber thoroughly to remove excess liquid. Place in the dressing and stir well to thoroughly coat the cucumber and shallot. Cover and refrigerate for a minimum of 12 hours.

## Redcurrant and Balsamic Relish

*An easy-to-make relish that is great with roast lamb, cutlets and pork.*

**Serves 4**

| | |
|---|---|
| 125 g fresh or frozen redcurrants | **Per serve** |
| 1 firm red apple (such as Jonagold or Braeburn), cored and chopped medium-fine | Energy 356 kJ (85 cal) |
| 3 green shallots*, trimmed and chopped | Protein 0.8 g |
| 4 tbs (60 mL) balsamic vinegar* (ingredient check—Vinegar; ◯) | Total fat 0.1 g |
| 3 tbs (45 mL) water | Saturated fat <0.1 g |
| 35 g caster sugar | Carbohydrate 19.0 g |
| 12 juniper berries | Total sugars 18.5 g |
| ¼ tsp ground coriander | Dietary fibre 2.5 g |
| 10 fresh mint leaves, finely chopped | Sodium 5 mg |

1  Put all the ingredients except the mint in a small pan over a high heat. Bring to the boil, reduce the heat until simmering gently. Cook for 10 minutes, stirring occasionally, or until the relish thickens.

2  Stir through the mint. Serve hot or cold.


## Seasoned Sun-Dried Tomatoes in Olive Oil

*Commercially made sun-dried tomatoes are a jewel in the flavour department if you can eat them—but many preparations contain MSG, tons of garlic and various other additives that make them a 'No-Go' food (see Glossary—Ingredients, page 192) so I usually make my own! This recipe is equally good made with sun-dried, char-grilled or roasted capsicum\*—or a mixture. If using char-grilled or roasted capsicum, omit the rehydration step. Use the glorious oil marinade for stir-fries or to make a salad or steamed vegetable dressing. I tend to use extra-light olive oil so that I have a flavoured oil with a smoke point suitable for high temperature stir-fries and char-grilling (see Glossary—Oils).*

**Makes 2 cups**

| | |
|---|---|
| 150 g dehydrated sun-dried tomatoes* | **Per 30 g** |
| 125 mL (½ cup) extra-light* or virgin olive oil* | **(4–5 tomatoes drained of excess oil)** |
| 1 tsp paprika | Energy 313 kJ (75 cal) |
| ½ tsp coriander seeds, lightly crushed | Protein 1.0 g |
| ½ tsp fennel seeds, lightly crushed | Total fat 6.0 g |
| 1 tsp black peppercorns, lightly crushed | Saturated fat 1.0 g |
| 1 dried red chilli | Carbohydrate 4.0 g |
| 1 tsp dried oregano | Total sugars 4.0 g |
| 2 green shallots*, trimmed and roughly sliced | Dietary fibre 2.0 g |
| 1 tbs (15 mL) balsamic vinegar* (ingredient check—Vinegar; ◯) | Sodium 8 mg |
| 2 tbs (30 mL) white vinegar (ingredient check—Vinegar; ◯) | |

1  Sterilise a 500 mL preserving or heat-resistant jar with lid**.

2  Put the tomatoes in a bowl and cover with boiling water to rehydrate. Leave to stand for 12–15 minutes to soften (the tomatoes will become mushy if oversoaked). Drain and gently squeeze out any excess water. Place on kitchen towels to dry thoroughly.

3  While the tomatoes are soaking, put the oil in a pan with the spices, oregano and shallots over a low heat and warm very gently (do not overheat or the spices will burn, the oil must not boil). Add the dried tomatoes and cook for gently for 5 minutes. Stir through the vinegars and remove from the heat.

4  Transfer to the sterilised jar, ensuring the tomatoes are covered with the oil mix (add additional oil if required). Allow to cool, seal, label and refrigerate. The tomatoes will keep for months (if they last that long!).

## Vegetables

In the same way that a sauce is used to dress up a piece of meat or fish, a dish can be dressed up by including vegetables that have been prepared to add a different flavour dimension. Often these recipes are very simple, but can turn a basic meal into something quite delicious. Most of the following recipes include a serving suggestion for a complete dish.

### Ⓒ Bean Sprout, Snow Pea and Watercress Stir-Fry

Ⓕ *A quick and easy stir-fry of vegetables that is a great accompaniment to lightly poached chicken breasts with mango 'hedgehogs', or*
Ⓝ *other poultry dishes. Trimmed fresh asparagus, sugar snap peas, okra, Chinese cabbage, sliced button mushrooms make tasty additions*
Ⓥ *or substitutes—add the asparagus, sugar snaps, okra and mushrooms with the capsicum, the cabbage with the bean sprouts.*

**Serves 4**

| | |
|---|---|
| 5 g dried sliced shiitake mushrooms* | **Per serve** |
| 1 tsp apple juice concentrate* | **Energy 166 kJ (40 cal)** |
| 1 tsp balsamic vinegar* (ingredient check—Vinegar; Ⓒ) | **Protein 4.6 g** |
| freshly ground black pepper | **Total fat 0.4 g** |
| extra-light olive oil spray* (ingredient check) | **Saturated fat <0.1 g** |
| ½ red capsicum, seeded and finely sliced | **Carbohydrate 5.1 g** |
| 150 g snow peas, trimmed and halved | **Total sugars 3.9 g** |
| 250 g bean sprouts | **Dietary fibre 4.5 g** |
| 150 g watercress, trimmed and roughly chopped | **Sodium 20 mg** |

1   Place the shiitake mushrooms in a small bowl and cover with boiling water. Soak for 5 minutes, or until soft. Drain well.

2   Mix the apple juice concentrate, vinegar and black pepper together in a small bowl.

3   Very lightly spray a non-stick frying pan or wok with oil and place over a high heat. Add the capsicum and snow peas and cook for 1 minute, stirring frequently. Stir through the bean sprouts and mushrooms, and cook for 30–45 seconds. Stir though the watercress and cook until just starting to wilt (about 30–45 seconds).

4   Toss through the vinegar mix. Serve immediately.

### Ⓒ Braised Fennel and Tomatoes

Ⓕ *A delicious way to serve fennel—it makes an excellent accompaniment for roast meats and chops.*
Ⓝ

**Serves 4**

| | |
|---|---|
| 400 g fennel | **Per serve** |
| 1 tbs (15 mL) virgin olive oil* | **Energy 353 kJ (84 cal)** |
| 2 large green shallots*, trimmed and cut in thirds | **Protein 5.1 g** |
| 3 Roma tomatoes, peeled and chopped | **Total fat 4.4 g** |
| 50 g short-cut, rindless bacon (ingredient check; Ⓒ), roughly chopped | **Saturated fat 0.8 g** |
| 250 mL (1 cup) water | **Carbohydrate 5.4 g** |
| freshly ground black pepper | **Total sugars 5.4 g** |
| 10 okra or sugar snap peas, trimmed | **Dietary fibre 4.0 g** |
| | **Sodium 225 mg** |

Garnish
retained fennel tips

1   Cut the fennel into wedges lengthways through base, trim the core back carefully so that the wedge remains intact. Trim the tips and retain as garnish.

2   Place the oil in a heavy-bottomed pan over a high heat. When hot, add the fennel and shallots and cook for 4 minutes, shaking the pan regularly to prevent the vegetables catching.

3   Add the tomatoes and bacon and cook for 1 minute.

4   Add the water and black pepper, cover and simmer gently for 2–3 minutes or until the fennel is almost tender. Add the okra or sugar snap peas and simmer for 1–2 minutes or until the fennel is tender. Serve immediately garnished with the fennel tips.

## Carrot, Parsnip and Kumara Batons

*A simple mix of orange and white roast vegetables that is great with meat, poultry or fish. If serving with fish try adding 1 teaspoon fresh lemon thyme leaves to the oil mix. The quantities of the vegetables are approximate.*

**Serves 4**

| | |
|---|---|
| 2 tsp extra-light olive oil* | **Per serve** |
| 1 tsp paprika or ½ tsp sweet smoked paprika* or curry powder* (ingredient check) | **Energy 781 kJ (186 cal)** |
| freshly ground black pepper | **Protein 5.7 g** |
| 300 g carrots, peeled | **Total fat 2.5 g** |
| 450 g fine-skinned Desiree potatoes, cleaned | **Saturated fat 0.3 g** |
| 200 g parsnips, peeled | **Carbohydrate 34.8 g** |
| 300 g kumara or orange sweet potato, peeled | **Total sugars 11.1 g** |
| | **Dietary fibre 7.0 g** |
| | **Sodium 54 mg** |

1   Preheat the oven to 240°C (220°C fan forced). Line 2 baking trays with baking paper.

2   Put the oil, paprika and pepper in a mixing bowl and combine.

3   Cut the carrots and potatoes into 1 cm square x 5 cm batons, and cut the parsnips and kumara into 1.5 cm square x 5 cm batons and toss in the oil mix. Spread out on the lined baking trays and roast for 25–30 minutes or until starting to brown, turning once during cooking. Serve immediately.

## Coconut Rice

*Inclusion of the coconut and spices gives the rice a moister consistency and makes an excellent bed for satay sticks. Use a heavy-based pan or heat diffuser† to prevent the rice catching.*

**Serves 4**

| | |
|---|---|
| 275 g basmati* or other long-grain rice | **Per serve** |
| 250 mL (1 cup) light coconut milk* (ingredient check; ◌) | **Energy 1195 kJ (285 cal)** |
| 5 curry leaves* | **Protein 6.4 g** |
| ½ tsp freshly grated ginger | **Total fat 4.0 g** |
| ¼ tsp black mustard seeds | **Saturated fat 3.3 g** |
| 2 x 5 cm strips lemon zest | **Carbohydrate 55.3 g** |
| water (see Step 1) | **Total sugars 1.0 g** |
| | **Dietary fibre <0.1 g** |
| | **Sodium 11 mg** |

1   Put all the ingredients in a pan. Calculate the amount of water required based on the amount stated on the packet for 'absorption method' less 250 mL (1 cup) and add to the rice.

2   Cook as instructed on the packet, taking care not to let the rice catch or burn. When cooked, cover and set aside for 10 minutes. Fluff with a fork and serve immediately.

## (F) Corn Patties

(N)
(V) *A great accompaniment for bacon (ingredient check) and tomatoes for a Sunday morning brunch, or for chops. My crew will munch them as carbohydrate with any meal!*

**Makes 12—serves 4-6**

| | |
|---|---|
| 250 g Desiree potatoes (about 2 medium-sized), cleaned (skin on) | **Per serve** |
| 250 g raw corn kernels (if using canned, rinse and drain well) | **Energy 702 kJ (168 cal)** |
| 250 g creamed corn (ingredient check) | **Protein 5.3 g** |
| 1 tsp finely chopped coriander root* | **Total fat 1.2 g** |
| ½ red chilli, seeded and very finely chopped | **Saturated fat 0.1 g** |
| freshly ground black pepper | **Carbohydrate 33.3 g** |
| 1 cup quick-cook (instant) polenta* | **Total sugars 3.0 g** |
| extra-light olive oil spray* (ingredient check) | **Dietary fibre 4.7 g** |
| | **Sodium 133 mg** |

1 Place the potatoes in a pan of cold water over a high heat. Bring to the boil and simmer for 10 minutes or until just underdone when tested with a sharp knife. Drain and leave to cool. (The potatoes can also be cooked in the microwave: prick the skins with a sharp knife, wrap in kitchen towels and microwave on high for 3 minutes; turn over and microwave for 3 minutes or until just cooked when tested with a sharp knife.)

2 When cool, grate the potatoes into a mixing bowl (the skin acts as a holder for grating—discard after grating the flesh).

3 Mix through the corn, coriander, chilli and black pepper.

4 Spread the polenta out on a plate. Roll a dessertspoonful of the patty mix in the polenta to lightly coat, flattening the patty ball out as it is coated. Transfer the patty to a clean plate and repeat until all the patty mix is used up.

5 Cover the patties and chill thoroughly (this helps to keep the patty intact when it is cooked).

6 Lightly spray a non-stick frying pan with oil and place over a medium-high heat. When hot, place a single layer of patties in the pan and cook for 3–4 minutes on each side, or until lightly browned. Transfer to a pre-warmed plate, cover and keep warm until all the patties are cooked. Serve immediately.

## (C) 'Dilled' Celeriac and Carrots

(F)
(N) *This is a great way to serve these two vegetables, to provide a light, fresh-flavoured bed or accompaniment for fish or meat. The purée may be prepared in advance, covered and refrigerated; simply microwave to reheat immediately before serving.*
(V)

**Serves 4**

| | |
|---|---|
| 400 g celeriac, peeled and cubed (discard any soft centre) | **Per serve** |
| 150 g carrots, peeled and roughly sliced | **Energy 242 kJ (58 cal)** |
| water | **Protein 1.9 g** |
| 2 tsp margarine (Nuttelex brand)* or virgin olive oil* | **Total fat 2.5 g** |
| ¼ tsp chilli oil* (optional; ingredient check) | **Saturated fat 0.4 g** |
| 1 tbs finely chopped fresh dill tips | **Carbohydrate 4.8 g** |
| freshly ground black pepper | **Total sugars 4.7 g** |
| | **Dietary fibre 2.9 g** |
| Garnish | **Sodium 47 mg** |
| sprigs of fresh dill | |

1 Place the celeriac and carrots in a pan with enough boiling water to just cover them. Simmer, partially covered, for 15 minutes or until the vegetables are soft when tested with a sharp knife; do not overcook or the purée will be too liquid.

2 Drain the vegetables thoroughly (retain the stock for blending).

3 Place in a food processor (or use a Bamix blender) with ¼ of the retained liquid and all the remaining ingredients. Blend thoroughly, adding more of the stock as required to form a smooth but not runny purée. Season to taste.

4 Transfer to a warmed serving bowl if the purée is to be served as an accompaniment, and garnish, or spoon on to plates to form a bed for the fish or meat of choice immediately before serving.

## Fragrant Rice

*Try one of these three simple mixes to lift the flavour and colour of long-grain rice—basmati\*, parboiled long-grain (Sungold brand)\* or jasmine\*—with the addition of a few fragrant spices. Scale the quantities of the ingredients according to the number of serves of cooked rice you require. For Mix 1, the spices are cooked with the rice and so it must be cooked by the absorption method. For Mixes 2 and 3, the rice is dressed once it is cooked, so it may be cooked by any of the methods recommended on the packet. Mix 3 is also suitable for dressing short-grain sushi rice for making sushi rolls.*

**Serves 4**

2 cups rice of choice, washed and drained

Mix 1—Fragrant Yellow Rice

1 tsp ground turmeric

5 cardamom pods, lightly crushed

5 cloves

1 cinnamon quill

Mix 2—Sesame and Lime Rice

2 tbs (24 g) sesame seeds

1 tbs (15 mL) pure sesame oil\*

finely grated zest of ½ lime

2 tsp lime juice

⅛ tsp sambal oelek\* (optional; ingredient check)

Mix 3—Pickled Ginger and Nori Rice

2 tbs sushi-style pickled ginger\*, finely chopped (ingredient check—Ginger; ○)

3 tbs (45 mL) brown rice vinegar\* (ingredient check—Vinegar)

3 tbs (45 mL) mirin\* (ingredient check)

1 tsp grated palm sugar\* or soft brown sugar

¼ cup kizami nori\* or ½ sheet roasted nori\* shredded

**Per serve (Mix 1)**

Energy 1378 kJ (329 cal)

Protein 8.0 g

Total fat 0.4 g

Saturated fat 0.1 g

Carbohydrate 72.2 g

Total sugars 0.1 g

Dietary fibre <0.1 g

Sodium <0.1 mg

1 *For Mix 1* Place the rice and spices in a large, heavy-based pan (use a heat diffuser†) or in a rice cooker†. Cook following the packet or rice cooker instructions for the 'absorption method'. Fluff with a fork before serving.

2 *For Mixes 2 and 3* Cook the rice following the packet or rice cooker instructions. While the rice is standing after cooking:

*Mix 2* Place the sesame seeds in a small pan over a low heat and dry roast for 3–4 minutes or until golden, tossing regularly. Remove from the heat and allow to cool slightly. Add the oil, lime zest, juice and sambal oelek, if using, and mix well. When the rice has stood for the required time, add the dressing and fork through the rice to fluff and dress the rice.

*Mix 3* Combine all the dressing ingredients in a small bowl. When the rice has stood for the required time, add the dressing and fork through the rice to fluff and dress the rice.

## Grilled Basil and Olive Polenta

*A very tasty recipe for polenta that isn't brimming with cheese and butter—the lemon-infused olive oil lifts the fresh flavours of the basil and black olives. Try making it with lemon thyme in place of the basil, too.* ① *use vegetable stock.*

**Serves 6-8**

| | |
|---|---|
| extra-light olive oil spray* (ingredient check) | **Per serve** |
| 700 mL chicken* or vegetable stock* (ingredient check—Stock) | Energy 458 kJ (109 cal) |
| 175 g quick-cook (instant) polenta* | Protein 2.6 g |
| 1 tbs (15 mL) lemon-infused olive oil* | Total fat 3.3 g |
| 45 g black olives, pitted and chopped (ingredient check) | Saturated fat 0.5 g |
| 1 tbs finely chopped fresh basil leaves or 1 tsp finely chopped fresh lemon thyme leaves | Carbohydrate 17.1 g |
| freshly ground black pepper | Total sugars 1.0 g |
| | Dietary fibre 3.0 g |
| | Sodium 46 mg |

1 Very lightly oil a 20 cm square or round non-stick baking tin and line the base with baking paper.

2 Place the stock in a pan over a medium heat and bring to a simmer.

3 Add the polenta in a thin stream and cook, stirring continually, for 3–5 minutes or until the mixture comes away from the side of the pan.

4 Stir through the remaining ingredients and spread out evenly in the prepared baking tin. Refrigerate for a minimum of 30 minutes or until firm.

5 Preheat a grill to hot. Slice the polenta into 6–8 pieces, very lightly spray with oil and grill for 5–6 minutes or until golden brown. Serve immediately. (The polenta can also be browned on a barbecue plate.)

## Kumara Purée

*This purée is very simple to prepare. The sweet, soft kumara (or orange sweet potato) makes an excellent bed for char-grilled lamb or a fish fillet such as Atlantic salmon (page 31), or try one of the variations at the end of the recipe. The herb used should complement the meat or fish, for example mint or rosemary with lamb, oregano with chicken and lemon thyme with fish. The purée may be prepared in advance and refrigerated until ready to serve.*

**Serves 4**

| | |
|---|---|
| 1 kg kumara or orange sweet potato, peeled and diced | **Per serve** |
| 1 tbs (15 mL) lemon-infused olive oil* | Energy 807 kJ (193 cal) |
|    or 1 tbs extra-virgin olive oil* plus finely grated zest of ¼ lemon | Protein 4.8 g |
| freshly ground black pepper | Total fat 3.6 g |
| 2 tsp finely chopped fresh herbs (see recipe introduction) | Saturated fat 0.4 g |
| | Carbohydrate 35.3 g |
| | Total sugars 14.0 g |
| | Dietary fibre 4.5 g |
| | Sodium 25 mg |

1 Place the kumara in a pan and just cover with cold water. Bring to the boil, reduce heat and simmer, partially covered, for 10–12 minutes or until the kumara is just soft when tested with a sharp knife (do not overcook or the purée will be runny).

2 Drain well, retaining the liquid for blending. Transfer the kumara to a food processor with the chopped herbs (or use a Bamix blender) with ⅓ cup retained liquid and the oil (and zest if using). Blend thoroughly, slowly adding more of the retained liquid as required to form a smooth but not runny purée. Season to taste.

3 Immediately before serving, reheat the purée in a microwave or on a cooktop, taking care not to allow the purée to catch and burn.

*Variations*

- Substitute 500 g of evenly chopped carrots or diced Sebago potato for half the kumara and mash (rather than purée) with the oil and seasoning.

- Boil 1 kg peeled, evenly chopped carrots until tender and mash with 2 tbs (30 mL) pure maple syrup, 2 tbs (30 mL) lemon juice and ½ teaspoon lightly bruised ajowan seeds*.

- Boil 600 g diced Sebago potatoes with 400 g peeled, sliced parsnips until tender and mash with oil, herb of choice and seasoning.

## Lemon Oil Infused Green Beans with Almonds and Bacon

*This quick and easy way to dress up green beans makes an ideal accompaniment for fish, lamb, pork and poultry dishes.*
*replace almonds with pepitas; omit bacon.*

**Serves 4-6**

| | |
|---|---|
| 100 g short-cut, rindless bacon (ingredient check; ), diced | **Per serve** |
| 600 g tender green beans, trimmed and halved | Energy 468 kJ (112 cal) |
| 60 g (½ cup) flaked almonds, dry roasted** | Protein 7.1 g |
| 1 tsp lemon-infused olive oil* | Total fat 7.9 g |
| freshly ground black pepper | Saturated fat 1.1 g |
| | Carbohydrate 2.9 g |
| | Total sugars 2.3 g |
| | Dietary fibre 3.8 g |
| | Sodium 246 mg |

1 Place the bacon in a non-stick frying pan over a medium-high heat and dry fry until browned and crisp. Transfer to kitchen towels to drain.

2 Place the green beans in a microwave-proof bowl with 1 teaspoon water, cover with plastic wrap and microwave on high for 3 minutes. Shake beans and microwave for a further 1–2 minutes or until cooked al dente. (The beans may also be cooked in a pan of fast-boiling water; do not overcook.)

3 Add the bacon to the beans, toss through all the remaining ingredients and serve immediately.

## Lemon Long-Grain Rice

*A great accompaniment for fish, lamb or chicken and mild curries. This recipe can easily be adapted for any rice that can be cooked by the absorption method: simply vary the amount of water used, the cooking and standing time according to the packet instructions. Use a heavy-based pan or heat diffuser† to prevent the rice catching. Tasty variations: add a teaspoon each of sumac* and finely chopped lemon thyme leaves with the lemon zest; a small can of tomato paste with the water or stock; or 10 finely sliced button mushrooms at the end of cooking. use vegetable stock.*

**Serves 4-6**

| | |
|---|---|
| 1 tsp virgin olive oil* | **Per serve** |
| 3 green shallots*, trimmed and finely sliced | Energy 1985 kJ (474 cal) |
| 1 tsp freshly grated ginger | Protein 11.0 g |
| zest of 2 lemons | Total fat 1.6 g |
| 4 tbs (60 mL) lemon juice | Saturated fat 0.3 g |
| 1 L (4 cups) water or 500 mL water plus 500 mL chicken* or vegetable stock* | Carbohydrate 101.9 g |
| (ingredient check; ) | Total sugars 1.6 g |
| 2 cups (400 g) parboiled long-grain rice (Sungold brand)* | Dietary fibre 2.0 g |
| freshly ground black pepper | Sodium 16 mg |

1 Place oil, shallots and lemon zest in a pan over a medium-high heat. Sauté for 1 minute. Add ginger, and cook for 1 minute.

**2** Add all the remaining ingredients, cover and bring to the boil. Reduce heat, cover and simmer for 25–30 minutes. Remove from the heat and leave to stand for 20–25 minutes, covered.

**3** Fluff rice with a fork and serve immediately.

## Minted and Spiced English Spinach

*Two quick ways of dressing up iron-packed spinach, which form an excellent bed for seared fish or a side dish for roast lamb. To serve hot, the spinach is best prepared immediately before serving. The second mix is also excellent chilled as a side salad, or as a bed for chilled, marinated fish.*

**Serves 4**

Mix 1

1 tsp virgin olive oil*

3 green shallots*, trimmed and roughly chopped

½ tsp yellow mustard seeds

pinch of ground nutmeg

1 bunch English spinach (about 350 g), trimmed, washed and roughly shredded

1 tbs (15 mL) lemon juice

20 fresh mint leaves, shredded

**Per serve (Mix 1)**

Energy 350 kJ (84 cal)

Protein 5.1 g

Total fat 5.2 g

Saturated fat 2.8 g

Carbohydrate 4.3 g

Total sugars 3.2 g

Dietary fibre 5.2 g

Sodium 52 mg

Mix 2

½ tsp virgin olive oil*

1 green shallot*, trimmed and finely chopped

¼ tsp sambal oelek* (ingredient check)

½ tsp tamarind paste* (ingredient check)

200 mL light coconut milk* (ingredient check; )

25 mL lemon juice

1 bunch English spinach (about 350 g), washed and stalks trimmed (retain for another dish)

**1** *Mix 1* Heat the oil in a wok or large, non-stick frying pan over medium heat. Add the shallots and mustard seeds and cook gently for 2 minutes, stirring occasionally. Add the nutmeg and spinach. Cook, stirring, until the spinach has just wilted (1–2 minutes). Mix through the lemon juice and mint, and serve immediately.

**2** *Mix 2* Heat the oil in a wok or large, non-stick frying pan over medium heat. Add the shallot, sambal oelek and tamarind paste and cook for 1 minute, stirring constantly. Add the coconut milk and lemon juice and simmer for 3–4 minutes. Add the spinach and toss until just wilting. Serve immediately, or set aside to cool, cover and chill.

## Minted Spiced Rice with Toasted Pine Nuts

*The herbs, spices, currants and pine nuts in this recipe combine to make a wonderfully flavoured and moist rice bed for fish, chicken, meat or a medley of steamed vegetables. The rice can be made in advance up to the addition of the pine nuts and mint, then reheated in a microwave before forking them through to finish the dish. The rice is also delicious served at room temperature.*

**Serves 4**

½ tsp virgin olive oil*

½ tsp cumin seeds

1 cinnamon quill

1 bay leaf

1½ cups parboiled long-grain rice (Sungold brand)*

3 cups (750 mL) water or volume specified on packet for absorption method

35 g currants (ingredient check—Dried fruit; )

¼ tsp ground turmeric

50 g pine nuts, dry roasted**

20 fresh mint leaves, finely shredded

**Per serve**

Energy 1504 kJ (359 cal)

Protein 6.8 g

Total fat 9.7 g

Saturated fat 0.7 g

Carbohydrate 60.7 g

Total sugars 6.2 g

Dietary fibre 2.6 g

Sodium 8 mg

1   Heat the oil in a heavy-based pan over a medium heat. Add the cumin, cinnamon and bay leaf. Cook for
    1 minute, stirring regularly, or until the cumin seeds are golden and fragrant.

2   Add the rice, stir-fry to coat with the oil–spice mix for 1 minute. Add the water, currants and turmeric, cover
    and bring to the boil. Reduce heat to low and simmer very gently for 15 minutes or until the liquid is absorbed.
    Cover and set aside to stand for 5 minutes.

3   Remove the cinnamon quill and bay leaf. Fork through the pine nuts and shredded mint. Serve immediately
    with topping of choice.

## Orange Zested Roast Parsnips

*While roast parsnips are delicious this simple recipe makes them special! They make a great accompaniment to a roast or a Christmas turkey.*

**Serves 6**

zest of 1 orange

1 tbs (15 mL) extra–light olive oil*

1 kg small parsnips, trimmed and peeled

3 fresh bay leaves, torn into quarters

Per serve

Energy 423 kJ (101 cal)

Protein 3.0 g

Total fat 2.4 g

Saturated fat 0.2 g

Carbohydrate 16.7 g

Total sugars 8.0 g

Dietary fibre 4.2 g

Sodium 32 mg

1   Toss the orange zest in 1 teaspoon of oil. Cover and set aside.

2   Preheat the oven to 220°C (200°C fan forced). Line a baking tray with baking paper. Add the remaining oil,
    parsnips and bay leaves and toss well to coat the parsnips and bay leaves.

3   Bake in oven for 15 minutes or until starting to brown. Toss through the orange zest/oil mix to coat the
    parsnips evenly and bake for a further 5 minutes or until lightly browned. Serve immediately.

## Oven–Roasted and Semi-Dried Roma Tomatoes

*Simple! By varying the cooking time you can produce succulent tomatoes that make a great side dish when served warm to accompany an entrée, a colourful and tasty garnish served chilled, a simple starter when served with fresh asparagus, or just a snack when served on suitable crackers or bread and topped with freshly ground black pepper and chopped fresh herbs. Cook for longer and turn out flavour-packed semi-dried tomatoes that you can store in oil and use in salads or pasta.*

**Makes about 20 halves**

(depending on the size of the tomatoes)

1 kg ripe but firm Roma tomatoes

4 tsp virgin olive oil*

1 tsp soft brown sugar

½ tsp sea salt

½ tsp ground cumin

1 tsp sumac*

freshly ground black pepper

Per tomato (2 halves)

Energy 125 kJ (30 cal)

Protein 1.0 g

Total fat 1.8 g

Saturated fat 0.2 g

Carbohydrate 2.4 g

Total sugars 2.3 g

Dietary fibre 1.2 g

Sodium 135 mg

1   Preheat the oven to 180°C (160°C fan forced).

2   Cut the tomatoes in half lengthways and place on a baking tray cut-side up. Drizzle the olive oil over the tomatoes and sprinkle remaining ingredients over the top. Roast in the oven for 30–40 minutes or until starting to shrivel slightly and the top is starting to brown.

3   For semi-dried tomatoes, extend the cooking time up to 2 hours or until the tomatoes are withered but not totally desiccated. Set aside to cool before transferring to a screw-top jar with any pan juices, top with extra olive oil, cover and store in the refrigerator for up to 2 weeks.

## Potato And Apple Pancake

*A great way to serve potatoes and dress up a chop or cutlet, be it meat or fish. A family favourite is Pork a-top a Pancake (page 53). The mix can be made either into a single pancake which is served by slicing into wedges, or as individual patties 8–10 cm in diameter.*

**Serves 4**

5 medium-sized Desiree potatoes (about 750 g), skin on and cleaned

1 firm red apple (such as Jonagold or Braeburn)

⅓ cup finely chopped fresh parsley

freshly ground black pepper

grated zest of ½ lemon (if serving with fish)

extra-light olive oil spray* (ingredient check)

**Per serve**

Energy 598 kJ (143 cal)

Protein 4.7 g

Total fat 0.2 g

Saturated fat <0.1 g

Carbohydrate 29.8 g

Total sugars 5.8 g

Dietary fibre 4.7 g

Sodium 8 mg

1   Place the potatoes in a pan of cold water over a high heat. Bring to the boil, cover, reduce the heat and simmer gently until slightly undercooked when tested with a sharp knife. Drain, place in a bowl and refrigerate for a minimum of 2 hours. (Note: The potatoes can be cooked in the microwave; this increases the waxiness of the potato when it is grated.)

2   Grate the cold potatoes into a mixing bowl (leave the skin on while grating the potato—it forms a ready-made holder—simply discard the skin once the flesh is grated!).

3   Peel the apple, leaving an area the diameter of the core unpeeled at the top and bottom (provides a non-slippery area to hold while grating) and grate coarsely, discarding the core. Toss the grated apple and potato together with the parsley, black pepper (and lemon if using).

4   Spread the mix out on a very lightly oiled dinner plate and press it together to form a pancake. (If making individual patties, roll 2 tablespoons of the mix into balls and flatten out to a diameter of 8–10 cm.)

5   Lightly spray a large, flat-bottomed non-stick frying pan and place over a high heat. When hot, gently slide in the pancake or patties. Cook the pancake until a golden-brown crust forms on the underside, shaking the pan every so often to prevent it sticking.

6   To turn over, place an upturned plate over the top of the pancake and, while holding your hand on the underside of the plate, invert the pan and the plate so that the pancake is lying on the plate, crust-side up.

7   Respray the pan with oil and return it to the heat. When the pan is hot, gently slide the pancake back into the pan, crust-side up. Cook the underside of the pancake until it is also golden-brown, then transfer the pancake to a pre-warmed plate and place in a slow oven or warming drawer until ready to serve.

## Roast Chat, Pink Fir and Kipfler Potatoes

*The skin on a new potato is delicious roasted, so instead of peeling, just clean the potatoes well, roast as is and retain all the nutrients stored just below the skin. The secret is to use a bare minimum of oil on baking paper in a fast oven to ensure the skins are crispy and fat intake next to zip! They are excellent for building a dish—use the semi-flattened potatoes as the first or second layer of a dish, such as Pork Fillet and Prosciutto Parcels on Cinnamon Poached Quince and Spinach Bed (page 54).*

**Serves 6**

1 kg chat potatoes (the smaller the better) or Kipfler, Pink Fir or Desiree chats

1–2 tsp extra-light olive oil*

Garnish

1 tsp finely chopped fresh herb (such as lemon thyme, parsley, rosemary; optional)

**Per serve**
Energy 480 kJ (115 cal)
Protein 4.0 g
Total fat 0.9 g
Saturated fat 0.1 g
Carbohydrate 22.0 g
Total sugars 0.8 g
Dietary fibre 3.3 g
Sodium 5 mg

1  Preheat the oven to 240°C (220°C fan forced). Line a baking tray with baking paper and add the oil.

2  Clean the potatoes thoroughly and remove any eyes. (For best results for potatoes of greater than 3–4 cm diameter, slice potatoes in half.)

3  Roll the potatoes in oil to lightly coat; for potatoes cut in half, place cut-side up.

4  Roast in the oven for 35–40 minutes or until potatoes are golden brown. Shake the tray twice during cooking to ensure the potatoes roast evenly.

5  Serve immediately as is, or garnished with the chopped fresh herb. To make a bed for char-grilled or barbecued meat, poultry or fish, arrange 3–4 potatoes (depending on size) in the centre of each serving plate. Lightly 'squash' the potatoes with a potato masher to semi-flatten. Top with the vegetable or meat layer of the dish to build the dish.

## Spiced Red Beans in Red Wine

*These are delicious served hot or cold. They are very versatile and can be eaten as a dip, either as is or puréed, on rice cakes or toast as a breakfast or light snack, or as a vegetable accompaniment to a meal. Prepare in advance and reheat as required.*

**Serves 4**

450 g cooked red kidney beans** (if using canned, ingredient check)

150 g tomato paste (ingredient check)

2 green shallots*, trimmed and finely sliced

1 tsp ground cumin

1 tsp paprika

½ tsp ground coriander

½ tsp sambal oelek* (optional; ingredient check)

freshly ground black pepper

100 mL red wine (ingredient check—Wine)

150 mL water

½ tsp dried oregano or 1 tsp shredded fresh oregano

⅓ cup finely shredded fresh flat-leaf (Italian) parsley

**Per serve**
Energy 574 kJ (137 cal)
Protein 11.0 g
Total fat 0.9 g
Saturated fat 0.2 g
Carbohydrate 18.2 g
Total sugars 5.5 g
Dietary fibre 10.2 g
Sodium 31 mg

1  Put all the ingredients except the parsley (and oregano if using fresh) in a pan. Cover and simmer over a low heat for 25–30 minutes, or until tender, stirring occasionally.

2  Stir through the parsley and any fresh oregano. Simmer for 1 minute. Serve immediately or set aside to cool.

## Salads

### ⓒ Warm Spiced Lentil Salad

ⓕ
ⓝ
ⓥ

*This salad uses du Puy green lentils (available from gourmet food shops and some supermarkets), which have quite a different texture and flavour to the more common red or brown lentils, as its base. This salad is a great, high-fibre alternative to rice or potatoes under char-grilled lamb, chicken or fish fillets. The salad can be prepared in advance without adding the fresh herbs and rocket. To serve, re-warm the lentils in a microwave, stir through the leaves and serve immediately. Any left-overs are delicious at room temperature. (For a cheaper version, you can substitute brown lentils.)*

**Serves 4**

Spiced Dressing
4 tsp extra-virgin olive oil*
1 tsp ground cumin
1 tsp ground turmeric
1 tsp ground coriander
pinch of ground cardamom
freshly ground black pepper
1 tbs (15 mL) apple cider vinegar*
1 tbs (15 mL) lime juice
1 tsp honey

Lentils
280 g du Puy lentils*
1 L water
1 tsp finely chopped fresh lemon thyme (with lamb, chicken or fish) or rosemary leaves (lamb)
1 cup wild rocket or baby rocket leaves

**Per serve**
Energy 1236 kJ (295 cal)
Protein 20.6 g
Total fat 4.7 g
Saturated fat 0.6 g
Carbohydrate 42.8 g
Total sugars 5.8 g
Dietary fibre 14.3 g
Sodium 5 mg

1   Put all the dressing ingredients together in a large bowl and mix well. Cover and set aside to infuse.

2   Place the lentils and water in a pan over a high heat and bring to the boil. Reduce the heat and simmer gently for 20–25 minutes or until the lentils are cooked al dente. Drain well and toss in the dressing.

3   Quickly stir through the fresh herbs and rocket. Serve immediately on warmed plates and top with meat or fish of choice.

### ⓒ White Bean, Mint and Rosemary Purée

ⓕ
ⓝ
ⓥ

*This purée makes an excellent bed for marinated char-grilled lamb. If you vary the blend of herbs and other flavouring agents, it is equally good served with beef or fish— replace the mint and rosemary with sun-dried tomatoes (ingredient check; ⓒ) and oregano for beef, or chives and curly parsley or lemon thyme with fish. You can make this purée with other beans, such as borlotti, butter or black eye ... they all have slightly different flavours and are packed with fibre and goodness.*

**Serves 4-6**

480 g cooked cannellini beans** (if using canned, ingredient check)
2 tsp lemon-infused olive oil* or 2 tsp extra-virgin olive oil* plus zest of ⅓ lemon
1 tsp very finely chopped fresh rosemary leaves
10 fresh mint leaves, finely shredded
freshly ground black pepper
6 tbs (90 mL) water plus extra as required

**Per serve**
Energy 351 kJ (84 cal)
Protein 6.6 g
Total fat 1.8 g
Saturated fat 0.3 g
Carbohydrate 11.3 g
Total sugars 0.6 g
Dietary fibre 5.6 g
Sodium 2 mg

1 Put all the ingredients in a food processor and blend to a smooth purée. Add additional water if required to form a thick but moist purée. Transfer to a microwave-proof bowl and cover.

2 Just before serving, heat in the microwave on high for 4 minutes. Remove, stir, cover again and heat for a further 3 minutes or until hot. Leave to stand for 3 minutes before serving.

## Asian Cucumber Salad

*A light salad to serve with satays (see Macadamia and Cashew Satay Sauce, page 77). The salad is best if the cucumber is left to marinate in the dressing for 1 hour before serving, but if time is short simply toss all the ingredients in the dressing and serve immediately. use pepitas instead of cashews.*

**Serves 4**

2 Lebanese cucumbers
1 cup bean sprouts
2 cups shredded Chinese cabbage
⅓ cup roughly chopped fresh coriander leaves
10 fresh mint leaves, finely shredded
50 g raw cashews or pepitas, dry roasted**

**Dressing**
1 tbs (15 mL) white vinegar (ingredient check—Vinegar; )
1 tsp grated palm sugar* or soft brown sugar
¼ tsp pure sesame oil*
1 tsp fish sauce* (ingredient check; )
¼ tsp sambal oelek* or chilli paste* (ingredient check; )

**Per serve**
**Energy 386 kJ (92 cal)**
**Protein 3.6 g**
**Total fat 6.6 g**
**Saturated fat 1.1 g**
**Carbohydrate 4.6 g**
**Total sugars 3.1 g**
**Dietary fibre 2.8 g**
**Sodium 154 mg**

1 Using a vegetable peeler, stripe peel the cucumber lengthways so about half the skin remains intact. Slice the cucumber in half lengthways. Remove the seeds with a teaspoon, slice thinly crossways and transfer to a serving bowl.

2 Mix the vinegar and sugar together in a small bowl, stirring until the sugar has fully dissolved. Mix in the remaining dressing ingredients and pour over the cucumber. Toss to coat, cover and chill for 1 hour.

3 Immediately before serving, toss through all the remaining salad ingredients.

## Black Rice Salad

*This is not the traditional way of cooking or serving black glutinous rice but it makes a very tasty and extremely colourful savoury salad which always looks great at a buffet.*

**Serves 4-6**

300 g black glutinous rice*
3 L cold water
150 g canned corn kernels, rinsed and drained well
2 large, vine-ripened or hydroponic tomatoes, diced
½ cup fresh flat-leaf (Italian) parsley, finely chopped

**Dressing**
1 tbs (15 mL) extra-virgin olive oil*
1 tsp cumin seeds
freshly ground black pepper

**Per serve**
**Energy 948 kJ (226 cal)**
**Protein 4.5 g**
**Total fat 2.6 g**
**Saturated fat 0.3 g**
**Carbohydrate 45.9 g**
**Total sugars 1.6 g**
**Dietary fibre 1.9 g**
**Sodium 38 mg**

Garnish
fresh flat-leaf (Italian) parsley leaves, finely shredded

1   Rinse the rice thoroughly with cold water and place in a large pan with the cold water over a high heat. Bring to the boil, reduce heat and simmer, stirring occasionally, for about 40 minutes or until the rice grains are al dente. (The rice should have the nutty consistency of cooked brown rice.)

2   Rinse thoroughly with cold water and drain well. Transfer to a mixing bowl.

3   Heat the oil in a small pan. When hot, add the cumin seeds and black pepper, and roast for 2 minutes or until the cumin seeds are golden and fragrant, shaking the pan regularly. Pour over the rice immediately (it will sizzle on hitting the grains) and fork through to mix.

4   Mix through the remaining ingredients, transfer to a serving bowl, cover and chill.

5   Gently re-mix the salad just before serving. Serve garnished with the finely shredded parsley.

## Ⓒ Buckwheat Tabouli

Ⓕ
Ⓝ   *A simple variation to the traditional tabouli salad, this recipe is based on nutty-flavoured buckwheat instead of burghul (cracked wheat)—and avoids any risk of 'onion breath' associated with the usual raw onion-based salad! It makes a simple tasty bed for*
Ⓥ   *grilled or barbecued fish or meat and is a great filler for wraps, tacos or anywhere a fresh, citrusy salad base is required.*

**Serves 4**

| | |
|---|---|
| ½ cup kibbled buckwheat* | **Per serve** |
| 500 mL (2 cups) warm water | **Energy 364 kJ (87 cal)** |
| 3 Roma tomatoes, seeded and diced | **Protein 4.1 g** |
| ¾ cup finely chopped fresh flat-leaf (Italian) parsley | **Total fat 0.9 g** |
| ½ cup finely chopped fresh coriander | **Saturated fat 0.2 g** |
| ½ bunch chives, finely chopped | **Carbohydrate 16.9 g** |
| 1 small green shallot*, trimmed and finely chopped | **Total sugars 2.2 g** |
| 3 tbs (45 mL) lemon juice | **Dietary fibre 4.4 g** |
| ½ tsp lemon zest | **Sodium 19 mg** |
| ¼ tsp ground cumin | |
| ¼ tsp paprika | |
| freshly ground black pepper (lots!) | |

1   Put the buckwheat in a bowl and cover with the warm water. Set aside to soak for 30 minutes (the buckwheat should be softened but not soft), stirring occasionally. Drain, rinse with cold water and set aside for 5 minutes to drain well, shaking occasionally to remove any water.

2   Put the drained buckwheat and the remaining ingredients in a bowl and mix thoroughly. Season to taste. Cover and chill well before serving.

## Ⓒ Melon and Brazil Nut Salad

Ⓕ   *This refreshing, simple salad is best served chilled. It is a lovely accompaniment to a good steak with jacket potatoes, or replace the*
Ⓥ   *coriander with mint and serve with lamb.*

**Serves 4**

| | |
|---|---|
| ½ large or 1 small honeydew melon, seeded, peeled and cut into 2 cm dice | **Per serve** |
| 12 brazil nuts, dry roasted** and roughly chopped | **Energy 775 kJ (185 cal)** |
| ¼ cup finely shredded fresh coriander or mint leaves | **Protein 4.2 g** |
| ½ tsp ground cinnamon | **Total fat 5.5 g** |
| tiny sprinkle of cayenne pepper or chilli powder | **Saturated fat 0.9 g** |
| ¼ tsp lime juice | |

Garnish
fresh coriander or mint leaves

Carbohydrate 29.7 g
Total sugars 29.5 g
Dietary fibre 5.3 g
Sodium 195 mg

**1** Put all the ingredients in a serving bowl and mix together gently. Cover and chill for a minimum of 1 hour.

**2** Serve garnished with the coriander leaves.

## Orange and Green Olive Salad

*A refreshing and unusual combination of flavours to set off lightly grilled or barbecued fish fillets.*
*⊙ use olive oil instead of macadamia or walnut oil.*

**Serves 4**

3 medium or 2 large oranges
2 radishes, trimmed and finely sliced
10 green olives, pitted and sliced (ingredient check)
1 tbs sushi-style pickled ginger* (ingredient check—Ginger; ⊙)
¼ cup roughly chopped fresh parsley
1 tbs (15 mL) macadamia* or walnut* or extra-virgin olive oil*
¼ tsp caster sugar
¼ tsp paprika
¼ tsp ground cumin
freshly ground black pepper

Per serve
Energy 531 kJ (127 cal)
Protein 1.5 g
Total fat 4.9 g
Saturated fat 0.5 g
Carbohydrate 17.7 g
Total sugars 17.1 g
Dietary fibre 7.0 g
Sodium 110 mg

**1** Slice off all the orange peel and pith with a sharp knife. Dice the oranges, discard any pips and catch any juice in a small bowl. Put the diced oranges in a serving bowl.

**2** Add the radishes, olives, ginger and parsley.

**3** Add the oil, sugar and spices to the orange juice and whisk to combine. Toss through the orange mix. Cover and refrigerate for a minimum of 1 hour before serving.

## Potato and Tomato Salad

*A potato salad with a difference—the turmeric gives the potatoes a wonderful yellow-orange hue to contrast with the red of the tomatoes and green of the herbs. This salad is excellent with grilled fish or lamb. Select potatoes with smooth skins if you leave them unpeeled (my preference).*

**Serves 4**

400 g chat potatoes (Coliban or Desiree), cleaned and cut into 1.5-2 cm dice
1 tsp ground turmeric
⅓ cup shredded fresh flat-leaf (Italian) parsley
    (to accompany lamb, ¼ cup parsley plus 10 fresh mint leaves)
1 tbs capers*, drained (ingredient check; ⊙)
3 medium-sized vine-ripened or hydroponic tomatoes, peeled and cut into eighths
juice of 1 lemon
½ lime, peeled and very finely diced
1 tsp extra-virgin olive oil*
2 tbs (30 mL) mirin* (ingredient check)
freshly ground black pepper

Per serve
Energy 425 kJ (101 cal)
Protein 3.5 g
Total fat 1.4 g
Saturated fat 0.1 g
Carbohydrate 15.8 g
Total sugars 2.8 g
Dietary fibre 3.1 g
Sodium 27 mg

1  Put the potatoes and turmeric in a pan of cold water. Bring to the boil and cook for 6–7 minutes or until just tender. Drain well and leave to cool and air dry.

2  Combine potatoes and all remaining ingredients in a mixing bowl. Arrange in the centre of 4 serving plates as a bed for the grilled or barbecued fish or lamb cut of choice.

## Prosciutto, Mushroom and Cashew Salad

*A tasty salad that can be served alone as a starter or as an accompaniment to an entrée.*

**Serves 4**

| | |
|---|---|
| 3 tbs (45 mL) macadamia oil* | **Per serve** |
| 1 tbs (15 mL) balsamic vinegar* (ingredient check—Vinegar; ◯) | **Energy 1008 kJ (241 cal)** |
| 200 g button mushrooms, cleaned and trimmed | **Protein 7.3 g** |
| 4 slices prosciutto*, trimmed of fat (ingredient check; ◯) | **Total fat 21.3 g** |
| 75 g raw cashews, dry roasted** | **Saturated fat 2.7 g** |
| 75 g cherry tomatoes, halved | **Carbohydrate 4.7 g** |
| 100 g baby spinach leaves | **Total sugars 1.9 g** |
| sprinkle of caraway seeds | **Dietary fibre 2.8 g** |
| freshly ground black pepper | **Sodium 245 mg** |

Dressing
1 tsp balsamic vinegar* (ingredient check—Vinegar; ◯)
1 tsp macadamia oil*

1  Combine the oil and vinegar in a bowl. Add the mushrooms and toss to coat. Set aside for 10 minutes.

2  Heat a non-stick frying pan over a medium-high heat. When hot, add the prosciutto and cook for 2–3 minutes to crisp. Set aside on a paper towel to drain and cool. Chop roughly.

3  Add the mushrooms to the pan and cook for 2–3 minutes, or until just starting to soften. Set aside to cool.

4  Immediately before serving, put mushrooms, any pan juices and remaining salad ingredients in a serving bowl. Drizzle over the dressing vinegar and macadamia oil and toss the salad gently.

## Warm Roast Vegetable Salad

*This salad is delicious served as an accompaniment to red meat, or on round of suitable crispy warm bread as a light lunch. It may be prepared in advance and warmed in a microwave just before serving.*

**Serves 4–6**

| | |
|---|---|
| 3 green shallots*, trimmed and roughly sliced | **Per serve** |
| 500 g diced eggplant | **Energy 554 kJ (132 cal)** |
| 500 g Roma tomatoes, halved | **Protein 5.1 g** |
| 1 green capsicum (about 200 g), seeded and sliced | **Total fat 7.5 g** |
| 3 tbs (45 mL) extra-light olive oil* | **Saturated fat 0.9 g** |
| 2 tsp balsamic vinegar* (ingredient check—Vinegar; ◯) | **Carbohydrate 10.5 g** |
| ½ tsp ground cumin | **Total sugars 5.3 g** |
| 200 g cooked chickpeas** (if using canned, ingredient check) | **Dietary fibre 5.5 g** |
| ¼ cup shredded fresh flat-leaf (Italian) parsley | **Sodium 17 mg** |
| freshly ground black pepper | |

1  Preheat the oven to 200°C (180°C fan forced).

2   Put the shallots, eggplant, tomatoes and capsicum in a baking tray. Add the oil, vinegar and cumin and toss to coat. Roast in the oven for 25–30 minutes or until the vegetables are tender, turning once during roasting. Toss through the chickpeas and roast for a further 5 minutes.

3   Transfer the vegetables to a serving bowl. Mix through the parsley and black pepper. Cover and set aside to rest for 5 minutes. Serve immediately.

## Watercress, Rocket and Marigold Salad

*This is a spicy and colourful salad, ideal to serve with more strongly flavoured meat such as lamb or kangaroo.*

*Balsamic and Mustard Vinaigrette—balsamic vinegar may contain caramel (ingredient check).*

**Serves 4**

1 bunch watercress, trimmed and roughly shredded (discard any thick stems)

150 g baby rocket leaves

3 marigold flowers—preferably different colours, such as orange, yellow, variegated

1 quantity Balsamic and Mustard Vinaigrette (page 106) or Orange and Ginger Dressing (page 108)

**Per serve**

Energy 661 kJ (158 cal)

Protein 3.2 g

Total fat 14.4 g

Saturated fat 1.6 g

Carbohydrate 3.1 g

Total sugars 2.7 g

Dietary fibre 3.3 g

Sodium 46 mg

1   Rinse the watercress and rocket leaves and drain thoroughly. Put in a salad bowl.

2   Pick the marigold petals off the flowers and toss through the watercress and rocket.

3   Toss the dressing through the salad immediately before serving, or serve on the side.

## White Cabbage, Tomato and Pickled Ginger Salad

*A light, crunchy salad to serve with red meat or fish. If you're a pickled ginger freak like me, increase the amount of ginger added, to give a bit more bite!*

**Serves 4-6**

¼ white cabbage (about 425 g), medium to finely shredded

3 hydroponic, vine-ripened or Roma tomatoes (about 350 g), diced

2 tsp lemon juice

2 tsp sushi-style pickled ginger*, finely chopped (ingredient check—Ginger; ◯)

2 tsp pickled ginger juice* (ingredient check—Ginger; ◯)

¼ cup finely chopped fresh parsley (retain some for the garnish)

freshly ground black pepper

Garnish

retained chopped parsley

**Per serve**

Energy 102 kJ (24 cal)

Protein 1.3 g

Total fat 0.1 g

Saturated fat <0.1 g

Carbohydrate 3.1 g

Total sugars 3.0 g

Dietary fibre 2.0 g

Sodium 13 mg

1   Mix all the ingredients together in a serving bowl, cover and refrigerate.

2   Just before serving, re-mix the salad and garnish with chopped parsley.

## Dressings

So often a simple dressing or marinade is all that is required to transform an 'ordinary' dish into something special. Serving or meal suggestions are given for each of the recipes included below to get you started. To reduce oil and calorie intake, make vinaigrettes from milder vinegars like balsamic, champagne, fruit, or rice wine vinegar—because they are less pungent, you can use a higher ratio of vinegar to oil. You will find most of these dressings are based on a reduced oil:vinegar ratio.

### Balsamic and Mustard Vinaigrette

*A classic balsamic vinaigrette with the added flavour kick of a seeded mustard. It is excellent served over a mesclun salad mix or cress salad.*

**Makes ½ cup**

| | |
|---|---|
| 2 tsp wholegrain mustard (ingredient check—Mustard) | **Per 100 mL** |
| 2 tbs (30 mL) balsamic vinegar* (ingredient check—Vinegar; ) | **Energy 1812 kJ (432 cal)** |
| 1 tbs (15 mL) lemon juice | **Protein 0.9 g** |
| 4 tbs (60 mL) extra-virgin olive oil* | **Total fat 44.2 g** |
| 1 tsp honey | **Saturated fat 5.2 g** |
| freshly ground black pepper | **Carbohydrate 5.7 g** |
| | **Total sugars 5.3 g** |
| | **Dietary fibre 0.4 g** |
| | **Sodium 8 mg** |

1  Whisk all the ingredients together well to combine.

### Basil and Tomato Vinaigrette

*A flavour-packed, chunky-style vinaigrette to dress up char-grilled or barbecued lamb or over a mixed leaf salad.*

**Makes 1 cup**

| | |
|---|---|
| 50 mL extra-virgin olive oil* | **Per 100 mL** |
| 50 mL mirin* (ingredient check) | **Energy 849 kJ (203 cal)** |
| 50 mL red wine vinegar* (ingredient check—Vinegar; ) | **Protein 1.2 g** |
| ½ tsp balsamic vinegar* (ingredient check—Vinegar; ) | **Total fat 18.1 g** |
| ¼ tsp ground cumin | **Saturated fat 2.2 g** |
| freshly ground black pepper | **Carbohydrate 3.3 g** |
| 3 Roma tomatoes, peeled and finely chopped | **Total sugars 3.1 g** |
| 10 fresh basil or mint leaves, finely shredded | **Dietary fibre 1.4 g** |
| | **Sodium 19 mg** |

1  Whisk the oil, mirin, vinegars, cumin and black pepper together to combine. Add the tomatoes and basil or mint leaves. Leave to stand at room temperature. Stir well before spooning over the meat.

### Caper Dressing

*Get away from serving smoked salmon with straight capers—dress the salmon up as a starter with this easy caper dressing. Try serving the salmon on a bed of baby rocket leaves and diced honeydew melon, then drizzle the Caper Dressing over the top.*

**Serves 4**

| | |
|---|---|
| ⅛ preserved lemon (about 5 g rind, see below)* (ingredient check) or zest of ½–1 lemon | **Per serve** |
| juice of ½ lemon | **Energy 152 kJ (36 cal)** |
| 2 tbs capers* (about 20 g), roughly chopped (ingredient check; ) | **Protein 0.2 g** |
| 1 tbs chopped chives | **Total fat 3.4 g** |
| 1 tbs chopped fresh dill tips | **Saturated fat 0.4 g** |
| | **Carbohydrate 1.1 g** |

1 small green shallot*, trimmed and very finely sliced

¼ tsp caster sugar

1 tbs (15 mL) extra–virgin olive oil*

freshly ground black pepper

Total sugars 1.1 g

Dietary fibre 0.2 g

Sodium 33 mg

**1** Remove the flesh and pith from the preserved lemon and discard. Rinse well under cold water, pat dry and dice very finely.

**2** Combine the diced lemon with the remaining ingredients and serve over smoked salmon or grilled fish.

## Coconut and Chilli Dressing

*A simple dressing to serve over a chicken, prawn or pasta salad, or a cold vegetable salad such as blanched green beans, sugar snap and snow peas with celery, fennel and grape tomatoes.*

**Makes ¾ cup**

100 mL light coconut milk* (ingredient check; ◯)

⅓ cup finely shredded fresh coriander leaves

zest of ½ lime

2 tbs (30 mL) lime juice

1 tbs (15 mL) fish sauce* (ingredient check; ◯)

1 small chilli, seeded and very finely chopped

freshly ground black pepper

Per 100 mL

Energy 205 kJ (49 cal)

Protein 1.9 g

Total fat 3.3 g

Saturated fat 2.8 g

Carbohydrate 2.7 g

Total sugars 1.9 g

Dietary fibre 1.0 g

Sodium 856 mg

**1** Put all the ingredients in a small bowl and mix well. Cover and refrigerate to chill lightly.

**2** To serve, spoon over salad.

## Green Olive Dressing

*Excellent spooned over shredded crisp iceberg or cos lettuce to accompany poached or char-grilled white fish—or for something special try it with Fig and Pancetta Parcels (page 18).*

**Makes ⅓ cup**

2 tbs (30 mL) extra–virgin olive oil*

2 tbs (30 mL) apple cider vinegar*

2 tbs (30 mL) lemon juice

1 tsp apple juice concentrate*

50-55 g green olives, pitted and finely chopped (ingredient check)

1 tsp finely chopped fresh oregano or thyme leaves

Per 100 mL

Energy 1551 kJ (370 cal)

Protein 1.2 g

Total fat 39.0 g

Saturated fat 5.1 g

Carbohydrate 9.3 g

Total sugars 5.2 g

Dietary fibre 12.9 g

Sodium 486 mg

**1** Put all the ingredients together in a glass jar and shake well.

**2** Pour over lettuce just before serving.

## Hummus Dressing

*A Lebanese-style dressing that is great as an alternative to mayonnaise for coleslaw and potato salad, or over falafel or green leafy salads with marinated, char-grilled meat. There are brands of canned puréed chickpeas available; check ingredients carefully if using in place of whole chickpeas. For potato salad, lightly boil chat potatoes with mint until al dente, drain and allow to cool slightly before adding dry roasted sesame seed, diced avocado tossed in lemon juice and finely sliced green shallots\*. Add dressing and toss to coat. Serve garnished with the sliced green shallot tops.*

**Makes ½ cup**

| | |
|---|---|
| 50 g cooked chickpeas\*\* (if using canned, ingredient check) | **Per 100 mL** |
| 2 tbs (30 mL) lemon juice | Energy 607 kJ (145 cal) |
| 1 tbs (15 mL) tahini\* | Protein 7.1 g |
| ¼ tsp ground cumin | Total fat 8.8 g |
| ½ tsp paprika | Saturated fat 1.4 g |
| freshly ground black pepper | Carbohydrate 8.1 g |
| water | Total sugars 1.2 g |
| | Dietary fibre 4.0 g |
| | Sodium 6 mg |

1  Put all the ingredients except the water in a food processor and blend. Slowly add enough water while processing to form a smooth, pourable dressing.

2  Chill for a minimum of 1 hour before serving.

## Mango Mayonnaise

*A light mayonnaise-style sauce which is excellent served with poached or grilled white fish or chicken fillets, or Chickpea Patties (page 15). It also makes a good dip to serve as a nibble with fresh fruit, vegetables. ⓝ replace almond meal with 1 tbs rice crumbs (Orgran brand)\*.*

**Makes ½ cup**

| | |
|---|---|
| 3 tbs (45 mL) light coconut milk\* (ingredient check; ⓥ) | **Per 100 mL** |
| 150 g fresh, ripe mango flesh (from 1 small mango) or 170 g can mango pulp | Energy 865 kJ (206 cal) |
| 1 tsp freshly grated ginger or sushi–style pickled ginger\* (ingredient check—Ginger; ⓥ) | Protein 5.5 g |
| zest of ½ lemon | Total fat 12.2 g |
| 1 tbs (15 mL) lemon juice | Saturated fat 2.7 g |
| 3 tbs almond meal | Carbohydrate 17.8 g |
| freshly ground black pepper | Total sugars 16.4 g |
| | Dietary fibre 3.7 g |
| | Sodium 11 mg |

1  Put all the ingredients in a blender and process until smooth. Cover and chill.

2  Serve spooned over fish, chicken or burgers.

## Orange and Ginger Dressing

*A zesty dressing suitable for carrot or dark green leafy salads.*

**Makes ½ cup**

| | |
|---|---|
| 1 tsp freshly grated ginger | **Per 100 mL** |
| 1 small green shallot\*, trimmed and very finely chopped | Energy 1666 kJ (398 cal) |
| 2 tbs (30 mL) fresh orange juice, strained | Protein 0.4 g |
| 1 tbs (15 mL) red wine vinegar\* (ingredient check—Vinegar; ⓥ) | Total fat 43.2 g |
| tiny pinch of caster sugar | Saturated fat 4.0 g |
| freshly ground black pepper | Carbohydrate 2.7 g |

2 tbs (30 mL) macadamia oil*

2 tbs (30 mL) grapeseed* or avocado* or virgin olive oil*

Total sugars 2.6 g

Dietary fibre 0.5 g

Sodium 11 mg

1 Combine all the ingredients except the oils together in a small mixing bowl.

2 Whisk in the oils until thoroughly blended. Chill before serving.

## Pesto Vinaigrette

*A tasty dressing to serve over wild rocket, a mixed green salad or pasta.*

**Makes ⅓ cup**

3 tbs (45 mL) white wine vinegar* (ingredient check—Vinegar; ◯)

4 tsp (20 mL) Vietnamese Mint Pesto (page 85)

2 tbs (30 mL) extra-virgin olive oil*

freshly ground black pepper

Per 100 mL

Energy 1616 kJ (386 cal)

Protein 1.9 g

Total fat 39.9 g

Saturated fat 4.9 g

Carbohydrate 2.5 g

Total sugars 1.6 g

Dietary fibre 1.7 g

Sodium 38 mg

1 Put all the ingredients in a small bowl or jug and stir to combine.

2 Cover and refrigerate until ready to use.

## Sun-Dried Tomato Dressing

*This is a thick, creamy dressing to serve with rocket and lettuce-based salads, bean salads or simply tossed through pasta.*

**Makes ¾ cup**

8 dehydrated sun-dried tomatoes*

4 tbs (60 mL) tomato passata* (ingredient check) or 1 tbs tomato paste (ingredient check) plus 3 tbs water

2 tsp tomato paste (ingredient check)

4 tbs (60 mL) balsamic vinegar* (ingredient check—Vinegar; ◯)

4 tbs water

1 tsp finely chopped fresh oregano leaves (dried can be substituted but fresh is best)

1 large red chilli, seeded (optional)

3 tbs (45 mL) extra-virgin olive oil*

extra 3-4 tbs water, to thin to taste

freshly ground black pepper

Per 100 mL

Energy 1069 kJ (255 cal)

Protein 2.2 g

Total fat 22.2 g

Saturated fat 2.7 g

Carbohydrate 7.4 g

Total sugars 7.0 g

Dietary fibre 2.8 g

Sodium 22 mg

1 Rehydrate the tomatoes by placing in a bowl and covering with boiling water. Leave to stand for 12–15 minutes to soften (be alert, as the tomatoes will become mushy if oversoaked). Drain, gently squeezing out any excess water.

2 Put the tomatoes, passata, tomato paste, vinegar, water, oregano and chilli if using in a food processor. Blend until smooth.

3 With the processor running, stream in the olive oil and process until thoroughly mixed through the tomato base. Add additional water and black pepper to taste.

## Sweet Chilli Dressing

*This is excellent served warm or at room temperature as a dipping sauce or dressing for patties—take your pick of fish, potato or corn—or as a spunky dressing to go with a strong-leafed salad such as rocket or watercress. If serving at room temperature, add gelatine or agar powder\* to the pan after simmering as this will suspend the chilli, ginger and lemon grass.*

**Makes ¼ cup**

| | |
|---|---|
| 3 tbs (45 mL) lime juice | **Per 100 mL** |
| 1 tbs (15 mL) soft brown sugar | **Energy 380 kJ (90 cal)** |
| 1 tsp freshly grated ginger | **Protein 1.0 g** |
| ½–1 bird's eye chilli, seeded and very finely chopped | **Total fat 0.2 g** |
| 1 tbs finely chopped lemon grass\* (white part only) | **Saturated fat <0.1 g** |
| ¼ tsp fish sauce\* (ingredient check; ◯) | **Carbohydrate 20.0 g** |
| 1 tsp gelatine (or ¼ tsp agar powder\*) | **Total sugars 19.7 g** |
| | **Dietary fibre 0.4 g** |
| | **Sodium 218 mg** |

1  Put all the ingredients in a small pan over a medium heat, stirring until the sugar has dissolved. Simmer for 1 minute to reduce slightly. If serving at room temperature, add gelatine or agar powder and stir to dissolve.

2  Serve warm, at room temperature or chilled.

## Marinades

## Asian Marinade

*Versatile plus! This is an excellent oyster sauce\*-free dressing for Thai Beef Salad (page 23) or other cuts of beef or lamb (for instance, fillet, backstrap or cutlets) where the meat is marinated after it has been barbecued or char-grilled rather than before. Allow the meat to cool before slicing (if required) and then place in the marinade for a minimum of 1 hour before serving chilled or at room temperature. It is equally good used to marinate meat, such as kebabs, prior to barbecuing.*

**Makes 135 mL—serves 6–8**

| | |
|---|---|
| 3 tbs (45 mL) dry vermouth (ingredient check—Wine) | **Per serve** |
| 3 tbs (45 mL) fish sauce\* (ingredient check; ◯) | **Energy 235 kJ (56 cal)** |
| 3 tbs (45 mL) pure sesame oil\* | **Protein 0.7 g** |
| ¼ tsp shrimp paste\* (ingredient check; ◯) | **Total fat 5.1 g** |
| ½ tsp tamarind paste\* (ingredient check) | **Saturated fat 0.7 g** |
| ½ red bird's eye chilli, seeded and very finely chopped (optional) | **Carbohydrate 0.8 g** |
| | **Total sugars 0.6 g** |
| | **Dietary fibre <0.1 g** |
| | **Sodium 609 mg** |

1  Mix all ingredients together well.

2  Coat the cooled, char-grilled meat thoroughly in the marinade. Cover and refrigerate for a minimum of 1 hour.

3  Serve the meat chilled or at room temperature on top of bed of salad or refreshed blanched vegetables of choice, drizzled with the remaining marinade.

## BBQ Leg of Lamb 'Marinade'

*More like a stuffing than a marinade, this cooks to form a wonderful crust when the lamb is roasted slowly on a barbecue or in the oven, and the resulting meat juices add a wealth of flavour to a gravy.*

**For up to a 2 kg leg of lamb**

zest of 2 lemons

juice of ½ lemon

6 sun-dried tomatoes*, finely chopped (ingredient check; ◎)

2 tsp sun-dried tomato oil* (ingredient check; ◎) or extra-light olive oil*

1 sprig of fresh rosemary, leaves picked and very finely chopped

5 kaffir lime leaves*, very finely chopped

freshly ground black pepper

| Per serve | |
|---|---|
| Energy 65 kJ (15 cal) | |
| Protein 0.2 g | |
| Total fat 1.4 g | |
| Saturated fat 0.2 g | |
| Carbohydrate 1.0 g | |
| Total sugars 0.4 g | |
| Dietary fibre 0.6 g | |
| Sodium 3 mg | |

**1** Put all the marinade ingredients in a small bowl and mix well.

**2** Trim the lamb of any excess fat. Using a sharp knife, score 0.5–1 cm deep cuts diagonally across the top surface, 2–2.5 cm apart. Repeat the scoring at right angles to the first, to form a diamond pattern over the meat.

**3** Stuff the scores with the marinade. Cover and refrigerate for a minimum of 2 hours or overnight before barbecuing or roasting as usual.

## Curried Coconut Marinade

*A simple marinade for white fish fillet, prawns or prawn meat and fish kebabs. A dash of curry powder always enhances the natural sweetness of prawns.*

**Makes ⅔ cup**

125 mL light coconut milk* (ingredient check; ◎)

juice of ½ lime

1 tbs curry powder* (ingredient check)

1 tbs (15 mL) fish sauce* (ingredient check; ◎)

freshly ground black pepper

| Per 100 mL | |
|---|---|
| Energy 287 kJ (68 cal) | |
| Protein 1.9 g | |
| Total fat 4.7 g | |
| Saturated fat 3.9 g | |
| Carbohydrate 4.6 g | |
| Total sugars 2.3 g | |
| Dietary fibre 0.1 g | |
| Sodium 966 mg | |

**1** Put all the ingredients in a mixing bowl and whisk to combine.

**2** Add the fish or prawns and marinate for a minimum of 1 hour or overnight.

## Pomegranate Molasses and Red Wine Marinade

*The naturally tart flavour of the concentrated pomegranate juice makes this simple marinade excellent for any cut of lamb before char-grilling or barbecuing. It is also delicious with quail.*

**Serves 4**

2 tbs (30 mL) full-bodied red wine, such as merlot (ingredient check—Wine)

1 tbs pomegranate molasses*

1 tsp extra-light olive oil*

1 tsp grated palm sugar* or soft brown sugar

2 fresh bay leaves, bruised

zest of ½ orange

| Per serve | |
|---|---|
| Energy 103 kJ (25 cal) | |
| Protein 0.1 g | |
| Total fat 1.1 g | |
| Saturated fat 0.1 g | |
| Carbohydrate 2.3 g | |

¼ tsp dry mustard powder* (ingredient check)

freshly ground black pepper

Total sugars 0.4 g

Dietary fibre <0.1 g

Sodium 1 mg

1 Mix all the ingredients together in a bowl.

2 Add the lamb, toss to coat, cover and marinate for a minimum of 2 hours or overnight.

## Preserved Lemon Chermoula

*An excellent marinade for lamb, poultry, and fish—simply baste these well with the chermoula, cover and refrigerate for a minimum of 1 hour for meat and 30 minutes for fish before char-grilling, barbecuing or baking. If using as a marinade for whole fish, score the skin and flesh first so that the flavours permeate the fish, wrap in foil or baking paper to retain all the juices. When char-grilling or barbecuing ensure the chermoula does not burn.*

**Makes ¾ cup**

¼ preserved lemon* (ingredient check)

zest of 1 lime

1 tbs (15 mL) lime juice

1 tsp extra–light olive oil*

½ cup finely chopped fresh coriander leaves

½ cup finely chopped fresh flat–leaf (Italian) parsley leaves

3 green shallots*, trimmed and very finely chopped

¼ tsp sambal oelek* or chilli paste* (ingredient check; )

¼ tsp ground cumin

good pinch of ground cinnamon

freshly ground black pepper

Per 100 mL

Energy 187 kJ (45 cal)

Protein 1.9 g

Total fat 2.6 g

Saturated fat 0.3 g

Carbohydrate 2.7 g

Total sugars 2.4 g

Dietary fibre 3.3 g

Sodium 32 mg

1 Remove the flesh and pith from the preserved lemon and discard. Rinse the rind thoroughly under cold running water, pat dry and dice finely. Place in a glass or ceramic bowl.

2 Add all the remaining ingredients and mix well

## Satay Marinade

*Marinate your beef, chicken or lamb satays or kebabs for 1–2 hours before char-grilling—or best of all, barbecuing over charcoal—and serve with Macadamia and Cashew Satay Sauce (page 77) for a great starter, or a main serve with steaming jasmine rice* and an Asian Cucumber Salad (page 101).*

**Marinade for up to 1.5 kg of meat**

2 tbs (30 mL) honey

½ tsp ground coriander

½ tsp ground turmeric

freshly ground black pepper

1 tsp sambal oelek* (ingredient check)

4 tbs (60 mL) lemon juice

5 tbs (75 mL) light coconut milk* (ingredient check; ◉)

1 tbs (15 mL) fish sauce* (ingredient check; ◉)

Per serve

Energy 88 kJ (21 cal)

Protein 0.3 g

Total fat 0.5 g

Saturated fat 0.4 g

Carbohydrate 3.9 g

Total sugars 3.7 g

Dietary fibre <0.1 g

Sodium 167 mg

1 Put the spices in a large mixing bowl with 2 tablespoons lemon juice. Stir to combine. Mix in all the remaining ingredients. Coat the meat in the marinade, cover and chill for a minimum of 2 hours. Place bamboo skewers in water to soak.

2 Thread the meat onto the skewers and place on hot char-grill or barbecue, basting the meat with remaining marinade during cooking.

Desserts, Cakes and 'Puddings'

## Basic Flour Mix and Basic Self-Raising Flour Mix

*Nutritionally, this flour mix is a good source of protein, fibre and vitamins, being based on a legume (chickpeas), and a cereal flour (rice). When doing a lot of baking, I find it is easier to make the flour up in bulk rather than measuring out the different ingredients each time I want to bake. Mixing the flours thoroughly is a critical step to ensure the four flours are evenly blended. Flour storage is likewise critical—I store the mix in a loose-top container so that it can breathe as this prevents the flour from sweating and becoming rancid or providing the ideal home for weevils. Paper and calico bags are also ideal. See Glossary—Ingredients for flour suppliers.*

**Makes 1.5 kg**

Plain Flour

500 g potato flour

500 g besan flour*

250 g fine white rice flour*

250 g arrowroot

Self-raising Flour

gluten-free/wheat-free baking powder (Ward's brand* or home-made;
   see Glossary—Basic Flour Mix)

**Per 100 g**

**Energy 1502 kJ (358 cal)**

**Protein 10.8 g**

**Total fat 2.5 g**

**Saturated fat 0.3 g**

**Carbohydrate 74.1 g**

**Total sugars 1.9 g**

**Dietary fibre 2.6 g**

**Sodium 41 mg**

1 Put all the flours together in a large, strong plastic bag. Hold the top of the bag closed and toss to work the flours together. Sift the flour into a second bag. Sift twice more to ensure the flour is thoroughly mixed and lump free. The flour will not need to be sifted prior to use.

2 Transfer plain flour to chosen storage container and store in a cool, dry place.

3 *Self-raising flour* Add baking powder to plain flour as required—1 teaspoon per 125 g.

## Apples Poached in Golden Syrup Citrus Sauce

*Easy—and equally good served with oranges, pears or a combination of fruits! The fruit may be served warm or at room temperature, as is or accompanied by a sorbet or gelato of choice.*

**Serves 4**

4 red apples, stalks intact

Sauce

3 tbs (75 g) golden syrup (ingredient check; ◎)

zest of 1 lemon

4 tbs (60 mL) lemon juice

200 mL water

Garnish

lemon zest

shredded fresh mint leaves

**Per serve**

**Energy 579 kJ (138 cal)**

**Protein 0.6 g**

**Total fat 0.2 g**

**Saturated fat <0.1 g**

**Carbohydrate 34.5 g**

**Total sugars 33.7 g**

**Dietary fibre 3.2 g**

**Sodium 26 mg**

1 Place all the sauce ingredients in a pan over a medium heat and simmer for 4 minutes, stirring to combine.

2 While the sauce is simmering, peel and core the apples, leaving stalks intact. Place in the sauce, cover and simmer for 6–8 minutes, or until the apples are just softened when tested with a sharp knife, turning them in the sauce 3–4 times during cooking.

3 Transfer the apples to 4 serving plates. Boil the sauce over a high heat for 2 minutes to reduce. Drizzle the sauce over the apples and serve garnished with the lemon zest and mint.

## ⓒ Black Rice Pudding with Mango Sauce

Ⓕ  *The black rice has a lovely nutty taste and is best sweetened with palm sugar\*. The simple mango sauce provides a wonderful*
Ⓝ  *flavour and colour contrast to this rice; it may be made without the coconut milk, in which case reduce the ginger to 10–15 g*
Ⓥ

**Serves 4-6**

Rice

100 g black glutinous rice\*

50 g white glutinous rice\*

750 mL (3 cups) water

30 g grated palm sugar\* or soft brown sugar

Mango Sauce

175 g ripe mango flesh (about 1 small mango)

50 g sushi-style pickled ginger\* (ingredient check—Ginger; ⓒ)

100 mL light coconut milk\* (ingredient check; ⓒ)

zest of ½ lime

Garnish

washed bougainvillea flowers or equivalent

Per serve

Energy 591 kJ (141 cal)

Protein 2.1 g

Total fat 1.0 g

Saturated fat 0.9 g

Carbohydrate 31.0 g

Total sugars 10.2 g

Dietary fibre 0.9 g

Sodium 8 mg

**1**   Put the rice in a sieve and rinse thoroughly under cold running water. Drain well.

**2**   Place the rice and water in a heavy-bottomed pan over a medium heat and bring to the boil. Reduce the heat and simmer for 30 minutes or until the rice is just al dente, stirring occasionally.

**3**   Stir in the sugar and continue to simmer very slowly until almost all the liquid is absorbed; the last of the liquid will be absorbed as the rice cools. Transfer to a bowl, cover and chill.

**4**   To make the mango sauce, place all the sauce ingredients in a food processor and blend to a purée. Cover and chill.

**5**   To serve, spoon the rice onto dessert plates. Top with the mango sauce and garnish with a flower.

## ⓒ Blackberry and Cassis Tart with Fresh Mixed Berries

Ⓕ  *The tart simply melts in your mouth, drizzled with the blackberry-cassis sauce. The recipe is equally good made with strawberries*
Ⓝ  *or boysenberries.  ⓒ use guar gum; check cordial if added vitamin C is a problem (see Avoiding Corn, page 161).*
Ⓥ

**Serves 6**

Pastry

120 g Basic Flour Mix (page 113)

50 g tapioca flour\*

30 g caster sugar

½ tsp xanthan\* or guar gum\*

¼ tsp ajowan seeds\* or caraway seeds

75 g margarine (Nuttelex brand)\*

35 g rice syrup\* (ingredient check)

3-4 tsp extra-light olive oil\*

Blackberry and Cassis Filling

1 x 425 g can blackberries in syrup

4 tbs (60 mL) light coconut milk\* (ingredient check; ⓒ)

zest of ½ lemon, very finely grated

2 tbs (30 mL) Monin Cassis Syrup\* or blackcurrant cordial, such as Bickford's brand

Per serve

Energy 1387 kJ (331 cal)

Protein 3.2 g

Total fat 13.2 g

Saturated fat 2.7 g

Carbohydrate 50.9 g

Total sugars 26.0 g

Dietary fibre 3.0 g

Sodium 74 mg

1¼ tsp agar powder*

125 mL (½ cup) boiling water

Syrup

1 tbs (15 mL) Monin Cassis Syrup* or blackcurrant cordial

2 tsp arrowroot plus 2 tbs (30 mL) water, mixed to a smooth paste

Berries

180 g fresh mixed berries

1 tbs pure icing sugar, for dusting

1   Preheat the oven to 160°C (140°C fan forced). Lightly grease a 20 cm round, non-stick cake tin and line the base with baking paper.

2   Place the flours, sugar, gum and seeds in a mixing bowl and stir to combine. Add the margarine and work it through the flour with a spoon. Add the rice syrup and work through with the spoon, repeatedly covering it with the flour until it is broken up and no longer sticky. Add 3 teaspoons of oil and work through the flour pulling the mix together; add an additional teaspoon of oil if required to form the pastry into a ball. Knead lightly.

3   Roll the pastry out to a 22–23 cm disc between 2 sheets of baking paper. Using the base of the tin as a guide, cut out a 20 cm disc with a sharp knife. Remove the excess pastry. Use the bottom sheet of paper to invert the pastry into the base of the tin. Bake for 25–30 minutes or until just starting to brown very lightly. Set aside to cool for 2–3 minutes.

4   While the pastry is baking, prepare the filling. Drain the blackberries in a metal sieve, retaining the juice for the syrup. Press the berries through the sieve into a mixing bowl and discard the seeds. Add the coconut milk, lemon zest and cassis. Sprinkle the agar over the water and stir to dissolve. Stir through the berry mix, pour it onto the flan base and chill for 2 hours or until set.

5   To make the syrup, place the juice (should be about ¾ cup) and cassis in a small pan over a medium heat. When hot, stir through the arrowroot paste and simmer for 1–2 minutes or until the sauce thickens. Transfer to a small jug, cover and chill.

6   Serve a wedge of tart topped with the fresh berries, drizzled with the sauce and dusted with the icing sugar.

## Brandied Fruit Compote

*You can poach a combination of seasonal fruits—our favourite is blood oranges with pitted sour cherries—or just a single fruit. The fruit is wonderful served with a suitable ice-cream or gelato, or dressed up served in individual ginger snap baskets—see Ginger Snaps and Baskets (page 152).*

### Serves 4

| | |
|---|---|
| 3 blood oranges (when in season, or navels, tangelos, ruby grapefruit, etc.) | **Per serve** |
| zest and juice of 2 oranges | Energy 886 kJ (211 cal) |
| 4 tbs (60 mL) brandy (ingredient check—Spirits; ◯) | Protein 3.8 g |
| 1 cinnamon quill | Total fat 0.4 g |
| 1 tbs grated palm sugar* or raw sugar | Saturated fat <0.1 g |
| 2 tbs redcurrant jelly (ingredient check) | Carbohydrate 39.9 g |
| 150 g canned sour pitted (morello) cherries or about 30 fresh cherries, pitted | Total sugars 38.3 g |
| 1 tsp arrowroot plus 1 tbs water, mixed to a smooth paste | Dietary fibre 6.9 g |
| | Sodium 12 mg |

1   Peel the oranges, removing any pith. Break into segments and cut into thirds, removing any pips. Place the orange and any juice in a pan with the all the remaining ingredients except canned cherries (add fresh cherries if using) and arrowroot paste. Cover and cook over a low heat for 10 minutes.

**2** Add canned cherries and arrowroot paste and cook for 1–2 minutes or until the arrowroot is cooked and the sauce thickened. Remove from the heat, transfer to a glass or ceramic bowl, cover and set aside to cool before chilling.

**3** Serve with suitable ice-cream, yoghurt or in Ginger Snap Baskets.

## Brandy and Orange Panna Cotta

*'Panna cotta' means cooked cream. Try this delicious dairy-free version: serve with fresh fruit, such as mixed berries (marinated in Cointreau and passionfruit juice for a real treat, see Sozzled Strawberry Terrine, page 130)—or Raspberry and Lime Sauce (page 140). For a non-alcoholic version, replace the brandy with 2 tablespoons Monin Macadamia or Hazelnut Syrup\* (not for nut-free) and omit the icing sugar.*

**Serves 4**

| | |
|---|---|
| extra-light olive oil spray* (ingredient check) | **Per serve** |
| 4 tsp powdered gelatine | **Energy 472 kJ (113 cal)** |
| 3 tbs (45 mL) water | **Protein 3.6 g** |
| 300 mL light coconut milk* (ingredient check; 🅒) | **Total fat 4.4 g** |
| 1 tsp orange zest | **Saturated fat 3.9 g** |
| 200 mL fresh orange juice | **Carbohydrate 12.4 g** |
| 4 tsp brandy (ingredient check—Spirits; 🅒) | **Total sugars 11.2 g** |
| 3 tbs (45 mL) pure icing sugar, sifted | **Dietary fibre 0.1 g** |
| ¼ tsp ground cinnamon | **Sodium 27 mg** |

**1** Very lightly grease 4 x 1-cup capacity moulds with oil.

**2** Sprinkle the gelatine over the water and set aside.

**3** Place all the ingredients except the gelatine in a small pan over a low-medium heat and bring to the boil. Reduce the heat and simmer gently for 3–4 minutes, stirring regularly (the simmering step is important to prevent the custard separating on cooling). Add the gelatine mix and stir until fully dissolved; do not boil.

**4** Divide the coconut mixture between the moulds and refrigerate for 3–4 hours or until set.

**5** To serve, dip the moulds into a pot of hot water for a few seconds and invert onto a serving plate. Serve with fruit or drizzled with sauce.

## Chilled Strawberry Soup with Nectarines

*To repeat the comments of my son and his friends, 'this soup is to die for'! It is equally delicious served as a starter or as a dessert. It is best served in wide, flat bowls rather than traditional soup bowls, to show off the fruit. If nectarines are out of season, substitute with fruits such as mixed berries (fresh or frozen) or kiwi fruit.*

**Serves 6**

| | |
|---|---|
| 3 large passionfruit | **Per serve** |
| 500 g hulled strawberries, washed and drained | **Energy 398 kJ (95 cal)** |
| 20 g caster sugar | **Protein 2.7 g** |
| 5 fresh mint leaves, shredded | **Total fat 0.2 g** |
| 125 mL (½ cup) dessert wine (ingredient check—Wine) | **Saturated fat <0.1 g** |
| 3 ripe nectarines, chilled | **Carbohydrate 14.6 g** |
| | **Total sugars 14.6 g** |
| Garnish | **Dietary fibre 5.6 g** |
| sprigs of fresh mint | **Sodium 10 mg** |

**1** Put the passionfruit pulp in a food processor and blend for 20–30 seconds to release the juice from the seeds. Press through a sieve with the back of a metal spoon into a glass or ceramic mixing bowl and discard the seeds.

**2** Put the strawberries, sugar and mint leaves in the food processor and blend until smooth. Press though the sieve into the passionfruit juice. Add the dessert wine and stir to combine. Cover and chill well.

**3** Just before serving, stone and dice the nectarines. Arrange half a diced nectarine in the centre of each bowl. Spoon the strawberry soup around the nectarines. Serve immediately garnished with the mint sprigs.

## Chocolate, Orange and Rum Mud Cake

*This wonderfully moist dessert cake is delicious served chilled or at room temperature. For a dinner party serve it topped with the Cashew and Chocolate Cream (page 140; not nut-free) and fresh berries or nectarines and Raspberry and Lime Sauce (page 140). The cake is equally good with fresh fruit and with a suitable ice cream or gelato—or try it with chilled Hot Chocolate Sauce (page 140). Other beans, such as adzuki beans, can be used in place of the chickpeas.*

**Serves 8–10**

3 heaped tsp egg substitute (No Egg or Egg-Like brands)*
5 tbs (75 mL) water
400 g cooked chickpeas** (if using canned, ingredient check)
100 g soft dark brown sugar
30 g pure cocoa powder
20 g ground rice*
1 tsp gluten-free/wheat-free baking powder (Ward's brand)*
zest of 1 orange
125 mL (½ cup) fresh orange juice
2 tbs (30 mL) rum (ingredient check—Spirits; ) or water

Chocolate Icing (or 1 quantity Cashew and Chocolate Cream, page 140)
125 g pure icing sugar, sifted
2 tsp margarine (Nuttelex brand)*
1 tbs (15 mL) fresh orange juice
4 tsp pure cocoa powder

Garnish
1 quantity Raspberry and Lime Sauce (page 140)
300 g fresh or frozen raspberries

| Per serve |
| --- |
| Energy 905 kJ (216 cal) |
| Protein 4.8 g |
| Total fat 2.5 g |
| Saturated fat 0.6 g |
| Carbohydrate 41.8 g |
| Total sugars 30.3 g |
| Dietary fibre 5.1 g |
| Sodium 61 mg |

**1** Preheat the oven to 210°C (190°C fan forced). Very lightly grease a 20 cm round, non-stick cake tin.

**2** Place all the cake ingredients in a food processor and process to mix thoroughly. Pour into the cake tin.

**3** Bake for 35–40 minutes or until cooked when the centre of the cake is tested with a skewer; the top will have formed a light and slightly cracked crust. Set aside in the tin to cool completely before turning out on to a plate.

**4** Prepare the Chocolate Icing, (if using, otherwise see page 140) by placing all the ingredients in a small pan over a low heat and warming while stirring to form a smooth icing. Allow to cool.

**5** Prepare the Raspberry and Lime Sauce as described on page 140.

**6** Ice the top with selected icing and top with the raspberries. Serve at room temperature or chilled, drizzled with the Raspberry and Lime Sauce.

## Christmas Pudding

*This rich, moist Christmas pudding may be prepared up to 7 days in advance and stored refrigerated. Reheat in the microwave or by re-steaming and serve accompanied by Brandy Butter (page 138) and Vanilla Custard (page 141). baby apple contains—and apple juice may contain—added vitamin C (see Avoiding Corn, page 161); use Basic Flour Mix and guar gum. use rice crumbs.*

**Serves 8**

3 heaped tsp egg substitute (No Egg or Egg-Like brands)*

5 tbs (75 mL) water

50 g margarine (Nuttelex brand)*

100 g soft brown sugar

zest of 1 orange

200 g raisins (ingredient check—Dried fruit; ), chopped if large

200 g natural sultanas

150 g diced dates

50 g currants (ingredient check—Dried fruit; )

75 g mixed peel* (ingredient check; )

75 g almond meal or 20 g rice crumbs (Orgran brand)*

100 g baby apple (Heinz brand)

½ tsp bicarbonate of soda

125 g gluten-free/wheat-free plain flour (Orgran brand)*, sifted, or Basic Flour Mix (page 113)

2 tsp mixed spice

½ tsp xanthan* or guar gum*

150 mL dry sherry (ingredient check—Wine; ) or pure, unsweetened apple juice

**Per serve**

Energy 2289 kJ (546 cal)

Protein 4.3 g

Total fat 10.8 g

Saturated fat 1.5 g

Carbohydrate 91.6 g

Total sugars 73.1 g

Dietary fibre 6.6 g

Sodium 162 mg

**1** Mix the egg substitute and water to form a smooth paste. Set aside. Very lightly grease a 1-litre capacity Pyrex pudding basin.

**2** Cream the margarine, sugar and orange zest in a bowl. Stir through the egg substitute paste. Add all the remaining ingredients except the sherry (apple juice) and mix to combine. Stir through the sherry (apple juice). Spoon into the basin and smooth the top.

**3** Cut a circle of baking paper with a diameter at least 8 cm larger than the diameter of the top of the basin. Make a pleat in the middle and secure over the top of the basin with string.

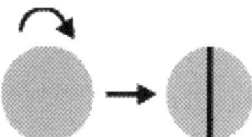

**4** Cover with foil, place in a pan and fill pan with water to halfway up the side of the basin. Bring to the boil, cover and reduce heat until simmering steadily. Cook for 1¼ hours.

**5** Remove the basin from the pan. If storing, set aside to cool in basin, then refrigerate. If serving immediately, set aside in the bowl for 10 minutes before turning out onto a plate to slice and serve with hot custard, ice-cream or Brandy Butter.

**6** If reheating in a microwave, remove foil and paper covers and turn the pudding out onto a plate. Re-cover with a double layer of plastic wrap and refrigerate. Allow to warm to room temperature before reheating in the microwave for 7–8 minutes on high, or until hot. Serve immediately.

**7** If reheating by steaming, leave the pudding in the bowl. Allow to return to room temperature before steaming as described in Step 4 for 30–40 minutes. Turn out onto a plate to serve.

## Cinnamon and Coconut Sweet Brown Rice

*This recipe is based on brown mochi gome, Japanese sweet brown rice\*, which is naturally glutinous. The rice is delicious served warm alone or topped with fresh or marinated fruit such as Marinated Mint and Orange Duet (page 123). The rice is best cooked using a heat diffuser† under the base of the pan to prevent the rice catching. ○ use pepitas or cinnamon to garnish instead of almonds.*

**Serves 4**

| | |
|---|---|
| 210 g sweet brown rice\* | **Per serve** |
| 625 mL (2½ cups) water | **Energy** 584 kJ (139 cal) |
| 1 cinnamon quill | **Protein** 2.3 g |
| 250 mL (1 cup) light coconut milk\* (ingredient check; ○) | **Total fat** 3.7 g |
| 2 pinches of mace or nutmeg | **Saturated fat** 3.3 g |
| 35 g currants (ingredient check—Dried fruit; ○) | **Carbohydrate** 24.4 g |
| 1 tbs (15 mL) pure maple syrup | **Total sugars** 9.4 g |
| | **Dietary fibre** 1.1 g |
| Garnish | **Sodium** 16 mg |
| 15-20 g flaked almonds or pepitas, dry roasted\*\*, or ground cinnamon | |

1   Place the rice, water and cinnamon quill in a medium-sized pan on the heat diffuser over a low-medium heat. Cover and bring to simmering point, reduce the heat and simmer very gently for 25–30 minutes or until the water is almost absorbed.

2   Add the coconut milk, mace and currants and simmer very gently, stirring regularly, until the rice is soft and glutinous. Stir through the maple syrup, garnish and serve immediately.

## Citrus and Coconut Flan with Lemon Syrup

*The wonderful tart lemon syrup is a perfect foil for this flan. Serve it alone, with suitable ice-cream, Marinated Mint and Orange Duet (page 123) or fresh berries. The flan self-crusts as it cooks—the outer 2 cm rises and browns more rapidly than the inner section, giving the flan the appearance of having a crust when cooked. For the best result the correct oven temperature and rotating the cake while baking are very important. I have also included a recipe for Passionfruit Syrup to use instead of the Lemon Syrup, as it is equally delicious with the flan. ○ use glutinous white rice flour\*.*

**Serves 8-10**

| | |
|---|---|
| 4 heaped tsp egg substitute (No Egg or Egg–Like brands)\* | **Per serve** |
| 6 tbs (90 mL) cold water | **Energy** 1523 kJ (363 cal) |
| 200 g caster sugar | **Protein** 3.6 g |
| 50 g margarine (Nuttelex brand)\* | **Total fat** 15.0 g |
| 100 g slivered almonds or almond meal | **Saturated fat** 2.6 g |
| 60 g desiccated coconut | **Carbohydrate** 55.1 g |
| 2 tbs lemon zest | **Total sugars** 45.6 g |
| 100 mL lemon juice | **Dietary fibre** 3.6 g |
| 2 tbs orange zest | **Sodium** 31 mg |
| 150 mL orange juice | |
| 250 mL (1 cup) light coconut milk\* (ingredient check; ○) | |
| 30 g gluten-free/wheat-free self-raising flour (Orgran brand)\* or 30 g glutinous white rice flour\* | |
| 30 g brown rice flour\* | |

Lemon Syrup

100 g caster sugar

100 mL fresh lemon juice, strained

zest of 1 lemon (long shreds if using a zester)

150 mL water

Passionfruit Syrup
¼ cup (185 mL) passionfruit pulp (about 9 small passionfruit)
4 tbs (60 mL) lime juice
125 g caster sugar
¼ tsp vanilla extract* (ingredient check; ◯)

1  Preheat the oven to 170°C (150°C fan forced). Lightly grease a 28 cm diameter flan dish.

2  Mix the egg substitute and water to a smooth paste and place in a food processor with all the remaining flan ingredients. Blend until well combined (the mixture is quite liquid until cooked).

3  Pour the mixture into the greased flan dish and bake, rotating every 15 minutes, for 1 hour or until lightly browned round the edges, a lightly cracked crust has formed over the top and it is cooked when its centre is tested with a skewer. Set aside to cool before refrigerating to chill thoroughly.

3  To make the lemon syrup, place the syrup ingredients in a small pan over a medium heat. Bring to the boil, stirring constantly, until the sugar has dissolved. Reduce the heat and simmer for 5 minutes. Transfer to a jug, cover and chill well.

4  To make the passionfruit syrup, put the passionfruit in a food processor and blend for 30 seconds to release the juice from the seeds. Place the lime juice and sugar in a small pan over a low-medium heat and stir until the sugar has dissolved. Strain the passionfruit juice into the pan, add the vanilla and stir to combine. Simmer gently for 10 minutes without stirring. Transfer to a jug, cover and chill well.

5  Slice the flan into wedges and serve drizzled with the lemon or passionfruit syrup, with accompaniment of choice.

## ◯ Coconut and Vanilla Risotto

*This 'risotto' can be served topped with toasted shredded coconut or sesame seeds, or accompanied by a compote of seasonal fruits—or even with a suitable shaved dark chocolate! ◯ use olive oil instead of macadamia oil.*

**Serves 4**

| | |
|---|---|
| 4 tbs shredded coconut or sesame seeds | **Per serve** |
| 750 mL (3 cups) rice milk* (ingredient check) | **Energy 1914 kJ (457 cal)** |
| 200 mL light coconut milk* (ingredient check; ◯) | **Protein 5.5 g** |
| 1 tsp vanilla extract* (ingredient check; ◯) | **Total fat 15.5 g** |
| 2 tbs (30 mL) macadamia* or extra-light olive oil* | **Saturated fat 3.4 g** |
| 225 g arborio rice* | **Carbohydrate 73.7 g** |
| 1 tbs grated palm sugar* or soft brown sugar | **Total sugars 10.0 g** |
| | **Dietary fibre 1.2 g** |
| | **Sodium 128 mg** |

1  Place the shredded coconut (or sesame seeds) in a small pan over a low heat and toast for 5 minutes or until golden brown, tossing regularly. Set aside.

2  Place the rice and coconut milks and vanilla extract in a pan over a medium heat until the milk is hot but not boiling. Reduce the heat to keep the milk warm.

3  Heat the macadamia oil in a pan over a medium heat and add the rice. Cook for 3 minutes, stirring continuously, or until the rice becomes glassy and translucent.

4  Add 1 cup (250 mL) of the hot milk mix and stir continuously until the liquid has been absorbed. Repeat until all the milk has been absorbed. Stir through the sugar, cover and leave to stand for 3 minutes.

5  Serve immediately sprinkled with toasted coconut or sesame seeds, or accompanied by a fruit compote of choice.

## Crème Caramel

*Delicious served garnished with fresh mint or with fresh fruit of choice.* ○ *use agar powder.*

**Serves 4**

extra-light olive oil spray* (ingredient check)

100 g caster sugar

2 tbs fine yellow maize flour*

3 tbs cornflour (maize)

500 mL (2 cups) rice milk* (ingredient check)

250 mL (1 cup) light coconut milk* (ingredient check)

2 tbs (30 mL) pure maple syrup

¼ tsp ground cinnamon

2 tsp vanilla extract* (ingredient check)

10 drops yellow food colouring (optional)

1 tbs (10 g) powdered gelatine dissolved in 3 tbs boiling water or 1 tsp agar powder*

Garnish

sprigs of fresh mint

**Per serve**

Energy 1279 kJ (305 cal)

Protein 3.7 g

Total fat 5.1 g

Saturated fat 3.4 g

Carbohydrate 61.4 g

Total sugars 37.1 g

Dietary fibre 0.2 g

Sodium 99 mg

1   Very lightly oil 4 x 1-cup capacity moulds.

2   Sift the sugar into a small, heavy-bottomed pan over a medium-high heat. Heat the sugar, stirring regularly, until it melts. Continue to heat gently until the syrup starts to colour to a light golden-brown, swirling around the pan to ensure even caramelisation. Quickly remove from the heat (it will continue to cook, so remove on the light side of golden brown to prevent the caramel burning or becoming brittle on cooling) and divide between the moulds, swirling the moulds so that the caramel coats the bottom evenly. Set aside.

3   To make the custard, place the flours and about 5 tablespoons rice milk in a small jug and mix to a smooth paste.

4   Place the remaining rice milk and coconut milk in a pan over a medium heat and stir through the maple syrup, cinnamon, vanilla extract and food colouring, if using; if using agar sprinkle over top of milk mixture and stir through to combine. Heat until near boiling and stir through the flour paste. Return to simmering point and simmer for 1–2 minutes, stirring constantly, or until the custard has thickened.

5   Remove the custard from the heat and add the gelatine mixture (if using) and stir until dissolved.

6   Pour into prepared moulds and chill for 1–2 hours or until set. To serve, invert moulds on serving plates and spoon any caramel in the bottom of the mould over the top of the custard. Serve immediately with fresh fruit and garnished with fresh mint.

## Flambéed Figgy Pudding with Brandy Butter

*Serve this deliciously moist figgy pudding with hot Vanilla Custard (page 138). To turn it into a Christmassy pudding, add 2 tablespoons of brandy (ingredient check—Spirits) to the pudding batter and serve with Brandy Butter (page 138) and hot custard. For that extra special meal, pour a measure of brandy over the pudding and flambé it immediately before serving.*

**Serves 4-6**

2 heaped tsp egg substitute (No Egg or Egg-Like brands)*

6 tbs (90 mL) water

375 g soft dried figs, stalks removed

200 mL full-bodied red wine, such as merlot (ingredient check—Wine)

6 tbs (90 mL) water

4 tbs (100 g) golden syrup (ingredient check)

120 g margarine (Nuttelex brand)*

**Per serve**

Energy 3901 kJ (931 cal)

Protein 4.4 g

Total fat 36.7 g

Saturated fat 8.5 g

Carbohydrate 134.0 g

Total sugars 92.3 g

100 g soft brown sugar

45 g rice crumbs (Orgran brand)*

120 g gluten-free/wheat-free self-raising flour (Orgran brand)*, sifted

½ tsp xanthan gum*

zest of 1 orange

½ tsp mixed spice

½ tsp ground cinnamon, sifted

½ tsp ground ginger, sifted

2 tbs (30 mL) brandy (optional; ingredient check—Spirits)

Serving

2 tbs (30 mL) brandy (optional, for flambéing)

1 quantity Brandy Butter (page 138)

1 quantity Vanilla Custard (page 141)

Dietary fibre 9.6 g

Sodium 280 mg

1  Mix the egg substitute and water to form a smooth paste. Set aside. Very lightly grease a 1-litre capacity Pyrex pudding basin. Line the base with a circle of greased baking paper.

2  Place the figs, wine, water and golden syrup in a pan over a low heat. Simmer gently for 10 minutes. Remove the figs with a slotted spoon and set aside. Increase the heat to high and boil for 2–3 minutes to reduce the sauce to a syrup.

3  Slice enough figs in thirds crossways to cover the bottom and 1–2 cm up the side of the basin. Pour the syrup over the top. Dice the remaining figs.

4  Cream the margarine and the sugar. Stir in the 'no-egg' paste. Fold in the diced figs and all the remaining ingredients. Spoon into the basin on top of the fig base and smooth top.

5  Cut a circle of baking paper with a diameter at least 8 cm larger than the diameter of the top of the basin. Make a pleat in the middle and secure over the top of the basin with string (see diagram on page 118).

6  Cover with foil, place in a pan and fill pan with water to halfway up the side of the basin. Bring to the boil, cover and reduce heat until simmering steadily. Cook for 1 hour.

7  Remove the basin from the pan and set aside to rest for 10 minutes. Turn out onto a warmed plate, pour over the brandy and quickly light. Serve immediately with the Brandy Butter and hot custard.

## Lemon Custard Tart with Candied Lemon Peel Garnish

*This delicious tart can be topped with the candied lemon slices or any combination of fresh fruits in season, or tinned fruits glazed with melted rose petal, quince or redcurrant jelly.*

**Serves 6**

Pastry

120 g Basic Flour Mix (page 113)

50 g tapioca flour*

30 g caster sugar

½ tsp xanthan gum*

75 g margarine (Nuttelex brand)*

35 g rice syrup* (ingredient check)

3-4 tsp extra-light olive oil*

Lemon Custard Filling

1 quantity Vanilla Custard (page 141)

**Per serve**

Energy 1830 kJ (437 cal)

Protein 3.4 g

Total fat 16.0 g

Saturated fat 4.4 g

Carbohydrate 70.0 g

Total sugars 31.7 g

Dietary fibre 1.3 g

Sodium 127 mg

zest of 1 large lemon, very finely grated
1 tsp agar powder*

Candied Lemon Peel
1 large lemon, cut into 0.25 cm slices and pips removed
375 mL (1½ cups) water
90 g caster sugar
125 mL (½ cup) water

1   Preheat the oven to 160°C (140°C fan forced). Lightly grease a 20 cm round, non-stick cake tin and line the base with baking paper.

2   Put the flours, sugar and gum in a mixing bowl and stir to combine. Add the margarine and work it through the flour with a spoon. Add the rice syrup and work it through with the spoon, repeatedly covering it with flour, until it is broken up and no longer sticky. Add 3 teaspoons oil and work through the flour pulling the mix together; add an additional teaspoon of oil if required to form the pastry into a ball. Knead lightly.

3   Roll out the pastry to a 22–23 cm disc between 2 sheets of baking paper. Using the base of the tin as a guide, cut out a 20 cm disc with a sharp knife. Remove the excess pastry. Use the bottom sheet of paper to invert the pastry into the base of the tin. Bake for 25–30 minutes or until just starting to brown very lightly. Set aside to cool for 2–3 minutes.

4   While the pastry is baking, prepare the custard as described on page 141, adding the lemon zest and agar to the pan with the milk before heating. Thicken as described and pour onto the flan base in the tin.

5   To candy the lemon peel, put the lemon slices and the 375 mL water in a pan and bring to the boil. Reduce the heat and simmer for 7–8 minutes or until the lemon rind is soft. While the lemon is simmering, put the sugar and remaining water in a pan over a medium heat. Stir until the sugar has dissolved and then boil for 7 minutes or until syrupy. Transfer the lemon slices to the syrup, reduce the heat and simmer for 5 minutes or until the lemon rind is becoming translucent. Allow to cool for 3–4 minutes.

6   Arrange the lemon slices on top of the tart and transfer the syrup to a small jug. Allow the flan to cool fully before chilling for 1–2 hours or until set. Serve wedges drizzled with the lemon syrup.

## Marinated Mint and Orange Duet

*This dish is best made with blood oranges and good navel oranges, to optimise the contrast in the duet of fruits. Likewise the duet combination of spearmint or peppermint with Vietnamese mint expands the blend of flavours. When blood oranges are out of season try substituting tangelo or ruby grapefruit. The oranges are delicious alone or can be served with Cinnamon and Coconut Sweet Brown Rice (page 119) or Citrus and Coconut Flan (page 119).*

**Serves 4**

12 fresh mint leaves, finely shredded
6 fresh Vietnamese mint leaves*, finely shredded
zest of 1 blood orange
3 blood oranges (if small, use 4–5)
3 navel oranges
1 cinnamon quill, halved
2 tbs (30 mL) Cointreau*
1 tbs Monin Macadamia Syrup*

Garnish
sprigs of fresh mint

**Per serve**

Energy 709 kJ (169 cal)
Protein 4.1 g
Total fat 0.4 g
Saturated fat <0.1 g
Carbohydrate 34.7 g
Total sugars 34.7 g
Dietary fibre 7.5 g
Sodium 13 mg

1 Mix the shredded mints with the orange zest. With a sharp knife, slice the skin and pith off the oranges and discard. Finely slice the oranges, discarding any pips, and arrange in alternating layers of blood and navel orange in a ceramic or glass bowl, sprinkling the mint–zest mixture between the layers. (If using tangelo or grapefruit, divide into segments rather than slicing.) Transfer any juice to a small bowl.

2 Push the cinnamon quill halves down the side of the oranges. Mix the Cointreau and Monin syrup with the retained juices and pour over the oranges. Cover and chill for a minimum of 3 hours, preferably overnight, to allow the juices to develop.

3 To serve, arrange the orange slices on plates, drizzle over the marinade and garnish with a mint sprig.

## Minted Tropical Fruit in Spiced Ginger Syrup

*A light and refreshing fruit salad to round off a meal. Vary the fruits used according to seasonal availability.*

**Serves 4**

| | |
|---|---|
| 1 small honeydew melon, cut into bite–sized dice | **Per serve** |
| 1 nashi pear, cored and diced | Energy 1056 kJ (252 cal) |
| 1 star fruit, sliced | Protein 3.4 g |
| 12 lychees, peeled and seeded (use canned if fresh unavailable) | Total fat 1.4 g |
| 1 prickly pear, peeled (use tongs to hold) and very finely diced | Saturated fat <0.1 g |
| 1 cup green seedless grapes, halved | Carbohydrate 58.3 g |
| 2 fresh mint leaves, finely shredded | Total sugars 54.0 g |
| | Dietary fibre 6.4 g |
| Syrup | Sodium 150 mg |
| zest and juice of 1 lime | |
| 6 tbs (90 mL) Ginger Refresher (Buderim brand)* | |
| 3 tbs (45 mL) water | |
| 60 g caster sugar | |
| ½ tsp freshly grated ginger | |
| ⅛ tsp Chinese Five Spice powder (ingredient check) | |

Garnish
fresh mint leaves

1 Gently combine the fruit and mint in a bowl.

2 Place all the syrup ingredients in a small pan over a medium heat and simmer gently for 5 minutes. Pour the hot syrup over the fruit and set aside to cool. Cover and refrigerate for a minimum of 2 hours, preferably overnight.

3 Serve garnished with mint leaves.

## Orange Almond Cake with Orange Syrup

*This is such a simple dessert cake to make—just throw everything in the food processor to mix and then bake in the oven. Served chilled, drizzled with the orange syrup. You only need a small slice, but I guarantee the cake won't last long! Great served with fresh fruit or a suitable ice-cream.*

**Serves 6-8**

| | |
|---|---|
| 2 heaped tsp egg substitute (No Egg or Egg–Like brands)* | **Per serve** |
| 3 tbs (45 mL) water | Energy 1187 kJ (283 cal) |
| 1 orange (about 200 g) | Protein 3.8 g |
| 60 g margarine (Nuttelex brand)* | Total fat 14.3 g |

100 g caster sugar

35 g gluten-free/wheat-free self-raising flour (Orgran brand)*, sifted

1½ tsp gluten-free/wheat-free baking powder (Ward's brand)*

120 g ground or slivered almonds

Syrup

100 g caster sugar

zest of ½ orange (long shreds)

150 mL fresh orange juice, strained

1 tbs (15 mL) lemon juice

150 mL water

Saturated fat 1.8 g

Carbohydrate 35.6 g

Total sugars 29.7 g

Dietary fibre 2.3 g

Sodium 121 mg

**1** Preheat the oven to 180°C (160°C fan forced). Grease a 20 cm round, non-stick cake tin and line the base with baking paper. Place a medium-sized pan of water on to boil.

**2** Mix the egg substitute and the water to a smooth paste.

**3** Put the orange in the pan of boiling water, cover and simmer for 10 minutes. Drain and leave until cool enough to handle. Chop roughly, removing any pips.

**4** Put the orange, 'no-egg' paste, margarine, sugar, flour, baking powder and almonds in a food processor and blend until smooth. Transfer the mixture to the tin and bake for 35–40 minutes or until golden and cooked when the centre of the cake is tested with a skewer. Set aside to cool. Transfer to a serving plate, cover and refrigerate for 1–2 hours to chill.

**5** To make the syrup, place all ingredients in a pan over a medium heat. Bring to the boil, stirring constantly, until the sugar has dissolved. Reduce the heat and simmer for 5 minutes. Transfer to a jug, cover and chill well.

**6** Serve wedges of cake drizzled with 1–2 tablespoons of the syrup.

## Passionfruit and Citrus Jellies with Drunken Fruits

*The tart freshness of the jelly in contrast to the drunken fruits makes this a perfect light dessert for a hot day. Keep orange as the base of the Drunken Fruits but the second fruit can be varied according to what's in season—or use frozen raspberries, blackberries or a combination of the two. The jellies may be prepared in glasses and served topped with the fruits and garnish, or in individual moulds and decanted on to serving plates immediately before serving.*

**Serves 4**

Jellies

juice from 3 passionfruit (about 50 mL), see below

375 mL (1½ cups) fresh orange juice

125 mL (½ cup) fresh lemon juice

125 mL (½ cup) water

75 g caster sugar

18 g powdered gelatine

Drunken Fruits

1 orange, peeled and all pith, membranes and pips removed

125 g strawberries, hulled and quartered or other berries or fruit of choice

¼ tsp caster sugar

2 tbs (30 mL) Cointreau*

2 fresh mint leaves, finely shredded

Garnish

small sprigs of fresh mint

Per serve

Energy 778 kJ (186 cal)

Protein 6.3 g

Total fat 0.4 g

Saturated fat <0.1 g

Carbohydrate 36.4 g

Total sugars 36.4 g

Dietary fibre 5.1 g

Sodium 30 mg

1 Process the passionfruit pulp in a food processor for 20–30 seconds to release the juice from the seeds. Press the passionfruit juice through a metal sieve into a glass or ceramic mixing bowl using the back of a metal spoon. Discard the seeds. Strain the orange and lemon juice into the bowl.

2 Heat the water in a small pan until just boiling. Reduce heat and slowly whisk in the caster sugar and gelatine; continue whisking until both are fully dissolved but do not boil. Remove from the heat and stir through the citrus juices. Wet the serving glasses or moulds by rinsing with cold water and shaking to drain. Pour in the jelly, cover and refrigerate for a minimum of 4 hours to set.

3 Cut the cleaned orange segments into quarters and place in a small bowl with the strawberries. Sprinkle over the caster sugar and stir through the Cointreau and shredded mint. Cover and refrigerate for a minimum of 1 hour.

4 To serve, spoon the drunken fruits on the top of the jelly in the glasses (or turned out of the moulds on serving plates) and garnish with mint sprigs.

## Pears Poached in Chocolate Syrup with Berry Garnish

*The hints of star anise and kaffir lime make this chocolate syrup perfect for poaching pears—or nectarines, peaches or green apples. Delicious served warm, at room temperature or chilled.*

**Serves 4**

| | |
|---|---|
| Syrup | **Per serve** |
| 500 mL (2 cups) water | **Energy 793 kJ (189 cal)** |
| 3 tbs (25 g) pure cocoa powder | **Protein 2.2 g** |
| 75 g caster sugar | **Total fat 1.0 g** |
| ½ tsp ground star anise | **Saturated fat 0.4 g** |
| 6 kaffir lime leaves*, bruised | **Carbohydrate 43.6 g** |
| | **Total sugars 36.1 g** |
| Fruit | **Dietary fibre 5.6 g** |
| 4 firmish pears, such as Packham or Beurre Bosc | **Sodium 4 mg** |
| 1 cup berries, such as: | |
| blackberries, raspberries, strawberries or mixed berries (frozen are fine) | |

1 Put all the syrup ingredients in a medium-sized pan and whisk to combine the cocoa powder and water. Bring to the boil over a medium heat, stirring continually until the sugar has fully dissolved. Remove from the heat.

2 Remove the core from the base of the pears using an apple corer, leaving the stalk intact, and then peel with a vegetable peeler. Place in the hot syrup. Return to the heat and simmer gently, uncovered, turning occasionally, for 15 minutes or until the pears are tender when tested with a sharp knife.

3 Using a slotted spoon, transfer the pears to a shallow dish. Cover with foil and keep warm if serving warm, or set aside to cool to room temperature, or refrigerate if serving chilled.

4 Increase the heat to high and boil the syrup, uncovered, for 10–12 minutes to reduce to half the original volume.

5 If serving warm, transfer the pears to serving dishes and drizzle the syrup over the top. If serving at room temperature or chilled, transfer the syrup into a jug and set aside to cool or chill.

6 Serve garnished with the berries.

## Persimmon and Tamarillo Compote

*A very different but delicious blend of fruits that is suitable to serve alone with a biscuit such as Lemon Myrtle and Macadamia Nut Biscuits (page 154), or drizzled over a sorbet or pure frozen fruit.*

**Serves 4**

2 tamarillos, peeled and quartered

1 persimmon, peeled and cut into eighths

125 mL (½ cup) white wine (ingredient check—Wine)

2 tsp grated palm sugar* or 1 tsp soft brown sugar

Per serve

**Energy 275 kJ (66 cal)**

**Protein 1.5 g**

**Total fat 0.1 g**

**Saturated fat <0.1 g**

**Carbohydrate 9.0 g**

**Total sugars 9.0 g**

**Dietary fibre 3.9 g**

**Sodium 11 mg**

1   Place all the ingredients in a pan over a low heat and simmer for 8–10 minutes or until the liquid is reduced by half and thickened.

2   Transfer the compote to a bowl and set aside to cool. Cover and chill before serving.

## Quandong Compote

*This is a simple way to prepare this subtle peachy-apricot-flavoured native fruit. The compote, served as is or puréed, not only makes a wonderful accompaniment to serve with sorbet or suitable ice-cream, but also forms the base for a number of savoury and dessert recipes featured in this book. The Quandong Compote should be refrigerated overnight after cooking to allow the fruit flavour to fully develop in the sauce. When using as a flan filling, thicken the compote with gelatine to form a jelly suitable for slicing.*

**Serves 6**

150 g dried quandongs*

150 g caster sugar

5 tbs (75 mL) lemon juice

750 mL (3 cups) water

Per serve:

**Energy 622 kJ (149 cal)**

**Protein 1.2 g**

**Total fat 0.1 g**

**Saturated fat <0.1 g**

**Carbohydrate 36.4 g**

**Total sugars 35.5 g**

**Dietary fibre 2.3 g**

**Sodium 10 mg**

1   Put the dried quandongs and water in a pan and set aside to soak for 1 hour or until soft (this step is important to ensure the fruit is soft when cooked since cooking more that 10 minutes will cause the fruit to discolour).

2   Add the sugar and lemon juice and gently simmer together, for no more than 10 minutes. Cover and set aside to cool. Refrigerate for at least 12 hours.

3   The compote may be served as is with ice-cream or sorbet or as a simple purée. To purée, use a Bamix blender or food processor, or press the fruit through a metal sieve. The purée may be served chilled over ice-cream or sorbet, or warm over shortbread.

## Quandong, Lemon and Roast Almond Flan

*The tart, apricotty flavour of the quandongs is complemented by the citrus tartness of the candied lemon peel. It is important to soak the quandongs well to soften them since, in order to retain their colour, they are only cooked for a short period. Serve with Vanilla Custard (page 141), a suitable ice-cream or gelato, or chilled light coconut milk\*. Stewed dried peaches or apricots can be used as a poor substitute for the quandongs. ○ omit almond garnish.*

**Serves 8–10**

Quandongs
110 g dried quandongs\*
500 mL (2 cups) water
75 g caster sugar
4 tbs (60 mL) lemon juice


Pastry
100 g margarine (Nuttelex brand)\*
75 g rice syrup\* (ingredient check)
200 g Basic Flour Mix (page 113)
30 g ground rice


Candied Lemon Peel
375 mL (1½ cups) water
8 very thin slices of lemon (discard any pips)
extra 6 tbs (90 mL) water
60 g caster sugar


Setting Mix
5 tsp powdered gelatine
5 tbs (75 mL) hot water


Garnish
50 g flaked almonds, dry roasted\*\*

**Per serve**
**Energy 1081 kJ (258 cal)**
**Protein 4.3 g**
**Total fat 8.6 g**
**Saturated fat 1.6 g**
**Carbohydrate 41.7 g**
**Total sugars 22.0 g**
**Dietary fibre 1.5 g**
**Sodium 59 mg**

1  Put the dried quandongs and water in a pan and set aside to soak until soft (usually 1 hour or more for best results).

2  Add the lemon juice and sugar to the pan, place over a medium heat and simmer gently for no more than 10 minutes. Cover and set aside to cool. Refrigerate after cooling for at least 12 hours or overnight, to allow flavour to develop.

3  To make the pastry, preheat the oven to 160°C (140°C fan forced). Very lightly grease a 24 cm flan dish. Put the margarine and rice syrup in a small pan and warm to melt the margarine. Stir through the flours with a wooden spoon and work until the dough comes away from the pan. Set aside to cool. Roll the pastry out to a 27–28 cm disc between 2 sheets of baking paper. Using the bottom sheet to lift the pastry, invert the pastry over the dish. Gently press into the dish, repair any tears and trim any excess pastry with a sharp knife. Bake in the oven for 25–30 minutes or until lightly browned and cooked. Set aside to cool.

4  To prepare the candied lemon, put the water in a pan over a medium heat. Add the lemon slices and simmer for 7–8 minutes or until the rind is soft. Combine the remaining water and sugar in a small pan over medium heat. Stir the sugar until dissolved and then boil for 7 minutes or until syrupy. Add the lemon slices, reduce heat and simmer for 5 minutes, or until the zest is becoming translucent.

5  Drain the quandong syrup juice into a small jug and arrange the quandongs in the flan base. Drain the lemon peel syrup into the quandong syrup. Roughly chop the lemon peel and scatter over the top of the quandongs.

6   Sprinkle the gelatine over the hot water and microwave for 5–10 seconds to fully dissolve; do not boil. Add to the quandong–lemon syrup. Stir though extra cold water if required to make up to ¾ cup. Pour over the tart and refrigerate for 1–2 hours or until set.

7   Sprinkle the almond garnish over the top immediately before serving. Serve wedges of the flan with accompaniment of choice.

## Red Bean and Apple Pie

*With a couple of simple additions a ready-made red bean paste makes the filling for this lovely moist pie! The lemon myrtle adds a piquancy to the flavour that is really complemented by the lime. Serve warm or at room temperature with suitable ice-cream or Vanilla Custard (page 141).*

**Serves 4-6**

| | |
|---|---|
| extra-light olive oil spray* (ingredient check) | **Per serve** |
| 1 quantity Sweet Shortcrust Pastry (page 155) | Energy 1392 kJ (332 cal) |
| 250 g sweetened red bean paste* (ingredient check) | Protein 7.4 g |
| zest of 1 lime | Total fat 18.7 g |
| 3 tbs (45 mL) lime or lemon juice | Saturated fat 3.4 g |
| 1 tsp ground lemon myrtle* | Carbohydrate 34.4 g |
| 1 tbs (15 mL) water | Total sugars 12.9 g |
| 1 firm red apple, peeled, cored and sliced into segments/crescents | Dietary fibre 3.7 g |
| 1 tsp honey or pure maple syrup | Sodium 101 mg |
| 1 tsp sesame seeds | |

1   Preheat the oven to 200°C (180°C fan forced). Lightly oil a 20 cm pie dish.

2   Prepare pastry as described on page 155 and divide into ⅔ and ⅓ portions. Wrap the smaller portion in a plastic bag and set aside. Roll out the remaining portion to a 25–26 cm disc between 2 sheets of baking paper. Using the bottom sheet, invert the pastry over the pie dish. Gently press into the dish, repairing any tears.

3   Place the red bean paste, lime zest and juice, and lemon myrtle in a bowl and mix together thoroughly. The paste should be firm but spreadable. If too dry, add up to 1 tablespoon water.

4   Spread the paste in the flan and level off the top, then trim excess pastry leaving a 0.5 cm lip around the edge for sealing the tart. Arrange the apple segments in a single layer on top of the paste.

5   Roll out the remaining pastry between the baking paper. Moisten the lip of the pastry base with water and invert the second sheet of pastry over the pie using the bottom sheet of baking paper.

6   Trim the top pastry sheet to size and press the two edges of the tart together with the end of a wooden spoon to seal and flute.

7   Glaze the top of the tart with the honey or maple syrup and sprinkle the sesame seeds over the top. Cut three 2–3 cm slits in the centre of the top of the tart.

8   Bake in the oven for 40 minutes or until the pastry is golden brown. Serve warm or at room temperature with ice-cream or custard.

## Self-Saucing Chocolate and Walnut Pudding

*The glorious fudgey chocolate sauce that forms the base of this pudding self-sauces the crisp-topped, walnut-filled, chocolate sponge. use Basic Flour Mix. replace the walnuts with 100 g chopped raisins (ingredient check—Dried fruit;) or natural sultanas.*

**Serves 4**

| | |
|---|---|
| extra-light olive oil spray* (ingredient check) | **Per serve** |
| 45 g walnut pieces | Energy 2047 kJ (489 cal) |
| 90 g gluten-free/wheat-free plain flour (Orgran brand)* or 100 g Basic Flour Mix (page 113) | Protein 4.5 g |
| 30 g besan flour* | Total fat 15.0 g |
| 1 tsp gluten-free/wheat-free baking powder (Ward's brand)* | Saturated fat 1.9 g |
| 150 g caster sugar | Carbohydrate 85.4 g |
| 1 tbs pure cocoa powder | Total sugars 57.6 g |
| 125 mL (½ cup) rice milk* (ingredient check) | Dietary fibre 1.2 g |
| 1 tsp vanilla extract* (ingredient check;) | Sodium 175 mg |
| 30 g margarine (Nuttelex brand)* | |
| 75 g soft brown sugar | |
| 2 tsp pure cocoa powder | |
| 250 mL (1 cup) boiling water | |
| pure icing sugar to dust | |

1  Preheat the oven to 200°C (180°C fan forced). Very lightly oil 4 x 1-cup capacity ramekins.

2  Put walnut pieces in a small pan over a low heat and toast for 5 minutes or until golden and fragrant, tossing frequently.

3  Sift the flours, baking powder, sugar and cocoa into a mixing bowl. Add the walnuts, rice milk, vanilla and margarine, and mix to a smooth batter. Pour into the prepared ramekins.

4  Mix the brown sugar and cocoa with the boiling water. Pour over the puddings.

5  Bake for 30 minutes or until the top of the puddings are crispy and springy when gently pressed.

6  Serve immediately, dusted with icing sugar or with a scoop of a suitable ice-cream.

## Sozzled Strawberry Terrine

*A fantastic dessert to create an impact at a lunch or dinner party, as it is a magic combination of a good sparkling strawberry wine with fresh berries. Fresita\* is my wine of choice because the depth of strawberry flavour from the natural strawberry pulp added to the wine really complements the fresh strawberries. The secret is to use a flat-bottomed plate or dish that is the same diameter as the inside of the tin you use for the terrine—this way the whole terrine can be weighted down evenly as it sets, so that the fruit is held together and it is easy to slice. For a non-alcoholic version, use a suitable sparkling strawberry wine (such as Robinvale\*) or replace the wine/gelatine/sugar mix with 1 packet of suitable strawberry jelly crystals and water, plus 10 g powdered gelatine and omit the sugar.*

**Serves 6-8**

| | |
|---|---|
| 1 kiwi fruit, peeled and finely sliced | **Per serve** |
| 500 g small strawberries, hulled | Energy 430 kJ (103 cal) |
| 150 g blueberries | Protein 4.7 g |
| zest of 1 lime | Total fat 0.2 g |
| 500 mL (2 cups) sparkling strawberry wine (such as Fresita\*) or blush champagne (ingredient check—see Wine) | Saturated fat <0.1 g |
| | Carbohydrate 18.5 g |
| 25 g powdered gelatine | Total sugars 18.4 g |
| 15 g caster sugar or 30 g if using blush champagne | Dietary fibre 5.0 g |
| juice from 6 large passionfruit (about 100 mL—see below) | Sodium 24 mg |
| 3 tbs (45 mL) Cointreau\* | |

Garnish
6-8 strawberries, fanned (slice the strawberries finely leaving the top and hull intact)

1   Put a 20 cm round, non-stick cake tin (1.5 litre capacity) on a flat surface. Place the kiwi fruit slices in a ring around the outside of the tin base. Arrange the strawberries and blueberries over the kiwi fruit and the rest of the base, the smallest and most perfect fruit first, sprinkling the lime zest in as you go. Finish with as even a surface as possible.

2   *If using the wine–gelatine mix:*

a   Heat 150 mL of the wine in a small pan until just boiling. Reduce the heat.

b   Whisk in the gelatine and caster sugar until fully dissolved; do not boil. Whisk in the remaining wine.

c   Pour over the fruit until almost covered; the fruit should not float off the bottom. Set aside any left-over jelly mix for later.

d   Cover with plastic wrap, place the flat-bottomed plate on top and weight with a pack of rice or equivalent. Refrigerate overnight. (If there is any additional jelly mix left over, refrigerate the terrine for 1 hour or until it has started to set, warm the left-over jelly in a microwave or in a basin of hot water to re-liquify and pour over the fruit mix until it is just covered. Re-cover with plastic wrap, replace the weight and refrigerate overnight.)

3   *If using the jelly:*

a   Put the jelly crystals and gelatine in a jug and add 250 mL boiling water. Stir until the jelly crystals and gelatine have dissolved totally. Make up to 500 mL with cold water, and set aside to cool slightly before pouring over the fruit.

b   Cover the fruit with the jelly mix and follow Step d, above.

4   To prepare the passionfruit juice, process the pulp in a food processor for 20–30 seconds to release the juice from the seeds. Press through a metal sieve into a small bowl with the back of a metal spoon. Discard the seeds. Stir through the Cointreau. Cover with plastic wrap and chill.

5   10–20 minutes before serving, dip the terrine tin in hot water very quickly and invert on a large serving dish. Return to the fridge to allow any liquid to reset.

6   Cut into wedges between kiwi fruit slices. Serve each wedge drizzled with 1–2 tablespoons of passionfruit sauce on a plate garnished with a fanned strawberry.

## Sticky Date Pudding with Butterscotch Sauce

*Another classic—with the added dimension of dates softened in red wine! Make your own Butterscotch Sauce (page 139) or use a suitable commercial one to drizzle over the pud.*

**Serves 6**

| | |
|---|---|
| 2 heaped tsp egg substitute (No Egg or Egg-Like brands)* | **Per serve** |
| 6 tbs (90 mL) water | Energy 3311 kJ (790 cal) |
| 375 g pitted dates | Protein 2.5 g |
| 200 mL full-bodied red wine, such as merlot (ingredient check—Wine) | Total fat 26.3 g |
| 5 tbs (75 mL) water | Saturated fat 6.2 g |
| 3 tbs (75 g) golden syrup (ingredient check) | Carbohydrate 135.4 g |
| 120 g margarine (Nuttelex brand)* | Total sugars 102.1 g |
| 100 g soft brown sugar | Dietary fibre 6.2 g |
| 45 g rice crumbs (Orgran brand)* | Sodium 181 mg |
| 120 g gluten–free/wheat–free self–raising flour (Orgran brand)*, sifted | |
| ½ tsp xanthan gum* | |
| ½ tsp mixed spice | |

½ tsp ground cinnamon, sifted

½ tsp ground ginger, sifted

1 quantity hot Butterscotch Sauce (page 139)

1 Mix the egg substitute and water to form a smooth paste. Set aside. Very lightly grease a 1-litre capacity Pyrex pudding basin. Line the base with a circle of greased baking paper.

2 Place the dates, wine, water and golden syrup in a pan over a low heat. Simmer gently for 10 minutes. Remove the dates with tongs and set aside. Increase the heat to high and boil the sauce for 1–2 minutes to reduce the sauce to a syrup.

3 Flatten enough dates to cover the bottom and 1–2 cm up the side of the basin. Pour the syrup over the top. Dice the remaining dates.

4 Cream the margarine and the sugar together. Beat in the 'no-egg' paste with a spoon. Fold in the diced dates and all the remaining ingredients except Butterscotch Sauce. Spoon into the basin on top of the date base and smooth the pudding top.

5 Cut a circle of baking paper with a diameter at least 8 cm larger than the diameter of the top of the basin. Make a pleat in the middle and secure over the top of the basin with string (see diagram on page 118). Cover with foil and place in a pan and fill pan with water to halfway up the side of the basin. Bring to the boil, partially cover and reduce heat until simmering steadily. Cook for 1¼ hours.

6 Remove the basin from the pan and set aside to rest for 10 minutes.

7 Turn out onto a pre-warmed plate. Serve immediately drizzled with the hot Butterscotch Sauce.

## Ⓕ Ⓝ Ⓥ Upside–Down Nectarine and Berry Cake with Berry Sauce

*A simple dessert cake served warm with berry sauce. Try substituting different fruits—a family favourite is fresh sweet pineapple (such as Sweet Gold) with fresh raspberries. The cake may be served in wedges with the fruit on the bottom as it is baked (my choice!), or inverted onto a plate just before serving so the fruit sits on top.*

**Serves 8–10**

| Cake | Per serve |
|---|---|
| 2 ripe nectarines, stoned and sliced or 200 g fresh pineapple pieces | **Energy 1549 kJ (370 cal)** |
| 150 g fresh raspberries | **Protein 1.7 g** |
| 3 heaped tsp egg substitute (No Egg or Egg-Like brands)* | **Total fat 16.6 g** |
| 5 tbs (75 mL) water | **Saturated fat 3.1 g** |
| 200 g margarine (Nuttelex brand)* | **Carbohydrate 53.9 g** |
| 200 g caster sugar | **Total sugars 28.6 g** |
| 175 g gluten-free/wheat-free self-raising flour (Orgran brand)* | **Dietary fibre 3.3 g** |
| 100 g brown rice flour* | **Sodium 103 mg** |
| ½ tsp gluten-free/wheat-free baking powder (Ward's brand)* | |

Sauce

1 x 425 g can boysenberries or raspberries in syrup

finely grated zest of ⅓ lime

2 tsp arrowroot powder plus 2 tbs (30 mL) water mixed to a smooth paste

1 Preheat the oven to 200°C (180°C fan forced). Line** a 19 cm springform tin with baking paper with a minimum of 5 cm above the sides of the tin.

2 Arrange the fruit over the base of the tin.

3   Mix the egg substitute and water to a smooth paste. Beat the margarine and sugar in a mixing bowl until light and creamy. Beat in the 'no-egg' paste. Sift the flours and baking powder into the bowl and fold through the mixture. Spoon the mix over the top of the fruit base and roughly smooth the top. Bake for 1 hour or until the centre of the cake is cooked when tested with a skewer, rotating the cake every 15–20 minutes to ensure it bakes evenly.

4   Leave to cool for 10 minutes in the tin before removing to serve (as is, or inverted onto a serving plate for an upside-down cake).

5   Prepare the sauce while the cake is baking. Press the canned berries and syrup through a metal sieve with the back of a spoon into a small pan. Discard the seeds. Add the lime zest and the arrowroot mix. Bring to simmering point over a medium heat, stirring constantly. Simmer gently for 1–2 minutes or until the arrowroot is cooked and the sauce has thickened.

6   Serve wedges of the cake surrounded by or (if the cake is inverted) topped with the berry sauce.

## Vermouth Poached Peaches with Blueberry and Toasted Almond Garnish

*A very simple dish—the blueberries turn this magic sauce into a deep crimson colour—and the blend of flavours makes it a great way to finish off any meal. Nectarines are equally delicious served this way. ○ substitute almond garnish with 3 tbs dry-roasted\*\*, shredded coconut (page 203).*

**Serves 4**

2 large peaches, washed, cut in half and stone removed

Sauce
2 tbs (30 mL) pickled ginger juice\* (ingredient check—Ginger; ○)
375 mL (1½ cups) apricot nectar (Berri brand)
zest of ½ lime
2 tsp lime juice
2 tbs (30 mL) dry vermouth (ingredient check—Wine)
16–20 blueberries

Garnish
⅓ cup slivered almonds, dry roasted\*\*
fresh mint leaves

| Per serve | |
| --- | --- |
| Energy 376 kJ (90 cal) | |
| Protein 1.2 g | |
| Total fat 0.5 g | |
| Saturated fat <0.1 g | |
| Carbohydrate 18.2 g | |
| Total sugars 17.8 g | |
| Dietary fibre 1.2 g | |
| Sodium 7 mg | |

1   Put the sauce ingredients in a large, flat-bottomed non-stick frying pan with the peaches, cut-side down. Simmer over a low-medium heat for 4 minutes, stirring occasionally. Turn the peaches over and simmer for a further 3 minutes. Transfer the peaches to 4 plates.

2   Return the sauce to a medium-high heat and cook to reduce the volume by half, stirring regularly. Drizzle over the peaches.

3   Serve immediately, garnished with the almonds and mint leaves.

## ⊙ Walnut and Caramel Pie

*The wonderful caramel sauce in which the walnuts are baked makes this a favourite every time! Simply serve as is—warm or cold—or with ice-cream or custard. For a change, substitute the walnuts with pecans, the more traditional filling, or chopped dates topped with LSA mix\*.*

**Serves 8-10**

1 quantity Sweet Shortcrust Pastry (page 155)

Filling
60 g margarine (Nuttelex brand)\*
275 g golden syrup (ingredient check; ⊙)
5 heaped tsp egg substitute (No Egg or Egg–Like brands)\*
5 tbs (75 mL) water
100 g soft brown sugar
2 tbs (30 mL) rum (ingredient check—Spirits; ⊙) or Monin Caribbean Rum Syrup\* or water
175 g walnut pieces

Per serve
Energy 1891 kJ (451 cal)
Protein 4.6 g
Total fat 27.0 g
Saturated fat 3.5 g
Carbohydrate 48.3 g
Total sugars 33.5 g
Dietary fibre 1.3 g
Sodium 115 mg

1 Preheat the oven to 200°C (180°C fan forced). Very lightly grease a 24 cm pie or flan dish.

2 Place the margarine in a small pan over a low heat. When melted, add the golden syrup and stir to combine. Set aside to cool.

3 While the syrup is cooling, prepare the pastry as described on page 155. Roll out the pastry to a 27–28 cm disc between 2 sheets of baking paper. Using the bottom sheet, invert the pastry over the pie dish. Gently press the pastry into the dish and repair any tears. Trim excess pastry with a sharp knife.

4 Mix the egg substitute and water to form a smooth paste. Add the sugar and rum or water and mix well. Stir through the cooled syrup.

5 Arrange the nuts in the bottom of the pie shell and pour the syrup mix over the top. Bake for 35–40 minutes or until the filling is just set. If the top or crust start to brown too rapidly, loosely cover the pie with aluminium foil until the filling is cooked.

## ⊙ Yorkshire Treacle Tart

*A variation on the usual treacle tart—the dried fruit and rice crumbs take the often overbearing sweetness of this classic. Serve warm or at room temperature with custard or a suitable ice-cream.*

**Serves 8**

Pastry
1 quantity Sweet Shortcrust Pastry (page 155)

Filling
1 large green apple, such as Granny Smith (about 200 g), washed and cored
zest and juice of 1 lemon
70 g rice crumbs (Orgran brand)\*
40 g mixed peel\* (ingredient check; )
70 g currants (ingredient check—Dried fruit; )
70 g raisins (ingredient check—Dried fruit; ⊙)
¼ tsp mixed spice
¼ tsp ground nutmeg
2 tbs (50 g) golden syrup (ingredient check; ⊙)

Per serve
Energy 1328 kJ (317 cal)
Protein 3.7 g
Total fat 13.0 g
Saturated fat 2.4 g
Carbohydrate 47.2 g
Total sugars 25.3 g
Dietary fibre 2.0 g
Sodium 98 mg

1 Preheat the oven to 200°C (180°C fan forced). Lightly grease a 24 cm pie dish.

2 Prepare the pastry as described on page 155. Roll out the pastry to a 27–28 cm disc between 2 sheets of baking paper. Using the bottom sheet, invert the pastry over the pie dish. Gently press the pastry into the dish and repair any tears. Trim off excess pastry with a sharp knife.

3 Coarsely grate the apple and mix through the lemon juice and zest.

4 Mix the rice crumbs, dried fruit and spices together in a bowl. Add the grated apple mix and the golden syrup and stir well to mix. Fill the pastry shell with the mix and smooth the top. Bake for 40 minutes in the oven or until the top of the pie is golden brown. Set aside to cool. Serve warm or cold with suitable custard or ice-cream.

Sorbets, Gelati and Ice-creams

## Banana Ice-Cream

*A smooth, creamy ice-cream for any banana fan!*

**Serves 4**

400 g peeled ripe bananas, roughly chopped
180 mL rice milk* (ingredient check)
1 tsp vanilla extract* (ingredient check; ◯)
3 tbs (45 mL) coconut cream* (ingredient check; ◯)
4 tsp tahini*

| Per serve | |
| --- | --- |
| Energy 718 kJ (171 cal) | |
| Protein 3.7 g | |
| Total fat 5.6 g | |
| Saturated fat 2.3 g | |
| Carbohydrate 26.4 g | |
| Total sugars 19.0 g | |
| Dietary fibre 2.9 g | |
| Sodium 31 mg | |

1 Put all ingredients in a food processor and blend until smooth.

2 *Either* chill the mixture thoroughly in the refrigerator before churning in an ice-cream machine† as per the manufacturer's instruction. Transfer to a freezer-proof, lidded container and leave to freeze completely.

3 *Or* pour the mixture into a freezer-proof container with lid and freeze until mushy and ice crystals are starting to form around the edge. Mash well with a fork to break up the ice crystals and return to the freezer. Repeat this process 2–3 times until the ice-cream has a fine texture. Leave to freeze completely.

## Chocolate, Mocha, Choc-Mint and Rum 'n' Raisin Sorbets

*These are sorbets to die for! Delicious served alone or with chilled fresh fruit such as nectarines or berries.*

**Makes 1 litre**

Chocolate Sorbet
100 g pure cocoa powder
200 g caster sugar
500 mL (2 cups) water
250 mL (1 cup) light coconut milk* (ingredient check; ◯)

| Per scoop (35 mL) | |
| --- | --- |
| Energy 186 kJ (44 cal) | |
| Protein 0.8 g | |
| Total fat 0.9 g | |
| Saturated fat 0.7 g | |
| Carbohydrate 8.1 g | |
| Total sugars 7.1 g | |
| Dietary fibre <0.1 g | |
| Sodium 2 mg | |

1 Sieve the cocoa into a medium-sized pan. Stir through the sugar. Gradually mix in the water to form a smooth paste. Add the remaining water, stirring constantly.

2   Place over a medium heat and bring to the boil, stirring constantly until the sugar dissolves. Reduce the heat and simmer gently for 10 minutes, stirring occasionally. Add the coconut milk, return to simmering point and simmer, while stirring, for 1 minute. Set aside to cool.

3   *Either* chill the mixture thoroughly in the refrigerator before churning in an ice-cream machine† as per the manufacturer's instruction. Transfer to a freezer-proof, lidded container and leave to freeze completely.

4   *Or* pour the mixture into a freezer-proof container with lid and freeze until mushy and ice crystals are starting to form around the edge. Mash well with a fork to break up the ice crystals and return to the freezer. Repeat this process 2–3 times until the sorbet has a fine texture. Leave to freeze completely.

*Mocha Sorbet* Reduce the water to 450 mL and add 3 tablespoons instant coffee granules dissolved in 5 tablespoons (75 mL) boiling water and 2 teaspoons vanilla extract* (ingredient check; ○) after the sugar has dissolved.

*Choc-Mint Sorbet* Add a few drops of mint extract or essence (to taste) to the cooled mixture.

*Rum 'n' Raisin Sorbet* Soak 200 g raisins (ingredient check—Dried fruit; ○) (chopped if large) in 125 mL (½ cup) rum (ingredient check—Spirits; ○) in a sealed screw-top jar overnight and stir through the cooled syrup before churning. Use Monin Caribbean Rum Syrup* in place of the rum for a non-alcoholic version.

## ○ Lime and Coconut, and Grapefruit Gelati

Ⓕ
Ⓝ   *This Lime and Coconut is a creamy tart gelato while the Grapefruit is milder and more subtle. They make an excellent*
Ⓥ   *accompaniment to any chilled fresh fruit—or try them with some of the sauce toppings or fruit compotes in this section.*

**Makes 0.75 litre**

Lime and Coconut Gelato

150 g caster sugar

200 mL water

400 mL light coconut milk* (ingredient check; ○)

finely grated zest and juice of 1 large lime

finely grated zest and juice of 1 lemon

Grapefruit Gelato

150 g caster sugar

200 mL water

200 mL light coconut milk* (ingredient check; ○)

300 mL fresh grapefruit juice, strained

6 fresh mint leaves, very finely shredded

**Per scoop (35 mL)**

**Energy 168 kJ (40 cal)**

**Protein 0.2 g**

**Total fat 1.1 g**

**Saturated fat 1.0 g**

**Carbohydrate 7.7 g**

**Total sugars 7.4 g**

**Dietary fibre <0.1 g**

**Sodium 3 mg**

1   Place the sugar and water in a small pan over a medium heat. Bring to the boil while stirring. Reduce the heat and leave to simmer for 5 minutes. Set aside to cool to room temperature.

2   Whisk the coconut milk and lime and lemon juices and zests, or grapefruit juice and mint into the cooled syrup.

3   *Either* chill the mixture thoroughly in the refrigerator before churning in an ice-cream machine† as per the manufacturer's instruction. Transfer to a freezer-proof, lidded container and leave to freeze completely.

4   *Or* pour the mixture into a freezer-proof container with lid and freeze until mushy and ice crystals are starting to form around the edge. Mash well with a fork or re-whisk to break up the ice crystals and return to the freezer. Repeat this process 2–3 times until the gelato has a fine texture. Leave to freeze completely.

# Mango and Passionfruit Sorbets

*These are always fought over! The mango is a smooth, creamy sorbet and contrasts wonderfully with the tart lightness of the passionfruit sorbet. Serve alone, together or with chilled fruits, or with a complementary gelato such as Lime and Coconut (page 136). If the passionfruit sorbet has been frozen for any period, leave in the refrigerator for 1–1½ hours to soften slightly before serving.*

**Makes 0.75 litre**

Mango Sorbet

75 g caster sugar

100 mL water

350 mL mango flesh (from 500–550 g mango, see below)

4 tbs (60 mL) lemon juice

2 tbs (30 mL) lime juice

150 mL water

Passionfruit Sorbet

150 g caster sugar

200 mL water

200 mL passionfruit juice—approximately 6 large passionfruit (see below)

4 tbs (60 mL) lemon juice

finely grated zest of ½ lemon

200 mL water

**Per scoop (35 mL)**

Energy 99 kJ (24 cal)

Protein 0.2 g

Total fat <0.1 g

Saturated fat <0.1 g

Carbohydrate 5.6 g

Total sugars 5.6 g

Dietary fibre 0.3 g

Sodium <1 mg

1   Place the sugar and water in a small pan over a medium heat. Bring to the boil while stirring. Reduce the heat and leave to simmer for 5 minutes. Set aside to cool to room temperature.

2   *Mango* Blend the mango flesh in a food processor and pass the pulp through a metal sieve (or press the flesh through a sieve—this requires a bit more elbow grease!).

3   *Passionfruit* Process the passionfruit pulp in a food processor for 20–30 seconds to release the juice from the seeds. Press the juice through a metal sieve in a mixing bowl using the back of a metal spoon. Discard the seeds.

4   Mix the mango flesh or passionfruit juice and the remaining ingredients through the cooled syrup.

5   *Either* chill the mixture thoroughly in the refrigerator before churning in an ice-cream machine† as per the manufacturer's instruction. Transfer to a freezer-proof, lidded container and leave to freeze completely.

6   *Or* pour the mixture into a freezer-proof container with lid and freeze until mushy and ice crystals are starting to form around the edge. Mash well with a fork to break up the ice crystals and return to the freezer. Repeat this process 2–3 times until the sorbet has a fine texture. Leave to freeze completely.

# Vanilla Ice-Cream

*The white bean base to this ice-cream makes it a high-fibre dessert—not a usual plus for an ice-cream! It is important to use beans that are cooked without any salt, so canned are not suitable for this recipe.*

**Makes 1 litre**

500 g cooked cannellini beans**

150 g rice syrup* (ingredient check)

250 mL (1 cup) water

1 tbs (15 mL) vanilla extract* (ingredient check; ◯)

3 tbs (45 mL) pure maple syrup

200 mL coconut cream* (ingredient check; ◯)

**Per scoop (35 mL)**

Energy 210 kJ (50 cal)

Protein 1.6 g

Total fat 1.2 g

Saturated fat 1.1 g

Carbohydrate 8.3 g

Total sugars 3.9 g
Dietary fibre 1.2 g
Sodium 3 mg

1  Cover and chill the cooked beans.

2  Place the rice syrup, water, vanilla extract and maple syrup in a small pan over a low-medium heat. Bring to the boil, reduce heat and simmer for 10 minutes, stirring occasionally. Set aside to cool.

3  Put the beans, syrup and coconut milk in a food processor and blend until smooth. Press the mixture through a metal sieve with the back of a metal spoon; discard the residual bean skins.

4  *Either* chill the mixture thoroughly in the refrigerator before churning in an ice-cream machine† as per the manufacturer's instruction. Transfer to a freezer-proof, lidded container and leave to freeze completely.

5  *Or* pour the mixture into a freezer-proof container with lid and freeze until mushy and ice crystals are starting to form around the edge. Mash well with a fork or to break up the ice crystals and return to the freezer. Repeat this process 2–3 times until the ice-cream has a fine texture. Leave to freeze completely.

## Sweet Sauces

These simple sauces are designed to drizzle over fresh fruit, ice-cream or cakes—to turn something simple into something special. See also recipes for blueberry sauce in Vermouth Poached Peaches with Blueberry and Toasted Almond Garnish (page 133), Golden Syrup Citrus Sauce (page 113), lemon and passionfruit syrups in Citrus and Coconut Flan with Lemon Syrup (page 119), orange syrup in Orange Almond Cake with Orange Syrup (page 124), mango sauce in Black Rice Pudding and Mango Sauce (page 114) and spiced ginger syrup in Minted Tropical Fruit with Spiced Ginger Syrup (page 124) for other delicious sauces and serving suggestions.

## Brandy Butter

*A classic accompaniment for Christmas Pudding (page 118) or Flambéed Figgy Pudding (page 121). Store in the freezer and remove immediately before serving.*

**Serves 8–10**

125 g margarine (Nuttelex brand)*
75 g soft brown sugar
75 g pure icing sugar plus extra if required
½ tsp vanilla extract* (ingredient check; ◯)
½ tsp lemon zest
3 tbs (45 mL) brandy (ingredient check—Spirits; ◯)

Per serve
Energy 636 kJ (152 cal)
Protein <0.1 g
Total fat 10.0 g
Saturated fat 1.9 g
Carbohydrate 13.7 g
Total sugars 13.6 g
Dietary fibre <0.1 g
Sodium 49 mg

1  Put the margarine in a mixing bowl. Sift in the sugars and mix to cream.

2  Blend in the remaining ingredients, adding extra icing sugar if required to make a stiffish cream. Transfer to a freezer-proof container. Cover and freeze.

## Butterscotch Sauce

*Delicious served hot drizzled over Sticky Date Pudding (page 131), and when it is chilled it forms a gloriously rich, thick sauce to serve over ice-cream, fruit or whatever you fancy! The addition of the schnapps gives the sauce that extra kick! The sauce keeps refrigerated for up to 3 weeks.* ◯ *use rice syrup.*

**Makes 2 cups**

150 g soft dark brown sugar

4 tbs (60 mL) light corn syrup or rice syrup* (ingredient check)

60 g margarine (Nuttelex brand)*

180 mL light coconut milk* (ingredient check; ◯)

1 tsp vanilla extract* (ingredient check; ◯)

1 ½ tsp lemon juice

3 tbs (45 mL) De Kuyper Butterscotch Schnapps* or water

| Per 100 mL | |
| --- | --- |
| Energy 1232 kJ (294 cal) | |
| Protein 0.3 g | |
| Total fat 11.7 g | |
| Saturated fat 3.7 g | |
| Carbohydrate 45.4 g | |
| Total sugars 38.6 g | |
| Dietary fibre <0.1 g | |
| Sodium 84 mg | |

1   Place the sugar, syrup and margarine in a small, heavy-based pan over a medium heat and stir until the sugar has dissolved. Boil the syrup, without stirring, for 5–6 minutes (should measure 135°C on a candy thermometer).

2   Remove from the heat and stir in the remaining ingredients carefully to avoid the very hot sauce spitting. Stir until smooth. The sauce will thicken as it cools. Serve hot, at room temperature or chilled.

## Caramel Sauces

*Different dishes require different caramel sauces—here are two beauties. Sauce 1 is a thick, very rich sauce and a generous teaspoon is all you need on a dessert such as a sparkling wine jelly with fresh fruit. Sauce 2 is a thinner sauce ideal for pouring over a fresh fruit salad.*

**Serves 4**

Sauce 1

6 tbs (90 mL) coconut cream* (such as Kara brand) (ingredient check; ◯)

10 g margarine (Nuttelex brand)*

15 g golden syrup (ingredient check; ◯)

Sauce 2

125 mL (½ cup) light coconut milk* (ingredient check; ◯)

15 g margarine (Nuttelex brand)*

75 g golden syrup (ingredient check; ◯)

15 g soft dark brown sugar

| Per serve (Sauce 1) | |
| --- | --- |
| Energy 274 kJ (65 cal) | |
| Protein 0.4 g | |
| Total fat 5.7 g | |
| Saturated fat 3.8 g | |
| Carbohydrate 3.4 g | |
| Total sugars 3.2 g | |
| Dietary fibre <0.1 g | |
| Sodium 18 mg | |

1   *Sauce 1* Combine all the ingredients in a small heatproof bowl. Place over a pan of boiling water and stir frequently for 15 minutes or until the sauce changes to a golden brown-caramel colour and thickens. Serve warm or chilled, spooned over dessert of choice.

2   *Sauce 2* Combine all the ingredients in a small pan over a low-medium heat and cook gently for 3 minutes or until the margarine has melted and the ingredients combined to a smooth sauce. Set aside to cool slightly. Pour over fresh fruit and serve immediately or chilled.

## Cashew and Chocolate Cream

*This cream makes a wonderful cake filling or icing—such as on a Chocolate, Orange and Rum Cake (page 117) or Vanilla Kisses (page 157).*

**Makes ⅓ cup**

2 tbs (30 mL) pure cashew spread* (Naytura brand)

1 tbs (15 mL) pure maple syrup or honey

¼ tsp vanilla extract* (ingredient check; ⓒ)

1 tbs (15 mL) fresh orange juice

2 tbs pure cocoa powder

extra 1-2 tbs (15-30 mL) fresh orange juice

**Per teaspoon**

Energy 80 kJ (19 cal)

Protein 0.6 g

Total fat 1.2 g

Saturated fat 0.2 g

Carbohydrate 1.8 g

Total sugars 0.8 g

Dietary fibre <0.1 g

Sodium 1 mg

1   Put all the ingredients except the cocoa and the extra orange juice in a small bowl and mix to a smooth cream.

2   Add the cocoa and mix thoroughly to a stiff paste. Add extra orange juice as required to form a spreadable paste. Use as a filling or icing.

## Hot Chocolate Sauce

*A delicious sauce to serve hot or chilled over ice-cream, rice puddings, dessert cakes such as Chocolate, Orange and Rum Cake (page 117), or Fruit Kebabs (page 19). It is easily converted to a choc-mint sauce by adding a few drops of pure peppermint extract or essence, a mocha sauce by adding 100 mL strong coffee in place of the water, or an orange chocolate sauce by adding the zest of ¼ orange and replacing half the water with strained fresh orange juice.*

**Makes ½ cup—serves 4-6**

2 tsp extra-light olive oil*

3 tbs caster sugar

1 tbs pure cocoa powder, sifted

100 mL water

**Per serve**

Energy 179 kJ (43 cal)

Protein 0.2 g

Total fat 1.5 g

Saturated fat 0.2 g

Carbohydrate 7.3 g

Total sugars 7.1 g

Dietary fibre 0 g

Sodium 0.1 mg

1   Put all the ingredients in a small pan. Bring to the boil over a medium heat, while stirring.

2   Boil for 1 minute, stirring constantly. When ready, the sauce will darken slightly and become 'clearer' and glossy. Serve hot or chilled.

## Raspberry and Lime Sauce

*A simple fruit sauce (coulis style) ideal to serve over ice-cream, fresh fruit or with desserts such as Brandy and Orange Panna Cotta (page 116). The lime zest adds a lovely balance to the sweetness of the raspberries or boysenberries.*

**Makes 1½ cups—serves 6 as a sauce, 8 as a garnish**

1 x 425 g can raspberries or boysenberries in syrup

finely grated zest of ⅓ lime

2 tsp arrowroot powder plus 2 tbs (30 mL) water, mixed to a smooth paste

**Per serve**

Energy 222 kJ (53 cal)

Protein 0.4 g

Total fat 0.1 g

Saturated fat <0.1 g

Carbohydrate 12.8 g

Total sugars 11.9 g

Dietary fibre 1.8 g

Sodium 4 mg

**1** Press the berries and syrup through a metal sieve with the back of a metal spoon into a pan. Discard the seeds.

**2** Add the lime zest and the arrowroot paste. Bring to simmering point over a medium heat, stirring constantly. Simmer gently for 1–2 minutes or until the arrowroot is cooked and the sauce has thickened.

**3** Serve warm, at room temperature or chilled.

## Vanilla Custard

*This custard is great served hot or chilled, makes an easy custard base and is perfect for fruit flan fillings. Use 2 tablespoons cornflour for a thinner sauce, 3 tablespoons for a thicker one. For a flan, add 4 teaspoons powdered gelatine dissolved in 5 tablespoons (75 mL) boiling water (or 1 teaspoon agar powder\* sprinkled over rice milk mix in pan). ◯ use agar as setting agent.*

**Serves 4**

2 tbs fine yellow maize flour\*

2–3 tbs maize cornflour

500 mL (2 cups) rice milk\* (ingredient check)

250 mL (1 cup) light coconut milk\* (ingredient check)

2 tbs (50 g) pure maple syrup or golden syrup (ingredient check)

¼ tsp ground cinnamon

2 tsp vanilla extract\* (ingredient check)

10 drops yellow food colouring (optional)

**Per serve**

Energy 800 kJ (191 cal)

Protein 1.6 g

Total fat 5.0 g

Saturated fat 3.4 g

Carbohydrate 33.9 g

Total sugars 12.1 g

Dietary fibre 0.2 g

Sodium 90 mg

**1** Put the flours and about 4 tablespoons of rice milk in a small jug and mix to a smooth paste.

**2** Put the remaining rice and the coconut milks in a pan over a medium heat and stir through the maple syrup, cinnamon and vanilla extract and, if using, the agar and food colouring. Heat until near boiling and stir through the flour paste. Return to simmering point and simmer for 1–2 minutes, stirring constantly, or until the custard has thickened. If using as a custard, serve immediately.

**3** If using as a flan filling remove the custard from the heat and add the gelatine mixture (ignore if using agar) and stir until dissolved. Pour into prepared flan base, set aside to cool before chilling for 1–2 hours or until set.

*Variations*

*Coffee Custard* Omit the vanilla. Crush 10 g espresso-style coffee beans into coarse pieces, add to the milk and other ingredients, and heat until simmering. Remove from the heat and leave to infuse for 10 minutes. Strain through a fine sieve, return to the heat and thicken as described.

*Ginger Custard* Omit the vanilla. Very finely slice a 2 cm piece of peeled, fresh ginger, add to the pan with the milk and other ingredients, and heat until simmering. Remove from the heat and leave to infuse for 15–20 minutes. Strain, return to the heat and thicken as described.

*Lemon-vanilla Custard* Add 2 teaspoons very finely grated lemon zest to the pan with the rice milk. Bring to the boil slowly to allow the lemon zest to infuse. Thicken as described.

Cakes and Slices

## ◯ Barm Brack

*This is a traditional Irish fruit bread—serve as is or lightly spread with margarine and to be traditional, accompanied by a hot cup of tea! The secret is to bake the bread slowly so it cooks evenly without burning since it contains no fat or oil. Other dried fruits, such as raisins and dates, can also be used as part of the fruit base.* ◯ *use Basic Flour Mix; baby apple contains vitamin C (see Avoiding Corn, page 161).*

**Serves 12**

| | |
|---|---|
| 150 g natural sultanas | **Per serve** |
| 250 g currants (ingredient check—Dried fruit; ◯) | Energy 1131 kJ (270 cal) |
| 1 cup (250 mL) strong hot black tea (such as Irish Breakfast) | Protein 3.1 g |
| 1 heaped tsp egg substitute (No Egg or Egg–Like brands)* | Total fat 0.7 g |
| 2 tbs water | Saturated fat 0.1 g |
| 150 g caster sugar | Carbohydrate 53.5 g |
| 225 g Basic Flour Mix (page 113) plus 2 tsp gluten-free/wheat-free baking powder (Ward's brand)* or 250 g gluten-free/wheat-free self-raising flour (Orgran brand)*, sifted | Total sugars 38.3 g |
| | Dietary fibre 2.5 g |
| 110 g baby apple (Heinz brand) | Sodium 105 mg |
| 1 tsp mixed spice | |
| 2 tbs orange marmalade | |
| 1 tsp freshly grated ginger (optional) | |

1  Soak the fruit in the tea overnight.

2  Next day, preheat the oven to 170°C (150°C fan forced). Lightly grease and line a 20 cm square non-stick cake tin.

3  Mix the egg substitute with the water to form a smooth paste and combine with all the remaining ingredients. Add the fruit and stir through the mix gently to prevent the softened fruit breaking up.

4  Transfer to the cake tin and bake for 1¼–1½ hours or until cooked when tested with a skewer in the centre of the bread, rotating 2–3 times during cooking.

5  Cool in the tin before turning out. Serve slices lightly spread with margarine. Store in an airtight container.

## ◯ Chocolate and Brazil Nut Fudge Slice

*These are guaranteed not to last long! They also make a great dessert served with a scoop of suitable ice-cream or gelato. I use a square tin to make slices and a round tin to serve as a dessert.* ◯ *use Basic Flour Mix.*

**Makes 12**

| | |
|---|---|
| 1 heaped tsp egg substitute (No Egg or Egg–Like brands)* | **Per slice** |
| 2 tbs (30 mL) water | Energy 1037 kJ (247 cal) |
| 125 g margarine (Nuttelex brand)* | Protein 2.7 g |
| 135 g soft dark brown sugar | Total fat 13.1 g |
| 2 tbs pure cocoa powder | Saturated fat 2.6 g |
| 2 tbs (50 g) golden syrup (ingredient check; ◯) | Carbohydrate 31.2 g |
| 110 g Basic Flour Mix (page 113) plus 1 tsp gluten-free/wheat-free baking powder (Ward's brand)* or 100 g gluten-free/wheat-free self-raising flour (Orgran brand)* | Total sugars 20.2 g |
| | Dietary fibre 1.7 g |
| 50 g brown rice flour* | Sodium 91 mg |
| 100 g chopped, pitted or diced dates | |
| 75 g brazil nuts, dry roasted** and finely chopped | |
| 1 tsp lemon zest | |
| pure icing sugar, to dust | |

1 Preheat the oven to 170°C (150°C fan forced). Lightly grease a 20 cm square or round non-stick cake tin.

2 Mix the egg substitute and the water together to form a smooth paste.

3 Put margarine, sugar, cocoa and golden syrup in a small pan. Stir over a low heat until the margarine has melted and all the ingredients are well combined. Set aside to cool slightly before whisking in the 'no-egg' paste.

4 Sift the flours into a large bowl. Mix through the dates, brazil nuts and lemon zest. Pour in the cocoa sauce and mix well. Spread mixture evenly into the cake tin and bake for 35–40 minutes or until cooked when the centre of the slice is tested with a skewer, rotating twice during cooking.

5 Set aside to cool slightly. Cut into slices or wedges before leaving to cool completely in the tin. Transfer to an airtight container and store in the refrigerator.

6 Serve lightly dusted with icing sugar or accompanied by suitable ice-cream.


## Date and Apple Slices

*These wholesome, easy-to-make slices are delicious served chilled—simply store refrigerated in an airtight container.*

*use guar gum.*

**Makes 12**

| | |
|---|---|
| 100 g margarine (Nuttelex brand)* | **Per slice** |
| 50 g soft brown sugar | **Energy 893 kJ (213 cal)** |
| 2 firm green apples (about 300 g), peeled and finely chopped | **Protein 2.4 g** |
| 100 g chopped nuts, such as almonds, brazil nuts, walnuts or a mixture of nuts | **Total fat 12.9 g** |
| 100 g pitted dates, chopped | **Saturated fat 1.7 g** |
| 150 g brown rice flour* | **Carbohydrate 23.2 g** |
| 1 tsp mixed spice | **Total sugars 13.0 g** |
| 1/2 tsp xanthan* or guar gum* | **Dietary fibre 2.4 g** |
| 1 tsp gluten–free/wheat–free baking powder (Ward's brand)* | **Sodium 78 mg** |

1 Preheat the oven to 180°C (160°C fan forced). Lightly grease and line a 20 cm square cake tin.

2 Blend margarine and sugar in a bowl. Stir in the apples, nuts and dates.

3 Sift the flour, mixed spice, gum and baking powder into a separate bowl and mix well. Gradually stir the flour mixture into the apple mixture.

4 Spread the mix out into the cake tin. Bake for 25–30 minutes, or until cooked when tested with a skewer, rotating once during baking.

5 Leave to cool for 5 minutes. Cut into slices and transfer to a wire rack to cool completely. Store in an airtight container.

## Ⓖ Fruit and Nut Rock Buns

Ⓕ *The addition of chopped nuts and vanilla to the classic style of rock bun gives another taste dimension.*
Ⓝ *Ⓖ use Basic Flour Mix. Ⓝ replace nuts with additional dried fruit.*
Ⓥ

**Makes 18**

1 heaped tsp egg substitute (No Egg or Egg–Like brands)*
4 tbs (60 mL) water
125 g margarine (Nuttelex brand)*
100 g caster sugar
1 tsp vanilla extract* (ingredient check; Ⓖ)
110 g baby apple (Heinz brand; omit if using Basic Flour Mix)
200 g Basic Flour Mix (page 113) plus 1½ tsp gluten-free/wheat-free baking powder (Ward's brand)* or 180 g gluten-free/wheat-free self-raising flour (Orgran brand)*, sifted
60 g mixed pecans and walnuts, chopped
100 g natural sultanas or 75 g dried fruit medley (ingredient check—Dried fruit; Ⓖ)
50 g raisins (ingredient check—Dried fruit; Ⓖ), chopped if large

| Per bun | |
| --- | --- |
| Energy | 811 kJ (193 cal) |
| Protein | 1.9 g |
| Total fat | 8.2 g |
| Saturated fat | 1.2 g |
| Carbohydrate | 21.3 g |
| Total sugars | 12.5 g |
| Dietary fibre | 1.0 g |
| Sodium | 76 mg |

1  Preheat the oven to 200°C (180°C fan forced). Line a baking tray with baking paper.

2  Mix the egg substitute with water to a smooth paste. Cream the margarine and sugar with a wooden spoon. Mix through the 'no-egg' paste, vanilla and baby apple (omit if using Basic Flour Mix).

3  Fold in flour and baking powder until well combined. Fold through the nuts and dried fruit.

4  Drop tablespoonfuls of the mixture onto the baking tray, allowing space for spreading.

5  Bake for 15–20 minutes or until starting to brown, rotating once during cooking. Allow to cool before transferring to a wire rack to cool completely. Store in an airtight container.

## Ⓖ Moist Pumpkin Fruit Cake

Ⓕ *Simple to make, this moist fruit cake ends up with a lightly crunchy crust—a lovely contrast to the soft, fruity interior. Store in an*
Ⓝ *airtight container. Do not overcook the pumpkin or it will become sludgy; when cooked, it should be just soft enough to mash easily.*
Ⓥ *Ⓖ use Basic Flour Mix. Ⓝ omit walnuts or substitute with pepitas or sunflower seeds.*

**Serves 10**

2 heaped tsp egg substitute (No Egg or Egg–Like brands)*
4 tbs (60 mL) water
200 g margarine (Nuttelex brand)*
125 g soft brown sugar
210 g Basic Flour Mix (page 113) plus 2 tsp gluten-free/wheat-free baking powder (Ward's brand)* or 225 g gluten-free/wheat-free self-raising flour (Orgran brand)*, sifted
2 tsp mixed spice
350 g cooked, well-drained pumpkin (such as Aussie sweet pumpkin), mashed
1 tbs (6 g) psyllium*
150 g natural sultanas
50 g currants (ingredient check—Dried fruit; Ⓖ)
60 g mixed peel* (ingredient check; Ⓝ)
30 g walnut pieces or 25 g sunflower seeds or pepitas
10 walnut halves or 25 g pepitas or sunflower seeds

| Per serve | |
| --- | --- |
| Energy | 1715 kJ (409 cal) |
| Protein | 4.7 g |
| Total fat | 21.5 g |
| Saturated fat | 3.4 g |
| Carbohydrate | 51.4 g |
| Total sugars | 32.8 g |
| Dietary fibre | 2.8 g |
| Sodium | 207 mg |

1  Preheat the oven to 180°C (160°C fan forced). Line** a 19 cm springform tin with a double layer of baking paper leaving a 5 cm overlap at the top of the tin.

**2** Mix the egg substitute and water to a smooth paste. Set aside.

**3** Cream the margarine and sugar in a mixing bowl. Mix through the 'no-egg' paste. Fold through the flour, mixed spice, pumpkin and psyllium. Stir through the dried fruit and walnut pieces (or seeds). Allow to stand for 10 minutes for the psyllium to absorb the moisture and thicken the mix.

**4** Remix, transfer to the lined tin, and smooth the top. Evenly space the walnut halves around the edge of the cake (or seeds over the top) and gently press into the mixture.

**5** Bake in the preheated oven for 1¼–1½ hours or until the centre of the cake is cooked when tested with a skewer, rotating 2–3 times during cooking. Leave to cool in the tin for 10 minutes before transferring to a wire rack to cool completely. Store in an airtight container.

## Morello Cherry, Apple and Coconut Slice

*The cherry filling can be substituted with any fruit of choice, such as apples, apricots or peaches—but make sure that the fruit is really well drained on kitchen towels before arranging on the slice base so that the base does not become soggy. To make a date and lemon slice, replace the filling with 250 g chopped, pitted dates, 100 g caster sugar, 125 mL water, zest of ½ lemon and 5 tablespoons (75 mL) lemon juice; combine in a small pan, bring to the boil and boil, stirring, for 3–4 minutes or until the dates have softened. ⓞ replace the almonds with extra 30 g gluten-free/wheat-free/nut-free cornflakes.*

**Makes 16**

Base

1 heaped tsp egg substitute (No Egg or Egg-Like brands)*

2 tbs (30 mL) water

3 tbs (45 mL) light coconut milk* (ingredient check)

100 g caster sugar

75 g margarine (Nuttelex brand)*

225 g Basic Flour Mix (page 113)

2 tsp gluten-free/wheat-free baking powder (Ward's brand)*

75 g desiccated coconut

Filling

400 g green apples (about 3), peeled, cored and very finely sliced

2 tsp lemon juice

3 tbs cherry or other fruit jam

1 x 720 g jar of sour pitted (Morello) or sour cherries, drained and halved

Topping

75 g margarine (Nuttelex brand)*

40 g gluten-free/wheat-free cornflakes, coarsely crushed (ingredient check; ⓞ)

35 g shredded coconut

45 g slivered almonds

25 g soft brown sugar

½ tsp ground cinnamon

**Per slice**

Energy 1157 kJ (276 cal)

Protein 3.3 g

Total fat 14.2 g

Saturated fat 1.8 g

Carbohydrate 35.6 g

Total sugars 20.6 g

Dietary fibre 3.3 g

Sodium 126 mg

**1** Preheat the oven to 180° C (160°C fan forced). Lightly grease an 18 x 28 cm slice tin and line with baking paper, allowing the paper to overhang.

**2** Mix the egg substitute and water to a smooth paste. Mix through the coconut milk and set aside. Put the sugar and margarine in a mixing bowl and beat to a smooth, creamy paste. Add the 'no-egg' paste while beating to combine. Gradually stir in the flour, baking powder and coconut with a wooden spoon to form a dough. Transfer to the cake tin and spread out evenly over the base with a palette knife. Bake in the oven for 20 minutes or until risen and cooked through. Set aside to cool.

3  While the base is cooking, put the apples in a small pan with the lemon juice, cover with a lid and cook over a low heat for 10 minutes or until softened.

4  Spread the jam evenly over the top of the base and top with the cooked apple. Arrange the cherry halves evenly over the top.

5  To make the topping, melt the margarine in a small pan. Remove from the heat and stir through all the remaining ingredients. Sprinkle over the top of the fruit and return to the oven for 10 minutes or until the topping is crisp and golden.

6  Set aside to cool for 10 minutes before slicing and allowing to cool completely. Store in an airtight container.

## 'Oatmeal' Slice

*The 'oatmeal' only describes the moist, oaty texture of this slice—there are no oats in the ingredients! The slice can be made as a semi-savoury or sweet slice by varying the type of syrup used to bind the mix. To convert to a sweet slice simply replace the rice syrup with additional golden syrup.*

**Makes 8**

30 g rolled rice*

5 tbs (75 mL) boiling water

60 g margarine (Nuttelex brand)*

30 g golden syrup (ingredient check; ⓖ)

30 g rice syrup* (ingredient check)

65 g Basic Flour Mix (page 113)

2 tsp (4 g) psyllium*

30 g desiccated coconut

½ tsp mixed spice

½ tsp gluten–free/wheat–free baking powder (Ward's brand)*

| Per slice | |
| --- | --- |
| Energy 574 kJ (137 cal) | |
| Protein 1.3 g | |
| Total fat 8.7 g | |
| Saturated fat 1.2 g | |
| Carbohydrate 14.5 g | |
| Total sugars 4.8 g | |
| Dietary fibre 1.3 g | |
| Sodium 69 mg | |

1  Preheat the oven to 180°C (160°C fan forced). Lightly grease a 20 cm round baking tin and line the base with baking paper.

2  Stir the boiling water through the rolled rice and set aside for 1 hour or until the water has been absorbed and the rice flakes softened.

3  Place the margarine and the syrups in a medium-sized pan over a low heat to melt, stirring to combine. Stir through the flour, psyllium, coconut, mixed spice and baking powder. Add the softened rice flakes and stir until well combined. Pour into the baking tin and smooth the surface. Set aside for 5 minutes to allow the psyllium to swell.

4  Bake for 18–20 minutes or until golden brown, rotating once during cooking. Remove from the oven and immediately cut into 8 wedges with a sharp knife. Allow to cool in tin for 10 minutes before transferring to a wire rack to cool completely. Store in an airtight container.

## ◯ Panforte

*A delicious variation on this classic—the mixed peel, dried fruit and nuts are a flavour-packed alternative to the usual glacé-fruit filled version—but you'll only manage a small slice at a time!* ◯ *use Basic Flour Mix.*

**Serves 10**

150 g whole blanched almonds, dry roasted**

140 g hazelnuts, dry roasted** and skinned (rub well in a tea towel or kitchen paper)

60 g gluten-free/wheat-free self-raising flour (Orgran brand)*, sifted, or 50 g Basic Flour Mix (page 113) plus ½ tsp gluten-free/wheat-free baking powder (Ward's brand)*

40 g brown rice flour*

1½ tsp ground coriander

½ tsp ground cinnamon

¼ tsp ground ginger

½ tsp nutmeg

200 g mixed peel* (ingredient check)

150 g Craisins* (dried cranberries) or raisins (ingredient check—Dried fruit; ◯)

150 g caster sugar

250 g honey

pure icing sugar, for dusting

**Per serve**

Energy 1903 kJ (454 cal)

Protein 5.9 g

Total fat 17.2 g

Saturated fat 1.1 g

Carbohydrate 71.3 g

Total sugars 61.7 g

Dietary fibre 5.4 g

Sodium 62 mg

1 Preheat the oven to 160°C (140°C fan forced). Line** a 19 cm springform tin (or use 2 x 10 cm tins to make 2 smaller cakes).

2 Coarsely chop the nuts and put in a bowl. Sift the flours and spices into the bowl and add the fruit. Mix well.

3 Combine the sugar and honey in a pan. Slowly bring to the boil, and cook for 3–4 minutes over a medium heat until the mixture reaches the 'soft ball stage' (a drop of the mixture forms a distinct, soft ball when dropped into a cup of cold water).

4 Pour the syrup over the cake mixture immediately. Stir well with a wooden spoon to mix all the ingredients together thoroughly. Press into the cake tin.

5 Bake in the preheated oven for 1–1¼ hours or until an even golden colour. (If the cake rises significantly during cooking, press back into the tin with the back of a wooden spoon.) Leave the cake to cool in the tin before turning out onto a wire rack to completely cool. Dust with icing sugar to serve. Store in an airtight container.

## ◯ Rich Fruit Cake

*Simple to make, this rich fruit cake can be served as is during the year, or covered with almond paste and iced during the festive season. If storing for any period, moisten by making holes in the base with a skewer and 'topping up' with additional sherry or unsweetened apple juice every 1–2 weeks.* ◯ *baby apple contains and apple juice may contain vitamin C (see Avoiding Corn, page 161); use gelatine in place of xanthan gum; use Basic Flour Mix.*

**Serves 10–12**

3 heaped tsp egg substitute (No Egg or Egg-Like brands)*

5 tbs (75 mL) water

50 g margarine (Nuttelex brand)*

100 g soft dark brown sugar

zest of 1 orange

150 g baby apple (Heinz brand)

½ tsp bicarbonate of soda, sifted

2 tbs (30 mL) apple juice concentrate*

200 g raisins, chopped if large (ingredient check—Dried fruit; ◯ )

**Per serve**

Energy 1592 kJ (380 cal)

Protein 2.9 g

Total fat 7.2 g

Saturated fat 1.0 g

Carbohydrate 61.6 g

Total sugars 49.6 g

Dietary fibre 4.3 g

Sodium 104 mg

200 g natural sultanas

150 g diced dates

50 g currants (ingredient check—Dried fruit; ⊙)

50 g mixed peel* (ingredient check)

75 g almond meal

120 g gluten-free/wheat-free plain flour (Orgran brand)*, sifted,

or 110 g Basic Flour Mix (page 113)

2 tsp mixed spice

½ tsp xanthan gum* or 1 tsp powdered gelatine plus 3 tablespoons (45 mL) boiling water

150 mL dry sherry (ingredient check—Wine; ⊙) or pure, unsweetened apple juice

   (Note: if using gelatine, reduce to 100 mL)

**1** Preheat the oven to 180°C (160°C fan forced). Line** a 19 cm round springform tin with a double layer of baking paper leaving a 5 cm overlap above the top of the tin.

**2** Mix the egg substitute and water to form a smooth paste. Set aside.

**3** If using gelatine, sprinkle the gelatine over the water in a small bowl or cup. Warm in the microwave for 5–10 seconds or until the gelatine has dissolved; do not boil.

**4** Cream the margarine, sugar and orange zest in a large mixing bowl with a wooden spoon. Stir through the 'no-egg' paste. Add all the remaining ingredients except the sherry (or apple juice) and mix to combine. Stir through the sherry (or apple juice). Spoon into the prepared cake tin and smooth the top.

**5** Bake in the centre of the oven for 1½–1¾ hours or until cooked when tested with a skewer, rotating cake every 30 minutes to ensure even cooking. Loosely cover with aluminium foil if the edges start to brown too rapidly. Leave to cool in the tin before turning out onto a wire rack to cool completely. Store in an airtight container.

## Ⓕ Sesame and Tahini Cake

Ⓥ *This is a heavier-style cake which is excellent served either at room temperature or warm with Vanilla Custard (page 141).*

**Serves 10-12**

1 tsp margarine (Nuttelex brand)*

3-4 tbs sesame seeds

250 g tahini*

150 g caster sugar

50 g soft brown sugar

zest of 2 oranges

125 mL (½ cup) fresh orange juice

225 mL rice milk* (ingredient check)

200 g gluten-free/wheat-free self-raising flour (Orgran)*, sifted

120 g gluten-free/wheat-free plain flour (Orgran brand)*, sifted

1 tsp ground allspice

100 g pistachio kernels (chopped)

6 dates, pitted and chopped

3 tbs sesame seeds, extra

**Per serve**

**Energy 1678 kJ (400 cal)**

**Protein 9.9 g**

**Total fat 20.4 g**

**Saturated fat 3.0 g**

**Carbohydrate 45.0 g**

**Total sugars 19.1 g**

**Dietary fibre 4.8 g**

**Sodium 17 mg**

**1** Preheat the oven to 170°C (150°C fan forced).

**2** Grease a 20 cm square non-stick cake tin with the margarine and sprinkle with the sesame seeds to coat. Set aside.

**3** Beat the tahini, sugar and orange zest together until creamy with an electric mixer. Add the orange juice and rice milk and continue to beat until combined.

4 Sift the flours and spice into the bowl. Add all the remaining ingredients and fold through to mix thoroughly. Spoon the mix into the prepared tin and smooth the top. Bake in the oven for 45–60 minutes, or until the centre of the cake is cooked when tested with a skewer.

5 Leave to cool for 5 minutes before turning out on to a wire rack to cool completely. Store in an airtight container.

## Surprise Fruit Cup Cakes

*These delicious little cakes can be made with a variety fresh or canned fruit, or fruit jam—I like to mix it up, with 2–3 flavours in a batch. The cake mix rises around the fruit as it bakes, resulting in a sweet, moist, fruity centre.*
◯ *baby apple and canned fruit contain vitamin C (see Avoiding Corn, page 161).*

**Makes 18**
2 heaped tsp egg substitute (No Egg or Egg–Like brands)*
4 tbs (30 mL) water
3 tbs (45 mL) light coconut milk* (ingredient check; ◯)
100 g caster sugar
75 g margarine (Nuttelex brand)*
225 g Basic Flour Mix (page 113)
1 tbs gluten–free/wheat–free baking powder (Ward's brand)*
220 g baby apple (Heinz brand)

Fruit Fillings
select one of the following:
18 canned apricot halves in natural juice (Goulburn Valley brand)
36 pitted sour (Morello) cherries
150 g fresh blueberries or raspberries
18 pitted prunes
18 peaches slices in natural juice (Goulburn Valley brand)

**Per cake**
**Energy 729 kJ (174 cal)**
**Protein 1.5 g**
**Total fat 3.8 g**
**Saturated fat 0.8 g**
**Carbohydrate 19.1 g**
**Total sugars 8.4 g**
**Dietary fibre 0.7 g**
**Sodium 103 mg**

1 Preheat the oven to 180°C (160°C fan forced). Set up 18 large patty cases on a baking tray or in muffin trays.

2 Mix the egg substitute and water to a smooth paste. Mix through the coconut milk and set aside. Cream the sugar and margarine in a mixing bowl. Blend in the 'no-egg' paste. Fold through the flour, baking powder and baby apple.

3 Spoon the mix into the muffin trays and place an apricot half (or other filling of choice) on top of each.

4 Bake in the oven for 20–25 minutes or until golden and cooked when tested with a skewer, rotating once during baking. Set aside to cool. Store in an airtight container

Biscuits and Pastries

## Almond Crescents

*These lovely biscuits are based on the traditional Greek biscuits 'almond pears'.*

**Makes 15**

2 heaped tsp egg substitute (No Egg or Egg–Like brands)*

2 tbs (30 mL) water

135 g almond meal

100 g caster sugar

3 drops natural almond essence (ingredient check)

¼ tsp lemon zest

extra ½–1 tsp water

50 g flaked almonds

3 tbs pure icing sugar

**Per biscuit**

Energy 466 kJ (111 cal)

Protein 2.7 g

Total fat 6.7 g

Saturated fat 0.6 g

Carbohydrate 10.0 g

Total sugars 9.0 g

Dietary fibre 1.2 g

Sodium 2 mg

1  Preheat the oven to 180°C (160°C fan forced). Line a baking tray with baking paper.

2  Mix the egg substitute with the water to form a smooth paste.

3  Put the almond meal, sugar, almond essence and lemon zest in a bowl and mix well. Add the egg paste and stir until the mixture forms a firm paste—if the mixture is too dry add the extra water, ½ teaspoon at a time, working it into the mix well before adding any additional water.

4  Put the flaked almonds on a plate. Roll a tablespoon of the mix in the almonds into a 7–8 cm long roll. Bend into a crescent shape and place on the baking tray. Repeat with the remaining mixture. Press any residual flaked almonds into the top of the biscuits.

5  Bake in the oven for 15–17 minutes or until starting to brown lightly, rotating once during cooking. Leave to cool fully on the tray before transferring to an airtight container for storage. Serve dusted with sifted icing sugar.

## Anzac Biscuits

*These Aussie classics are made using poha, beaten or rolled rice flakes of Indian origin, in place of the usual oats. Thin poha flakes are softer than the rolled rice flakes found in health food shops and so do not require pre-processing. Gluten-free cornflakes make an excellent alternative. ○ use Basic Flour Mix and poha.*

**Makes 18**

125 g margarine (Nuttelex brand)*

1 tbs (25 g) golden syrup (ingredient check; ○)

55 g thin poha* or 85 g gluten–free/wheat–free cornflakes* (ingredient check; ○)

120 g gluten-free/wheat-free plain flour (Orgran brand)*, sifted,

  or Basic Flour Mix (page 113)

60 g caster sugar

50 g desiccated coconut

½ tsp bicarbonate of soda

1 tbs (15 mL) boiling water

**Per biscuit**

Energy 505 kJ (120 cal)

Protein 0.5 g

Total fat 7.4 g

Saturated fat 1.1 g

Carbohydrate 13.3 g

Total sugars 4.4 g

Dietary fibre 0.6 g

Sodium 60 mg

1  Preheat the oven to 170°C (150°C fan forced). Line 2 baking trays with baking paper.

2  Place the margarine and golden syrup in a medium-sized pan over a low heat to melt, stirring to combine. Add the poha and cook for 2 minutes, stirring regularly (do not add cornflakes if using).

3  Add the flour, sugar and coconut (and cornflakes if using), and stir until well combined. Dissolve the bicarbonate of soda in the boiling water and stir through the mix.

4  Spoon tablespoonfuls of the mix onto the baking tray, allowing room for spreading.

5  Bake for 15 minutes or until golden brown, rotating once during cooking. Allow to cool on tray before transferring to a wire rack to cool completely. Store in an airtight container.

## Coconut and Almond Macaroons

*These easy-to-make almond macaroons can also be made with other nut meals such as hazelnut, cashew or even ground LSA mix\* to ring a change!*

**Makes 18**

|  | | |
|---|---|---|
| 1 heaped tsp egg substitute (No Egg or Egg–Like brands)\* | **Per biscuit** | |
| 2 tbs water | **Energy 307 kJ (73 cal)** | |
| 100 g almond meal | **Protein 1.6 g** | |
| 100 g caster sugar | **Total fat 4.7 g** | |
| 30 g desiccated coconut | **Saturated fat 0.3 g** | |
| 2 drops natural almond essence (ingredient check) | **Carbohydrate 6.6 g** | |
| 18 blanched almonds | **Total sugars 5.9 g** | |
| | **Dietary fibre 0.9 g** | |
| | **Sodium 2 mg** | |

1  Preheat the oven to 180°C (160°C fan forced). Line a baking slide with baking paper.

2  Mix the egg substitute and water together until a smooth paste.

3  Mix the almond meal, sugar and coconut together in a bowl. Stir through the almond essence and 'no-egg' paste (do not over mix).

4  Roll 2 teaspoonfuls of the mixture into a ball, place on the slide and flatten out slightly. Repeat until all the mixture has been used, placing the balls 3 cm apart. Press an almond into the top of each and lightly dust with icing sugar.

5  Bake in the oven for 12–15 minutes or until lightly browned, rotating once during cooking. Allow to stand for 5 minutes before transferring to a wire rack to cool completely. Store in an airtight container.

## Echidnas

*These delicious nibbles can be stored in an airtight container in the refrigerator—normally they don't stay there for long!*

**Makes 50**

|  | | |
|---|---|---|
| 150 g pitted dates | **Per echidna** | |
| 4 tbs (60 mL) water | **Energy 164 kJ (39 cal)** | |
| 125 g rice crumbs (Orgran brand)\* | **Protein 0.6 g** | |
| 40 g almond meal | **Total fat 1.2 g** | |
| 150 g natural sultanas | **Saturated fat 0.1 g** | |
| 2 tbs pure cocoa powder | **Carbohydrate 6.8 g** | |
| 1 tsp vanilla extract\* (ingredient check; ◯) | **Total sugars 4.4 g** | |
| | **Dietary fibre 0.7 g** | |
| Coating | **Sodium 2 mg** | |
| ½ cup desiccated coconut and/or dry-roasted\*\* sesame seeds | | |

1  Place the dates and water in a small pan over a low-medium heat and simmer for 5 minutes to soften.

2  Put the softened dates and all the remaining ingredients except the coating in a food processor and blend until a ball has formed.

3  Place half the coating of choice on a small plate. Roll a teaspoonful of the mix into a ball in your hand. Roll it in the coating and transfer to a clean plate. Repeat until all the mixture has been used. Cover and chill. Store refrigerated in an airtight container.

## ⊙ Flourless Choc–Nut Cookies

Ⓕ *These delicious flourless cookies will keep in an airtight container for up to 2 weeks.* ⊙ *use guar gum.*

Ⓥ **Makes 25**

| | |
|---|---|
| 1 heaped tsp egg substitute (No Egg or Egg–Like brands)* | **Per biscuit** |
| 2 tbs (30 mL) water | **Energy 520 kJ (124 cal)** |
| 300 g raw cashews, dry roasted** | **Protein 2.8 g** |
| 100 g walnut pieces | **Total fat 8.9 g** |
| 1 tsp extra–light olive oil* | **Saturated fat 1.3 g** |
| 3 tbs pure cocoa powder | **Carbohydrate 8.6 g** |
| 150 g caster sugar | **Total sugars 6.8 g** |
| ¼ tsp xanthan* or guar gum* | **Dietary fibre 1.0 g** |
| 1 tsp rum (optional; ingredient check—Spirits; ⊙) | **Sodium 3 mg** |

1  Preheat the oven to 180°C (160°C fan forced). Line 2 baking trays with baking paper.

2  Mix the egg substitute and water together to form a smooth paste and set aside.

3  Put the cashews, walnut pieces and oil in a food processor and blend until the mixture starts to form a paste. Add the all the remaining ingredients and process until the mixture comes together.

4  Roll a tablespoonful of the mixture into a ball and place on a lined tray. Repeat with all the remaining mixture, placing balls about 3 cm apart to allow for spreading. Use the back of a spoon to slightly flatten each cookie.

5  Bake in the oven for 10–12 minutes or until starting to brown round the edges, rotating once during cooking. Remove from the oven and leave to cool for 10 minutes before transferring to a wire rack to cool completely. Store in an airtight container.

## Ⓕ Ginger Snaps and Baskets

Ⓝ *Quick and easy—prepare as flat biscuits, as a small roll garnish or wider roll to fill as a brandy snap. For something special use the*
Ⓥ *mix to make Ginger Snap Baskets, which are perfect for loading with ice-cream or gelato of choice and macerated fruit or fruit compote. The secret of getting really 'snappy' wafers is to cook the mixture until it is bubbling and golden brown.*

**Makes over 20 biscuits and rolls, or 8 baskets**

| | |
|---|---|
| 50 g soft brown sugar | **Per biscuit** |
| 50 g golden syrup (ingredient check) | **Energy 132 kJ (31 cal)** |
| 15 g margarine (Nuttelex brand)* | **Protein 0.1 g** |
| 1 tsp lemon juice | **Total fat 0.6 g** |
| 50 g gluten-free/wheat-free plain flour (Orgran brand)*, sifted | **Saturated fat 0.1 g** |
| 1 tsp ground ginger, sifted | **Carbohydrate 6.5 g** |
| | **Total sugars 4.3 g** |
| | **Dietary fibre 0.1 g** |
| | **Sodium 7 mg** |

1  Preheat the oven to 190°C (170°C fan forced).

2  Line 2 baking trays with baking paper. Put the sugar, golden syrup, margarine and lemon juice in a small pan and warm, stirring continually until the sugar is dissolved. Fold through the flour and ginger.

3  *To make the biscuits* Place teaspoonfuls of the mixture 10–12 cm apart on the baking trays. Bake in the oven for 5–7 minutes or until bubbling and golden brown. Remove and set aside to cool.

4  Repeat until all the mixture is used up. If the mixture has cooled too much to spoon out, gently re-warm over a low heat until soft enough to handle.

5 *To make the rolls or brandy snaps* Grease the handle of a wooden spoon or 2 cm diameter plastic handle or cylinder, respectively. Prepare and bake the mixture as described for the biscuits but only cook 1 tray of biscuits at a time. As soon as the cooked biscuits have cooled enough to handle (about 15–20 seconds), quickly and carefully pick up one up and roll it around the handle or cylinder. Slip off and set aside to cool. Quickly repeat with the remaining biscuits.

6 Repeat until all the mixture is used up, re-warming the mixture over a low heat as described in Step 4.

7 *To make the baskets* Cut 8 x 16 cm square pieces of baking paper. Arrange 4 of the squares on 2 baking trays. Very lightly grease the bottom and sides of 4 ramekins (5–6 cm diameter) or tea cups. Prepare the biscuit ginger mix as described above and place 2 teaspoonfuls of the mixture on each of the 4 baking paper squares. Bake in the oven for 5–7 minutes or until bubbling and golden brown. Remove the top tray from the oven and place a ramekin in the centre of one ginger base. Carefully pick up the baking paper square and invert it over the ramekin. Gently press the ginger base around the side of the ramekin to form a fluted basket. Set aside to cool. Repeat quickly with the remaining 3 ginger discs.

8 Repeat with the remaining mixture, removing the first batch of cooled baskets from the ramekins to a wire rack, to re-use the ramekins as moulds. Re-warm the mixture gently as described in Step 4 if it has cooled too much to spoon easily.

9 Store wrapped in kitchen paper in an airtight container. To serve, dust the serving plates with pure icing sugar (optional). Place a basket in the centre of each plate. Place 1–2 scoops of ice-cream in the basket and top with the macerated fruit.

## Hazelnut Shortbread

*This wonderfully nutty shortbread can be prepared as individual biscuits or as a more traditional round. The nut-meal base can be varied to taste—using a pre-ground nut meal results in a denser, firmer shortbread. If you cut slightly larger slices or rounds, the shortbread makes a great base for a simple dessert of sliced fresh fruits such as peaches, nectarines and kiwi fruit, accompanied by a scoop of sorbet! ◯ use Basic Flour Mix and guar gum.*

**Makes 20 biscuits or 8 slices**

| | |
|---|---|
| 50 g raw nuts—hazelnuts, cashews, macadamia nuts, brazil nuts or blanched almonds, dry roasted** (or substitute a pre-ground nut meal) | **Per slice** |
| | Energy 292 kJ (70 cal) |
| 75 g margarine (Nuttelex brand)* | Protein 0.5 g |
| 60 g pure icing sugar, sifted | Total fat 4.8 g |
| 50 g gluten-free/wheat-free self-raising flour (Orgran brand)*, sifted, or 50 g Basic Flour Mix (page 113) | Saturated fat 0.9 g |
| | Carbohydrate 6.3 g |
| 40 g brown rice flour*, sifted | Total sugars 2.6 g |
| ¼ tsp xanthan* or guar gum* | Dietary fibre 0.4 g |
| | Sodium 16 mg |

1 Preheat the oven to 170°C (150°C fan forced). Line a baking tray with baking paper or lightly grease a 22 cm fluted flan dish and line the base with baking paper.

2 If using hazelnuts or brazil nuts, remove their papery skins after dry roasting by rubbing them in a tea towel. Put nuts in a food processor and blend to a meal (skip if using a nut meal).

3 Blend margarine and sugar well in a bowl. Gradually work in the sifted flours, xanthan gum and the nut meal with the back of a metal spoon until a ball of dough is formed.

4 Roll the dough out between 2 sheets of baking paper to a thickness of 5–6 mm. Either cut into biscuits with a 5 cm pastry cutter and transfer to the baking tray, reworking the left-over shortbread until it is used up, or, if baking in the flan dish, use the bottom sheet of paper to lift the shortbread into the dish and gently press it into the dish, repairing any tears. Using a sharp knife, cut into 8 wedges. Lightly prick the surface of the shortbread with a fork.

**5** Bake the biscuits for 10 minutes and the whole shortbread for 15–20 minutes or until cooked and lightly browned. Recut the wedges for the whole shortbread immediately on removing from the oven. Set aside to cool for 10 minutes before transferring to a wire rack to cool completely. Store in an airtight container.

## Lemon Myrtle and Macadamia Biscuits

*These are a very light, short biscuit with the delicate hint of lemon myrtle as a background flavour.* ○ *use guar gum.*

**Makes 18 biscuits**

| | |
|---|---|
| 100 g margarine (Nuttelex brand)* | **Per biscuit** |
| 45 g caster sugar | **Energy 372 kJ (89 cal)** |
| ¼ tsp xanthan* or guar gum* | **Protein 0.6 g** |
| 30 g raw, unsalted macadamia nuts, coarsely ground | **Total fat 6.6 g** |
| 100 g brown rice flour*, sifted | **Saturated fat 1.0 g** |
| 1 tsp ground lemon myrtle* | **Carbohydrate 7.1 g** |
| 20 g desiccated coconut | **Total sugars 2.6 g** |
| | **Dietary fibre 0.6 g** |
| | **Sodium 23 mg** |

**1** Preheat the oven to 200°C (180°C fan forced). Line a baking tray with baking paper.

**2** Cream the margarine and sugar. Stir through the gum evenly through the mixture. Add the ground nuts, flour and lemon myrtle and mix together thoroughly. Spoon heaped teaspoons of the mixture onto the tray. Flatten the top of each biscuit slightly and sprinkle with desiccated coconut.

**3** Bake in the oven for 10–12 minutes or until a light golden colour, rotating once during cooking. Allow the biscuits to cool slightly before transferring to a wire rack to completely cool. Store in an airtight container.

## Savoury Biscuit Assortment

*Made on a shortcrust pastry base, these biscuits melt in your mouth. By dividing the pastry mix into portions and adding a different flavour to each you can bake a biscuit assortment in one go.* ○ *use guar gum.*

**Makes 30 biscuits**

| | |
|---|---|
| 1 quantity Shortcrust Pastry (page 155) | **Per biscuit base without** |
| | **flavourings** |
| Flavourings | **Energy 240 kJ (57 cal)** |
| select one of the following (or reduce proportionately if making two or more flavours | **Protein 0.9 g** |
| per batch of pastry): | **Total fat 3.4 g** |
| 1 tsp caraway, cumin or dill seeds | **Saturated fat 0.6 g** |
| 1 tsp curry powder* (ingredient check) | **Carbohydrate 5.9 g** |
| 2 tsp ras el hanout* | **Total sugars 0.2 g** |
| 1 tsp Italian herbs (ingredient check) | **Dietary fibre 0.2 g** |
| | **Sodium 19 mg** |

**1** Preheat the oven to 180°C (160°C fan forced).

**2** *If only using one flavouring* Put the margarine, flour and gum and flavouring in a mixing bowl and work together using a knife. Add the water and mix through with a knife. Work the mix by kneading gently until it comes away from the bowl and forms a ball. Roll the pastry out between 2 sheets of baking paper until about 2–3 mm thick.

**3** *If using more than one flavouring* Divide unflavoured pastry into the desired number of portions. Work with one portion at a time, wrapping remaining portions in a plastic bag to prevent the pastry drying out. Remove the top sheet of paper and sprinkle the selected flavouring over the top. Fold the pastry up over the flavouring and work into a ball to distribute the flavouring evenly. Replace the paper and roll the pastry out until 2–3 mm thick.

4   Using a 6 cm pastry cutter (shapes or fluted) cut out the biscuits. Remove the excess pastry from between the biscuits and using a spatula, gently transfer the biscuits to the baking tray. Re-work the excess pastry and cut into biscuits. Repeat until the pastry is used up.

5   Repeat with remaining portions of pastry and selected flavouring.

6   Bake for 12–15 minutes or until golden, rotating once during cooking. Set aside to cool. Store in an airtight container.

## ⚪ Shortcrust and Sweet Shortcrust Pastry

*This is a very short, light pastry that can easily be used as is as the base for savoury flans or tartlets, or see Savoury Biscuit Assortment (page 154) to convert the pastry into a batch of biscuits. Adding icing sugar and natural flavourings, such as lemon myrtle or wattle seed, converts the pastry into a wonderful base for sweet flans and tarts. (For a sweet shortcrust pastry suitable for baking unfilled see Quandong, Lemon and Roast Almond Flan, page 128.) ⚪ use guar gum.*

**Makes 1 x 24 cm flan base (serves 8–10) or 45 x 5 cm tartlet bases**

| | |
|---|---|
| 120 g margarine (Nuttelex brand)* | **Per serve** |
| 240 g Basic Flour Mix (page 113) | Energy 721 kJ (172 cal) |
| ¼ tsp xanthan* or guar gum* | Protein 2.6 g |
| 3 tbs (45 mL) water | Total fat 10.2 g |
| | Saturated fat 1.9 g |
| **Sweet Shortcrust Pastry** | Carbohydrate 17.8 g |
| 3 tbs pure icing sugar, sifted, or replace water with apple juice concentrate* | Total sugars 0.5 g |
| | Dietary fibre 0.6 g |
| | Sodium 58 mg |

1   Put the margarine, flour and gum (plus icing sugar if making sweet pastry, and any dry flavourings) in a mixing bowl and work together using a knife. Add the water (or apple juice concentrate if using in place of icing sugar) and mix through with the knife. Work the mix by kneading gently until it comes away from the bowl and forms a ball.

2   Roll the pastry out to a 27–28 cm disc between 2 sheets of baking paper.

3   If using the pastry as a flan base, use the bottom sheet to pick up the pastry and invert over the flan dish. Gently press the pastry into the dish, repairing any tears. Trim the excess pastry with a sharp knife. Fill and bake according to the recipe instructions.

4   For tartlet bases, preheat oven to 200°C (180°C fan forced). Use a 5 cm pastry cutter to cut the bases, removing the excess pastry from round the discs. Transfer the bases to a lined baking tray. Rework the left-over pastry until all the pastry has been used up. Bake in oven for:
    10–12 minutes or until very lightly coloured if the bases will be rewarmed with a topping before serving, or
    12–15 minutes or until golden if serving at room temperature using a pre-cooked topping.

Try these simple tartlet toppings; spread pastry with a scrape of margarine and top with:

• Green prawns poached in macadamia oil*, lemon juice and sambal oelek* (ingredient check) and chilled in the sauce; top with freshly ground black pepper;
• Coriander salsa (see Seared Crusted Salmon with Coriander Salsa, page 39);
• Smoked Mackerel and Butter Bean Pâté (page 28) or Beetroot Pâté (page 26).

## Sweet Biscuit Assortment

*These melt-in-the-mouth biscuits are made on a shortcrust pastry-style base. By dividing the pastry dough into portions and adding a different flavour to each portion, you can bake a biscuit assortment in one go. If selecting only one flavouring, add it to the mixing bowl with the flours; if using 2 or more, add after dividing the pastry into portions as described below. ⊙ use guar gum.*

**Makes 36 biscuits**

180 g Basic Flour Mix (page 113)

75 g tapioca flour*

45 g caster sugar

½ tsp xanthan* or guar gum*

110 g margarine (Nuttelex brand)*

55 g rice syrup* (ingredient check)

3–4 tsp extra–light olive oil*

pure icing sugar to dust (optional)

**Per biscuit base without flavourings**

Energy 251 kJ (60 cal)

Protein 0.5 g

Total fat 2.9 g

Saturated fat 0.5 g

Carbohydrate 8.0 g

Total sugars 2.1 g

Dietary fibre 0.1 g

Sodium 16 mg

Flavourings

select one of the following (or reduce proportionately if making two or more flavours per batch of pastry):

100 g currants (ingredient check—Dried fruit; ⊙)

50 g flaked almonds (not for nut–free)

1 tsp cinnamon plus finely grated zest of 1 orange

1 tsp ajowan* seeds

2 tbs sesame seeds, dry roasted**

1 tsp mixed spice

1 tsp ground lemon myrtle*

1  Preheat the oven to 180°C (160°C fan forced). Line 2 baking trays with baking paper.

2  *If only using one flavouring* Put the flours, sugar and gum and seed or spice flavourings (add currants and nuts with the oil) in a mixing bowl and stir to combine. Add the margarine and work it through the flour. Add the rice syrup and work through with your fingers covering it with the flour until it is broken up and no longer sticky. Add currants or nuts, if using, and 3 teaspoons of the oil and work through the flour pulling the mix together; add an additional teaspoon of oil if required to form the pastry into a ball. Knead lightly. Roll the pastry out between 2 sheets of baking paper until about 2–3 mm thick.

3  *If using more than one flavouring* Divide unflavoured pastry into the desired number of portions. Work with one portion at a time, wrapping remaining portions in a plastic bag to prevent the pastry drying out. Remove the top sheet of paper and sprinkle the selected flavouring over the top. Fold the pastry up over the flavouring and work into a ball to distribute the flavouring evenly. Replace the paper and roll the pastry out until 2–3 mm thick.

4  Using a 6 cm pastry cutter (shapes or fluted) cut out the biscuits. Remove the excess pastry from between the biscuits and using a spatula, gently transfer the biscuits to the baking tray. Rework the left-over pastry until the pastry is used up.

5  Repeat with remaining portion(s) of pastry and selected flavouring(s).

6  Bake for 12–15 minutes on until golden, rotating once during cooking. Set aside to cool. Serve as is or lightly dusted with icing sugar. Store in an airtight container.

## Vanilla Kisses

*These dainty little biscuits dissolve in your mouth and can be made with one or more icing flavours per batch, or simply eaten as is. By reducing the size of the biscuit to about 7.5 g each, the little kisses can be assembled as a double biscuit using the icing as a filler.*

**Makes 30**

125 g margarine (Nuttelex brand)*
40 g pure icing sugar, sifted
½ tsp vanilla extract* (ingredient check)
65 g gluten-free/wheat-free self-raising flour (Orgran brand)*
75 g maize cornflour
20 g fine white rice flour*

Icing
80 g pure icing sugar, sifted
zest of 1 lemon
1 tsp margarine (Nuttelex brand)*
2–3 tsp lemon juice

Per biscuit
Energy 264 kJ (63 cal)
Protein 0.1 g
Total fat 3.5 g
Saturated fat 0.7 g
Carbohydrate 7.9 g
Total sugars 3.4 g
Dietary fibre 0.1 g
Sodium 17 mg

1 Preheat the oven to 160°C (140°C fan forced). Line a baking tray with baking paper.

2 Put the margarine and sugar in a bowl and mix with a metal spoon until creamy. Blend in the vanilla extract. Sift in the flours and work through the mix with the spoon until a dough is formed. Roll into walnut-sized balls (about 10 g each) and place on the tray. Flatten the balls with the back of a fork. (Alternatively, the mixture may be piped onto the trays.)

3 Bake in the oven for 25–30 minutes. Cool on the trays for 5 minutes before transferring to a wire rack to cool completely.

4 To make the icing, combine the icing sugar, lemon zest and margarine in a small bowl and gradually add the lemon juice, mixing well between additions, until a stiff icing is formed.

5 Ice the top of each biscuit with ½ teaspoon of the icing mix. Store in an airtight container.

*Variations*

*Almond Kisses* Replace vanilla extract with 3 drops natural almond essence*. (Not for nut-free.)

*Chocolate Icing* 75 g pure icing sugar, 4 teaspoons pure cocoa powder, 2–3 teaspoons boiling water (or use Cashew and Chocolate Cream, page 140; not for nut-free).

*Chocolate Kisses* Replace rice flour with 2 tablespoons pure cocoa powder, then ice with chocolate, lemon or orange icing.

*Coconut Kisses* Replace vanilla extract with ½ teaspoon suitable coconut essence.

*Orange Icing* replace lemon zest with zest of ¾ orange, and lemon juice with orange juice.

## Wonton, Mezzelune and Ravioli Wrappers

*This dough is very versatile and amazingly resilient—it can be boiled, steamed, fried or baked. Take care to add the last 2 tablespoons of liquid slowly and work it into the dry ingredients really well before adding extra, to prevent the pastry becoming too wet and tacky. Prepare the filling before rolling out the pastry or the pastry may dry out and become brittle.*

*The pastry can be stored at room temperature in a plastic bag for 24 hours (do not refrigerate). The wrappers can be used to make the usual style of Asian wonton, stuffed with a savoury meat filling and served in a good broth, Italian mezzalune or ravioli with meat, poultry, fish or vegetarian filling of choice, or with a lemon myrtle red bean paste (see Red Bean and Apple Pie, page 129) to make a sweet dainty. The secret is to roll the dough out very thinly.*

**Makes 25–30 wonton or mezzalune wrappers, 12–15 ravioli wrappers**

| | |
|---|---|
| 35 g fine white rice flour* | **Per wrapper** |
| 25 g maize cornflour | **Energy 58 kJ (14 cal)** |
| 25 g glutinous white rice flour* | **Protein 0.2 g** |
| 35 g fine maize flour* | **Total fat <0.1 g** |
| ½ tsp xanthan gum* | **Saturated fat <0.1 g** |
| 6–7 tbs (90–105 mL) water or unsweetened apple juice (for sweet wontons) or chicken | **Carbohydrate 3.1 g** |
| stock* (ingredient check; for savoury wontons) | **Total sugars <0.1 g** |
| extra glutinous white rice flour, for dusting | **Dietary fibre 0.1 g** |
| | **Sodium 2 mg** |

1  Put all the dry ingredients in a sieve over a mixing bowl and sift 3 times to ensure complete mixing. Make a well in the middle and add 5 tablespoons of water (or juice or stock). Work the liquid through the flours with a fork to form a dough. Add extra liquid, 1 teaspoon at a time, until the dough just comes together when worked with your hand.

2  Place a sheet of baking paper on a benchtop, lightly flour and knead the dough for a 1–2 minutes until it is elastic and forms a tight ball. Cut the dough into 3 equal pieces and roll into balls. Place 2 balls in a plastic bag to keep moist.

3  Lightly flour a rolling pin and the baking paper work surface. Roll the third ball out evenly to a 22–24 cm round (the pastry should be between 1–2 mm thick), reflouring the rolling pin and baking paper lightly as required. For wonton and mezzalune wrappers, use a 7 cm diameter pastry cutter, or for ravioli wrappers a 6 cm diameter cutter. Remove the excess pastry and lift the pastry rounds onto a clean sheet of baking paper, floured side down. Cover with a damp tea towel.

4  Add the excess pastry to the second ball of pastry and repeat the process. Repeat with the third ball, reworking the excess pastry until the pastry is used up.

5  For wonton and mezzalune wrappers, place ½ teaspoon of filling in one half of the wrapper. Wet the edge of the pastry with cold water. Fold the wrapper in half over the filling and squeeze the edges together to seal. Place the filled wrapper on a tray and cover with a damp tea towel. Repeat with the remaining wrappers.

6  For ravioli, place ¾–1 teaspoon of filling in the centre of a wrapper. Wet the edge of the pastry with cold water. Place a second wrapper over the top and squeeze the edges together to seal. Place the filled wrapper on a tray and cover with a damp tea towel. Repeat with the remaining wrappers. Do not allow the wrappers to dry out.

7  To cook, bring a large pan of water to a fast boil, drop the pastries into the water and cook for 2 minutes after they rise to the surface for pre-cooked filling and 3–4 minutes for an uncooked, non-vegetarian filling, using a spider or slotted spoon to gently turn the pastries and remove them at the end of cooking.

8  Serve immediately in broth of choice or with pasta sauce of choice.

Avoiding 'No-Go' Foods and their Derivatives

Besides avoiding the foods that are a 'no-go', eating a wide range of suitable foods in a balance that will meet all your dietary requirements is fundamental to the success of your diet and your ongoing health. If you have recently found out you have an intolerance or allergy to one or more foods, or are shopping to feed a friend or family member with food problems, this section will help you identify the many forms in which the 'No-Go' foods are found commercially, and gives examples of where they may be hidden in commercially manufactured foods.

When you first start shopping and cooking to avoid one or more foods, it can seem an overwhelming challenge. What is there left to eat? It seems as though there is nothing you can buy—a basic food like wheat, dairy, soy or eggs appears to be included in the ingredient list on the label of *everything* that you used to buy. The difficulties are compounded when you discover a single food can appear under many different and often unpronounceable names in the ingredient list. You find a product that you thought was safe is, in fact, a 'no-go'—perhaps corn is described in the ingredient list as 'invert sugar' or 'glucono delta-lactone', while a non-dairy coffee whitener contains casein, one of the main milk proteins, so is very definitely not 'non-dairy'.

While these hidden forms of a 'No-Go' food are real problems, probably the most common reason people inadvertently eat a 'No-Go' food is contamination of a safe food. This can easily happen when the same serving utensils or cooking equipment are used in a salad bar, a take-away food outlet, café or restaurant. How often are cheese and meat sliced on the same slicer in a delicatessen without it being cleaned in between? Similarly, the machinery in a production line may not be properly cleaned down between different product runs, leading to the contamination of a safe food by the residue of 'No-Go' food in the previous run. Contamination by peanuts is a well-known example of this, but there is potential for such cross-contamination to occur in any manufacturing area where a range of products is made on the same machinery or where an ingredient may become airborne. The home environment is also not exempt—preventing cross-contamination of safe foods during preparation and while they are being stored is also essential (see Managing the Kitchen, page 201).

As of December 2002, the Australian and New Zealand Food Standards (FSANZ) Code (Standard 1.2.3, clause 4, www.foodstandards.gov.au/foodstandardscode), which sets out the standards for the labelling of commercially made food, now includes mandatory labelling requirements for a group of foods that are recognised as having the potential to cause adverse or allergic reactions in sensitive individuals. Manufacturers must list the following eight groups of ingredients, or ingredients derived from these foods, on the product label:

- cereals containing gluten and their products (namely, wheat, rye, barley, oats and spelt and their hybridised strains). Note: beer and spirits are exempt;
- crustacea and their products (the specific crustacean included must be nominated);
- egg and egg products;
- fish and fish products (the specific type of fish need not be nominated);
- milk and milk products;
- peanuts and peanut products;
- soybeans and soybean products;
- tree nuts (the type must be specifically named) and sesame seeds and their products.

While there are some exemptions to this requirement—for example if the food is not sold in a package, or is made and packaged on the premises from which it is sold—this labelling change has assisted consumers in unravelling the nightmare of ingredient content to a large extent. Additionally, where there is the risk of cross-contamination of a product by one of these foods, the manufacturer is required to list this on the product label. Manufacturers must now also list any alternative ingredients they may use in a product—overcoming their ability to swap ingredients without flagging a change to the consumer.

There are still problems in some areas. We are between two Food Standard Codes, although by the time this book is published the problems caused by the transition should be largely overcome, with only some long-life foods (such as canned foods) being labelled under the old standard until 20 December 2004; all other food labels should comply—with of course the exception of wine vintages and other aged beverages bottled prior to December 2002, the labelling requirements of which are still under active debate. However, application is already before FSANZ to water down these labelling requirements, because they are too onerous for food manufacturers. The proposal is to limit the mandatory declarations to the presence of the eight nominated food groups and any protein-containing derivatives of these foods, on the basis that it is only the protein component of these foods that can provoke an adverse reaction in sensitive individuals. This would preclude declaration of ingredients such as oils, lecithin, starch, sugars, flavourings or colours (such as caramel) derived from these foods, if they were deemed to be protein-free, and would be a real setback for people sensitive to the non-protein fractions of the foods.

In addition, people with sensitivities to any of these eight food groups must deduce if a product is suitable by the *omission* of the food names on the label, rather than by specific declaration of the food origin of an ingredient. For example, the generic name 'vegetable oil' without qualification on a label indicates that the oil has not been derived from wheat, soy, peanut, tree nut or sesame—if it was, then the current Code requires that the food origin be stated. Of course, this does not help people whose sensitivities extend to foods such as corn. So when a label's ingredient list includes a generic name such as 'vegetable oil', consider the product's suitability carefully in light of your specific dietary needs—and use the lists on the following pages to help you work out the likely food origin of these generically described ingredients.

Flavourings still pose a potential problem. The Code only requires they be disclosed on a label as 'flavour' or 'flavourings'—but they are still subject to the mandatory ingredient disclosure requirements for the eight food groups listed above. Wherever these all-encompassing terms appear be wary and check—the ingredients used in their manufacture are often kept secret as proprietary information by the flavouring manufacturer rather than the food manufacturer, and if the food manufacturer is unaware of the derivation of the flavour, it is possible that the 'flavour' includes an ingredient that should be disclosed. In this situation I avoid any commercially made food that includes the word 'flavouring', 'flavour', 'natural flavour' and so on, unless I have confirmation from the manufacturer that the flavour is not derived from and does not contain any of my 'No-Go' foods.

Caramel added as a colouring (caramel, 150 a–d) is an example of potential labelling problems. Most caramel used in the food and beverage industry is derived from dextrose, invert sugar, lactose, malt syrup, molasses, starch hydrolysates or sucrose—and ultimately, from corn, wheat, sugar cane or dairy. Under the mandatory labelling requirements, where the caramel is a wheat or dairy derivative, it should be described as such on the label. Absence of such a declaration only excludes a wheat or dairy source; it does not exclude corn (maize), for example. Alcoholic beverages are the exception—for standardised alcoholic drinks, manufacturers are not required to declare the presence of caramel on the label of wines or spirits; if caramel does pose a problem then individual brands and vintages need to be checked for suitability (see the entries in the Ingredients section for suitable brands and vintages of wines, spirits and liqueurs used in these recipes).

Likewise the declaration of garlic can be hidden, since it is legitimately included under the umbrella of 'spices' if it is present as a flavouring rather than in larger quantities as a food ingredient *per se*. Even a small amount of hidden garlic can cause significant problems to sensitive individuals, and the problem can be compounded if a sensitive person unknowingly eats a range of foods in which it is hidden.

So the bottom line is:
- if you are uncertain about the food origin of an ingredient on a product label, don't use that product unless you have confirmed the origin with the manufacturer;
- if the ingredient list includes an umbrella name such as 'spices', 'flavours' and one of your 'No-Go' foods may be included under that name, don't use the product unless you have confirmed its absence with the manufacturer;
- if the product doesn't carry an ingredient listing, don't use the product;
- if you react to a product that didn't include one of your 'No-Go' foods in its ingredient list, it is possible that the product was cross-contaminated by another food made in the same area of the factory, or the ingredient list is incomplete. Check back with the manufacturer.

To report a labelling problem with a food, go to the Environmental Health Officer at your local council or the Senior Food Officer in your State or Territory Health Department; FSANZ does not handle infractions.

The following pages include lists of:
- the different names or guises in which each of the 'No-Go' foods can appear on labels; and
- the most common commercially made foods in which they may be found.

Don't panic—in many cases you will find the same commercially made foods listed simply because of the repetitive use of 'No-Go' foods (the same few basic ingredients or so-called 'staples') across their food range by manufacturers.

## Avoiding Corn

'Corn' in this book specifically refers to any maize-based or -derived product and *not* wheat starch. Confusingly, wheat starch can be labelled as 'cornstarch' on some products but under the requirements of the Food Standards Code wheat-derived cornstarch should now be labelled accordingly.

A large proportion of processed foods is made with corn syrup, cornstarch or corn meal—in fact, most regular pantry items contain some corn-derived ingredient. So, as with any food avoidance, careful label reading is the key to avoid corn successfully.

Usually corn avoidance involves avoiding the foods or ingredients included in the two following lists. However, a few of the recipes in this book include an additional note referring to corn avoidance in specific ingredients, such as fruit juices, which can contain added vitamin C as additives—sodium ascorbate (301) and ascorbic acid (300); these may be derived from corn and may cause problems for people who are very highly sensitive to corn. Other food additives which may be derived from corn but rarely cause problems for corn-sensitive individuals are the food acids—such as citric (330), lactic (270) and acetic (260) acids—and other acidity regulators such as calcium lactate (327) and gluconate (578). These may be included in some brands of commercially made ingredients used in the recipes in this book and reference to them is included in the respective ingredient entry in the Glossary (page 173). Given the very low incidence of sensitivity to these additives, the corn-free flag ⊚ on recipes using a product that usually contains one or more of these additives is *not* marked as a ◯. If in doubt, please check with your healthcare practitioner whether any of these additives need to be excluded from your diet, and mark the affected ingredients in the recipes accordingly.

## Avoid

All corn and corn-derived foods, including products with any of the following labelled ingredients (★ unless suitable origin specified):

- caramel, caramel colour or flavour★;
- corn, baby corn, corn cuts, creamed corn, kernels;
- corn alcohol, extract or oil;
- corn sugars, syrup or syrup solids, or sweeteners ;
- cornflour, cornstarch or starch (unless specifically labelled as wheat-derived);
- cornmeal;
- dextrose, dextrin or dextrates;
- edible starch★;
- fructose or high fructose corn syrup;
- flavour, or natural flavour or flavouring★;
- glucono delta-lactone;
- glucose or glucose syrup★;
- golden syrup (unless labelled from cane sugar);
- grits;
- hominy;
- hydrolysed corn, corn or vegetable★ protein;
- icing or confectioner's sugar (unless labelled 'pure');
- lecithin★;
- invert sugar or syrup★;
- maize, maize meal or thickener;
- malt or malt syrup★;
- maltodextrin★;
- modified corn, starch or food starch★;
- monosodium glutamate★;
- polenta;
- popcorn;
- pregelatinised starch★;
- thickener★;

- treacle (unless specified as pure molasses);
- unmodified starch★;
- vegetable gum, starch, shortenings or other derivative★;
- vanilla extract or vanillin (check corn syrup free);
- xanthan gum;
- zein.

### Possible Hidden Sources of Corn

Note: This list is a guide—please read all labels of commercially prepared food carefully before using, to ensure the food is corn-free.

- beverages—soft and fruit drinks sweetened with corn syrup or artificial sweetener, glucose, etc., fruit juice concentrates, frozen juice, instant teas, sports drinks, alcoholic beverages (see Glossary—Wines, and Spirits and Liqueurs);
- breads and pastries—biscuits and biscuit mixes, cakes and cake mixes, doughnuts, frostings, many breads, muffins;
- breakfast cereals—cereals sweetened with corn syrup, cornflakes, puffed corn;
- dairy products—cream, cheese (including cottage and ricotta), frozen yogurt, imitation cheeses, sour cream, ice cream;
- meat, fish and poultry—bacon, canned tuna, cold cuts (turkey, roast beef, corned beef and silverside) cured meat (ham, bacon), fish sticks, hot dogs, luncheon meat, imitation seafood;
- pastas—canned spaghetti, udon noodles (may be made from wheat);
- puddings and desserts—canned, steamed or instant puddings, custards, custard powder, custard tarts;
- snacks and sweets—corn chips, crispy foods such as french fries, jams, jelly, lollies sweetened with corn syrup or dusted with icing sugar, marshmallows, nachos, peanut butter, potato puffs and chips, tacos, tortillas;
- take-away food—Chinese food (routinely thickened with cornstarch), breads, fried foods, hot dogs, cross-contamination from corn-containing foods prepared in the area;
- vegetables—baked beans, canned and frozen vegetables in sauce, thickened tomato products;
- other foods—baking powder, bottled sauces and ketchups, canned soups, gravy browning, margarine, pickles, salad dressings, sauce mixes;
- other items—adhesives and gummed paper, artificial sweeteners, bleached white flour, distilled white vinegar, iodised salt, plastic wrap, paper cups and plates may be coated with corn oil, toothpaste, many medications and vitamins, including capsules, solid and liquid medications, ointments, suppositories and lozenges.

## Avoiding Dairy

People who need to avoid dairy—because of a lactose intolerance or a reaction to one of the milk proteins—will find that dairy, like wheat, corn and soy, appears in a huge range of commercially made foods. Not only is milk usage widespread, but milk derivatives such as butter, cream, yoghurt, or a fraction of milk (such as casein or lactose) appear in many food ingredient lists, as well as pharmaceuticals, so care must be taken when shopping or eating out to avoid it.

There are a number of alternatives to dairy available through supermarkets (Western and Asian) and health food shops. The majority of these are based on soy—which is fine if you like or can tolerate soy—and range from milks to cheese, yoghurt and so on, but be careful to check many of these soy-based products are really dairy-free. Other milks are based on rice and oats (the latter is only suitable if you can tolerate gluten). There is a range of dairy-free margarines available through supermarkets; the recipes in this book are based on Nuttelex because it suits the widest range of food intolerances and is a light, neutral-tasting spread.

White beans (cannellini) and coconut milk make good non-dairy bases. The beans are excellent because they provide a lot of texture and fibre, and are a natural thickener. I love using coconut milk, but it is important to take care in selecting a brand in order to minimise the amount of saturated fat routinely used in your cooking (see Glossary, page 176).

Whether you can or can't tolerate dairy, ensuring an adequate calcium intake is important. Many calcium-enriched, non-dairy products, including fruit juices, cereals, rice and soy (if tolerated) beverages, are now widely available. They can be used in addition to naturally calcium-rich foods such as fish with edible bones, green leafy vegetables, oranges, almonds and ground sesame seed paste (tahini) to boost your daily calcium intake. Your calcium requirements will vary at different stages of your life, so do check with your healthcare practitioner to ensure you are getting a balanced diet with sufficient calcium to meet your body's needs.

## Avoid

All dairy, dairy-derived and 'au-gratin' foods (including cow, goat, sheep, buffalo and horse unless tolerated) and products with any of the following labelled ingredients (★ if dairy-derived, the Food Standards Code requires declaration of the dairy-based origin):

- artificial butter and cream★;
- butter or butter fat;
- buttermilk, buttermilk flavour or solids;
- calcium or sodium caseinate;
- caramel, caramel colour or flavour★;
- casein or caseinate;
- cheese and cheese flavour;
- condensed or evaporated milk;
- cream (single/double/whipping);
- crème fraiche;
- curd;
- dried milk or milk solids;
- galactose (breakdown product of lactose rarely associated with dairy sensitivity);
- ghee;
- ice-cream (dairy-based);
- lactalbumin;
- lactoglobulin;
- lactic acid (270—can be produced from fermentation of milk, but is usually dairy free)★;
- lactose;
- milk protein or solids;
- non-fat or sour milk solids;
- pasteurised milk;
- rennet;
- skim milk or milk powder;
- sour cream or solids;
- whey, whey powder or protein concentrate;
- yoghurt;
- other descriptors—'animal fat', 'high protein/protein enriched', hydrolysed vegetable protein, 'natural ingredients or flavouring', 'non-dairy'★.

## Possible Hidden Sources of Dairy

Note: This list is a guide—please read all labels of commercially prepared food carefully before using to ensure the food is dairy-free.

- beverages—beverage whitener, cream liqueurs, instant drinks (dandelion coffee, etc.), malted milk flavouring (Milo, etc.), high-protein drink powders and food supplements, slimming meal replacers, alcoholic beverages (see Glossary—Wines, and Spirits and Liqueurs);
- breads and pastries—baked goods (brushed on), biscuits and biscuit mixes, bread, cakes and cake mixes, cookies, croissants, doughnuts, flans, meringues, muffins, pastry, pies, rusks, tarts;
- breakfast cereals—high protein cereals, including muesli;
- meat, fish and poultry—canned fish and meat, deli meat, frankfurters, hot dogs, luncheon meats, pies, salami, sausages;
- pastas—ready-made pasta dishes with cream, cheese or butter-based sauces and dressings;

- puddings and desserts—frozen dessert coatings, creamed rice, instant puddings, junket, pancakes and mixes, rice pudding, soufflés, waffles and mixes, whipped desserts and toppings, Yorkshire puddings;
- snacks and sweets—butterscotch and caramel lollies, chewing gum, chocolate, frozen juice ice blocks or creams, fudge, lollies, nougat, sherbet, savoury and flavoured snack foods (e.g. corn and potato chips), toffee;
- take-away food—a wide range of take-away foods based on the other food groups listed, battered foods (e.g. fish), sauces, cross-contamination from dairy-containing foods prepared in the same area;
- vegetables—canned or frozen vegetables in sauce (e.g. creamed mushrooms), commercially prepared salads (e.g. potato salad dressed with mayonnaise), frozen french fries or chips, mashed potato, soy cheese, vegetable fat, vegetarian cheese;
- other foods—chicken broth, cream-based and creamy soups and sauces, bouillon, gravy and gravy mixes, mayonnaise, packaged soups and sauces, peanut butter, pickles, salad dressings;
- other items—artificial sweeteners, coconut milk powder, cream substitutes, imitation sour cream, low-fat spreads, margarine, peanut butter, some medicines and vitamins contain lactose.

## Avoiding Eggs

Besides the obvious presence of eggs in quiche and other egg-based dishes, and as a binder to prevent baked foods such as cakes and pastries from crumbling, a number of components of eggs are found in a wide range of commercially made foods. They are used as emulsifiers, coagulants, preservatives and glazes (on goods such as pretzels and bagels)—and are not always obvious when looking at a food item. So check labels carefully, and take extra care when buying unlabelled goods from a bakery or other food vendor or where there is any risk of cross-contamination—when buying food from gourmet food shops and take-away food outlets or in restaurants. Egg proteins are also found in cosmetics, shampoos and pharmaceuticals.

Fortunately, the binding function of eggs can be replaced in recipes with good results, usually up to a maximum of three eggs in one recipe. I have used widely available egg substitutes (No Egg and Egg-Like) in many recipes; they are easy to use and leave no aftertaste. One tablespoon (10 g) powdered gelatine mixed with 2 tablespoons warm water immediately before use also works well as a binder in many recipes, as do xanthan* and guar gums*.

### Avoid

All eggs and egg-derived food, including products with any of the following labelled ingredients (★ if egg-derived, the Food Standards Code requires declaration of the egg-based origin):

- albumin;
- binder★;
- coagulant★;
- dried egg;
- egg powder, protein, solids, white yolk or yellow;
- emulsifier★;
- globulin;
- lecithin★;
- livetin;
- lysozyme;
- ovalbumin;
- ovoglobulin;
- ovomucin;
- ovomucoid;
- ovovitellin or vitellin;
- pasteurised, powdered or whole egg.

## Possible Hidden Sources of Egg

Note: This list is a guide—please read all labels of commercially prepared food carefully before using, to ensure the food is egg free.

- beverages—Advocaat, eggnog, malted cocoa drinks (e.g. Ovaltine), root beer or coffee if clarified with egg, alcoholic beverages (see Glossary—Wines, and Spirits and Liqueurs);
- breads and pastries—baked goods (most, some breads are exceptions) and baking mixes, including biscuits, cakes, choux pastry, cookies, doughnuts, macaroons, meringues, muffins, pastry, pavlova, waffles, glazed bakery items such as bagels, breads rolls and pie crusts, French toast;
- breakfast cereals—some breakfast cereals;
- meat, fish and poultry, etc.—omelettes, processed meats (e.g. bologna, meat balls, meat loaf, meat jellies, meat moulds), quiche, meat jellies, sausages, sausage rolls;
- pastas—pastas, spaghetti and noodles such as egg noodles, prepared pastas such as macaroni, and lasagne;
- puddings and desserts—baked and steamed puddings and desserts, creamy fillings, custards, fruit whips, ice-cream, marzipan, milk puddings, pancakes, pavlova and pavlova powder mix, pikelets, some icings, sorbet, soufflés, whips;
- snacks and sweets—glazed baked snacks such as pretzels, jelly beans brushed with egg whites, marshmallows, sweets and candies, such as fondant creams, truffles, Turkish delight;
- take-away food—battered and crumbed foods (e.g. fish), coating mixes, fried rice, clear soups and broths clarified with egg (many Asian broths and stocks), cross-contamination from egg-containing foods prepared in the same area
- vegetables—battered or breaded vegetables, Caesar salad, canned and frozen vegetables in sauce, croquettes;
- other foods—bouillon, broths and stocks (clarified with egg), commercial sauce mixes, dressings such as creamy salad dressings, fat substitutes, mayonnaise, soups such as turtle or mock turtle soup, chicken and sweet corn soup or other egg drop soup, any soup with egg noodles or macaroni, tartare sauce, sauces such as bearnaise and hollandaise, some soups and consommés;
- other items—lemon curd, egg substitutes, egg protein shampoo, laxatives.

# Avoiding Fish

This book includes both fish (F) and shellfish (S) (crustaceans) in the classification 'fish-free'; if you are able to eat fish but not shellfish or vice versa, modify your food avoidance list accordingly, annotating which fish- or shellfish-based recipes in the book suit you. Whether you have to avoid all fish or shellfish, or particular types of either, will depend on your individual sensitivity. While, in many cases, the inclusion of fish in a food may be obvious, highly processed foods may contain hidden fish or shellfish—for example, fish is often used as the basis of imitation shellfish such as crab. As with other foods sensitivities, the risk of cross-contamination with fish or shellfish proteins may warrant avoiding restaurants and food outlets that serve these.

## Avoid

*Fish*

All fish and any fish-derived foods products labelled with any of the following ingredients (★ if fish-derived, the Food Standards Code requires declaration of the fish-based origin):

- anchovies, anchovy sauce or extract;
- disodium inosinate (fish- or meat-derived flavour enhancer, food additive 631)★;
- fish—all or specified types according to individual sensitivity;
- fish oil, sauce and stock;
- fish collagen;
- fish roe, caviar or tarama;
- imitation crab, lobster, shrimp (see 'surimi' below);
- omega-3 fortified foods★;
- roe (fish eggs);
- seelachs;
- surimi (fish muscle reshaped to make imitation seafood—almost any species can be used. It is commonly found in imitation crab legs, lump crabmeat, crab cakes, imitation lobster products and imitation scallops).

*Shellfish*

All shellfish and any shellfish-derived product labelled with any of the following ingredients:

- abalone, clam, cockle, crab, crayfish, crevette, langoustine, lobster, molluscs, mussels, oyster, periwinkle, prawns, scallops, sea urchin, shrimp;
- imitation seafood;
- oyster sauce;
- shrimp paste.

## Possible Hidden Sources of Fish or Shellfish

Note: This list is a guide—please read all labels of commercially prepared food carefully before using to ensure the food is fish (F) and/or shellfish (S) free.

- Asian dishes (F/S);
- Caesar salad (F);
- dips and spreads (F/S);
- dressings (may contain anchovies or anchovy extract) (F);
- health food products often contain fish oil (F);
- hot dogs, pizza toppings, bologna and ham can contain 'surimi' (see 'surimi' above) (F/S);
- marinara sauce (F/S);
- paella (F/S);
- prawn crackers (F/S);
- spring rolls (F/S);
- soups (F/S);
- sushi (F);
- tapenade (F);
- taramosalata (F);
- wine—isinglass (a protein derived from fish) and chitin (extracted from the shells of crabs or lobsters) are used to clarify alcoholic beverages including wine (see Glossary—Wine, and Spirits and Liqueurs) (F/S);
- Worcestershire sauce (F);
- some shampoos, conditioners and skin-care products (F).

## Avoiding Garlic and Onions

Avoiding garlic in commercially made foods is indeed a challenge; you are safer to assume a product is guilty until proven innocent and that garlic will most likely be present in any savoury sauce, condiment, pre-prepared meal, etc. The issue is complicated as garlic would normally be considered a 'food' and warrant inclusion in the ingredient list but its presence is often hidden under the generic terms 'spices' or 'natural flavour'. This necessitates contacting manufacturers about individual products to check whether or not garlic is included. Some manufacturers are prepared to give out information on its inclusion in a product as a spice, while others consider this proprietary information and will advise 'they cannot disclose the spice content of a product', sometimes with the qualification 'if you are allergic to garlic or onions then avoid the product'. Additionally, there is no requirement under the current Food Standards Code that any change to a 'spice' in a product, to include or remove garlic, be reflected in a change to the ingredient listing. Usually, onion is declared as a food ingredient and so is generally easier than garlic to identify in foods; however, it can be included in a product and described in the ingredient list as 'natural flavour'.

Various forms of garlic and onion may be included in commercially prepared foods, ranging from the whole bulb or clove, garlic or onion extract, powder, minced or granulated garlic, to garlic oil; all of these can cause a reaction in anyone sensitive to the ubiquitous bulbs.

Additionally, where sensitivity to garlic is high, asafoetida or hing may also cause a similar reaction, even though it is not related to garlic or the lily family. Asafoetida is made from the dried resinous sap of a variety of giant fennel and has a very strong, foetid odour; it is available in two powdered forms—brown or yellow—which usually include wheat starch as a bulking and anti-caking agent. It is used in Indian vegetarian meals and pickles (such as lime pickle) to add a garlic-like flavour with onion overtones.

## Avoiding Peanuts

Peanuts (also known as groundnuts and monkey nuts) are well known for evoking severe, life-threatening reactions in very sensitive individuals—often only the most minute traces of peanuts can cause a reaction. Specialist dietary guidance is essential for anyone with peanut allergy because of the widespread use of peanuts and their derivatives in manufactured foods, and because of the potential consequences of inadvertent consumption of even a trace.

Although peanuts are not a true nut, instead being a legume, management of a peanut allergy often includes the avoidance of all types of nuts. This is based on the potential for contamination of nuts with peanut products and because of potential co-existing allergies to tree nuts (most commonly to brazil nuts, almonds, hazelnuts and walnuts) which may not have been identified. It is also possible that other members of the legume family—including beans such as soy, green or kidney, green peas and lupins—may be a problem. Check with your healthcare practitioner about which additional foods, if any, you may need to avoid.

In effect, because of the widespread inclusion of peanuts in commercially made products, any manufactured food should be considered a source of peanuts (or tree nuts) until it is known that it is not. It is now a legal requirement that any product which might feasibly contain peanut traces must be labelled to that effect. Likewise, eating out and take-away food can be very difficult when trying to guarantee a peanut-free diet—in addition to the widespread usage of peanuts in food, peanuts tend to leave a residue on utensils and containers, greatly increasing the risk of cross-contamination of an otherwise safe meal.

### Avoid

All peanuts and peanut-derived foods, including products with any of the following labelled ingredients (★ if peanut-derived, the Food Standards Code requires declaration of the peanut-based origin):

- almond, arachis, groundnut, hazelnut and walnut oils;
- almond essence or extract;
- artificial or artificially flavoured nuts (made from deflavoured peanuts, reshaped and reflavoured with nuts such as almonds, pecans or walnuts);
- ground nuts;
- hydrolysed plant or vegetable protein★;
- mixed nuts;
- natural flavour★;
- nuts, nut butter, flour, meal, pastes and spreads;
- peanuts;
- peanut butter, flakes, flour, granules;
- peanut extracts, flour, protein or protein hydrolysate;
- peanut oil, and cold-pressed, expelled or expressed peanut oil.

### Possible Hidden Sources of Peanuts

Note: This list is a guide—please read all labels of commercially prepared food carefully before using to ensure the food is peanut-free.

- beverages—Amaretto and Frangelico, nut-flavoured coffees, nut syrups;
- breads and pastries—many baked goods and baking mixes, Bakewell tarts, biscuits, cookies, crackers, frangipan(e), macaroons, pastries, *all* cakes and pastries with unknown ingredients, particularly 'health cakes' such as carrot cake, pumpkin cake or pie, fruit and nut rolls, etc.;
- breakfast cereals—cereals bars, any breakfast cereal especially fruit and fruit and nut cereals, muesli;
- dairy products—ice-cream, ice-cream topping and flavourings, frozen yoghurts, nut-containing or nut-coated cheeses;
- meat, fish and poultry—Asian food, particularly Chinese, Thai and Indonesian (including satay) African and other ethnic dishes, kebabs;
- pastas—chilli and spaghetti sauces (peanuts may be used as a thickener), instant noodles, pesto sauce;
- puddings and desserts—desserts, dessert toppings;
- snacks and sweets—dips, lollies and other confectionery, chocolate (particularly compounded, as in Easter

eggs, health food bars, premium and imported chocolates), 'health' bars, marzipan, noisette, praline, savoury snacks;
- take-away food—battered foods, egg rolls, kebabs;
- vegetables—mixed salads, meat substitutes, vegetarian products including those containing hydrolysed vegetable protein, wild rice;
- other foods—Asian/Oriental sauces including satay sauce, bouillon, gravy (peanut butter may be used as a shortening or oil), margarine, salad dressings, soups, Worcestershire sauce;
- other items—Prometrium (progesterone cream derived from peanuts), food additive 322 (lecithins) may contain peanut or soy, vitamin tablets (especially A, D and E), shampoos, shaving cream, health-care products may contain peanut and almond oil, sunscreen lotion, some brands of lipsticks and foundations containing loramine wax and peanutamide, animal and bird feeds.

## Avoiding Soy

Soy is used as an ingredient in about two-thirds of all commercially made food products, including bakery goods, beverages, breakfast cereals, confectionery, ice-cream, margarine, pasta, processed meats and seasoned foods. Soy oil usage is likewise very widespread in the food industry, as are the numerous fractions of soy. It can appear as a stabiliser, thickener, emulsifier and flavouring agent, to extend the shelf life of products, to add colour or to boost protein content. As with the other 'No-Go' ingredients, soy appears on food labels under a wide range of names. This said, manufacturers are required under the Food Standards Code to declare the soy origin when applying a generic label, such as 'lecithin' or 'natural flavour'. Again, in the absence of such a declaration, I always check with the manufacturer in case of any oversight.

### Avoid

All soy and soy-derived foods including products with any of the following labelled ingredients (★ if soy-derived, the Food Standards Code requires declaration of the soy-based origin):
- carob;
- emulsifier, thickener, stabiliser, bulking agent★;
- hydrolysed plant or vegetable protein★;
- hydrolysed soy protein;
- lecithin★;
- miso;
- mono- and di-glycerides★;
- monosodium glutamate★;
- natto;
- natural and artificial flavouring★;
- okara★;
- protein or protein extender;
- soy beans, bran, curds, fibre, flour, fruits, granules, grits, isolate, milk, nuts, panthenol, protein, spreads, sprouts, yoghurt;
- soy sauce, shoyu, tamari, teriyaki;
- tempeh;
- textured soy protein or flour;
- textured vegetable protein (TVP)★;
- tofu;
- vegetable broth, oil, protein;
- Vitamin E★;
- yuba★.

## Possible Hidden Sources of Soy

Note: This list is a guide—please read all labels of commercially prepared food carefully before using to ensure the food is soy-free.

* beverages—hot chocolate mix, infant formula, liquid meal replacers;
* breads and pastries—biscuits and cookies, bread improver, cakes, most breads and rolls (especially high protein);
* breakfast cereals—cereal baby foods, muesli and other breakfast cereals;
* dairy products—artificial cheese, butter substitutes, ice-cream, margarine;
  meat, fish and poultry—black pudding, canned meat and fish in sauces, hamburgers, meat extender, meat pies, pâtés, processed meats, sausages, stews;
* pastas—soy pasta, prepared pasta sauces;
* puddings and desserts—non-dairy frozen desserts, pie crusts, steamed puddings;
* snacks and sweets—chocolates (cream centres), crackers, 'health' foods and high-protein foods, snack bars;
* take-away food—Asian and other take-away food;
* vegetables—canned and frozen vegetables, meat substitutes, vegetable oils;
* other foods—bouillon, broths, canned and packet soups, salad dressings, flavouring and spice blends, gravy powders, marinades, mayonnaise, sauces and sauce mixes, seasoned salt, stocks and stock cubes, Worcestershire sauce;
* other items—puréed baby foods, shortenings, inks, linoleum, paints, plastics, soap, glue.

# Avoiding Tree Nuts

Tree nuts are increasingly being used in commercially made and processed foods such as barbecue sauces, cereals, crackers and ice-creams, so careful label reading is essential, as is averting the risk of any cross-contamination of a food in the home, or inadvertent ingestion through cross-contamination in shops where bulk items are sold, or in restaurants and take-away food outlets. Additionally, for many people the need to avoid nuts involves avoiding all tree nuts and products made with them, rather than simply one or two different nuts. Coconut is not included in this category since it is not usually associated with a cross-sensitivity to tree nuts, nor are nutmeg and chestnut. Please also refer to Avoiding Peanuts (page 167) in case of any cross-reactivity with peanuts.

## Avoid

Avoid foods that contain any of the following ingredients (★ if nut-derived, the Food Standards Code requires declaration of the nut-based origin):

* almonds;
* artificial nuts (made from deflavoured peanuts reflavoured with nuts such as pecan or walnut);
* beer nuts;
* brazil nuts;
* candlenuts;
* cashews;
* chestnuts;
* emulsifier★;
* hazelnuts (filberts);
* gianduja (a mixture of chocolate and chopped nuts found in premium or imported chocolate);
* hickory nuts;
* hydrolysed plant or vegetable protein★;
* imitation or artificially flavoured extracts★;
* macadamia nuts;
* marzipan/almond paste;
* mixed nuts;
* natural flavours and extracts, e.g. pure almond extract, natural wintergreen extract (hazelnut allergic);
* nut butters, pastes and spreads (e.g. cashew or almond butter, cashew paste);
* nut meal or crushed nuts;

- nut oil;
- pecans;
- pine nuts (pignolia, pinion);
- pistachios;
- vegetable oil and shortenings★;
- walnuts.

### Possible Hidden Sources of Tree Nuts

Note: This list is a guide—please read all labels of commercially prepared food carefully before using to ensure the food is tree nut-free.

- beverages—Amaretto, Frangelico, nut-flavoured coffees, nut syrups (e.g. Monin);
- breads and pastries—all biscuits, biscotti, cakes and pastries with unknown ingredients, fruit and nut rolls and breads;
- breakfast cereals—fruit and nut cereals, muesli (check labels for possible cross-contamination of all cereals);
- dairy products—nut-flavoured ice-creams, yoghurt;
- meat, fish and poultry—dishes including nuts such as almond chicken, many Asian dishes including satays, stir-fries with cashews, etc.;
- pastas—hot and cold pasta dishes with nuts such as pine nuts;
- puddings and desserts—flourless cakes, frozen yoghurt, ice-cream, sundae toppings, pie crusts;
- snacks and sweets—breakfast and health food bars, chocolate (particularly compounded, e.g. Easter eggs, fancy and imported), popcorn, praline, nougat;
- take-away food—Asian food (such as satay, Indonesian, Thai), egg rolls, spring rolls;
- vegetables—salads, vegetarian dishes including meat substitutes, nut meats, burgers and sausages;
- other foods—Asian sauces, barbecue sauces, bouillon, pesto sauce, satay and other sauces containing crushed nuts, salad dressings, Worcestershire sauce;
- other items—shampoos, shaving creams and health-care products contain almond oil, some animal and bird feed contain peanuts and other nuts.

## Avoiding Wheat, Gluten and Gluten-like Proteins

Wheat and gluten intolerance and avoidance pose a major dietary challenge, since wheat starch and gluten not only form the basis of many of our staple foods, such as bread, but they are used in varying quantities in a vast number of commercially made products.

Having a wheat or gluten intolerance is not one and the same thing. For people with a wheat intolerance, all the non-wheat members of the cereal family—including rye, oats, barley, millet, rice and corn, and their derivatives—can be eaten without problem and offer a viable alternative in most situations. A sensitivity to gluten is far more of a problem. Gluten is the protein that confers the glue-like and elastic properties on a dough when wheat flour is mixed with a liquid. The result—a dough can be kneaded, it can rise as it traps the gas produced by a raising agent such as yeast, and it prevents the pastry or bread from crumbling when cooked. Several other grains, including rye, barley, spelt, triticale and oats (although there is continued debate about the suitability of oats) contain gluten-like proteins which must also be avoided by people with a gluten sensitivity. For simplicity these proteins will also be called 'gluten'. Rice, millet and corn are suitable for gluten-sensitive people to eat, but care must be taken when buying a product containing cornstarch, to ensure it is derived from maize and not wheat.

The following lists, 'Avoid' and 'Possible Hidden Sources of Wheat and Gluten', include cereals— and ingredients derived from them—which must be avoided, together with the types of manufactured goods which may include wheat and/or gluten. Remember to check product labels carefully, as under the Food Standards Code manufacturers are required to declare the inclusion of wheat and other gluten-containing grains. Contact the Coeliac Society in your State for a very useful, comprehensive listing of suitable and to-be-avoided ingredients (see Useful Contacts, page 207).

The main problem in replacing wheat and gluten in cooking is that no other single flour provides the same elasticity or glue to food in which it is used. Thus for best results a number of different ingredients must be combined to obtain a similar end dish, from both workability and texture viewpoints. Suitable replacement flours include rice (white, brown, glutinous*), corn (maize), arrowroot, buckwheat*, millet, pea, lentil, polenta, potato, sweet potato, besan*, chickpea, sago, tapioca (cassava), amaranth, quinoa, chestnut, suitable gluten-free flour mixes (both home made—see Basic Flour Mix (page 113)—or commercially made, such as Orgran) and soy (if suitable). Flours from non-wheat grains are also suitable *for wheat-free diets only*.

The addition of tapioca starch, glutinous white rice flour* and warm liquids help to give structure to a flour mix. Vegetable gums such as xanthan* or guar*, or a small amount of oil, can add elasticity and help to bind a mix together, allowing it to be rolled out and cut without crumbling after baking. Other elasticisers include gelatine, psyllium* and pectin. Grated apple, banana and egg (if tolerated) can also be of use in certain mixes.

## Avoid

Note: All wheat and gluten-contaning grains, and foods derived from same, including products with any of the following labelled ingredients (★ If wheat- or gluten-contaning grain derived, the Food Standards Code requires declaration of the grain-based origin):

- grains, flours and brans—wheat (including wholegrain, bran, cracked or kibbled, burghul or bulgur, durum, wheat-based cornflour, couscous, semolina, wheat germ and oil, wheat starch), barley, kamut, oats, rye, spelt (dinkel), triticale;
- binders, fillers, excipients and extenders★;
- caramel 150 a–d (check for wheat-free diet; gluten-free—no detectable gluten even wheat-derived)★;
- Farina and thickeners including additive numbers 1400–1450★;
- flavour and flavourings—natural, artificial, and enhancers numbers 620–625 (including MSG)★;
- flour (including wholemeal, bakers, graham, granary, white, brown, strong, atta, rye, barley, spelt)★;
- flour treatment enzyme #1100 (alpha-amylase);
- hydrolysed plant protein—HPP★;
- hydrolysed vegetable protein—HVP★;
- hydrolysed wheat protein;
- malt, maltose and malt extract, flavouring, sugar, syrup, dextrin, maltodextrin and any 'malted' ingredient;
- starch—edible, food, modified (food), cornstarch★;
- texturised vegetable protein—TVP★;
- vegetable fibre or extract★.

## Possible Hidden Sources of Wheat and Gluten

Note: This list is a guide—please read all labels of commercially prepared food carefully before using to ensure the food is wheat- or gluten-free.

- beverages—barley waters and soft drinks containing malt extract, beverage whitener, cereal-based coffee substitutes, instant drinks from vending machines, malted beverages (e.g. Milo, Ovaltine), milk flavourings, soy milk with maltodextrin, some alcoholic beverages including beer, ale, stout, lager, some wines and spirits (see Glossary—Wines, and Spirits and Liqueurs for details of suitable products);
- bread and pastries—bread including wheat, rye, sourdough, spelt, flatbreads, etc., biscuits (biscuit crumbs), buns, breadcrumbs, croissant, crumpets, muffins, pastries and pies, pikelets, tarts, wheat-based tortillas and burritos, suet, ice-cream cones and wafers, waffles;
- breakfast cereals—containing wheat, oats, semolina, barley and malt extract, rye, wheat bran, oat bran, cornflakes, Rice Bubbles;
- dairy products—cheese mixtures, blue cheese, pastes and spreads, grated cheese, malted milks (including soy), ice-creams with cone/wafer, thickened cream or other dairy products, artificial cream, low-fat cheese, yoghurts containing grains;
- meats, fish and poultry—foods prepared or thickened with flour, batter, crumbs, stuffing, rusk or suet, burgers, canned or frozen meats, fish and poultry, corned beef, frozen dinners, meat pies, most processed meats and fish, salami, sausages and smallgoods;
- nuts—some nut mixes, beer nuts, dry-roasted nuts;
- pastas—instant pasta meals, pasta, soba (some), spaghetti, vermicelli, wheaten noodles;

- puddings and desserts—commercially thickened fruit-pie fillings, custard, desserts containing flour, semolina, breadcrumbs and suet, etc., many frozen desserts, icing sugar mixture, using baking powder containing wheat starch;
- snacks and sweets—chocolate bars containing biscuit (e.g. Twix), confectionery sprinkles, fondant, marzipan, packet savoury snacks (e.g. flavoured corn chips, potato chips, rice crackers, etc.), sweets rolled in flour (e.g. licorice, marshmallows), unwrapped sweets;
- take-away food—battered foods, chips (may be coated with flour), crumbed foods, gravies and thickened sauces, etc., hamburgers, pasties, pies, pizza, sausages, savoury pastries, sausages rolls, souvlaki, stuffed roast chickens;
- vegetables—baked beans and other thickened, processed legumes (e.g. in sauce), canned or frozen vegetables in sauce (e.g. creamed mushrooms), commercially prepared salads (e.g. potato salad dressed with mayonnaise, tabouli, etc.), creamed corn (check label), crumbed or rolled in flour, frozen french fries or chips, vegetarian products containing TVP, tofu burgers;
- other foods—chutneys, gravies, pickles, ready-mixed gravy powders, curry and spice mixes (including garlic powder), malt vinegar or vinegar of unspecified origin, miso, mustard (prepared and powder), oyster sauce, pepper mixes (white or black) using flour as a filler or to prevent caking, relishes, sauces, seasonings, soups, soy sauce (shoyu), stocks or stock cubes thickened or flavoured with wheat, rye, barley or pasta, yeast extract spreads (e.g. Vegemite, Promite, Marmite);
- other items—some medicines and vitamins contain flour as a filler, communion wafers, brewers yeast.

Glossary of Foods and Ingredients

This glossary is designed to provide both information on many of the ingredients used in this book and, where the ingredient is flagged with '(ingredient check)' in a recipe, information on what to watch out for when selecting that ingredient—such as which of the 'No-Go' foods may be included in some brands of the ingredient. I have nominated a number of specific product brands, not only for their quality, but also for what they don't contain as much as what they do! These brand suggestions are provided as a guide—you certainly may substitute with other suitable brands as you choose. Also included in the Glossary, where relevant, are the manufacturer's or distributor's details to help you track the ingredient down in the event it is not readily available in your local area. You will find many manufacturers are very helpful, providing details of local suppliers (obviously this is in their interest!); some also provide a mail order facility for which freight costs are not exorbitant and which, for some of the bush tucker products for example, is invaluable. The brands suggested do not include all brands that may be suitable, but in some cases alternative manufacturers have been contacted and their product found to contain an unsuitable ingredient (even though it may not be disclosed on the label at this stage despite its disclosure being required by the current Food Standards Code; see www.foodstandards.gov.au/foodstandardscode).

Remember that when you are avoiding a specific food always check the ingredients on the label *carefully* to ensure that the ingredients have not changed from the time my recipe was developed or this book went to print. When in doubt, check with the manufacturer or avoid the product.

## Ingredients

**Agar** (agar agar, kanten, Japanese gelatine) Agar is produced from red algae or seaweed and is used as a vegetarian setting agent in place of animal gelatine. It is widely used in Asia. Commercially, it is used as used as a stabilising or texturising agent, emulsifier, and thickener in ice-cream, sherbets, jellies, soups, sauces, canned soups, meat and fish. It is also used as a clarifying agent in winemaking and brewing. Agar is tasteless and has slightly stronger gelling properties than gelatine, but unlike gelatine, does not need to be refrigerated to gel, setting above room temperature at about 35°C. Once gelled, it does not melt below 85°C. Agar is available as a powder or flake from health food shops and Asian grocers (as a general rule, 1 teaspoon agar powder is equivalent to 1 tablespoon or 15 mL or agar flakes). It is worth checking the gelling property of the brand you use since this can vary; for an agar powder that states a gelling rate of 25 g agar powder per 3 L water, 1 teaspoon per 500 mL produces a firm jelly. However, the higher the acidity of the food, the more agar is required to set it, with 1½–2 teaspoons required to set 500 mL; fruits such as kiwi fruit, mango and papaya totally break down agar's gelling ability.

**Ajowan seeds** Also known as bishop's weed or carom, ajowan is related to dill, caraway and cumin, and is mostly found in Indian cooking. The greyish-green seeds are striped and curved, often with a fine silk stalk attached, and are usually sold whole. The seeds are delicious chewed whole (medicinally—used for their relief of indigestion and colic), having a spicy, aromatic, thyme-like flavour, with their essential oil, thymol, leaving the tongue temporarily numb! Lightly bruise the seeds before using—the flavour mellows on cooking. Available from good spice outlets (see Suppliers—Herbs and Spices).

**Almond essence** A few drops in a biscuit mix add a lovely almond flavour. Natural almond essence is based on a bitter almond oil, extracted peach seeds (check suitability for peanut-free, see page 167). Queen Fine Foods (www.queen.com.au, (07) 3356 7344) makes a natural almond essence, the alcohol base of which is derived from sugar cane.

**Anchovy fillets** These tiny fish are generally filleted, salt-cured and canned or bottled in oil. They are used sparingly as a fish-salt flavouring agent in many dishes, such as Pasta Putanesca, or as a garnish. To reduce saltiness, soak the fillets in cold water for about 30 minutes, drain and pat dry with paper towels. Check label to ensure a suitable oil, such as olive, has been used to preserve them and no other unsuitable additives are present.

**Apple cider vinegar** *see* Vinegar.

**Apple juice concentrate** (Pureharvest brand) A preservative-free concentrate of apple juice that is a good substitute for sugar in cooking. Combined with apple cider vinegar and a dash of fish sauce (optional), it makes a good mock soy sauce in dishes such as Mock Soy Stir-fried Chicken with Cashews (page 66). Available from supermarkets and health food shops. (Pureharvest: www.pureharvest.com.au, (03) 5625 1111.)

**Arborio rice** *see* Rice.

**Artichoke hearts in brine** Select artichoke hearts in a brine, both to reduce fat intake (some brands include soy oil) and to avoid added flavours including garlic. A food acid such as citric acid is usually included (see Avoiding Corn, page 161). Admiral brand (Riviana Foods, www.rivianafoodservice.com, (03) 9765 5100) is available from supermarkets.

**Bacon** Check packet label carefully for ingredient listing. Most bacon is treated with dextrose which is usually derived from corn. KR bacon (Darling Downs Foods, 1800 155 150) is cured with sucrose and is corn-free (any dextrose used in their products is derived from tapioca). Some bacon products, such as Hans (www.hans.com.au (07) 3395 9999), are specifically labelled as 'gluten free'. These products are available from supermarkets.

**Baking powder** Check the flour base of commercially available brands. Ward's brand is gluten-free and made on a rice flour base. To make baking powder, combine ⅓ cup bicarbonate of soda (baking soda), ⅔ cup cream of tartar, ⅔ cup arrowroot, potato or white rice flour. Add 1 teaspoon baking powder to every 125 g plain flour (see Basic Flour Mix, below) for self-raising flour.

**Basic Flour Mix** *see* recipe on page 113. A highly nutritious flour mix based on besan*, potato, arrowroot and fine white rice flours*, originally developed by Lola Workman (Lola's Wheat Free World). Besan flour and arrowroot are available from supermarkets, potato flour is available from Asian grocery and health food shops, fine white rice flour is available from health food shops or see Suppliers—Flours (page 197) for retail outlets and mail order. This flour mix also makes an excellent gravy when used to thicken a suitable stock mixed with fresh thyme and mint (or herbs of choice), paprika, tomato paste, freshly ground black pepper and any meat juices. Use Queen Parisian Essence—contains corn-derived (maize) caramel—from supermarkets to colour as required (Queen Fine Foods www.queen.com.au, (07) 3356 7344).

**Basmati rice** *see* Rice.

**Bean–thread vermicelli** *see* Pasta.

**Beef stock** *see* Stock.

**Besan flour** This is a textured, finely milled flour made from lightly roasted chickpeas; it has a better flavour than the more bitter raw chickpea flour when used in baking. Chickpeas are a member of the legume family and so yield a highly nutritious flour which is very rich in dietary fibre, protein, complex carbohydrates, vitamins and minerals. The raw flour is pale yellow in colour and has a strong aftertaste before cooking. Besan flour is used extensively in Indian cooking. Available from some supermarkets, health food shops and Middle Eastern grocery shops, or see Suppliers—Flours (page 197) for mail-ordering.

**Bonito flakes** Bonito is a relative of mackerel and tuna and is used in extensively in Japanese cookery as a base for dashi or as a garnish. Fresh bonito fillets are dried until they are rock hard before they are shaved to make the wispy aromatic flakes used to make the dashi stock. Available from Japanese and Asian grocery shops.

**Brown rice** *see* Rice.

**Brown rice vinegar** *see* Vinegar.

**Buckwheat**  A highly nutritious kernel, rich in protein, that is unrelated to wheat or other members of the cereal family as it is a member of the rhubarb family. It has a distinct earthy, nutty flavour, and is most commonly ground into a dark, gritty flour and used to make everything from pancakes to soba noodles*; the kibbled variety, available from health food shops and some supermarkets, makes an excellent replacement for burghul in tabouli.

**Buckwheat pasta** *see* Pasta.

**Bush tomato**  Also known as akudjura or the 'desert raisin', the bush tomato is a native of the central Australian desert, and was an important staple food for the desert Aboriginal tribes. The berry is left to dry on the bush which intensifies the uniquely different, natural spicy flavour. Only a small amount of ground bush tomato is required to flavour a dish—too much in a dish and it will leave a bitter aftertaste. Use a maximum of 1 part ground bush tomato to 10 parts other ingredients. It is excellent in tomato sauces such as Bush Tomato Tartlet (page 14), or added as a seasoning and thickening agent to stews and casseroles. Available from some gourmet food shops and spice shops, or see Suppliers—Herbs and Spices (page 197).

**Butter beans** *see* Canned beans.

**Canned beans**  Using canned red kidney, butter (lima), cannellini or other white beans, lentils or chickpeas is a great time saver and way to add fibre and nutrients to any casserole or stew. Select the brand carefully to minimise sodium intake, and always rinse thoroughly under running water and drain well. In the recipes, stated ingredient weights for beans are the *cooked, drained* weight; a 400 g can of beans typically yields 240 g rinsed, drained beans. Some canned beans may contain traces of soybeans, so check the label carefully. Most brands of canned legumes contain a food acid, such as citric acid, as a preservative (see Avoiding Corn, page 161). BioNature brand (available from supermarkets or contact Leo's Imports for outlets www.leosimports.com.au, (03) 9359 0658) uses organically grown beans and peas, contains no food acids, and has a low sodium content.

**Cannellini beans** *see* Canned beans.

**Capers**  Originating as a condiment in ancient Greece, capers are the unopened, olive-green flower bud of a prickly shrub native to the Mediterranean, Middle East and Northern Africa. Capers vary in size from very tiny (baby or lilliput) to the size of a pea. They are used to add a sharp, sour flavour to fish dishes—probably best known with smoked salmon—and are excellent in salads, wraps, dressings such as Caper Dressing (page 106), Bruschetta Mix (page 27) and as a garnish. They are available commercially in three forms, preserved in:

*Vinegar or food acid and brine*—this is the most commonly available and cheapest form but the capers do tend to lose some their flavour and texture in the vinegar–salt solution. Check the vinegar source carefully to ensure no risk of residual gluten, for example, barley-derived vinegar. Sandhurst Foods (www.sandhurstfinefoods.com.au, 1800 500 362) produces capers pickled in a food acid (acetic acid) solution (see Avoiding Corn, page 161). Other brands, such as Colavita (www.basile.com.au, 1800 635 268), and Sacla (www.congafoods.com.au) are pickled in wine vinegar and are available from supermarkets. Some brands may contain added vitamin C (see Avoiding Corn, page 161).

*Salt*—preservation under sea salt retains the natural delicate flavours and texture of the capers. They must be rinsed thoroughly with cold water before using to remove excess salt. Available from gourmet food shops.

*Extra-virgin olive oil*—these are the most expensive of the preserved caper range. Often they are soaked in wine vinegar and dried before they are preserved under extra-virgin olive oil. The oil takes up some of the aroma and intense flavour of the capers so can be used as a seasoned oil for dressings or to toss through pasta. Always store covered with oil. Available from gourmet food shops.

**Cashew and macadamia spread**  While a bit pricey, this is a good paste if you don't want to make your own. Naytura brand is available from Woolworths and Safeway supermarkets, or other suitable brands from health food shops. To make your own, lightly dry roast (see Cooking Hints, page 201) 2 cups raw, unsalted cashews or macadamia nuts, allow to cool and blend in a food processor with 1–2 tablespoons extra-light olive oil*. Store refrigerated.

**Char-grilled capsicum and oil**  The flavour and sweetness of red capsicum is enhanced when char-grilled; the tender red flesh then makes an excellent base for bruschetta (page 000), pastas, salsas, dressing and garnishes. The capsicum is delicious when marinated in a good seasoned oil, imparting some of its flavour to the marinade, making the oil a great starting point for a simple salad or pasta dressing, or to use in place of a regular oil for a stir-fry. There is a wide range of char-grilled capsicum in oil products on the market but they are all loaded with garlic and many contain MSG. Char-grill capsicum at home on:
- a charcoal barbecue (preferred method, since it gives additional flavour to the flesh);
- a rack over a gas flame;
- a rack under a hot grill.
- a rack in an oven preheated to 220–240°C (200–220°C fan forced);

Turn the capsicum to blacken and blister the skin all over. Immediately place the capsicum in a plastic bag and set aside for 5–10 minutes to sweat and cool. Peel off the skin, remove the stalk, seeds and membrane and discard these. The capsicum can be used as is or marinated in seasoned oil (see Seasoned Sun-dried Tomatoes in Olive Oil, page 192).

**Chicken stock**  *see* Stock.

**Chilli oil**  *see* Oils.

**Chilli paste**  This can be used in place of fresh chillies in sauces and marinades. I use chilli paste or sambal oelek (see below) and find they save the risk of accidentally wiping my eye with chilli juice on my fingers! The paste includes the chilli seeds so use sparingly, adding extra to achieve the desired level of 'heat'. Check label for potential cross-contamination with peanuts and inclusion of xanthan gum and food acid (see Avoiding Corn, page 161).

**Chinese five spice powder**  A classic blend of star anise, fennel seed, cassia, pepper and cloves that is used to complement stir-fry dishes and grilled and roast meats. Commercially available blends may contain wheat starch; Herbie's brand is compounded with only the pure spices (see Suppliers—Herbs and Spices, page 197).

**Cider**  Fermented from apples. Historically most ciders are clarified (fined) using gelatine or other animal-derived products. Strongbow ciders (Bulmer Australia Ltd., (02) 4625 8711) are clarified using an ultrafilter and no animal- or earth-derived products are used in their production.

**Coconut milk and light coconut milk**  Coconut milk is widely used in Asian cooking and makes a good substitute for dairy and soy in many recipes. However, since coconut milk contains a relatively high level of saturated fat, care must be taken when using it frequently to select a brand that maintains the creamy consistency and rich coconut flavour while minimising the level of saturated fat. Typically the level of saturated fat per serve (80 mL) of regular coconut milk ranges from 9.6–28 g, while that of a light (often seen as 'lite' on labels) coconut milk ranges from 4.0–9.0 g, making the latter a healthier option. Additionally, some coconut milks contain a stabiliser or thickener, such as xanthan gum* (see Avoiding Corn, page 161), guar gum* (e.g. A Taste of Thai, my favourite) or carboxymethylcellulose, an emulsifier such as polysorbate, or a food acid (see Avoiding Corn, page 161), so check the ingredient listing carefully before using. Coconut milk is widely available from supermarkets and Asian grocery shops.

**Coconut cream** Typically this contains a much higher level of saturated fat than coconut milk (18–20 g per 80 mL) and so must be used sparingly. It is used to give a thicker consistency to a dish. The same check as for coconut milk applies regarding inclusion of a suitable stabiliser or thickener; Kara brand, for example, contains a range of stabilisers including xanthan gum* (see Avoiding Corn, page 161), guar gum* and carrageen, while Ayam brand contains none.

**Coriander** Also known as cilantro and Chinese parsley. Its lovely refreshing, aromatic flavour is widely incorporated in Thai cooking. Always buy fresh coriander with the roots intact since the trimmed roots and lower section of the stems impart a depth of flavour not present in the leaves. The roots should be rinsed well before using. Dry extra roots and store frozen in a plastic ziplock bag. The roots and stems are chopped, ground or minced and used in stocks and curries, or incorporated into curry and chilli pastes. The leaves are added to sauces and soups immediately before serving so the flavour is not dissipated by cooking, or eaten raw in salads, noodle or rice dishes. Interestingly, about one in eight people cannot tolerate the flavour of coriander; so either omit the coriander from the recipe or substitute with flat-leaf (Italian) parsley, lemon thyme or other herb of choice.

**Cornflakes** Check these are free of malt or other gluten-containing ingredients and any traces of nuts.

**Craisins** Sweetened dried cranberries (Ocean Spray brand) available from supermarkets. These make a great cranberry base for Panforte (page 147) and Cranberry Relish (page 87).

**Cream of tartar** Tartaric acid is a brownish-red acid powder that is precipitated onto the walls of casks used to age wine. When refined into a white acid powder, potassium hydrogen tartrate or 'cream of tartar', it is used in baking combined with baking soda or sodium bicarbonate to make baking powder. Baking powder is preferred to tartaric acid alone because it acts more slowly, giving a longer raising or leavening time.

**Creamed corn** Check can label that only a maize-based thickener is included.

**Curry leaves** The leaflets from a tropical member of the citrus family, which are used extensively in southern Indian and Sri Lankan cuisine. The leaves have a strong, warm curry aroma when bruised or rubbed but rather than imparting a strong curry flavour to a dish, their oils give a complementary refreshing tangy, citrus-like flavour. They are usually chopped and fried in oil at the start of making a curry. Fresh leaves are available from Asian grocery shops and some supermarkets. Store fresh leaves frozen in a plastic ziplock bag; they lose much of their flavour when dried. Curry leaves are not the same as curry powder!

**Curry powder** Commercially available curry powders may contain wheat flour, garlic and onion powder. Check ingredients carefully. Masterfoods brand mild curry powder, and Herbie's curry powders—except those containing asafoetida—are wheat, garlic and onion powder free (see Suppliers—Herbs and Spices). Or make your own; see recipe on page 81.

**Daikon** (white or Japanese radish) Daikon is larger and milder than its relative, the red radish. The Japanese serve it grated with sushi or sashimi, but it is also suitable to pickle, stir-fry, or slice and add to salads. Japanese daikon tends to be longer and thinner than the Chinese variety, but both can be used. Select roots that are firm and shiny. Available from supermarkets and Asian grocery shops.

**Dashi** Soup stock used extensively in Japanese cooking, usually made with bonito* flakes and kombu*. There are different kinds of dashi—it can be made from kombu (dried kelp), katsuo-bushi (dried bonito flakes), niboshi (dried small sardines) or hoshi-shiitake (dried shiitake mushrooms). Kombu dashi and mushroom dashi are good vegetarian stocks. Instant varieties usually contain MSG.

**Dried fruit** Many types of dried fruit are treated with vegetable oils to allow free-flowing during processing. Where possible, select natural dried fruit without vegetable oils, such as Angas Park brand raisins, currants and sultanas (www.angaspark.com.au, (08) 8564 2052). Angas Park vine fruits treated with vegetable oil contain rapeseed (canola) and/or sunflower oil only. Sun-dried apricots have a deeper, tarter flavour and are not treated with the preservative sulphur dioxide.

**Dried shrimp**  (goong haeng)  Small, shelled and salted sun-dried shrimps. Usually sold in plastic packets, they should be deep salmon-pink and yield only slightly to the touch. They are mildly salty with a fragrant aroma and should be soaked in warm water to soften before adding to salads, unless using ground. Store refrigerated in a sealed container. Check ingredients: they should only include shrimp, salt and, in some brands, an artificial colour. Available from Asian grocers and some supermarkets.

**Dry cider**  *see* Cider.

**Du Puy green lentils**  Named after Le Puy in Auvergne, France. Like all lentils, they are low in fat and high in protein and fibre, and do not require soaking prior to cooking. Du Puy lentils are the best, most delicate lentils, and have a distinct peppery flavour. They hold their shape well on cooking, making them excellent bases for salads and vegetable dishes, but they take longer to cook than other lentils. Salt and acidic ingredients further slow the cooking process so always add these at the end of cooking. Available from gourmet food shops.

**Egg substitute**  The recipes in this book have been developed using No Egg (Orgran brand— www.orgran.com, (03) 9776 9044) or Egg-Like (Country Harvest Products, (03) 9898 4999) which are available from supermarkets and health food shops. These egg substitutes do not leave any aftertaste and provide texture, acting as a binder in the cake and pudding recipes. Both brands contain citric acid which is derived from sweet potato, so they are suitable for people highly sensitive to corn derivatives (see Avoiding Corn, page 161).

**Extra-light olive oil spray**  *see* Oils.

**Fine white rice flour**  *see* Rice flour.

**Fish sauce**  A pungent, strong-flavoured watery sauce ranging in colour from ochre to dark brown. It is a staple in South East Asian cuisine, as a distinct flavouring agent in many dishes and as a condiment, being the base for dipping sauces and dressings. The Thai name 'nam bplah' literally means 'fish water' and, as the name describes, the sauce is made from the juice extracted from small fish, such as anchovies, which have undergone prolonged salting and fermentation. The best sauce is the juice from the first fermentation. Second- and third-grade sauce is made by further fermenting and boiling the fish; the flavour of these sauces is often enhanced either by adding some of the first-grade sauce, or by diluting the sauce with water coloured and flavoured with sugar, caramel, MSG, hydrolysed wheat protein, fructose or other natural or artificial flavourings and colouring, and thickener— so check the label carefully. Maggi and Knorr brands, available from supermarkets and Asian grocers, are made from anchovies or fish extract, sea salt, sugar and water.

**Fish stock**  *see* Stock.

**Flour**  The commercially available gluten- and wheat-free flour mix used in many of the recipes is the Orgran brand Plain All Purpose Flour or Self Raising Flour. Unlike many of the gluten-free/wheat-free flour mixes available, these do not contain soy, and include guar gum derived from guar seeds; however, these flours are not suitable for people with a corn (maize) sensitivity. They are available from supermarkets and health food shops (www.orgran.com, (03) 9776 9044).

**Fresita**  *see* Wines.

**Gai lum (Chinese broccoli)**  A leafy vegetable with small stems and green heads (which actually are flowers). It is suitable to stir-fry, steam or blanch, as you would broccoli. Available from supermarkets, greengrocers and Asian grocers.

**Galangal**  A valued spice, with a distinct ginger-like flavour and aroma, used in cooking since the early Middle Ages. It is a staple flavouring ingredient in many Thai dishes, including curry pastes. It is available fresh, as a ginger-like rhizome, or dried, in either a sliced or powdered form. Dried galangal is spicier than fresh; sliced, dried galangal needs to be rehydrated prior to cooking to release its flavours in a dish. Available from Asian grocers, some greengrocers and supermarkets.

**Ginger**  Ginger is a highly versatile ingredient that can be used fresh, either peeled and sliced for a milder, refreshing background flavour, or finely grated or puréed for a more direct flavour. Dried ground ginger provides a more intense, spicy flavour and can, in combination with vinegar, provide the background 'heat' to a curry, such as a vindaloo (see Goat Vindaloo, page 46). Other forms of ginger used in these recipes are Buderim brand available from supermarkets or mail order (www.buderimginger.com, 1800 067 686).

*Pickled ginger*—an invaluable flavouring ingredient, imparting a sharp, sweet, spicy depth to a range of sauces, salads, pasta dishes, sashimi, etc. The ginger juice can also be used as a flavouring agent in recipes such as Vermouth Poached Peaches with Blueberry and Toasted Almond Garnish (page 133). There are several brands of sushi-style pickled ginger available but many contain MSG and vinegar of an unspecified origin; Buderim brand (Salad Slices) uses vinegar derived from cane sugar and is MSG free. Buderim brand red pickled ginger straws, as well as making a great garnish, add that zesty ginger flavour to top off a dish.

*Glacé ginger* (Buderim brand)—preserved in a sugar syrup which allows concentration of the rich ginger flavours, making it a great addition to fruit chutneys.

*Ginger Refresher* (Buderim brand)—a rich, spicy, non-alcoholic ginger mixer that combines to make an excellent marinade for pork, fish, scallops or, with the addition of sparkling mineral water and gelatine, a refreshing jelly. It contains xanthan gum so is not suitable for people with a corn sensitivity.

**Glutinous black and white rice**  *see* Rice.

**Glutinous white rice flour**  *see* Rice flour.

**Green peas**  *Frozen*—Baby Minted Green Peas Bird's Eye brand (1800 061 279); flavour added is mint.

*Canned green peas*—an excellent base for making green pea mash; select a brand of peas canned in brine with no added colour, thickener or unspecified flavour, and with a low sodium content.

**Green and pink peppercorns**  These are packed in brine, vinegar or salt, or freeze-dried soon after they are picked. Select a brand that specifies a brine or suitable vinegar base, or lists acetic acid or acidulating agent (260) to avoid any residual gluten. For corn sensitivities, if acetic acid is a problem, select peppercorns packed in brine (see Avoiding Corn, page 161). Green peppercorns are true peppercorns but are picked when they are still soft and under-ripe (black peppercorns are picked when the berry has not fully ripened; white peppercorns are picked when the berry is fully ripe and are then hulled). Green peppercorns are milder than their riper counterparts, they are soft and can be eaten whole. Pink peppercorns are not true peppercorns but the dried berries from the baies rose plant, cultivated in Madagascar. The berries are pungent and slightly sweet. Available from delicatessens and some supermarkets.

**Green shallots**  A member of the onion and lily family, also known as green, spring or Chinese onions, scallions or shallots. They are immature spring onions, being harvested before a pronounced white bulb develops.

The white part has a very mild onion flavour and can be eaten raw, grilled or sautéed. The green part is used as a garnish, in soups, stir-fries and salads. For these recipes, select shallots ¾–1 cm in diameter or, if thinner, proportionately increase the number of shallots you use. To prepare, trim and discard the root and the top 5 cm of the green section. Trim off the remaining dark green section and retain as a garnish; use the remaining white–pale green section as described in the recipe.

**Golden syrup**  Check ingredient listing is cane sugar and water only.

**Ground rice**  A very fine, pure ground rice such as McKenzie's brand (available from supermarkets) is excellent as a filler or thickener to replace nut meal and coconut in recipes. To replace coconut, use an equal weight of ground rice as the coconut it is replacing plus a suitable coconut essence to taste.

**Guar gum**  A white to yellowish, odourless powder that is made by grinding the seeds from the guar plant, a member of the legume family. It is used in commercial food processing, cosmetics and pharmaceuticals as an emulsifier, thickener, and stabiliser. A common ingredient in ice-creams, where it prevents the formation of large ice crystals. Guar gum dissolves readily in hot water and, unlike cornstarch and other thickening agents, does not require cooking to thicken a liquid. Available from health food shops.

**Italian herbs**  Check they are free of garlic. McCormick brand (1800 802 223) contains dried herbs only.

**Jasmine rice**  *see* Rice.

**Kaffir lime leaves**  The dark green, glossy leaves of the kaffir lime infuse a wonderful citrus flavour to dishes and are widely used in Asian cooking. The leaves have a unique double shape—a double leaf being counted as two single leaves in most recipes. Since the dried leaves lose much of the intensity of flavour, always try to use fresh leaves in cooking. These are available from Asian grocers, some greengrocers and supermarkets, and can be stored frozen in plastic ziplock bags to retain their freshness and flavour. If using dried leaves, allow double the quantity required in a recipe.

**Kangaroo**  An excellent source of high-quality protein, as well as many important vitamins and minerals including iron and zinc. It is an extremely lean meat with a very low level of cholesterol and saturated fats, so no prior trimming of excess fat is required before cooking. Given that the meat is finely textured with little connective tissue and has a very low fat content, it requires minimal cooking at a high temperature. It should be served rare; overcooking dries the meat out very quickly. Available from good butchers and some supermarkets.

**Kizami nori**  *see* Nori.

**Kohlrabi**  Resembles a turnip but its flesh is sweeter and more delicately flavoured. It can be eaten raw or cooked. Select small bulbs and peel before using. Available from supermarkets and greengrocers.

**Kombu** (Konbu)  Also known as kelp. Like other sea vegetables, kombu is rich in minerals. It is used extensively in Japanese cooking as one of the two basic ingredients in the soup stock 'dashi', and is also used to flavour cooked foods, in sushi and as a pickle condiment. Kombu is usually sold dried, in strips or sheets. The white powder that develops on the surface is should not be removed before cooking as it contributes to the flavour imparted to the stock. Available from Japanese grocers and some health food shops.

**Lecithin**  *see* Margarine.

**Lemon-infused olive oil**  *see* Oils.

**Lemon grass**  Grows as long, blade-like leaves with succulent, heavily lemon-scented, non-acidic lower leaves. It is a common ingredient in Asian and Indian cooking. To use, remove the outer leaves and use only approximately 20 cm of the lower white part of the stem. The scent is best released by slicing very finely, but if removing before serving cut the stalks into large pieces and crush with the back of a knife. Trimmed lemon grass can be stored frozen and makes a good substitute for fresh; dried lemon grass (soaked in hot water) is only a fair substitute.

**Lemon myrtle**  The leaves of this native Australian rainforest tree are highly aromatic with a glorious aroma and the delicate flavour of a blend of lemon grass, lemon and lime. The leaves can be used either fresh or dried in cooking, with the dried ground leaf more readily available from some supermarkets, gourmet food shops or good herb outlets (see Suppliers—Herbs and Spices, page 197). It complements white fish and poultry dishes, but my favourite is as a flavouring in biscuits and pies such as Lemon Myrtle and Macadamia Biscuits (page 154), and Red Bean and Apple Pie (page 129). Add lemon myrtle close to the end of the cooking process to maximise its delicate flavour in the finished dish.

**LSA mix**  A mix of crushed linseed, granulated sunflower kernels and raw almond kernel meal, high in omega-3 and omega-6 fatty acids. This mix makes an excellent coating for fish cutlets and for adding extra goodness to cakes, waffles, etc. Available brands include Nu-Vit (www.nu-vit.com.au, 1800 625 658), available from supermarkets and health food shops.

**Macadamia oil**  *see* Oils.

**Macadamia spread**  *see* Cashew spread.

**Maize flour, meal and starch**  Maize flour and meal are made from whole corn kernels so are high in both starch and fibre (unlike maize-derived cornstarch or cornflour, which lacks the fibre). As the names suggest, the flour is a finely milled product and is suitable for making cakes, biscuits and pastry. Maize meal is available in coarse- and fine-ground varieties. For baking and custards, use fine maize meal to ensure a finely textured pastry. Available from health food shops.

**Margarine**  The recipes in this book are based on Nuttelex Poly-unsaturated Vege-Table Margarine (Edward Zorn and Company, (03) 9428 3585), which contains a mix of three oils: sunflower, canola and palm olein. Until early 2004 it was free of all the 'No-Go' foods with the exception of a small amount (0.06 per cent w/w) of soy-derived lecithin, which was incorporated as an emulsifier. While this level of lecithin, and the minute traces of soy protein it contained (to enable GM fingerprinting of the soybeans), could be tolerated by most people sensitive to soy, as of April/May 2004, a lecithin derived from sunflower seeds will be used, making the product suitable for anyone with a sensitivity to soy. Check the Nuttelex ingredient label for inclusion of the non-soybean lecithin if you are sensitive to soy. Available from supermarkets. If using other dairy-free margarines, check ingredient listing carefully for suitability.

Nuttelex can be frozen, so make a tub of herb butter in advance and freeze for later use—spread it on a suitable bun or bread, wrap in foil and warm in the oven, or simply serve a knob over steamed vegetables or in a fluffy jacket potato. For each 250 g margarine, mix through:

3 green shallots*, trimmed and very finely sliced
2 tsp dried oregano
2 tsp finely chopped fresh lemon thyme leaves
1 tbs finely chopped flat-leaf (Italian) or curly parsley leaves
freshly ground black pepper

Try adding 1 teaspoon finely grated lemon zest and 2 teaspoons finely chopped fresh rosemary in place of the oregano for char-grilled lamb, or 1 teaspoon finely grated lemon zest and 1 very finely chopped anchovy fillet to top grilled fish; and for a bit of a zing, add ¼ teaspoon sambal oelek* to any of the mixes.

**Mirin** A sweet rice wine used in Japanese cooking as a mild seasoning to flavour rice and sauces. Many mirins are seasoned and may contain gluten and other 'No-Go' food derivatives. Spiral Foods Mirin, which is available from supermarkets and health food shops (www.spiralfoods.com.au, (07) 9429 8655), is made from sweet brown rice, rice koji, sea salt and well water without any additional seasonings.

**Mixed peel** Angas Park brand (www.angaspark.com.au, (08) 8564 2052) contains food acid (see Avoiding Corn, page 161); check suitability of other brands some of which may contain traces of nuts.

**Monin Syrups** A wide range of non-alcoholic liqueur syrups manufactured in France which, with the exception of nut-derived syrups such as hazelnut, macadamia, almond, chestnut and bitters, are free of all the 'No-Go' foods. They contain caramel derived from sugar cane or beet, or wheat (certified gluten-free). These syrups are used in many cafés to flavour coffees and other beverages but make an excellent base for dessert sauces, etc. For information on distributors contact Posi Pour at posipour@bigpond.au or (07) 5563 2599; for details of the syrup range see www.monin.com.au/index.html.

**Mountain pepper** An aromatic native pepper, unrelated to true pepper, which grows in Tasmania and Victoria. Unlike true pepper, mountain pepper contributes both flavour and heat to a dish. The pepperberries are very fiery, but the ground pepperleaf is much milder and more flavoursome, adding a mild peppery-eucalypt background to a dish. To maximise flavour, add it as close to the end of the cooking process as possible. Available from some supermarkets and good spice outlets (see Suppliers—Herbs and Spices, page 197).

**Mustard** One of the oldest and most widely used spices. There are three kinds of different mustard seeds: the European white or yellow seeds are the mildest; the brown, originating in Asia, are more pungent; and the Southern European black seeds have the strongest flavour. Besides being used whole to spice dishes or as part of a pickling mix, mustard is commercially available in a number of different presentations, from dry mustard powder to ready-made mustards. The ready-mades range from smooth pastes—such as mild Dijon or hot English—to coarse wholegrain mustards, flavoured with a wide variety of herbs, spices and liquids. In addition to making a good condiment for meat, mustard is an excellent flavouring agent for sauces and marinades. Many commercially available mustards contain gluten, garlic (as a spice, see Avoiding Garlic, page 166), food acids (see Avoiding Corn, page 161) and wine (see Wine for details of finings). Either make your own mustard (see pages 85 or 82) or use a 'Make Your Own' mix such as Herbie's (see Suppliers—Herbs and Spices, page 197), or select from one of the following Masterfoods (www.masterfoods.com, 1800 816 016) range—Australian, Dijon, Hot or Mild English and Honey Wholegrain (French, German, Herb, and Wholegrain contain garlic). Commercially available dry mustard powder is finely ground, husked mustard seeds (usually a mix of yellow and brown) which may be combined with flour and colourings to obtain the desired flavour and appearance. Masterfoods, Keens and Ward's brands of mustard powder have no additives. Horseradish can be used as a substitute hot condiment, however many horseradish pastes have a dairy base and can contain other 'No-Go' foods. Eskal brand white and red horseradish available from supermarkets is dairy-free and contains a synthetic vinegar (www.trialiafoods.com.au, (03) 9701 1666). Or make your own from a pure powdered horseradish such as Herbie's (see Suppliers—Herbs and Spices).

**Nori** *Kizami nori* Toasted, finely sliced seaweed more commonly known as the seaweed sheet used to wrap sushi rolls. With a mildly marine, slightly sweet-salty flavour, kizami nori seaweed is high in fibre, protein, vitamins and minerals. In addition, compared with dairy products, seaweed provides up to ten times more calcium and iron by weight, and contains other important trace minerals. Make an instant, nutritious broth with 1 part shredded kizami nori to 6 parts water, or combine 1 part water to 1 part shredded nori for a tasty, deep-green spread or pâté. Add a flavour dimension and fibre to pastry pie crusts or use in pancakes, potato pancakes and fritters as a nutritious binder. Available from Japanese grocers; roasted nori sheets, finely shredded, can be substituted.

*Roasted nori* Yaki-nori or yaki sushi nori. Thin sheets made from the seaweed nori which are used to make sushi. When roasted the seaweed changes from a dark purplish-black to green, and acquires a pleasant, nutty flavour.

Available from supermarkets and Asian grocers. Roasted nori is also sold in strips and flakes as soup seaweed in Asian grocers.

**Oils**  Oils are extensively used in cooking as a lubricant and to facilitate browning, to soften, and to add richness, texture and flavour to foods. The selection of a type of oil depends on the intended use—be it to roast vegetables, sear meat on a hot grill, bake in a pastry or make a delicate dressing. As a general rule the less refined the oil, the lower the temperature the oil can withstand before it starts to smoke and break down. Likewise the plant origin, and hence the fat-type profile, of the oil affects its ability to tolerate heat. The temperature at which an oil starts to break down is known as the 'smoke point'; it is the temperature at which a visible gaseous vapour becomes evident. It is important not to heat oil past its smoke point since this can result in chemical changes in the oil that not only reduce its flavour and nutritional value, but may also be detrimental to one's health.

Proper packaging and storage of an oil are important to prevent spoilage and rancidity, and to preserve nutrients. Heat, oxygen and light can all damage vegetable oils. Oils properly sealed in glass containers, without oxygen trapped at the top, are stable until opened. As soon as the seal is broken, atmospheric oxygen begins to break down the oil. Likewise light can damage unrefined oils by reacting with certain components, such as chlorophyll, in the oil; refined oils are far less susceptible to light-induced damage. The effects of oxygen and light are accelerated as the temperature increases. So, as a general rule, oils are best stored in dark glass bottles in a cool, dark place or chilled (particularly if they have a high monounsaturated fat content). On chilling, some oils, such as olive, become cloudy and too thick to pour, but clear on warming to room temperature.

As explained under Healthy Eating Guidelines (page 198), the fat profile of a food is important in relation to whether it assists in maintaining a good blood cholesterol profile, be it by having a low saturated fat content, or by assisting in raising good HDL cholesterol or decreasing bad LDL cholesterol levels. The oils I use most frequently are listed below together with the reasons that I select and how I use them.

*Avocado oil*  A relatively new introduction to the cooking oil arena, avocado oil is a virgin, cold-pressed oil with a lovely, delicate flavour and a very good fat profile. It is excellent for Asian-style cooking, fish and chicken dishes, and dressings and vinaigrettes. It has the highest smoke point of all the cooking oils (about 270°C) and so is suitable for the full range of cooking techniques, from low-heat sautéing to the hottest searing. Available from gourmet food shops.

*Canola oil*  Made from rape seeds (hence its alternative name rapeseed oil). It has a good fat profile with a very low level of saturated fat (about 6 per cent—avocado and olive contain about 14 per cent and palm oil about 79 per cent), and has a good monounsaturated fat level (but lower than avocado, olive and macadamia). With its neutral, bland flavour and a smoke point of about 205°C, it is suitable for both cooking (baking, sauté, stir-frying) and making dressings where a tasteless oil base is required.

*Chilli oil*  A vegetable oil in which hot red chillies have been steeped to release their heat and flavour; it is a mainstay of Chinese cookery. Depending on the oil base, it will keep for up to six months at room temperature, but will retain its potency longer if refrigerated. It is an excellent way to add a dash of heat and flavour to a sauce, dressing, stir-fried or steamed vegetables. There are a variety of chilli-infused oils on the market—check that a suitable vegetable oil base, such as olive, has been infused and no unwanted additives, such as garlic or MSG, have been included. Use sparingly until you have got the measure of its spiciness since the heat varies significantly between brands.

To make your own, soak 5 whole dried chillies in warm water for 10 minutes. While the chillies are soaking, place a sprig of rosemary and a bay leaf in a small pan with 250 mL extra-light olive oil* over a very low heat. Drain the chillies, dry really well, chop roughly and add to the oil. Warm gently for 30 minutes—the oil must not simmer, smoke or boil. Allow to cool slightly before straining into a screw-top glass bottle and sealing. The oil will keep for months in a cool, dark place. For extra flavour, add 1 teaspoon pure sesame oil* while the oil is cooling.

*Grapeseed oil*  As the name suggests this oil is extracted from grape seeds. Some grapeseed oils have a light 'grapey' flavour and fragrance but most are bland and so are suitable to use when a tasteless oil is required, such as in dressings. It has a relatively high smoke point (252°C) so it is also good for sautéing. It may be stored at room temperature or in the refrigerator. Grapeseed oil is available from gourmet food shops and some supermarkets.

*Lemon-infused olive oil*   The wonderful fresh, zesty lemon flavour imparted by just a small amount of this oil adds a whole flavour dimension to fish, poultry, meat, vegetables, dressings and marinades—you name it! While it is not cheap, it is one item that is a must for elevating the flavour base of a simple dish. There are a number of brands on the market, some more lemony than others—try Valley Produce Company's oil which is available from gourmet food shops (www.vpc.com.au, 0438 226 609).

*Macadamia oil*   Extracted by cold pressing mature nuts. This oil has the highest level of monounsaturates of all the oils, a low level of saturates and is rich in Vitamin E. It has a wonderful soft, aromatic flavour making it ideal for dressings and vinaigrettes. With a smoke point of 200–210°C, it is suitable for stir-fries, sautéing and baking, retaining its lovely flavour through the cooking process.

*Mustard seed oil*   A hot, pungent oil expressed from mustard seeds. It can be used in stir-fries, salad dressings and marinades and sauces, adding a spicy flavour to your cooking. Like chilli oil, use sparingly until you have got the measure of its spiciness.

*Olive oil*   Pressed tree-ripened olives produce a flavour-rich, monounsaturated oil that is prized throughout the world both for cooking and for dressings. Like wine, the flavour, colour and fragrance of olive oil can vary dramatically depending on factors such as the growing region. Olive oils are graded based on their level of acidity; the lower the acidity the finer the oil.

- *Extra-virgin olive oil*   This, being the finest and fruitiest of the olive oils, is produced by the first cold pressing and contains only 1 per cent acid. In general, the deeper green/green-yellow the colour, the more intense the olive flavour of the oil. It has a low smoke point (about 208°C), being rich in heat-sensitive nutrients. It is not suited to cooking other than simple sauces at most, and is best added to a dish after cooking to optimise its wonderful flavour and nutritional value.
- *Virgin olive oil*   Also a first-press oil, with a slightly higher level of acidity of between 1 and 3 per cent and suited to low temperature cooking (smoke point about 215°C). Fino olive oil is a blend of extra-virgin and virgin oils.
- *Extra-light olive oil*   The newer 'extra-light olive oil' is not a low-calorie version, but olive oil that has been through an extremely fine filtration process. While it retains the same level of beneficial monounsaturates as regular olive oil, it is lighter in both colour and fragrance, and has little of the classic olive-oil flavour, making it perfect for baking and cooking where a stronger-flavoured olive oil might be undesirable. The filtration process also results in oil with a higher smoke point (up to 242°C) than regular olive oil, suitable for high-heat frying, whereas regular olive oil is better suited for low- to medium-heat cooking, as well as for many uncooked foods such as salad dressings and marinades.
- *Olive oil*   Products simply labelled 'olive oil' (once called 'pure olive oil') contain a combination of refined olive oil and virgin or extra-virgin oil.
- *Extra-light olive oil spray*   Very useful for reducing fat consumption, whether for lightly oiling a food before char-grilling or greasing a non-stick pan before sautéing. Select a spray that is 100 per cent pure, and does not contain an emulsifier such as lecithin or other 'No-Go' food, for example garlic. Alternatives include olive oil pump packs or a pastry brush to apply oil to pans. For high-heat sautéing and char-grilling, select an extra-light olive oil spray to prevent oil breakdown on cooking.

*Sesame oil*   An oil expressed from sesame seeds. It is high in polyunsaturates, ranking fourth behind safflower, soybean and corn oil. Two types of sesame oil are available, a light, unroasted and a dark, roasted oil. The light sesame oil has a light and delicious nutty flavour and is excellent for everything from salad dressings to sautéing. The darker, roasted sesame oil has a much stronger flavour and fragrance and is used as a flavouring in many Asian dishes. It has a low smoke point so is usually added at the end of cooking; it is the dark, roasted oil that is used in this book.

*Walnut oil* This has a distinctive nutty flavour and fragrance, but with a relatively low smoke point it is best used in salad dressings (usually combined with less flavourful oils), sauces, main dishes and baked goods, and for low-temperature sautéing. It can be found in gourmet food shops and some supermarkets. Best stored refrigerated to prevent rancidity.

**Okara** The residue that is left after the liquid is drained off when making soybean curd (tofu). It is used in Japanese cooking for making soups, vegetable dishes and even salads.

**Olive oil** *see* Oils.

**Olives** The bitterness of fresh olives is removed by processing with a sodium hydroxide and/or salt solution. After processing the olives may then be treated with a vinegar solution (typically kalamata olives) or marinated with various ingredients, such as lemon, herbs, spices and garlic, before being packaged in a brine, brine-oil or vinegar mix. Preservatives such as calcium gluconate (578) and lactic (270) or other food acids may also be added (see Avoiding Corn, page 161). Olives, given their salt-curing process, can also have a high sodium content so select brand carefully.

Always Fresh brand kalamata olives with balsamic vinegar (note—low sodium content), and Greek kalamata olives (contain xanthan gum*) include caramel colour derived from corn. These are available from supermarkets (Riviana Foods www.rivianafoodservice.com, (02) 9757 4722).

Green Valley brand Greek kalamata olives and Spanish marinated olives (Conga Foods www.congafoods.com.au, (03) 9487 9500) contain lactic acid (see Avoiding Corn, page 161). Viva brand kalamata olives ((08) 8584 5811) are pickled in a brine–white spirit vinegar derived from molasses, and olive oil with lactic acid (see Avoiding Corn, page 161). These are available from supermarkets.

**Oyster sauce** This is a pungent sauce that combines with other Asian ingredients such as fish sauce to make a wonderful marinade, or is used alone as a seasoning for stir-fried vegetable, meat, seafood and noodle dishes. It is made from an extract of oysters, as the name suggests, but typically will contain a thickener, such as corn or wheat starch, plus caramel or burnt sugar as a colour enhancer; many brands also contain MSG. Sinsin brand Original Oyster Sauce contains caramel derived from sugar cane and a maize-derived thickener; it is available from supermarkets and Asian grocers (www.pacific-food.com, (07) 3807 6000).

**Palm sugar** A rich, aromatic sugar produced by reducing the sap of several kinds of palm trees. Available from supermarkets and Asian grocers in a solid, cake-like form which is grated before use. Soft brown sugar can be used as a substitute but lacks the delicate, winey flavour.

**Pancetta** A pork product produced from the layer of fat and flesh along the pork belly, under the skin, which is cured with salt and air dried, the ageing process lasting 30–100 days. Some varieties of pancetta are prepared with cinnamon, cloves and other local spices in addition to salt and pepper (some brands may contain milk solids, soy protein, corn-derived dextrose and garlic). The hot variety is produced by adding crushed chilli to give it a distinctive flavour. Round pancetta is prepared by stripping the skin from the meat and making it into a roll. It is used in Italian cooking to flavour sauces, pasta dishes, forcemeats, vegetables and meats. Pancetta can be tightly wrapped and refrigerated for up to 3 weeks, or frozen up to 6 months. Dorsogna brand pancetta is 'No-Go' food suitable; for product details and outlets see www.dorsogna.com.au

**Parboiled rice** *see* Rice.

**Passata** *see* Tomato passata.

**Pasta** A number of good wheat-, gluten-, soy- and egg-free pastas are readily available from Western and Asian supermarkets, and health food shops. These pastas are based on rice, mung beans, buckwheat* or corn (maize). Additionally, there are varieties of pastas that combine rice and soy, for example, which may also be suitable for you. I select pasta based on the flavour and consistency I want it to contribute to the dish; see comments below. Remember, cooking wheat pasta al dente requires careful timing **but** this timing is even more critical with non-wheat based pastas—they are not in the least forgiving if they are over-cooked, and can easily be reduced to a soggy mass if you don't follow the manufacturer's instructions and watch the clock!

*Buckwheat pastas* A number of buckwheat pastas are available, including noodles and spirals (e.g. Orgran brand) from supermarkets and health food shops. Many Asian-sourced buckwheat noodles are *not* pure buckwheat, also containing wheat flour, so check ingredients carefully. Pure buckwheat (soba) noodles are available but tend to be expensive.

*Corn (maize) pastas* Corn-based pastas including lasagne and pasta shapes are available from supermarkets and health food shops. I find the texture of these inferior to many of the rice noodles.

*Bean-thread vermicelli* (or cellophane or glass noodles) These flat or thread-like noodles are made from the legume mung beans. To rehydrate, bring a large pan of water to the boil, turn off the heat, add the noodles and soak for 5 minutes or until softened and translucent. These noodles are robust and have a firm texture when eaten but do not tend to absorb sauces to the same extent as rice noodles. They may also be deep-fried to make a crispy garnish.

*Rice pastas* Available as fresh and dried varieties. Rice pasta typically does not have much flavour, but depending on the type of pasta you select offers a different consistency or texture to the meal. Overall rice pastas result in very light dishes—just compare a lasagne made with fresh rice pasta to one made with wheat.

- *Fresh rice noodles and vermicelli* Fresh rice noodles are lightly cooked, soft, wet noodles made from sweet glutinous rice and are found in most Asian grocers. They are available in a variety of sizes, including thick flat noodles, thin round noodles, spaghetti, flat sheets and rolls. They are suitable for using in soups and stir-fries, and the flat sheets can also be used to make lasagne-style dishes. Check the ingredients carefully since many contain 'cornstarch' and vegetable oil. Different Asian grocers carry different brands, so trial varieties until you find a brand you like. I prefer unoiled, pure rice spaghetti (such as Way Lup brand, (02) 9660 8793); it has the best texture and does not break down readily when placed in hot stock or water. Varieties of fresh rice noodles are also available in the chilled section of some supermarkets (such as Mr Lee's Kitchen brand)—these are also suitable for soups and stir-fries but tend to be 'stickier' than the noodles from Asian grocers. It is important that the rice pasta is fresh; it is best stored at room temperature since refrigeration makes it brittle and difficult to handle. Reheat in the microwave or by dipping in boiling stock or water in an Asian wire strainer, metal sieve or colander; these noodles are delicate and are easily overcooked.

- *Dried rice stick noodles and vermicelli* Found in both Western and Asian supermarkets and again come in a variety of thicknesses. As with the fresh rice pasta, the texture and resilience of the different brands of vermicelli makes it well worth trialling the range available in your area. The best brands are those prepared by cooking in boiling water for 3–5 minutes, rinsed with cold water and then cooked as chosen in soup, sauce or fried, as opposed to brands prepared by soaking in hot water (Jiang Xi brand, imported by BKK Australia Pty Ltd (02)9756 6855 and available from Asian grocers and some supermarkets, is excellent). If making a chilled vermicelli salad with pesto or dressing of choice, cover, refrigerate and re-drain before using, as the vermicelli will exude further moisture while chilling. Rice vermicelli can also be deep fried for a crispy garnish. Certain Asian grocers carry dried 100 per cent rice macaroni (Lân Vàng brand imported by Rockman, Australia, Pty Ltd, (02) 9756 0088) which is robust and has an excellent texture on cooking.

- *Rice, and rice and vegetable, pastas* A variety of dried rice-based pastas are available from supermarkets and health food shops; try Buonotempo macaroni or Naked Foods pastariso.

**Pickled ginger** *see* Ginger.

**Plain flour**  *see* Flour.

**Poha**  Flattened or beaten rice. It is imported from India and can take some tracking down. It is available from some Middle Eastern and Asian supermarkets or see Suppliers—Flour, page 197.

**Polenta**  A staple in northern Italy for centuries, polenta is a type of cornmeal made from ground maize. Generally, in Italy two common types are used, coarse and fine. Polenta can be served soft as a porridge type of dish topped with sauce and meat, or allowed to cool and harden and then served fried or grilled. Regular polenta typically takes 15–20 minutes to cook, but instant or quick-cook varieties are available which reduce the cooking time to 3–5 minutes. Polenta is usually made from yellow corn, but other varieties include a mix of cornmeal with buckwheat and a white corn polenta. Available from delicatessens and some supermarkets.

**Pomegranate molasses**  (concentrated juice)  A tart syrup of Middle Eastern origin and not to be confused with the very sweet grenadine. It adds a quite a different fruity, tartness to meat marinades and glazes, sauces, and soups—or an as ice-cream topping or non-alcoholic cordial to serve with ice and sparkling mineral water. Available from Middle Eastern grocers (Cortas brand—contact Harkola Pty Ltd at www.harkola.com.au or (02) 9737 8883 for outlets) or Herbie's Spices (see Suppliers —Herbs and Spices).

**Poppadums**  Usually made on a base of lentil or lentil and rice flours. Many brands also contain garlic included as a 'spice'; check for warnings of cross-contamination with tree nuts or peanuts, or other 'No-Go' foods. While traditionally poppadums are deep fried, many brands are also suitable to microwave, which minimises fat intake. Place in a single layer on the microwave plate and cook on high power for 1 minute or until crispy. Sharwood's Plain (www.sharwoods.com) are free of all the 'No-Go' foods; Changs (www.changs.com) contain asafoetida (see Avoiding Garlic and Onions, page 166); available from supermarkets.

**Preserved lemon**  A staple of Middle Eastern cuisine, these are lemons that have been preserved in salt and lemon juice marinade with a range of herbs and spices, such as cloves, cinnamon and allspice. It is the rind and not the flesh that is used to provide a wonderful mellow citrus flavour in a wide range of savoury dishes, including meat, poultry, fish, pasta, salads, vegetables and chermoula. Maggie Beer brand (www.maggiebeer.com.au, (08) 8563 0204) is free of all the 'No-Go' foods and is available from gourmet food shops.

**Prosciutto**  Like pancetta, prosciutto originates from Italy. It is an air-dried ham taking over 6 months to mature and is renowned for its delicate, salty flavour (some brands may contain milk solids, soy protein, corn-derived dextrose and garlic. It is usually available cut into paper-thin slices and is served raw, but also makes an excellent wrap for char-grilled meat, chicken and fish, producing a crispy, salty coat. Dorsogna brand prosciutto is 'No-Go' food suitable; for product details and outlets see www.dorsogna.com.au

**Psyllium**  (psyllium husk)  The seed of the plantago species native to Iran and India. It is naturally high in soluble dietary fibre and mucilage. The mucilage swells when in contact with water to form a gelatinous mass which is not broken down by enzymes in the digestive tract, nor is it absorbed. Psyllium has long been used by Chinese and Ayurvedic herbalists to regulate bowel movements and alleviate diarrhoea and constipation, and is now used worldwide for this purpose. It may also help with the regulation of blood cholesterol and blood sugar levels, while increasing dietary fibre intake. It can be easily added to cooking to act as a tasteless thickener—add a teaspoonful to a casserole or gravy, pastry or cake mix. It is important to maintain adequate fluid intake when using psyllium in amounts up to 10 g per day. Available from supermarkets.

**Quandongs**  These native Australian fruits, also known as wild peaches, desert peaches or native peaches, are found in the arid and semi-arid regions of all Australian mainland states. They were much favoured by indigenous Australians, who used to dry the winter crop for summer eating and use it for medicinal properties. Quandongs have a vitamin C content higher than oranges and almost certainly saved many early Australian explorers from scurvy. Quandong fruit can be dried and frozen for eight years or more without losing any flavour. It is well worth the effort to track them down—I buy the dried fruit by the kilo via mail order and store it in an airtight container in a cool, dark cupboard. See Suppliers—Bush Foods for outlets.

**Quandong jam**  There are a few brands of quandong jam available commercially (e.g. Beerenburg) which can be used as a substitute for cooked quandongs as a sauce base in some recipes. Available from some supermarkets and gourmet food shops.

**Quince paste**  A wonderful sweet paste made from slowly cooked quinces and sugar. Primarily it is served as a traditional accompaniment to cheese in Spain, Portugal and southern France, but can also be served as an after-dinner sweet with coffee. It is delicious served cut into small squares and tossed in cinnamon sugar or dipped in dark chocolate. Suitable brands include: Maggie Beer brand (www.maggiebeer.com.au, (08) 8563 0204), available from gourmet food shops; Corazón del Sol brand, available from some supermarkets.

**Ras el hanout**  As with any seasoning or spice mix, check ingredients carefully to ensure no wheat flour or garlic has been added. Available from Middle Eastern grocers and good spice shops (see Suppliers—Herbs and Spices, page 197).

**Red bean paste**  A thick paste of red beans sweetened with sugar which makes an ideal base for pies; check no other ingredients are added. Freeze any left-over paste. Available in cans from Asian grocers.

**Red kidney beans**  *see* Canned beans.

**Redcurrant jelly**  A condiment usually served with lamb, this jelly is also useful in cooking as a sweetener or gelling agent. It also makes a good glaze for fruit tarts when melted and lightly brushed over the top of the fruit after cooking. Select a brand, such as Nelsons, made with redcurrants or redcurrant juice, sugar and water, with pectin as the gelling agent; available from supermarkets. Some brands may contain food acid (see Avoiding Corn, page 161).

**Rice**  There are a number of varieties of rice available which not only offer a range of flavour and texture, but also have differing impacts on blood sugar levels because of differences in the rate of breakdown of the rice starch to glucose. Basmati and doongara rice, for example, are the best types of rice for maintaining steady blood glucose (they have the lowest Glycaemic Index). Rice can be divided into three basic categories based on the length of the grain, namely long, medium and short grain.

*Long-grain rice*  The slender grains typical of long-grain rice do not clump when cooked and include jasmine, basmati, doongara, white long-grain, parboiled rice (see below) and some brown rice, with the outer bran layer intact.

*Medium-grain rice*  The rice grains are shorter and fatter than long-grain. The grains fluff up and separate during cooking but clump as the rice cools, except a medium-grain brown rice where the bran layer keeps the grains separate.

*Short-grain rice*  Has the highest starch content and include types such as sushi, arborio, carnaroli, and the very sticky Asian black and white glutinous rice (see below), which are used to make desserts.

The following types have rice have been used in the recipes:

*Arborio rice*  Traditionally used for risotto because its high starch content gives the dish its requisite creamy texture.

*Basmati rice*  This aromatic, long-grain rice is grown in the foothills of the Himalayas and is especially popular in India. The cooked grains are dry and fluffy, and make a great bed for curries and sauces. Try Riviana brand Ezi-Cook Basmati Rice available through supermarkets for a failsafe basmati rice!

*Brown rice* This is not milled to the same extent as white and retains the bran and germ, making it a higher fibre and more nutritious grain. It does not fluff up like white rice when cooked, has a chewier texture and distinct nutty flavour. Brown rice also takes about twice as long as white rice to cook, and has a much shorter shelf life because of the oil in the germ. The shelf life can be extended by storing it in the refrigerator.

*Glutinous white and black rice* These contain no gluten, the 'glutinous' describes the 'sticky' texture of the rice when it is cooked. Glutinous white rice, unlike the black, cooks very rapidly. The black rice is best stored refrigerated. Both are available from Asian grocers.

*Jasmine rice* A long-grain rice produced in Thailand that is sometimes used as a cheap substitute for basmati rice. It has a lovely subtle floral aroma and is excellent cooked in a rice cooker (see Cooking Tools, page 204). Kumarnthong brand available from supermarkets is a favourite.

*Parboiled rice or converted rice* A good compromise between nutritious brown rice and tender, fast-cooking white rice. Converted rice is steamed before it is husked, a process that causes the grains to absorb many of the nutrients from the husk. When cooked, the grains are more nutritious, firmer, and less clingy than white rice grains (try Sungold or Uncle Ben's brands available from supermarkets).

*Sweet brown rice* (Japanese mochi gome) A pearly, short-grain rice. It is the brown rice equivalent of glutinous white rice but the grains do not stick together as well as the white when cooked. Additionally, the name is a misnomer, as it is not naturally sweet. Available from Japanese and some Asian grocers.

*Wild rice* This is not a true rice but the seed of an aquatic grass. It has a very distinct nutty flavour, with extra-long grains that open and curl on cooking. Wild rice, unlike arborio and other true rices, is not suitable to fry in oil before cooking since this seals the outer coat and prevents the grains absorbing water and softening as they cook. Wild rice blends, such as wild rice mixed with long grain or brown rice, are also available. For best results I prefer to cook, rinse and drain the two different types of rice separately before combining and reheating.

**Rice crumbs** These make a good substitute for breadcrumbs but tend to be crunchier. Orgran brand (www.orgran.com, (03) 9776 9044), available from supermarkets and health food shops, is made from 100 per cent crumbed rice; some brands can include additives such as sugar.

**Rice flour** There are four basic types of rice flour, each contributing different textures and properties to baking; they are *not* interchangeable in the recipes.

*Brown rice flour* This is a grittier type of rice flour since, as the name suggests, it is milled from brown rice and so retains the fibre and nutrients of the bran and germ. If stored in an airtight container it can become rancid very rapidly because of the retained oil; store in paper or calico bags for best results.

*Fine white rice flour* Finely milled white rice flour that retains more texture than the very starchy white rice flour used in Asian cooking. It is used in the Basic Flour Mix (page 113). Available from health food shops or see Suppliers—Flour (page 197).

*Glutinous white rice flour* A starchy, fine flour made from white glutinous rice. This flour, when added to other gluten-free flours, helps to bind the mix together with the addition of liquid. Available from supermarkets and Asian grocers.

*White rice flour* Resembles cornflour in texture and is available from the Asian section of most supermarkets and Asian grocers.

**Rice milk**  There are a few of brands of rice milk now available from supermarkets and health food shops. The flavour and texture varies between brands: Australia's Own (www.sonatural.com.au, (02) 9526 2555), has a rich, malty flavour, with a brown rice and canola oil base it is good for cooking custards, risottos and rice puddings; the lighter, whiter Aussie Dream brand (www.pureharvest.com.au, (03) 5625 1111) is a good alternative and will result in a lighter-coloured sauce or custard. Rice Dream (www.kadac.com.au, (03) 9584 3266), available as original, enriched and vanilla, contains barley-derived malt so is not suitable for people with wheat or gluten sensitivities. All are available from supermarkets and health food shops.

**Rice syrup**  A versatile sweetener made by culturing rice with enzymes to break down the starches, the resultant liquid being cooked to a thick, syrupy consistency. Unlike sugar and glucose, about 90 per cent of the syrup is made up of maltose (unrelated to barley malt and gluten-free) and soluble complex carbohydrates, which take up to three hours to be digested and so provide a steady supply of energy instead of the instant, unsustained burst from sugar. It is about half as sweet as honey or sugar and is useful as a binder in cooking. Some rice syrups contain barley malt as a flavouring so check labels carefully. Pureharvest brand (www.pureharvest.com.au, (03) 5625 1111), containing only rice and water, is available from supermarkets and health food shops.

**Rice vermicelli**  *see* Pasta.

**Roasted nori**  *see* Nori.

**Rolled rice**  Whole uncooked rice grains rolled and flattened to form flakes. Unlike poha*, the flakes are very crunchy and need to be processed to be readily palatable. Available from health food shops and some supermarkets.

**Salmon caviar**  Many brands of caviar, especially those based on lumpfish, contain a wide variety of additives. Springs brand (Springs Smoked Seafood, (08) 8398 2533) comprises salmon caviar and salt and is available in the refrigerated section of supermarkets.

**Sambal oelek (ulek)**  A finely minced hot chilli paste with a sharp smell and pungent taste, and like chilli paste is a great way to add chilli without having to take the usual precautions of chopping up a fresh chilli. Check the ingredient listing carefully for additional ingredients such as garlic, flour, and food acids (see Avoiding Corn, page 161). The heat of the paste varies between brands, so start by adding a small amount and then increase to taste. I use a brand such as TFC (The Food Company, (02) 9519 7799) which also includes the added flavour of tamarind, and is available from Asian grocers.

**Self-raising flour**  *see* Flour.

**Sesame oil**  *see* Oils.

**Shiitake mushrooms**  (Chinese mushrooms)  Originating in Japan and Korea, these delicious mushrooms are now being widely cultivated. They have a wonderful, full-bodied flavour and make an excellent addition to the flavour-base of stocks and sauces. If buying fresh, the stalks are often tough so are best removed before adding the shiitake cap to a dish; retain the stalks for stock. Shiitake mushrooms are also available dried—I prefer the cleaned, sliced variety from Asian grocers since the whole caps can be gritty and require cleaning thoroughly before using. Rehydrate by standing in boiling water for 5–10 minutes or until softened; the resulting stock can be added to a sauce.

**Shrimp paste**  (belcan, blachan, trassi)  A pungent paste made from finely ground shrimp that has been fermented in salt; these should be the only ingredients. The colour, aroma and texture vary depending on the brand, from pink and soft to dark brown and hard. While the aroma seems overwhelming, it is a vital component in Thai cooking and its strong flavour blends wonderfully with the robust flavours of chilli, fragrant spices, and aromatic roots and herbs. The paste should be cooked before eating—roast for 1–2 minutes in foil under a hot grill or in a pan over a low heat, either alone or as part of a premixed paste, being careful to ensure it does not burn. Store refrigerated in an airtight container after opening. Available from supermarkets and Asian grocers.

**Sichuan peppercorns**  These have a wonderful woody flavour with a strong, hot aftertaste. I like to use them in dry marinades in combination with black peppercorns and other spices such as cumin and sumac∗. They are not true peppercorns but the dried, burst seed pods of a prickly ash tree and are sold whole or ground. Available from some Western supermarkets, Asian grocers and good spice shops (see Suppliers—Herbs and Spices, page 197).

**Smoked salmon**  Naturally cured smoked salmon is usually prepared by cold smoking using true wood smoke (such as a mix of Tasmanian hardwoods), although some manufacturers also produce a hot smoked product which is smoked at a higher temperature and results in a cooked product rather than a smoke-cured product. Select a brand that is 100 per cent salmon naturally smoked, such as Tassal brand (www.tassal.com.au, (03) 6211 9611), available from supermarkets.

**Smoked sweet paprika**  Originating from Spain. As the name suggests it is made by smoking the pepper with natural wood smoke before grinding. This results in a very distinctive robust aroma and flavour so only small quantities are required to give a whole new flavour dimension to soups, stews and casseroles. Available from good spice outlets or see Suppliers—Herbs and Spices, page 197.

**Spirits and liqueurs**  Checking the suitability of a spirit and liqueur is important since it may:
- have been derived from a grain such as wheat or corn, and despite having been distilled may pose a problem for very sensitive individuals;
- contain caramel added as a colouring which may have been derived from sugar cane, wheat, dairy or corn. If the caramel is wheat-derived, the processing it undergoes results in no gluten being detectable in the final product and is classified as acceptable for people with a gluten sensitivity. (Manufacturers are not required to declare the inclusion of caramel on the label of an alcoholic beverage under the current Food Standards Code);
- have been conditioned in casks that had previously held sherry, which may have been clarified with animal-derived finings, including a milk, egg or fish product (see Wine, below). Examples include malt whisky, some blended whiskies and Spanish brandies.

The following list includes brands of spirits and liqueurs used in selected recipes that have been classified as free of all 'No-Go' foods by the respective manufacturer unless otherwise qualified in the product entry.

*Brandy and cognac*  Barossa Brandy contains caramel derived from gluten (see note above regarding wheat-derived caramel; Fosters Group, www.fosters.com.au, contact through 'Help', (03) 9633 2000).

Hardy's Black Bottle Brandy and XO Brandy contain caramel derived from sugar cane (www.hardywines.com.au, (08) 8392 2222);

McWilliam's brandies: Chairmans Reserve Deluxe Brandy NV, Max Brandy NV and Show Reserve Deluxe Liqueur Brandy NV contain no caramel (www.mcwilliams.com.au, (02) 9722 1265);

Remy Martin Cognac contains no caramel (Maxxium Australia, www.maxxium.com/main.htm, (02) 9418 5000).

*Butterscotch Schnapps*  De Kuyper contains synthetic caramel (no animal or plant origin; De Kuyper Royal Distillers, The Netherlands, 0011 311 427 9700); Quality Brands International (Australia), (02) 9690 1911).

Note: De Kuyper uses synthetic caramel in schnapps and caramel derived from sugar cane in other products containing caramel.

*Cointreau*  (Maxxium Australia, www.maxxium.com/main.htm, (02) 9418 5000).

*Rum* Bacardi Rum made from cane molasses and special strains of yeast and filtered on wood-derived charcoal and on cellulose and synthetic pads (Quality Brands International, (02) 9690 1911).

Bundaberg Rum is made from molasses with caramel colour derived from corn (maize) added (Bundaberg Distilling Co. (07) 4131 2900).

**Stock** Many commercially available stocks contain one or more of the 'No-Go' foods, so check the ingredient list carefully for suitability before using. Try making bulk batches of stock in bulk, or routinely boil up or microwave any left-over chicken carcass or meat bone (see recipes for quick-and-easy and more traditional-style stocks on pages 9–13) so that you can keep a store of stock in the freezer to use as required. Never just discard prawn heads and shells—turn them into a tasty stock in a few minutes (see Prawn Stock, page 11). When roasting a chicken, wrap it in aluminium foil and drain the juices into a jug when you open the foil to brown the chicken for the last 10–15 minutes of cooking. Refrigerate the juices after cooling, to allow the fat to settle and solidify on top. The resulting jelly makes an excellent concentrated stock base for gravies, soups and sauces.

If tolerated, miso can be used as a simple substitute for stock. There are a number of types of savoury miso which are based on fermented soybeans—obviously, not suitable for anyone with a soy sensitivity. To use, simply replace the volume of stock listed in the recipe with an equivalent volume of water and add the miso paste, starting with 1 teaspoon per litre of water and increasing to taste. By varying the mixture of grains added and the fermentation time, the colour, texture and aroma of the resulting miso is varied. These include:

- hatcho miso—made from soybeans;
- genmai miso—made from soybeans and brown rice;
- kome miso—made from soybeans and white rice;
- soba miso—made from soybeans and buckwheat;
- mugi miso—made from soybeans and barley (*not* suitable for a gluten-free diet);
- awase miso—made from soybeans, rice and barley (*not* suitable for a gluten-free diet).

Massel brand stock concentrate is a vegetarian, low-fat, gluten- and lactose-free powder. It is *not* suitable for anyone sensitive to soy or onions. To use simply replace the volume of stock listed in the recipe with an equivalent volume of water and add 1 teaspoon of stock powder per 500 mL (2 cups) water. Other vegetable-based stock starters are available from health food shops; check ingredients for suitability.

If all else fails, simply replace the volume of stock in the recipe with the same volume of water and season the final dish to taste with extra freshly ground black pepper and a sprinkle of salt.

**Sumac** (sumak) In Middle Eastern cooking, sumac is used as a souring agent instead of lemon or vinegar. It is typically sprinkled on kebabs and used to garnish salads, especially those with tomatoes, parsley and onions. Sumac is a delicious addition to roast lamb, being rubbed into the lamb before cooking either alone and or mixed with paprika, pepper and oregano. The traditional blend of za'ater is made by blending sumac, thyme, toasted sesame seeds and salt, which is then sprinkled on flat bread with olive oil before toasting. Available from Middle Eastern grocers, some supermarkets or see Suppliers—Herbs and Spices, page 197.

**Sun-dried tomatoes and sun-dried tomato oil** Sun-dried tomatoes are wonderful additions to sauces, casseroles, pastas, salads and snacks. They are available unadulterated—dehydrated—or rehydrated and marinated in oil, herbs and spices. The drying process concentrates the sweetness and glorious flavours of tomatoes. There is a wide range of commercial marinated sun-dried tomatoes available but most are loaded with garlic and may contain MSG, so check the ingredient listing carefully. Carmelina brand contains no MSG or garlic and uses a wine vinegar (available from supermarkets or contact Leo's Imports for outlets, www.leosimports.com.au, (03) 9359 0658). Otherwise, buy unadulterated tomatoes and marinate them yourself (see Seasoned Sun-dried Tomatoes in Olive Oil, page 89). The tomatoes impart some of their flavour to the marinade, making the oil an excellent base for a simple salad or pasta dressing, or to use in place of a regular oil for a stir-fry. Unmarinated tomatoes are easily rehydrated: put in a bowl and cover with boiling water, leave to stand for 12–15 minutes to soften (the tomatoes will become mushy if oversoaked) before draining, gently squeezing out any excess water, and placing on kitchen towels to drain. Available from some supermarkets, gourmet food shops and grocery wholesale outlets.

**Sushi-style pickled ginger** *see* Ginger.

**Sweet brown rice** *see* Rice.

**Tahini** A paste made from white sesame seeds which is widely used in the Middle East to make hummus, baba ghanoush, dressings and sauces. It is available made from hulled or unhulled sesame seeds. Tahini is a good source of dietary calcium, since sesame seeds are naturally rich in calcium, but the body cannot utilise the calcium if the seeds are eaten intact. The sesame oil tends to rise to the top on standing, so stir well before using. Available from supermarkets and Middle Eastern grocers. Once opened, tahini is best stored refrigerated.

**Tamarind paste** Tamarind is a much-valued food ingredient in many Asian and Latin American recipes. Tamarind is the fruit pod produced by a tall, semi-evergreen tree grown primarily in India. The beans and pulp within the pod have virtually no smell, but have a very sour taste and so are using as a souring agent in many sauces. Tamarind is available as whole pods, a compressed block, a paste or concentrate and is available from supermarkets and Asian grocers. I use the paste or concentrate for convenience; select a brand that is contains pure tamarind extract only.

**Tapioca flour** A starchy flour extracted from the root of the cassava plant that behaves much like cornstarch when cooked and is used as a thickening agent for soups, fruit fillings, glazes, etc. Available from supermarkets, Asian grocery and health food shops.

**Tomato passata** (passato, passata di pomodoro) A smooth, rich, concentrated purée made from sieved tomatoes. It makes an excellent base for sauces since it is naturally richly flavoured and thicker than chopped or crushed tomatoes but not as sweet or concentrated as tomato paste. Usually available in 690–700 g bottles from some supermarkets, growers markets and gourmet food shops. Check ingredients carefully to ensure that only tomatoes and salt are included, and select a low-salt brand since the amount of sodium can vary significantly, from a low 18–20 mg/100 g (Aurora brand, Cosmo Foods (02) 9748 0299; Carmelina brand, Leo's Imports www.leosimports.com.au, (03) 9359 0658) to a high 350 mg/100 g. Tomato purée with no added salt (such as Ardmona brand), available from supermarkets, is also suitable. Other forms include 'passata rustica' or 'sugo' in which the tomatoes are crushed rather than sieved, resulting in a coarser sauce; sugo contains additional ingredients including garlic and/or onions.

**Tomato paste** The level of salt added to different brands of tomato paste can vary widely from brands with no added salt (such as Fountain brand 29 mg/100 g) or low added salt (La Gina brand 21 mg/100 g) to levels up to 835 mg/100 g plus. Select a brand with a concentrated flavour and minimum sodium levels for best results.

**Vanilla extract or essence** Check ingredient listing carefully; may contain corn syrup, alcohol of unspecified origin, etc. Queen Fine Foods (www.queen.com.au, (07) 3356 7344) make a natural vanilla extract that is alcohol-free, or see Suppliers—Herbs and Spices, page 197.

**Vegetable stock** *see* Stock.

**Vietnamese mint** Also known as Vietnamese coriander or laksa leaf, this has a strong, distinctive, minty, peppery flavour. To use, pick the leaves from the woody stems. Available from good greengrocers and Asian grocers, it is well worth tracking down for the lovely fresh, spicy flavour it gives a dish.

**Vinegar** There are many types of vinegar, the correct selection depends on the pungency of acetic flavour required in a dish, the length of cooking after addition of the vinegar, and what other aromatic flavours are required to complement the dish. The quality of a vinegar is determined by the quality of the primary ingredient, such as the wine, champagne or sherry, and the aging process, where appropriate; vinegar must age to become smooth and palatable—young vinegars taste rough but are inexpensive. Malt vinegar is unsuitable for anyone with a gluten intolerance, but a combination of white vinegar (ingredient check) with a balsamic and apple cider vinegar goes a long way to replacing the flavour and colour of a malt vinegar.

*Balsamic vinegar* Originating from Modena and the surrounding areas in Italy, this is a fruity, aromatic, syrupy vinegar made from pure grape 'must' (unfermented juice), aged in barrels of different woods, including chestnut, ash, mulberry, juniper and oak. Good balsamics are at least 12 years old and designated 'Aceto Balsamico Tradizinale di Modena'; the cheaper vinegars have been aged in stainless steel tanks or for much shorter periods in wood and may include caramel colouring (see Avoiding Wheat, Dairy, Corn, page 159) so check the label carefully. Cornwell's balsamic vinegar contains caramel derived from sugar cane (Goodman Fielder, 1800 638 112).

*Brown rice vinegar* A sweeter, less pungently flavoured vinegar than white spirit vinegars that is excellent when the dressing or marinade will not be cooked. Many rice vinegars are seasoned and may contain gluten and other 'No-Go' food derivatives. Try the delicate brown rice vinegar made by Spiral Foods (www.spiralfoods.com.au, (07) 9429 8655), made from a brown rice and water base; unlike some other brands, it does not use a gluten-based grain seed for the fermentation, the seed for subsequent batches being aged vinegar from the previous batch. It is available from supermarkets and health food shops.

*Cider or apple cider vinegar* Made from fermented apples, this vinegar has a distinct apple tang. The depth of flavour varies between brands and, hence, suitability for making a good vinaigrette or delicate sauce. I use a mild-flavoured cider vinegar for chutneys and marinades, but a brand such as Wild About Fruit when I want a vinegar with flavour and depth (www.wildaboutfruit.com.au, (03) 5694 4226, Gourmet Apple Vinegar and Sweet & Spicy Apple Vinegar). Available from supermarkets and gourmet food shops.

*Plum vinegar* Originating from Japan, ume or pickled plum vinegar is a very tart, salty vinegar made from umeboshi plums, which is typically used in dips and dressings. Red wine vinegar can be used as a substitute; additional salt may be required to balance the flavour of the dish. Spiral Foods brand (www.spiralfoods.com.au, (07) 9429 8655) is available from health food shops.

*White vinegar* The spirit base from which white vinegar is fermented varies (typically grains, including corn, or sugar cane) and where it is unspecified (i.e. not produced from one of the mandatory labelled foods) check the suitability of the base with the manufacturer. Cornwell's white vinegar is fermented from a sugar cane derived spirit (Goodman Fielder, 1800 638 112). When using vinegar to preserve foods (e.g. when pickling), check the level of acidity is a minimum of 5 per cent to preserve the food adequately.

*Wine vinegar* Red or white varieties take on the flavour of the grape variety base used in the wine, as well as their colour. Wine vinegars are milder and less acidic than cider or white vinegar, making them a good choice for dressings, sauces and marinades. There are several varieties, ranging from mild champagne vinegar, through the tangy white and red wine vinegars to the more assertive sherry vinegars. Select a milder, white wine vinegar for more delicate dishes, such as salads or as a base for home-made fruit or herb vinegars, but a stronger red one for deglazing pans, marinating meats and adding tang to sauces. The acidity of some wine vinegars may be increased by adding a fermented spirit-based vinegar, in which case the suitability of the spirit base must be checked (see White vinegar, above). Colavita brand wine vinegars (white, red, cabernet and champagne) are made only from fermented wine (the raspberry wine vinegar is made from the white wine vinegar plus a raspberry flavouring) and are clarified by filtration through a porous sedimentary rock (Diatomite) or non-animal derived filters (www.colavita.it). Cornwell's brand of red and white wine vinegars are not processed with any of the 'No-Go' foods or their derivatives; acidity is increased using a fermented sprit-based vinegar derived from sugar cane (Goodman Fielder, 1800 638 112).

**Walnut oil** *see* Oils.

**White corn tortilla**  San Diego brand are wheat- and gluten-free, and are available from some supermarkets (www.sandiego.com.au, (07) 5525 0433).

**White rice flour**  *see* Rice flour.

**Wild limes**  These tiny limes, 10–15 mm in diameter, are native to the semi-arid Queensland outback. They are a true citrus fruit with a delicate porous skin and a wonderful, intense, tart lime–grapefruit flavour. The whole fruit is used in making sauces, pickles and marmalades and they complement any fish, seafood, poultry or pork dish that uses lemon or lime. They are available frozen and keep for months stored frozen. Nothing replaces their glorious flavour, so make the effort to track them down. See Suppliers—Bush Foods for outlets.

**Wholegrain mustard**  *see* Mustard.

**Wild rice blend**  *see* Rice.

**Wine and fortified wine**  The use of animal-derived products in the process of winemaking is a widespread industry practice. Bottled wine is sold as a clean and clear liquid, that in most cases must maintain that clarity in the bottle. Clarification not only involves the removal of suspended matter in the fermented grape juice, but also reduction or removal of compounds, such as harsh tannins and bitter phenolics, that would adversely affect the flavour or palate of the finished product. For many winemakers, this clarification process is routinely assisted by adding animal-derived products or 'finings', including isinglass (a pure form of gelatine obtained from the bladders of fish), egg albumen, casein (from milk), chitin (from the shells of crustaceans) and gelatin. Given the subsequent filtration, decanting or other sediment-removal processes used in refining the final product, there is active debate about whether any of these finings remain in the wine and, if so, whether they are present at a level that could evoke a reaction in even the most sensitive individual.

With the changes to the Food Standards Code that came into effect in 2002, unless a wine manufacturer is certain that these substances have in fact been totally removed from the final product, the company is required to declare their usage on the label. It is important to note that the type and amount of fining used by a winemaker from vintage to vintage can vary dependent on the profile of the wine (see Australian Wine Research Institute www.awri.com.au and Australian Wine & Brandy Corporation www.awbc.com.au), so do not work on the basis that because one vintage was suitable that all vintages of the same wine will also be suitable. Additionally, vintages labelled prior to December 2002 did not have to carry these declarations. So you can either check with a winemaker regarding each brand *and* each vintage of a wine if you are catering for people with a marked sensitivity to these foods, or select a range of wines that are processed without any animal-derived finings. Such wines are processed using compounds such as bentonite, kieselguhr, kaolin and silica gel or solution, or simply by centrifugation and filtration. The majority of organic wines do not use animal-derived finings, but some do. There is a selection below of some suitable wines and non-alcoholic grape juices that are available.

*Wines*  Robinvale Organic Wines Australia, a small Victorian winery producing a wonderful selection of biodynamic and kosher wines, fortified wines (see Port below) and non-alcoholic flavoured grape juices (wonderful for jellies, the Sparkling Ginger for marinades). No animal-derived finings are used in making the wines. Available by mail order from www.organicwines.com.au, (03) 5026 3955, or for the following cities contact these distributors for retail suppliers (non-alcoholic juices only): Adelaide: Wilson's Organic (08) 8231 5014; Brisbane: United Organics, Rocklea (07) 3278 5997; Melbourne: Biodynamic Marketing, Footscray (03) 9689 1972; Sydney, Back to Eden, Homebush (02) 9746 0070.

Fresita Sparkling Wine contains natural strawberry pulp and is wonderful for making jellies and fruit terrines, as is its companion, a delicious passionfruit sparkling wine, Isla Noche. Serve over ice topped up with mineral water, or use as a fresh fruit marinade or to make jellies. Fresita is a Chilean wine clarified with bentonite (clay), available in: NSW: Woolworths; Liquorland and Theo's; Victoria: Liquorland, Safeway and Ritchies; Queensland: Liquorland, Liquor King and Giants or contact Vina Manquehue Pty Ltd, manque@ains.net.au, (03) 5962 6042, for outlets.

Hardy Wines (email customers@hardys.com.au) will provide information on specific wine vintages on request, for example Hardy's Reserve Merlot and R&R Merlot 3L 2002 vintage is suitable.

Jamieson's Run Chardonnay: Some of the 2001 red wines have been fined with egg white; this is flagged on the label as of December 2002 (www.jamiesonsrun.com.au, (08) 8736 3380).

Katlenburger sparkling fruit wines: A range of flavoured fruity wines available from Mac's Liquor and Liquorland (contact info@dr-demuth.de) with no animal-derived finings used in their production.

Peter Lehmann red wines: The range of white wines, sherries and ports are fined with milk (www.peterlehmannwines.com).

*Port* A fortified wine made from a variety of grapes which are blended and brandy added before fermentation is complete. Port is sometimes artificially coloured with caramelised wine or berry juice, or may have caramel added, but manufacturers are not required under the current Food Standards Code to declare its inclusion on the label.

Angove's Bookmark Tawny, Anchorage Old Tawny and Premium Vintage contain caramel derived from gluten (www.angoves.com.au, (08) 8580 3100).

Hardy Wines: Hardy Reserve 3 L Tawny Port and Whisker's Blake Port are fined with gelatine and contain caramel derived from sugar cane, their Vintage port is suitable (email customers@hardys.com.au).

McWilliam's Wines: McWilliam's ports are clarified by filtration; current vintages contain no caramel (caramel used by McWilliam's is derived from wheat and is certified as gluten-free, or from corn; www.mcwilliams.com.au, (02) 9722 1265).

Robinvale Organic Wines: Robinvale have a fortified cabernet port and Reserve Maurodaphne (no animal-derived finings used or caramel added); available by mail order from www.organicwines.com.au, (03) 5026 3955.

*Sherry* Many brands are fined with one or more of the listed fining agents and coloured with caramel but manufacturers are not required under the current Food Standards Code to declare the inclusion of caramel on the label.

Angove's: Angove's sherries (Oloroso Cream, Fino Dry Flor and Bookmark Dry or Sweet) contain caramel derived from gluten (www.angoves.com.au, (08 8580 3100).

McWilliam's Wines: McWilliam's sherries (dry, medium dry and sweet) are clarified by filtration and may contain caramel depending on the vintage; the caramel is derived from wheat and is certified as gluten-free, or from corn (www.mcwilliams.com.au, (02) 9722 1265).

*Vermouth* Cinzano Vermouth Bianco and Extra Dry: no animal-derived finings are used to process these (Tucker Seabrook www.tucker.com.au, (02) 9666 0000).

McWilliam's Wines: McWilliam's vermouths are clarified by filtration; the Sweet Vermouth contains caramel derived from wheat and certified as gluten-free, or from corn (www.mcwilliams.com.au, (02) 9722 1265).

**Xanthan gum** Produced from the fermentation of corn sugar and used as a thickener, emulsifier and stabiliser in foods such as dairy products and salad dressings. It also acts as a binder in gluten-free flour mixes when used in baking. Xanthan gum can result in abdominal discomfort if used in large quantities and in the absence of an adequate fluid intake, given its ability to absorb fluid. For people with a corn sensitivity, xanthan gum can be replaced on a weight for weight basis by guar gum. Available from health food shops and the Coeliac Society (see Useful Contacts, page 207).

**Yuba** The 'skin' that forms when soy milk is heated is removed and dried in sheets or sticks. It is often used in vegetarian dishes as a meat substitute or to wrap other foods that are then braised, deep-fried or steamed. The sticks are sometimes deep-fried to a crispy brown, to be eaten alone or broken into pieces for use in other dishes.

## Suppliers

### Bush foods

Australian Native Produce Industries (www.anpi.com.au), in South Australia, have a mail-order service for 1 kg packs of a range of native products, including wild limes, and can provide details of distributors in other states; email foods@anpi.com.au, (08) 8342 5099.

Vic Cherikoff Food Services Pty Limited stocks a wide range of native produce available in various pack sizes. For local distributors in your area, contact: (02) 9554 9477, www.cherikoff.net/cherikoff, email info@cherikoff.net.

*Kangaroo steak and eye fillet* Many good butchers carry fresh kangaroo or can order it on request. Southern Game Meat (www.sgm.com.au, (02) 9748 2261) has a wide range of cuts. Overseas Game Meat Export Pty Ltd, www.ogme.com/promotions/prom.htm produces a 500 g Frozen Bag which is available in some Queensland supermarkets or contact overgame@ozemail.com.au for distributors in your state.

### Flours

Lola's Wheat Free World at www.wheatfreeworld.com.au for a faxable order form for high quality besan, potato, maize and rice flours, etc.

Oriental and Continental, 41 Carlotta Street, Artarmon, NSW, (02) 9906 8990, carry a wide range of flours and grain products including poha*. They will pack an order for courier pick up if you are unable to get to the warehouse.

Kadac Pty Ltd supply a wide range of flours and LSA mix in addition to rice syrup, xanthan gum, and Orgran and Lotus brands. See their website (www.kadac.com.au) or contact Kadac at prodinfo@kadac.com.au or (03) 9583 1522 for outlets.

### Herbs and spices

Herbie's Spices carries a wide range of top quality herbs and spices and has a good mail order service available through its website at www.herbies.com.au, or call in at 745 Darling Street, Rozelle, NSW, (02) 9555 6035.

## Healthy Eating Guidelines

A healthy, balanced diet is one of the keys to achieving and maintaining good health. If you avoid one or more of the main food groups, understanding your dietary needs and ensuring your diet is correctly balanced becomes all the more important. The following section provides a brief overview of balancing your diet to achieve a sound nutritional base (full dietary guidelines for Australians are published by the National Health and Medical Research Council (see Useful Contacts on page 207) or contact your healthcare practitioner.

The bare basics are:

- eat a wide variety of nutritious foods;
- build a diet:
  - rich in wholegrain products, vegetables and fruit
  - low in total fat, saturated and cholesterol
  - with moderate sugar intake
  - with moderate in sodium and salt intake
  - with moderate alcohol intake (if you drink);
- exercise regularly;
- balance your food intake with your level of physical activity to maintain a healthy weight.

**Eat a wide variety of nutritious food** Aim to eat around 30 different foods each day. This is important because each food offers a different selection of the many nutrients our bodies need to function properly—the wider the range of nutritious foods you eat, the more complete the range of nutrients your body gets.

### Select foods from across all the five food groups

1 *Cereals* Rich in B group vitamins, carbohydrate and fibre, cereals also contain essential fatty acids, minerals and vitamin E.
2 *Vegetables* Vegetables, including legumes (such as lentils, dried and fresh beans and peas) are rich in Vitamin C, folate, fibre, and contain B group vitamins and minerals such as potassium, magnesium, calcium and iron. Legumes also contain phytochemicals.
3 *Fruit* Rich in Vitamin C, potassium and magnesium; many are also a good source of fibre.
4 *Calcium-rich foods* Dairy, calcium-enriched soy (both or either if tolerated) or orange juice, and other calcium-rich foods such as green leafy vegetables (spinach, broccoli, Chinese cabbage, bok choy), nuts (such as almonds and brazil), tahini* (sesame seed paste), canned fish with edible bones (such as salmon and sardines), dried fruit such as apricots and figs.
5 *Lean meat, poultry, fish, seafood, nuts and seeds* For protein, iron and zinc (red meat in particular), Vitamin $B_{12}$ (meat, poultry and fish) and omega-3 fats (fish and seafood).

**Each day aim to eat …** The following foods, in the right proportions to ensure you get the right balance of carbohydrate, protein, fats, minerals and vitamins:

- 6–11 servings of suitable cereals (wheat- and gluten-containing grains if suitable, rice, corn, millet, etc.), bread and pasta—preferably wholegrain;
- 3–5 servings of vegetables—a selection of green, orange and yellow, plus plenty of legumes;
- 2–4 servings of fruit;
- 2–3 servings of calcium-rich foods (dairy or soy products if suitable, or other substitutes, see below);
- 1–2 servings of meat, poultry, fish, seeds and nuts; meat 3–4 times per week, fish twice or more a week; $^1/_3$ cup nuts makes a great snack;
- only use fats, oils, salt, sugar and sweets sparingly; see below.

**Drink plenty of water** Since about two-thirds of our body weight is water, ensuring an adequate and regular supply is critical to many of the body's functions—assisting in the absorption of nutrients from food, transporting them round the body, flushing out the body's waste products and helping regulate the body's temperature through perspiration.

**Limit saturated fat and moderate total fat intake** Our bodies do require some fat in the diet to function properly, since fat supplies essential fatty acids and promotes absorption of the fat-soluble vitamins, A, D, E, and K. While it is now well recognised that a high fat diet increases the potential for weight gain, and the risk of heart disease and certain cancers, it is important to recognise that all fats do not present an equal health risk (see below).

Basically, oils and fats are classified according to their chemical structure as being either 'saturated' or 'unsaturated'. The unsaturated fats, or healthier fats, depending on their level of saturation, are further classified as 'monounsaturated' and 'polyunsaturated' fats. Unsaturated fats are derived primarily from plants and are liquid (in the form of an oil) at room temperature. Vegetable oils usually comprise a mix of both monounsaturated and polyunsaturated fats. Olive, canola and peanut are the most widely used oils that are high in monounsaturates, while polyunsaturated fats include safflower oil, soybean oil, corn oil and sesame oil (ranked in the order of most to least polyunsaturate content).

Omega-3 and omega-6 fatty acids are a particular classification of polyunsaturated fatty acids found in some plants (such as flax seed, walnuts and canola) and in the tissues of fish, such as salmon, herring, trout, mackerel and sardines. These special fatty acids have been found to be particularly beneficial for coronary health (purportedly lowering the bad LDL cholesterol and elevating the good HDL), as well as for brain growth and development, and the maintenance of cell membranes. High cooking temperatures (unlike microwave cooking) can destroy these fatty acids.

In general, saturated fats come from animal sources and are solid at room temperature, with the plant oils such as coconut and palm oil being well-known exceptions, both being highly saturated and semi-solid at room temperature. Saturated fats are classified nutritionally as 'bad fats' because of their impact on cholesterol levels and hence heart disease, and their association with some forms of cancer. Commercially, butter and lard are two of the most commonly used forms of saturated fat.

To limit total fat and saturated fat intake:
- select lean cuts of meat and trim off any excess fat;
- if you eat dairy products, select low- or reduced-fat products;
- use olive oil sprays to lightly oil a pan or the food rather than adding a volume of oil;
- roast vegetables at high temperatures to minimise fat uptake;
- char-grill food rather than pan frying in oil;
- avoid deep-fried and fatty foods;
- limit snack foods such as potato and corn chips;
- limit cakes, pastries and chocolates, etc. to 1–2 serves a week;
- check the levels of fat on product labels; products advertised as having reduced fat have 25 per cent less fat than regular food so are not necessarily 'low fat'; 'light' or 'lite' on a product label can mean lower fat or salt levels but again check the label carefully, since such products may contain excess sugar.

**Ensure you eat plenty of fibre** Fibre is found in plant foods like wholegrain cereals, legumes, and other vegetables and fruits. Fibre is not only important for proper bowel function but it may also lower the risk of developing heart disease and some cancers. Different plant food groups—such as cereals and legumes—contain different types of fibre, such as soluble and insoluble, and our body functions best when provided with the full range of dietary fibres. It is also best to eat fibre in a whole food rather than using a dietary supplement, since other nutrients in the food may likewise play an important role in providing these protective health benefits.

**Minimise salt** Select foods with low salt content or no added salt (low-salt foods contain less than 120 mg sodium per 100 g), and moderate the amount of salt added to food. Sodium plays an essential role in the body in the regulation of fluids and blood pressure, and many studies have shown that a high sodium intake is associated with higher blood pressure, particularly in conjunction with being overweight and lacking regular exercise. Adults need less than 2300 mg sodium per day—equivalent to only 1 level teaspoon of salt a day! So check food labels carefully for sodium content, and use freshly ground black pepper, dried and fresh herbs, spices, lime, lemon, mustard, vinegar and chilli, for example, to enhance the flavour of your food instead of adding salt.

**Minimise sugar** Consume only a moderate amount of sugar and foods containing added sugar. Since sugar is high in kilojoules but contains no essential nutrients, it basically provides empty energy to the body. By having a high sugar intake, the sugar effectively pushes out healthier foods from the diet. The net effect is the body fails to get its full complement of essential nutrients while trying to manage an increased kilojoule intake. Foods containing added sugar such as cakes, pastries, cordials, soft drinks and lollies should be considered as 'extra' foods, to be eaten only occasionally—particularly when the sugary food is also high in saturated fat.

**Limit alcohol intake (if you drink)** Excess alcohol can cause serious health risks including liver damage, certain cancers and raised blood pressure, and so increase the risk of heart disease and stroke.

**Monitor your fats and carbohydrates** While current dietary recommendations for a balanced diet include the key food groups be eaten in the following proportions, remember the types of carbohydrates (sugars versus starchy and fibrous) and fats (saturated versus unsaturated) eaten can greatly influence the impact your diet has on your blood glucose and fat levels, and hence your energy levels and body weight:

- 15–20 per cent protein;
- 65–75 per cent carbohydrate, containing 30–40 g dietary fibre per day;
- 10–15 per cent fat (comprising < 10 per cent saturated fat, < 10 per cent polyunsaturated and > 10 per cent monounsaturated fat); and in addition,
- 2 litres of fluid, preferably water or equivalent daily—more depending on the weather and your level of activity.

**Eat smart** Keep your servings moderate in size—don't put more food into your body than it needs!

Cooking Hints and Methods

**Managing the kitchen—avoiding cross-contamination of safe foods**  Cross-contamination of safe foods with 'No-Go' foods can easily occur in the home if care is not taken to avoid the problem. Obviously the most straightforward approach is to eliminate any 'No-Go' foods or products containing them from the home. This approach is not always practical for economic or logistical reasons, so effective means of avoiding cross-contamination must be implemented.

The way you control the risk of cross-contamination will in part depend on the nature of the 'No-Go' food to be controlled. For example, flours—such as wheat, corn or soy—can be particularly problematic since they can become airborne when handled and coat other utensils, clothing and so on in areas not in the immediate workspace. Liquids can be similarly challenging since they can be readily spilt and spread. Wherever 'No-Go' foods are handled, be it in the work area, with utensils or the cooking equipment they come in contact with, there is the potential for sufficient residue to remain to cause problems for a sensitive individual. It is, therefore, recommended that wherever possible a separate set of utensils is specifically dedicated to cooking 'No-Go' free foods. Care must be taken to ensure that any residue, such as crumbs, from 'No-Go' foods is thoroughly cleaned from all food preparation areas, as well as toasters, grillers, cake tins, sieves, chopping boards, food processors—basically anything used to cook, cut, mix or serve foods. Similarly, cleaning items, such as sponges and dishcloths, can easily transfer food residue if not meticulously managed.

There is also a significant risk of cross-contamination if communal foods such as margarine or jam are not carefully managed—a crumb-covered knife dipped back in for a second serve easily transfers particles of food ready for the next user to inadvertently pick up and eat. If, because family members or housemates fail to rigidly follow a single-dipping principle, you cannot be assured that this is not a risk, dedicate a specific tub or jar for the food-sensitive members that is off limits to anyone else.

It is good practice to store safe foods quite separately from any foods containing 'No-Go' foods and to ensure that any containers of foods, such as flours and biscuits, are clearly marked—preferably colour coded—to save any risk of confusion. The same applies to goods frozen for later use: mark and colour code the bags or containers so that there is no chance of confusion when they are defrosted for use.

Lastly, it is essential that all family members or housemates understand just what the correct food handling and storage procedures are and why they are necessary—what the consequences of inadvertent consumption of a 'No-Go' food by the sensitive family member means from a health and safety point of view.

The secret is to get organised, be organised and stay organised—and to make sure everyone involved fully understands and cooperates with the process.

**Simplifying recipe preparation**  When cooking, I work on the basis of 'time spent up front saves time later'. While it may seem time-consuming to do all your preparation work before you start cooking, time spent preparing your ingredients and equipment properly up front will save you lots of time in the long run—and often means you produce a better result! Here are a few tips for organising your preparation.

- Read your selected recipe through from start to finish before you begin.
- Assemble and prepare your equipment—such as greasing or lining. Don't wait until you are halfway through a recipe to discover you need a 28 cm and not a 20 cm tin to cook the dish properly.
- Check and assemble all the required ingredients—make sure you have everything you need.
- Check all perishable foods, to make sure they are still fresh.
- Have your recipe to hand when you are ready to cook—don't rely on your memory!
- Look for ingredients that overlap. If you are making several recipes at a time and they all call for chopped shallots or herbs, chop enough in one go.
- Choose a logical workspace. For example, prepare salads near a sink so that you can wash the vegetables, or prepare a cake mix near the mixer.
- Don't rush, take your time and do it right first time. Do whatever preparation you can well ahead of time so you don't feel rushed when actually cooking a dish, even if this is a day ahead for a special meal, or a week or more ahead if the dish can be frozen.

- Weigh all your ingredients into containers at the start of cooking, so that they can be transported on a tray to a second work area, such as a cooktop, and easily added to a dish as specified in the recipe. A dish can spoil if you have to prepare the ingredients as you go.
- Only measure the ingredients that you have to. Ingredients such as oils and vinegars can be poured from the bottle when an exact measurement is not called for. Others may be poured or measured straight into the mixing bowl if a number of ingredients will be sifted or combined in one recipe step (this is where electronic scales with a tare facility are invaluable).
- Clean up as you go so that the kitchen doesn't look as though a bomb has hit it when you've finished—and not every kitchen utensil you own is piled in the sink, if they've made it that far! Throw out unwanted scraps as you go, or cover and refrigerate them for later use.
- Note any modifications you want to remember on the recipe so that you can duplicate them next time round!

## Checking Oven Temperatures, Dry Roasting, Sterilising and More

**Checking oven temperature**  Setting the oven to the temperature specified in the recipe is critical for many recipes, particularly baked foods such as cakes and biscuits. However, the actual oven temperature may vary by several degrees from the temperature set on the dial, resulting in an apparent recipe failure, with undercooked food or food burnt on the outside and uncooked inside, depending on whether the oven is running below or above the set temperature. To get the best out of your baking, place an oven thermometer on the oven shelf you will be using and preheat the oven for a minimum of 15 minutes to allow the oven temperature to stabilise. Check the temperature and adjust the temperature dial, if necessary, until the oven stabilises at the required temperature. The thermometer can also be used to check for hot and cold spots in the oven, to identify how often or whether the food needs to be rotated while baking to ensure even cooking and browning.

Fully preheating an oven fully before baking is essential to ensure that the food is cooked by hot air at a stable temperature, with the element reheating infrequently and for a minimum period to maintain the temperature. While an oven is heating from cold there is radiant heat instead of hot air, which tends to brown or char the tops of cakes.

When using a fan-forced oven, the oven is set at a temperature 20°C lower than a regular oven. For best baking results, rotate the dish through 180° while baking or roasting once during a 30-minute cooking time, twice during a 60-minute cooking time, and so on, in order to ensure even cooking and browning. This allow for temperature differences in the oven due to air circulation (particularly in a fan-forced oven) or hot and cold spots (see Oven thermometer—Cooking Tools, page 204).

**Cooking beans**  Dried beans, unlike lentils, split peas and mung beans, need to be soaked prior to cooking. This is important not only to reduce the cooking time, but also to improve their digestibility by destroying any toxins that may be present. As a rule of thumb, 1 cup dried beans will yield at least 2 cups cooked beans. To save time cook an entire packet at once, rinse well with cold water, drain thoroughly and freeze any cooked beans not required immediately.

To cook, rinse the beans, lentils or peas well and pick over and discard any foreign matter. For each cup of beans cover with 3–4 cups water and leave to soak for at least 4 hours or overnight. (To shorten the soaking time, the beans can be brought to the boil after washing, again allowing 3–4 cups water per cup of dried beans, removed from the heat and set aside to soak for 1½–2 hours.) After soaking, rinse well, add the same volume of water, bring to the boil and simmer until tender. The cooking time varies according to the type of legume:

- borlotti, butter, cannellini, lima and red kidney beans, chickpeas and brown lentils require 1–1½ hours;
- split peas ¾–1 hour;
- red lentils 15 minutes.

Do not add additional ingredients such as salt, bicarbonate of soda or any acidic ingredient, for example chilli, while cooking since these can destroy valuable nutrients or toughen the coats, preventing the legumes from softening.

**Dry roasting/toasting**  To lightly brown seeds, nuts, spices, etc. without any fat. The method of dry roasting is determined by the size of the nut or seed to be roasted. Larger nuts are best roasted in a very slow oven, while smaller nuts, seeds and coconut can be roasted in a pan on a cooktop. Whichever method is used, toss the food regularly to ensure the roasting is even; watch the process carefully—with the high natural fat content of the nuts or seeds, cooking proceeds very quickly once started and they are easily overcooked or burnt. Roasted nuts may be stored in an airtight container for up to 2 weeks.

- *Pan roast:* almonds (whole, flaked or slivered), cashews (whole and pieces), sesame and sunflower seeds, pepitas and coconut (shredded or desiccated).
  Place the nuts or seeds in a dry, heavy-bottomed pan over a low–medium heat, and roast for 5 minutes or until golden and aromatic, tossing shaking or stirring constantly (the time will vary according to the quantity and the size of the nuts or seeds). Remove from the heat and transfer to a paper towel to cool completely before using. (If cooling in the pan, continue to shake occasionally until the pan cools and cooking stops.)
- *Oven roast:* brazil, hazel and macadamia nuts.
  Preheat the oven to 180°C (160°C fan forced). Spread nuts in a baking tray lined with baking paper and roast in the oven for 7–15 minutes or until starting to brown lightly, shaking regularly and checking carefully to ensure they roast evenly and do not burn. When cool remove any skins by rubbing the nuts in a clean tea towel.
- *Microwave:* nuts and coconut.
  Place the nuts or coconut in an oven bag and twist tightly to close. Cook on high for 1 minute, remove bag and shake gently. Repeat 4–5 times or until the nuts or coconut are lightly roasted.

**Lining baking tins**  Lining a springform tin can be a challenge! For a 19 cm diameter springform tin, open the tin hinge and place the side section flat on a benchtop. Cut one piece of baking paper 70 x 30 cm, fold it in half lengthways, form the paper into a circle with a 5 cm overlap and with the folded side facing down, slip it into the tin so the folded edge rests on the benchtop. Cut a 30 x 30 cm square of baking paper and fold it over the bottom of the tin. Slip the base into the tin side and fit into the bottom. Close the hinge and pull the bottom paper square taut over the base. This forms a 5 cm plus overhang at the top of the tin to allow for a cake rising.

**Low-fat cooking**  *see* Healthy Eating Guidelines, page 198.

**Pin-boning**  To remove the fine bones in a fish fillet. Lay the fillet flat on a benchtop and run your index finger along the surface of the fish to locate any bones. Remove the bones with a pair of tweezers and discard. Repeat until all bones have been removed.

**Preheating the oven**  *see* Checking Oven Temperature, page 202.

**Resting meat**  The length of time meat should rest is determined by the size of the piece of meat, and the method and temperature at which it was cooked. For example, rest steak (or equivalent) for 3–4 minutes, a whole roasted chicken for 15 minutes, and a beef roast for 20–30 minutes, covering the meat loosely with aluminium foil to prevent the surface from cooling too fast. For thick or large cuts of meat that have been roasted at high temperatures, the residual heat of cooking will continue to cook the meat during this resting period; this must be taken into account when calculating the actual cooking time so the meat is not overcooked when served.

**Sterilising**  It is important to sterilise containers and their lids before using them to store food for any period beyond 2–3 days in order to kill micro-organisms, such as bacteria, on the container that could contaminate the food. Glass jars with lids are best suited to food storage. If using a metal screw-top lid, place a cellophane preserve disc over the top of the jar before sealing, particularly if the food being bottled is acidic. Make sure you label the food with the relevant dates—date made, date ready and use-by date.

*Glass jars:*
1. Preheat the oven to 120°C (100°C fan forced).
2. Wash the jars thoroughly in hot, soapy water.

3 Rinse thoroughly and leave to drain; do not dry with a tea towel.
4 Place the jars on a baking tray lined with baking paper and dry in the oven for 30 minutes.
5 Leave the jars in the oven until ready to fill.
6 Fill with the prepared food and seal with the prepared lids (see below).

*Lids:*
1 Plastic lids and rubber seals cannot be sterilised and dried in the oven. Wash lids and seals as per the jars.
2 Place in a pan, cover with water and bring to the boil over a high heat. Reduce the heat and leave to simmer for 10 minutes. Drain and leave to air-dry on a clean tea towel.

Alternatively, use the rinse cycle at the hottest temperature in the dishwasher without adding any dishwasher powder.

## Cooking Tools

**Baking paper** Non-stick baking paper not only saves on the washing up but can be used to:
- line baking tins and sheets to prevent baked items from sticking and/or burning during cooking;
- reduce the amount of oil required to roast vegetables;
- ease rolling of pastry and its transfer to a pie dish;
- make paper pouches for oven-baking fish, keeping the fish moist and retaining the added sauce or resulting juices.

**Baking tins, flan and pie dishes** 19 cm non-stick springform tin; 20 cm round and square non-stick cake tins; 22, 24 and 28 cm fluted flan dishes; 18 x 28 cm lamington tin.

**Blender/food processor** A hand-held, electric Bamix blender is the simplest way to pulp, purée and pulverise and is excellent for blending a soup in the pan it has been cooked in—saving washing up! Mini-food processors are ideal for making spice pastes and small volumes of blended food, saving waste that accumulates on the side of larger food processor bowls. A food processor offers the flexibility of being able to blend, knead, mix, slice and chop. I primarily use the blending function for making cakes, large volumes of pastes, relishes and such like. It may seem excessive to have all three items, but when you need to cook almost all your food from basics, time-saving devices like these are invaluable.

**Casserole dish** A 3-litre and 5-litre capacity dish with lid will be sufficient for all the casserole recipes in this book, from the smaller cuts such as chicken thighs to larger cuts such as chicken maryland—with room for plenty of rich sauce.

**Chopping board** *see* Knives.

**Citrus zester** The simplest way to harvest the zest from citrus fruit for use as a flavouring, or to prepare long shreds of zest garnish.

**Char-grill/grill pan** There is a wide range of electric char-grills available with a single non-stick cooking surface, or press-style grills to cook both sides of a food at once. These grills allow very simple, low-fat cooking needing a minimum of oil brushed on the surface of the food—be it fish, meat or vegetables—before cooking. Alternatively a heavy-based grill pan can be used on a cooktop.

**Coffee grinder** Invaluable for grinding whole spices. Cheap electric grinders are available in some supermarkets.

**Gravy separator (or bulb baster)**  This is an invaluable tool for minimising fat and oil intake. Available from specialist kitchenware shops, it is basically a measuring jug with a spout at the base. Transfer your sauce, gravy or pan juices into the jug, the fat will settle out on top, then you can pour the fat-reduced juices back into the pan. Choose a jug with a strainer lid for ease for separating sauces with vegetables. A bulb baster can also be used to suck off any surface fat.

**Heat diffuser**  A metal plate placed on a gas or electric burner that conducts heat evenly under the entire surface of the pan eliminating scorching and hot spots. Invaluable when cooking risotto, rice by the absorption method and for very slow-simmered sauces. Available from some $2 or specialist kitchenware shops.

**Ice-cream maker**  If you are into making your own ice-creams, sorbets or granitas, an ice-cream maker saves the repeated re-forking of the mix as it freezes to break up the forming ice crystals. There are two types of machines available: the cheaper models require the churning bowl to be pre-frozen; the more expensive models don't, but as long as you remember plan ahead, the cheaper models do a brilliant job.

**Kitchen scales**  Gluten-free flours are far more unforgiving when being cooked than a wheat flour, with its built-in glue and elasticity. Weighing ingredients accurately in this type of cooking is, therefore, far more critical. A set of electronic scales which allow you to tare (to re-set the scales to zero in between weighing ingredients, thus allowing ingredients to be successively weighed into one mixing bowl without mental arithmetic!) allows for accurate and simplified measuring. Diet scales can be used as a substitute, but are limited by the 250 g maximum weight and have no tare facility.

**Knives**  Good sharp knives are a must. Use them only on a yielding board such as wood (not a hardwood—this can blunt as fast as ceramic, glass or marble) or polyethylene. My favourite knives are a 'beaky' or curved paring knife, and a small cleaver (from Asian grocers) which is excellent for chopping, skinning fish, and the like, and easily resharpened with a whetstone. I also use small kitchen scissors extensively—not being able to chop and slice with a knife with anything like dexterity of a chef, the scissors stand me in good stead!

**Mandoline**  A super-sharp slicing device that may be adjusted to prepare foods to various cuts and thicknesses. Professional, stainless steel mandolins are expensive, but there a number of low-cost alternatives available. They are invaluable for thinly and uniformly slicing vegetables such as cucumbers for pickles, potatoes for rosti toppings and fruits for tarts. Some slicers include interchangeable plates to shred, waffle and grate. Always use the finger guard to enable a clean slicing action without risk of injury.

**Measuring spoons and cups**  Accurate measurement is critical to the success of many recipes in this book. Use a set of spoons ranging from ¼ teaspoon size to 1 tablespoon (in this book a tablespoon is a 15 mL measure). Always make sure the food being measured is free of air spaces and the top of the spoon is levelled off with the back of a knife. Having a couple of sets of spoons is handy if you are cooking more than one dish simultaneously. When measuring by cups, use the correct cup size measure rather than trying to estimate a ½ cup in a whole cup measure, for example.

**Moulds**  1-cup capacity (250 mL) moulds for individual jellies (savoury and dessert), crème caramel and panna cotta, or substitute suitably shaped tea cups.

**Oven thermometer**  Relatively inexpensive thermometers are available at Kmart and Big W or specialist kitchenware shops; see Checking Oven Temperature in Cooking Hints and Methods, page 202.

**Ramekins**  Ovenproof 1-cup capacity ceramic pots for cooking individual-serve pies, savoury or dessert.

**Rice cooker**  These are worth their weight in gold for producing great rice every time. They cook rice by the absorption method and offer the advantage that the rice may be cooked in advance and kept warm and fluffy until required (within reason of course!). A rice cooker also makes flavouring rice a cinch—the herbs and spices can be added with the rice and water and left to gently infuse the rice as it cooks.

**Saucepans**  Of all the pans, I find a really good, heavy-based, high-sided, non-stick frying pan with a lid is the most valuable. The non-stick, heavy base means cooking is done with a bare minimum of oil, at high or low temperatures without fear of the food catching and spoiling. It can be used for sautées, stir-fries, sauces, poaching, searing, dry roasting, and more.

A heavy-based, 6-litre stainless steel stockpot with lid is invaluable for making large amounts of sauces, cooking pasta and rice, blanching vegetables, making soups, and so on. If you do a lot of cooking, having two of these pans is a real time saver.

A heavy-based, 2.5-litre pan with lid is ideal for risottos, smaller amounts of sauces, soups, curries, and custards.

**Scissors**  If you find chopping like the chefs a physical impossibility, a good pair of small scissors is a life saver. I normally have about three pairs on the go, so I always have a clean pair handy. They save me a lot of time— and the ends of my fingers!

**Sieve**  A good metal sieve used in conjunction with the back of a metal spoon is essential for preparing finely puréed soups, fruit coulis and suchlike. I find a variety of sieve and mesh sizes handy depending on the sifted/sieved result I want.

**Springform tin**  A round, straight-sided baking tin the sides of which are formed by a hoop that can be unclamped and detached from its base.

**Vegetable peeler**  A good vegetable peeler is not only a time saver but can be used to prepare finely sliced vegetables for salads, pickles and garnishes. There are two types on the market, the basic difference being the orientation of the blade, either running in line with the handle (traditional model) or the 'Y'-style, where the blade runs perpendicular to the handle—my preference is always the 'Y'-style.

**Other useful items**  Apple corer, bamboo steamer, colander, small metal whisks, spatulas for scraping out mixing bowls, wooden spoons (lots!).

Useful Contacts

**All Allergy**  A comprehensive set of website links to information about allergy, asthma and intolerance (www.allallergy.net).

**Allergy New Zealand**  Support and education group for people with allergies (www.allergy.org.nz, freecall 0800 34 0800 in New Zealand or 649 303 2024 from overseas).

**AllergySupport**  Links to information and articles of a wide range of allergies (www.allergysupport.org).

**Anaphylaxis Australia Inc** (Formerly FACT—Food Anaphylactic Children Training and Support Association) An Australian, not-for-profit, patient support organisation that provides information, training and emotional support to food anaphylactic children and their families (www.allergyfacts.org.au, 1300 728 000) and a member of the Food Allergy and Anaphylaxis Alliance (www.foodallergy.org).

**Australasian Society for Clinical Immunology and Allergy** (ASCIA)  Information on allergy, asthma and immune diseases (www.allergy.org.au).

**Australian Wine and Brandy Corporation**  Information on the industry position regarding mandatory labelling of allergens under the Food Standards Code for wine and brandy (www.awbc.com.au).

**Better Health Channel**  A good source of information on health and diet run under the auspices of the Victorian Department of Health (www.betterhealth.vic.gov.au).

**Coeliac Society**  Coeliac societies are run in each State by people with first-hand experience of either coeliac disease or dermatitis herpetiformis, with the Australian Coeliac Society acting as the umbrella society for the State societies and providing a forum to promote the national welfare of coeliacs throughout Australia. The State societies provide information on the disease, a gluten-free diet, permitted ingredients and where to buy them, cooking and recipes, overseas travel, medicines that are gluten-free, education material, and more.
NSW and ACT: www.nsw.coeliac.org.au; (02) 9411 4100;
Queensland: www.qld.coeliac.org.au; (07) 3854 0123;
SA and NT: www.sa.coeliac.org.au; (08) 8365 1488;
Tasmania: www.tas.coeliac.org.au; (03) 6427 2844;
Victoria: www.vic.coeliac.org.au; (03) 9808 5566;
WA: www.wa.coeliac.org.au; (08) 9444 9200 or freecall 1800 449 200.

**Diabetes Australia**  Information about diabetes and support for diabetics and their carers: (www.diabetesaustralia.com.au).

**Food Allergy and Anaphylaxis Network** (FAAN)  An international advocacy and education group for people affected by food allergies and anaphylaxis (www.foodallergy.org).

**Food Standards Australia and New Zealand** (FSANZ)  Information about labelling requirements and approved additive code numbers is produced by FSANZ. The list of approved food additives and their usage can be downloaded from the FSANZ website at www.foodstandards.gov.au; (02) 6271 2222.

**Heart Foundation**  Comprehensive information on healthy lifestyle habits and heart disease at: www.heartfoundation.com.au.

**National Health and Medical Research Council**  Publishes dietary guidelines for all Australians, which are available online at their website www.nhmrc.gov.au/publications.

**New Zealand Food Safety Authority**  New Zealand equivalent of FSANZ; www.nzfsa.govt.nz; (64 4) 473 9942 from overseas.

**Nutrition Australia**  Provides scientifically based information on nutrition. Visit the website and take the food variety test to see how well you score in food variety in your diet; www.nutritionaustralia.org.

General Index

All the recipes listed below are free of all the 'No-Go' foods, namely: wheat, gluten, dairy, eggs, peanuts, soy, garlic and onions.

Additionally, the recipes are individually flagged to indicate whether they are: corn-free ⓒ, fish-free ⓕ, tree nut-free ⓝ, and/or vegetarian ⓥ.

Wherever care in selecting a ingredient is required, the ingredient is flagged in the recipe, and information is either included in the recipe introduction or is cross-referenced to the specific ingredient entry in the Glossary (page 173).

# General Index

## Recipe Index

# Recipe Index